FEDERAL ENVIRONMENTAL LAW
THE USER'S GUIDE

Second Edition

By

OLGA L. MOYA
Professor of Law
South Texas College of Law

ANDREW L. FONO
Environmental Attorney
Haynes and Boone, L.L.P.

D1484626

WEST
GROUP

ST. PAUL, MINN., 2001

COPYRIGHT © 1997 WEST PUBLISHING CO.
COPYRIGHT © 2001 By WEST GROUP
        610 Opperman Drive
        P.O. Box 64526
        St. Paul, MN 55164–0526
        1–800–328–9352

ISBN 0–314–24108–6

 *TEXT IS PRINTED ON 10% POST CONSUMER RECYCLED PAPER*

DEDICATIONS

To:

Leanessa and Taylor, and all of my family for your never ending love, support, and encouragement; and to John Whitmire for your friendship and support.

OLGA L. MOYA

To:

My wife Stephanie, my three daughters, Alissa, Taylor and McKenna and our Border Collie, Lucy, for all the love, joy and support they bring to my life.

ANDREW L. FONO

ACKNOWLEDGMENTS

In preparing this book, we received invaluable help from various individuals and entities. We wish to thank South Texas College of Law, Dean Frank "Tom" Read and the Law Librarians for their generous support of this project from inception to completion. We also wish to thank and acknowledge the law students from South Texas College of Law who conducted numerous hours of research in support of this project: Bobby Bourlon, Preston Cunningham, Michael Goodman, Lana Martin, Kelton Tonn and Jim Viola. We also wish to thank Major Shannon Shy, United States Marine Corps for his assistance in reviewing and editing our NEPA Chapter and Mr. Edward Powers for his assistance in formatting and coding the numerous headings and citations to this book. Finally, we wish to thank West Publishing Company for allowing us to continue to assist others in understanding the world of environmental law.

PREFACE

Welcome to the exciting and challenging field of environmental law. Almost anyone encountering environmental statutes and regulations for the first time will agree that this area of the law can be confusing and often intimidating. We would like for you to use *The User's Guide* as a tool to help you better understand some of the basic tenets that imbue environmental law. We hope this book will enhance your understanding of environmental law and enable you to comfortably discuss and apply its principles.

This Second Edition to *The User's Guide* is a simple guide to federal environmental law. The idea for *The User's Guide* emerged in the Spring of 1992 at South Texas College of Law. Although there are other environmental resources available, none provide students with a simple, yet comprehensive text that walks them through each of the environmental statutes, related regulations, law reviews and journals, and case holdings. Most texts are either complex legal casebooks, or student aids that are far too limited in their scope and resources. *The User's Guide* is very different because it attempts to blend the simplicity of a student guidebook with the diversity of resources needed to further one's understanding of its contents.

The User's Guide is designed specifically for engineers and technicians who are routinely faced with federal environmental regulations; students at the graduate and undergraduate levels who study environmental science and technology; law students; and attorneys who are beginning their practice of environmental law. This book will also be useful to legislators; government officials; business owners and operators; public health officials; federal, state, and local agency personnel, and their trainers; teachers; and professors.

As a quick resource, *The User's Guide* provides citations to regulations, executive orders, court cases, and numerous law reviews, journal articles and textbooks. In addition, *The User's Guide* provides a list of acronyms, a glossary of terms, and a detailed index. This book should not be used as primary authority, nor for an update on the current status of environmental law in the United States. It should, however, be used to help you understand and digest the basic tenets contained in the federal environmental statutes and regulations.

The User's Guide contains six chapters covering: Administrative Law, the National Environmental Policy Act, the Resource Conservation and Recovery Act, the Comprehensive Environmental Response, Compensation and Liability Act, the Clean Air Act, and the Clean Water Act.

v

We sincerely encourage each of you to write us with ideas about how we can improve *The User's Guide*. We welcome your comments. Your ideas will help us provide you with the best environmental law guide available.

OLGA L. MOYA
ANDREW L. FONO

October, 1997 First Edition
January, 2001 Second Edition

FEDERAL
ENVIRONMENTAL LAW
THE USER'S GUIDE
Second Edition

TABLE OF CONTENTS

DEDICATIONS iii

ACKNOWLEDGEMENTS iv

PREFACE v

CHAPTER 1: ADMINISTRATIVE LAW 1

I.   **INTRODUCTION** 1

II. **THE RELATIONSHIP BETWEEN ADMINISTRATIVE LAW AND ENVIRONMENTAL LAW** 2
    A.   PUBLIC POLICY 2
    B.   ENVIRONMENTAL STATUTES 3
    C.   UNITED STATES ENVIRONMENTAL PROTECTION AGENCY (EPA) 3
        1.   Policy 3
        2.   History 4
        3.   EPA Today 4
    D.   AGENCY POWERS, FUNCTIONS AND ACCOUNTABILITY 5
        1.   Agency Powers and Functions 5
            a.   Legislative Functions 6
            b.   Judicial Functions 6
            c.   Executive Functions 6
        2.   Agency Accountability 7
            a.   The Administrative Record 7
            b.   Judicial Review 7

III. **RULEMAKING** 7
    A.   IN GENERAL 7
    B.   INFORMAL RULEMAKING 9
    C.   HYBRID RULEMAKING 10
        1.   Negotiated Rulemaking 11
        2.   Public Legislative Hearing 11
    D.   FORMAL RULEMAKING 12

IV.	**ADJUDICATION**	13
	A.	IN GENERAL	13
	B.	INFORMAL ADJUDICATIONS	14
	C.	FORMAL ADJUDICATIONS	15

V.	**ENFORCEMENT**	16
	A.	IN GENERAL	16
	B.	ADMINISTRATIVE REMEDIES	17
		1. Notice Letters	18
		2. Consent Agreements and Consent Decrees	18
		3. Modifications or Revocations of Permits	19
		4. Administrative Fines	19
		5. Injunctions	20
		6. Administrative Orders	20
	C.	CIVIL REMEDIES	21
		1. In General	21
		2. Injunctions	22
	D.	CRIMINAL REMEDIES	23
		1. Policy and History	23
		2. Historical Trends in Criminal Enforcement	24
		3. Elements of Environmental Crimes	25
		4. Penalties and Sanctions	26
		5. Burden of Proof	26
	E.	CITIZEN SUITS	27
		1. Purpose	27
		2. Types of Citizen Suits	28
		3. Statutory Authority	28
		4. Citizens Suits	29
		5. Litigation Costs	29
		6. Conclusion	30

VI.	**THE ADMINISTRATIVE RECORD**	30
	A.	POLICY	30
	B.	STATUTORY AUTHORITY	31
	C.	REGULATORY AUTHORITY	31
	D.	CONTENTS	32
	E.	JUDICIAL INTERPRETATIONS	33

VII.	**JUDICIAL REVIEW**	35
	A.	IN GENERAL	35
	B.	UNREVIEWABILITY	35
	C.	JURISDICTION	37
	D.	STANDING	37

		1.	Rule of Presumption of Judicial Review	38
		2.	Express Preclusion of Reviewability	38
		3.	Standing Created by the APA	39
	E.	TIMING	40
		1.	The Ripeness Doctrine	40
		2.	The Final Order Rule	41
		3.	The Exhaustion Doctrine	41
		4.	The Mootness Doctrine	42
	F.	THE PRIMARY JURISDICTION DOCTRINE	42
	G.	SCOPE AND STANDARD OF REVIEW	44
		1.	APA Provisions on Scope and Standard of Review	46
		2.	*De Novo* Review	47
		3.	Arbitrary and Capricious Standard	47
		4.	Substantial Evidence Standard	48
		5.	Strict Scrutiny Standard	49
	H.	REMEDIES	49
		1.	Actions Not Consistent with Prior Agency Policies	50
		2.	Action is Unconstitutional, Outside Legal Authority or Procedurally Flawed	50
		3.	Action is Not Supported by Substantial Evidence .	50

VIII. CONCLUSION . . . . | 51

CHAPTER 2: NATIONAL ENVIRONMENTAL POLICY ACT . . . . . | 52

I. INTRODUCTION . . . . | 52

II. POLICY . . . . | 53
	A.	STATUTORY APPROACH	54
		1.	Congressional Declaration of Purpose	54
		2.	Congressional Declaration of National Environmental Policy	54
		3.	Federal Government's Responsibility	55
		4.	Citizen's Responsibility	55
	B.	JUDICIAL INTERPRETATION	55
		1.	Environmental Consequences Must be Considered	56
		2.	The Hard Look Doctrine	56
		3.	Waiver of Sovereign Immunity	58
		4.	No Substitutes for an Environmental Assessment or an Environmental Impact Statement	58
		5.	NEPA Requires Alternatives	59

III.	**PRACTICAL APPLICATION**	59
	A.	THE ENVIRONMENTAL ASSESSMENT (EA)	60
	B.	THE FINDING OF NO SIGNIFICANT IMPACT (FONSI)	61
	C.	THE ENVIRONMENTAL IMPACT STATEMENT (EIS)	62
IV.	**APPLICATION OF NEPA**	63
	A.	IS AN EIS REQUIRED?	63
		1. Federal Agency Review	63
		2. Conditions that Mandate an EIS	63
		a. The Action Must be Federal	64
		b. The Action Must be Major	65
		c. The Action Must Significantly Affect the Human Environment	66
	B.	JUDICIAL INTERPRETATION OF "SIGNIFICANT" . .	70
		1. Significantly Affect	71
		2. Cumulative Effects May be Significant	71
	C.	CATEGORICAL EXCLUSIONS (CATXs)	72
V.	**NEPA'S PROCEDURAL STEPS**	73
	A.	PREPARE AN EA	74
	B.	DETERMINE WHETHER TO PREPARE AN EIS OR FONSI	75
		1. FONSI	75
		2. Challenges to the FONSI	76
	C.	FOLLOW THE CEQ REGULATIONS THROUGHOUT THE NEPA PROCESS	78
		1. Issuing the EIS	79
		a. Rule of Reason Test	79
		b. Timing	79
		2. Notice of Intent	80
		3. Scoping	80
		a. Lead Agency	81
		b. The Scoping Process	81
		c. Implementing The Scoping Process	82
	D.	CREATE AN ADMINISTRATIVE RECORD	90
		1. Regulatory Authority	91
		2. Contents	91
		3. Judicial Review	92
VI.	**CONCLUSION**	92

CHAPTER 3: RESOURCE CONSERVATION AND RECOVERY ACT 93

I.   **INTRODUCTION** 93
     A.   BACKGROUND 94
     B.   LEGISLATIVE HISTORY 95
     C.   ORGANIZATION OF SWDA & RCRA 96

II. **SUBTITLE C: HAZARDOUS WASTE** 98
     A.   SOLID WASTE DETERMINATION 98
          1.   Exemptions 99
          2.   Discarded Material 100
          3.   Recycled Material 100
          4.   Non-Solid, "Solid" Waste 102
     B.   HAZARDOUS WASTE 102
          1.   Types of Hazardous Waste 103
               a.   Listed Hazardous Waste 103
               b.   Characteristic Hazardous Wastes 106
          2.   Mixtures of Hazardous and Non-Hazardous
               Waste 108
          3.   Hazardous Waste Exclusions 111
          4.   Residue From Empty Containers 113
     C.   HAZARDOUS WASTE REGULATION 114
          1.   Overview 114
               a.   Cradle-to-Grave System of Regulation . . 114
               b.   State Authorization to Regulate
                    Hazardous Waste 115
          2.   Generators of Hazardous Waste 115
               a.   Types of Generators 116
          3.   Formal Generator Responsibilities 118
               a.   Hazardous Waste Identification 119
               b.   EPA Generator Identification Number . . 119
               c.   Prepare a Manifest 120
               d.   Packaging and Labeling Hazardous
                    Waste 121
               e.   Accumulating or Storing Hazardous
                    Waste 122
               f.   Prepare Reports 123
               g.   Recordkeeping 124
               h.   Generator Liability 124
          4.   Transporters of Hazardous Waste 125
          5.   Formal Transporter Responsibilities 125
               a.   EPA Identification Number 125

	b.	Manifesting	125
	c.	Handling	126
	d.	Recordkeeping	126
	e.	Spill Response Requirements	126
	f.	Transporter Becomes a Generator	126
6.		Treatment, Storage and Disposal Facilities (TSDFs)	127
7.		Permitting Procedures for TSDFs	128
	a.	Hazardous Waste Permit	129
	b.	Applicable Permit Standards	129
	c.	Permit by Incorporation	129
	d.	Additional Requirements	129
	e.	Permit Application Form and Procedures	130
	f.	Permit Modifications	130
8.		Facilities Operating under Interim Status	131
	a.	Submission of Part A and Interim Status	131
	b.	Submission of Part B	131
	c.	Changes During Interim Status	132
	d.	Loss of Interim Status	132
9.		Formal TSDF Responsibilities	133
	a.	EPA Identification Number	133
	b.	Required Notices	134
	c.	Waste Analysis	134
	d.	Security	134
	e.	Inspections	135
	f.	Personnel Training	135
	g.	Manifesting, Recordkeeping and Reporting	136
	h.	TSDF Preparedness and Prevention	136
	i.	Groundwater Monitoring Requirements .	137
	j.	Closure and Post-Closure Requirements .	138
	k.	Financial Responsibility Requirements Under Closure Operations	139
	l.	Liability Coverage Requirements	139
	m.	Corrective Action	140
10.		The Land Ban	144
	a.	Schedule For Land Disposal Restrictions	144
	b.	Treatment Standards	145
	c.	Variances and Exceptions	146
	d.	Effect of the Land Ban on Storage	146

III.   **SUBTITLE D: SOLID WASTE MANAGEMENT** 147
    A.   INTRODUCTION 147
    B.   DISPOSAL FACILITIES 148
        1.   Sanitary Landfill 148
        2.   Open Dump 150

IV.   **ENFORCEMENT REMEDIES** 150
    A.   ADMINISTRATIVE REMEDIES 150
        1.   Administrative Compliance Orders 150
        2.   Interim Status Corrective Action Orders 151
        3.   Monitoring, Analysis and Testing Orders 151
    B.   CIVIL REMEDIES 152
    C.   CRIMINAL ENFORCEMENT AUTHORITY 152
    D.   CITIZEN SUITS 154
        1.   Scope of Citizen Suit Authority 154
        2.   Notice Requirements 155

V.   **JUDICIAL REVIEW** 155
    A.   PROMULGATOIN OF REGULATIONS 155
    B.   PERMIT DECISIONS 156
    C.   OTHER FINAL AGENCY ACTIONS 156

VI.   **CONCLUSION** 156

**CHAPTER 4: COMPREHENSIVE ENVIRONMENTAL RESPONSE,
             COMPENSATION, AND LIABILITY ACT** 158

I.   **INTRODUCTION** 158
    A.   LOVE CANAL 159
    B.   CONGRESS ENACTS CERCLA 160
    C.   SUPERFUND AMENDMENTS AND REAUTHORIZATION
        ACT (SARA) 161

II.   **POLICY** 162

III.   **THE SUPERFUND PROCESS** 163
    A.   IDENTIFYING ABANDONED SITES 163
        1.   Hazardous Substances Under CERCLA 164
        2.   Notification of Releases at Active Sites 165
        3.   CERCLIS 166
    B.   PRELIMINARY ASSESSMENT (PA) 166
    C.   THE NATIONAL PRIORITIES LIST (NPL) 168
    D.   INVESTIGATION 169

      E.   REMEDIAL ACTIONS 170

IV. **SECTION 107 LIABILITY AND COST RECOVERY**
     ACTIONS 171
     A.   INTRODUCTION TO COST RECOVERY ACTIONS . 171
          1.   Causation 171
          2.   Elements 173
     B.   PROPERTY MUST BE A VESSEL OR FACILITY 173
          1.   Vessel 173
          2.   Facility 174
     C.   POTENTIALLY RESPONSIBLE PARTIES 176
          1.   Current Owners and Operators 177
               a.   Owner 178
               b.   Operator 179
               c.   Special Conditions and Exemptions
                        From Liability 182
          2.   Prior Owners and Operators: CERCLA's
              Retroactive Provision 184
          3.   Generators 185
          4.   Transporters 188
     D.   THERE MUST BE A HAZARDOUS SUBSTANCE . . . 189
     E.   THE PETROLEUM EXCLUSION 190
     F.   RELEASE, OR THREAT OF RELEASE AND THE
          INCURRENCE OF RESPONSE COSTS 192
          1.   Release 192
          2.   Threat of a Release 193
          3.   Incurrence of Response Costs 193
                a.   Response Costs 193
               b.   All Costs of Removal or Remedial
                        Actions 195
               c.   Any Other Necessary Costs of
                        Response 199
               d.   Damages for Loss of Natural Resources . 200
               e.   Health Assessments 201
     G.   NECESSARY AND CONSISTENT WITH THE NATIONAL
          CONTINGENCY PLAN (NCP) 202
          1.   The NCP 202
          2.   CERCLA-Quality Cleanup 204
     H.   EXTENT OF LIABILITY 204
          1.   Individual Liability 206
          2.   Organizational Liability 208
          3.   Retroactive Liability 208
          4.   Strict Liability 210
          5.   Joint and Several Liability 211

        a.   Contribution 212

        b.   Divisibility 214

   I.   DEFENSES 214

       1.   Act of God: Force Majeure 215

       2.   Act of War 216

       3.   Act of a Third Party 217

       4.   Innocent Landowner 218

       5.   Lender 220

       6.   Inheritance or Bequest 222

   J.   SETTLEMENTS 222

       1.   Mixed-Work Settlements 223

       2.   Mixed-Fund Settlements 223

       3.   Non-Binding Preliminary Allocation of
            Responsibility (NBAR) 224

       4.   De Minimis Settlements 226

       5.   Cash-Out Settlements 228

       6.   Covenants Not To Sue 229

V.   GOVERNMENT CLEANUP OPTIONS 229

   A.   SECTION 104 CLEANUP ACTIONS 231

   B.   SECTION 106 ORDERS 233

       1.   Enforcement Remedies 233

       2.   Violations of Section 106 Orders 234

VI.   CONCLUSION 234

CHAPTER 5: THE CLEAN AIR ACT 236

I.   INTRODUCTION 236

   A.   NEW PROGRAMS 237

       1.   Mobile Source Regulations 237

       2.   Acid Rain Regulations 238

       3.   Stratospheric Ozone Protection 239

   B.   MAJOR PROGRAMS 240

       1.   New Source Performance Standards (NSPS) . . . 240

       2.   National Ambient Air Quality Standards
            (NAAQS) 240

       3.   Nonattainment Areas (NA) Program 241

       4.   Prevention of Significant Deterioration (PSD) . . 242

       5.   National Emission Standards for Hazardous
            Air Pollutants (NESHAPs) Program 242

II.   NEW SOURCE PERFORMANCE STANDARDS (NSPS) . . . 242

   A.   INTRODUCTION 242

B. STATUTORY SCHEME 243
    1. Relevant Statutory Section 243
    2. The Federal Role 244
        a. List of Categories 244
        b. Standards of Performance 244
        c. Program Delegation 245
    3. The State Role 246
        a. Program Delegation 246
        b. Permit Requirements 246
        c. Waivers 246
C. JUDICIAL INTERPRETATIONS 247
    1. Arbitrary and Capricious Standards of Review . . 247
    2. NSPS and the Bubble Policy 247

III. NATIONAL AMBIENT AIR QUALITY STANDARDS
(NAAQS) 248
A. INTRODUCTION 248
B. STATUTORY SCHEME 249
    1. Relevant Statutory Sections 249
    2. The Federal Role 250
        a. Air Pollutants List 250
        b. Air Quality Criteria 250
        c. Air Pollution Control Techniques 251
        d. Setting the Standards 252
        e. Approval of State Implementation Plans
           (SIPs) 253
    3. The State's Role 255
        a. Air Quality Control Regions (AQCRs) . . 255
        b. Contents of a SIP 256
        c. Submission of SIPs to EPA 257
C. CURRENT NAAQS POLLUTANTS 257
    1. CO: Carbon Monoxide 257
    2. Pb: Lead 257
    3. Nox/NO_2: Nitrogen Oxides 258
    4. O_3: Ozone 258
    5. PM_{10}: Particulate Matter 258
    6. SO_2: Sulfur Dioxide 259

IV. NONATTAINMENT AREAS (NA) PROGRAM 260
A. INTRODUCTION 260
B. STATUTORY SCHEME 261
    1. Relevant Statutory Sections 261
    2. The Federal Role 261
        a. Standards of Performance 261

b.   EPA Designates and Classifies Areas . . . 261

c.   Review and Approve State Permit
Programs 262

3.   The State Role 262

a.   SIP Submission to EPA 262

b.   Section 172(c) Requirements 263

c.   Section 173 Permit Requirements 264

C.   JUDICIAL INTERPRETATIONS 266

1.   Partial SIP Approval Allowed 266

2.   SIP Provisions Disallowed 266

3.   Bubble Policy Allowed 266

4.   Denial of County Redesignation Upheld 267

V.   **PREVENTION OF SIGNIFICANT DETERIORATION
PROGRAM (PSD)** 267

A.   INTRODUCTION 267

B.   STATUTORY SCHEME 268

1.   Relevant Statutory Sections 268

2.   The Federal Role in Subclassifying Geographic
Areas 269

a.   Class I Areas 269

b.   Class II Areas 270

c.   Class III Areas 270

3.   The State Role 270

a.   Listing 271

b.   Area Class Redesignation 271

c.   PSD and the State Implementation Plan . 272

d.   Section 165 Permit Requirements 272

C.   JUDICIAL INTERPRETATIONS 274

1.   Air Deterioration Prohibited 274

2.   Judicial Review of PSD Regulations 275

3.   New Refinery Allowed in a PSD Area 275

4.   Redesignation to Class I Area Allowed 275

5.   Nonattainment Area Redesignated as a PSD
Area 275

VI.   **NATIONAL EMISSION STANDARDS FOR HAZARDOUS
AIR POLLUTANTS (NESHAPs)** 276

A.   INTRODUCTION 276

B.   STATUTORY SCHEME 277

1.   Relevant Statutory Section 277

2.   The Federal Role 278

a.   Hazardous Air Pollutants List 278

b.   Categories and Subcategories List 278

		c.	Emission Standards for Major Sources . .	278
		d.	Emissions from Area Sources to be Studied	279
	3.		The State Role	279
		a.	State HAPs Program	279
		b.	Permit Requirements	279
C.			JUDICIAL INTERPRETATIONS	280
	1.		Emission Standards Required for Listed HAPs . .	280
	2.		EPA Interpretations Upheld	280

VII. ENFORCEMENT PROVISIONS 281

A.			INTRODUCTION	281
B.			GENERAL PERMIT REQUIREMENTS	284
	1.		Introduction	284
	2.		Relevant Statutory Sections	285
		a.	Definitions	285
		b.	Permit Contents	285
		c.	Timelines for Permit Applications	286
		d.	Permit Conditions	286
		e.	Notifications	286
		f.	Self Regulation by States	286
		g.	Compliance Assistance for Small Businesses	286
C.			GOVERNMENT ACTIONS	287
	1.		Administrative Remedies	287
	2.		Civil Remedies	289
	3.		Criminal Remedies	289
D.			CITIZEN ACTIONS	291
E.			JUDICIAL INTERPRETATIONS	293
	1.		SIP Enforcement Allowed	293
	2.		Aerial Photography Allowed Without a Warrant .	293
	3.		EPA Must Issue Final Standards	294

VIII. CONCLUSION 294

CHAPTER 6: THE CLEAN WATER ACT 295

I. INTRODUCTION 295

A.			SOURCES OF POLLUTION	297
	1.		Point Sources	297
	2.		Nonpoint Sources	300
B.			TYPES OF POLLUTANTS	301
	1.		Conventional Pollutants	301
	2.		Toxic Pollutants	302

        3.   Nonconventional Pollutants 302

   C.   STATUTORY SCHEME 303

        1.   Person 303

        2.   Discharge 304

        3.   Pollutants 305

        4.   Navigable Waters of the United States 306

II.   **STATE WATER QUALITY STANDARDS** 308

   A.   DESIGNATING USES 308

        1.   Antidegradation Policy 308

        2.   Five Designated Uses 309

   B.   TESTING WATER QUALITY AND MIXING ZONES . 310

   C.   DOWNGRADING DESIGNATED USES 310

III.   **FEDERAL EFFLUENT LIMITATIONS** 312

   A.   FEDERAL ROLE 312

   B.   STATE ROLE 312

IV.   **THE NATIONAL POLLUTION DISCHARGE ELIMINATION SYSTEM (NPDES) PERMIT PROGRAM** 313

   A.   STATE DELEGATION 314

   B.   PERMIT CONDITIONS 315

        1.   Broad Discretion 315

        2.   Application 315

        3.   Permit Issuance Process 316

        4.   Term 318

        5.   Anti-Backsliding Policy 318

   C.   STANDARDS OF PERFORMANCE 319

        1.   Best Conventional Pollutant Control Technology (BCT) 320

            a.   BCT Applied 321

            b.   Factors Considered 321

        2.   Best Available Technology Economically Achievable (BAT) 321

            a.   BAT Applied 322

            b.   Factors Considered 323

        3.   Best Demonstrated Control Technology (BDT) . . 323

            a.   BDT Applied 324

            b.   Factors Considered 325

            c.   NEPA Applies 325

        4.   Treatment Levels 326

            a.   Primary Treatment Levels 326

            b.   Secondary Treatment Levels 326

            c.   Tertiary Treatment Levels 327

		5.	Individual Control Strategies (ICS)	327
	D.		PRETREATMENT STANDARDS	328
		1.	Implementation	328
		2.	Three Types of Standards	328
			a. General Prohibitions	328
			b. "Specific Prohibitions"	329
			c. Categorical Pretreatment Standards	329
		3.	Removal Credits Program	329
	E.		VARIANCES	330
		1.	Nonconventional Pollutants Variances	331
		2.	Fundamentally Different Factors (FDF) Variance	332
		3.	Thermal Discharge Variance	332
		4.	Pretreatment Standard Variance	333
		5.	Deepwater Discharge Variance	333
	F.		DEFENSES	334
		1.	Bypass	335
		2.	Upset	335

V.		WETLANDS PROTECTION AND THE DREDGE AND FILL PERMIT PROGRAM	336
	A.	DREDGE AND FILL PERMIT	337
	B.	EXEMPTIONS	339

VI.		OIL SPILL PROGRAM	340
	A.	NO DISCHARGE POLICY	341
	B.	REGULATIONS	341
	C.	ENFORCEMENT	342

VII.		NONPOINT SOURCE POLLUTION PROGRAM	342
	A.	NONPOINT SOURCE MANAGEMENT PROGRAMS .	343
	B.	AREA WIDE WASTE TREATMENT PROGRAMS . . .	344
	C.	TRANSBOUNDARY POLLUTION	344

VIII.		ENFORCEMENT PROVISIONS	345
	A.	INTRODUCTION	345
	B.	GOVERNMENT ACTIONS	346
		1.	Administrative Remedies	346
			a. Records, Reports and Inspections	346
			b. Compliance Orders	346
			c. Administrative Penalties	346
			d. Public Notice and Hearing Required . . .	347
		2.	Civil Remedies	348
		3.	Criminal Remedies	349

    C.   CITIZEN ACTIONS 351

IX.   CONCLUSION 353

TABLE OF CASES 354

ACRONYMS 359

GLOSSARY 364

INDEX 397

FEDERAL
ENVIRONMENTAL LAW
THE USER'S GUIDE
Second Edition

CHAPTER 1

ADMINISTRATIVE LAW

"Government is nothing but the balance of the natural elements of a country."

Jose Marti, *Our America*

CHAPTER 1: ADMINISTRATIVE LAW

I. INTRODUCTION

Environmental law is governed by administrative law. For this reason, you must master the concepts of administrative law before studying environmental law. To begin, administrative law has only developed in this country during the last century. The Federal Administrative Procedure Act (APA) was enacted by Congress in 1946 to designate general procedures to be used by federal agencies when exercising their rulemaking, adjudicatory, and enforcement powers.[1] This expanding area of the law defines how governmental organizations such as agencies, boards, and commissions develop and implement the regulatory programs they are legislatively authorized to create. Some of the many federal agencies that impact environmental issues include the Environmental Protection Agency (EPA), the Council on Environmental Quality (CEQ), the National Forest Service and the Bureau of Land Management.

For purposes of this book, we primarily refer to the Environmental Protection Agency (EPA) as the focus of our analysis. Administrative law applies to government agencies and to parties affected by agency actions. Many federal environmental programs are administered by the states under the authority of federal and related state laws. States often differ from both the federal

---

[1]   *See* Administrative Procedure Act, Pub. L. No. 89-554, 80 Stat. 381 (1946), Codified at 5 U.S.C.A. §§ 551-559.

1

government and each other in the way they interpret, implement, and enforce federal laws. In addition, each state has its own administrative guidelines that govern and define how state agencies act. All actions of federal agencies must comply with the federal APA.[2] However, each state in implementing federal programs must comply with both the federal APA and its own state APA. Most state APAs are modeled after the federal APA, though some distinctions exist.

II.   THE RELATIONSHIP BETWEEN ADMINISTRATIVE LAW AND ENVIRONMENTAL LAW

A.   PUBLIC POLICY

Public policy is the general principle by which our government branches[3] are guided in their management of public affairs. The legislature is directed to declare and shape national policy by passing legislation, which is the same as enacting law. The executive is directed to enforce the law while the judiciary interprets the law when a dispute arises.

When Congress considers certain conduct to be against public policy and against the public good, it passes legislation in the form of acts or statutes. Congress specifically regulates, controls or prohibits activity in conflict with public policy and attempts to encourage desirable behavior. Through legislation, Congress regulates behavior, selects agencies to implement new programs, and sets general procedural guidelines. This is where the relationship between administrative law and environmental law begins. The relationship between the two is so intertwined that one cannot exist without the other. When Congress passes environmental legislation it also declares and shapes our national environmental policy, thus fulfilling its policymaking function. The environmental statutes discussed in this book are primary examples of policymaking legislation.

---

[2]   *See* 5 U.S.C.A. § 551.

[3]   Government branches include, the legislative branch (Congress); the executive branch (the President); and the judicial branch (the Courts).

B.   ENVIRONMENTAL STATUTES

The environmental statutes discussed in this book include the National Environmental Policy Act (NEPA),[4] the Resource Conservation and Recovery Act (RCRA),[5] the Comprehensive Environmental Response, Compensation and Liability Act (CERCLA),[6] the Clean Air Act (CAA),[7] and the Clean Water Act (CWA).[8] These acts are broadly worded to identify existing problems that Congress believes can be corrected to protect human health, welfare, and the environment.

Protecting human health, welfare, and the environment is the national policy Congress chooses to encourage. For example, under NEPA, the national policy is to "promote efforts which will prevent or eliminate damage to the environment and biosphere and stimulate the health and welfare of man."[9] Similarly, under the Clean Air Act, the policy is "to protect and enhance the quality of the Nation's air resources so as to promote the public health and welfare and the productive capacity of its population."[10]

C.   UNITED STATES ENVIRONMENTAL PROTECTION AGENCY (EPA)

1.   Policy

Through statutes, Congress creates agencies with expertise to develop programs that best monitor and correct problem-causing conduct. Congress delegates regulatory authority to these agencies. Principally, agencies offer:

---

[4]   *See* National Environmental Policy Act, 42 U.S.C.A. §§ 4321-4349.

[5]   *See* Resource Conservation and Recovery Act, 42 U.S.C.A. §§ 6901-6992k.

[6]   *See* Comprehensive Environmental Response, Compensation and Liability Act, 42 U.S.C.A. §§ 9601-9675.

[7]   *See* Clean Air Act, 42 U.S.C.A. §§ 7401-7671(q).

[8]   *See* Clean Water Act, 33 U.S.C.A. §§ 1251-1387.

[9]   NEPA § 2; 42 U.S.C.A. § 4321.

[10]   CAA § 101; 42 U.S.C.A. § 7401.

1) specialized staffs that provide unique expertise and increased efficiency to analyze voluminous data and conduct precise research;

2) preventative programs that control unwanted behavior usually through permitting, license requirements, and the passage and enforcement of regulations; and

3) focused and continued attention on the agencies' regulatory and enforcement missions.

2.   History

In 1970, Congress created EPA.[11] The purpose was to consolidate functions previously carried out by several government agencies. These agencies included the Federal Water Quality Administration (within the Department of the Interior), and the National Air Pollution Control Administration and the Bureau of Solid Waste Management (both under the Department of Health, Education and Welfare). Consolidating these agencies into EPA has provided consistency for federal environmental planners and has eliminated the need to deal with numerous agencies.

3.   EPA Today

Today, EPA is one of the largest national administrative agencies. It has 10 regional offices spread throughout the nation and more than 17,000 employees. EPA has a budget of more than $6 billion, and it administers several programs implementing major environmental laws. Some of these laws include:

1) Clean Air Act (CAA);
2) Clean Water Act (CWA);
3) Comprehensive Environmental Response, Compensation, and Liability Act (CERCLA);
4) Resource Conservation and Recovery Act (RCRA);
5) Safe Drinking Water Act (SDWA);

---

[11] *See* Reorganization Plan No. 3 of 1970, 35 Fed. Reg. 15623 (1970), reprinted in 84 Stat. 2086 (1970).

6) Emergency Planning and Community Right-to-Know Act (EPCRA; SARA TITLE III);
7) Federal Insecticide, Fungicide, and Rodenticide Act (FIFRA);
8) Toxic Substances Control Act (TSCA);
9) Marine Protection, Research, and Sanctuaries Act (MPRSA), also known as the Ocean Dumping Ban Act (ODBA);
10) Uranium Mill Tailings Radiation Control Act (UMTRCA);
11) Indoor Radon Abatement Act (IRAA);
12) Coastal Zone Management Act (CZMA); and
13) The Pollution Prevention Act (PPA).

Through its 10 regional offices, its specialized staffs, and its visible enforcement programs, EPA offers the public a true representation of an administrative agency at work. It researches the causes and effects of specific problems and determines how to best regulate the activities causing the environmental problems. It often provides financial and technical assistance to states to encourage local implementation and enforcement of the federal environmental statutes. In some instances, EPA directly controls state programs. For example, EPA must approve certain state-issued permits such as those required under the CWA, CAA and RCRA.

In pursuit of its policy to protect human health and the environment, EPA issues regulations and sees that they are enforced. When a party fails to comply with the regulations, EPA has a wide range of enforcement remedies to ensure compliance such as fines, injunctions or even imprisonment. On the other hand, EPA must act fairly, efficiently, and within the confines and parameters of the APA at all times. If EPA fails to do so, Congress, the courts, and the public have ample opportunities to keep EPA within its legislatively authorized mission and the APA guidelines.

D. AGENCY POWERS, FUNCTIONS AND ACCOUNTABILITY

1. Agency Powers and Functions

For agencies to adequately regulate activity, Congress must grant them the power to carry out certain administrative functions. Agencies are given certain powers similar to those of the three branches of government. For example, agencies are given the power to draft rules, judge regulated activity, and enforce regulations. Thus agencies are often considered the fourth branch of government. Agencies have legislative functions (rulemaking), judicial functions (adjudication), and executive functions (enforcement).[12] These functions will be discussed briefly in this section and in more detail in later sections.

a.   Legislative Functions

In general, environmental statutes authorize EPA to draft rules and regulations that direct industry to protect human health, welfare, and the environment. Once regulations are declared final they have the force and effect of law. Thousands of federal agency regulations are enacted each year. These regulations are published daily in the Federal Register and codified annually in the Code of Federal Regulations (C.F.R.).

b.   Judicial Functions

EPA is also authorized to judge the regulated activity by making findings of fact and conclusions of law.[13] These findings and conclusions are developed in administrative hearings. Administrative hearings are conducted by administrative law judges (ALJs). These judges determine the applicability of a regulation to the conduct of a specific entity or individual. If someone is found guilty of a violation, then enforcement measures are taken to ensure compliance.

c.   Executive Functions

By its executive functions, EPA ensures compliance with environmental statutes. Executive functions are accomplished through specific enforcement powers including an agency's right to inspect facilities, review facility records, and issue licenses and permits. In addition, an agency may require periodic monitoring, sampling, and reporting of the regulated activity. When a party fails to comply, enforcement actions may result in administrative, civil, and criminal sanctions.

---

[12]   For discussion, *see*, Aman, Alfred C., Jr., Administrative Law in a Global Era: Progress, Deregulatory Change, and the Rise of the Administrative Presidency, 73 Cornell L. Rev. 1101 (1988).

[13]   International Telephone & Telegraph Corporation, Communications Equipment and Systems Division v. Local 134, International Brotherhood of Electrical Workers, AFL-CIO, 419 U.S. 428, 444; 95 S.Ct. 600, 610; 42 L.Ed.2d 558, 571 (1975).

2.   Agency Accountability

Agencies must be held accountable for failing to act within the scope of the authority Congress has delegated to it, and for failing to act within the parameters of the APA. Both the administrative record and judicial review foster agency accountability.

a.   The Administrative Record

Throughout the regulatory process, agencies are required to maintain a written record of their activities. This record includes significant research material, information, and proceedings that help formulate each agency's actions. The administrative record is available for public review and serves as substantial evidence that an agency acted reasonably and legally.

b.   Judicial Review

A party may seek judicial review when an agency action is not merited under the law. Judicial review is conducted by an outside authority, such as a court of law. This review is limited to an agency's administrative record. There are many legal parameters regarding the scope of review and the level of scrutiny a court can impose upon agency actions.

Agency powers are concepts borrowed from our three branches of government to help implement administrative laws. Administrative powers include rulemaking, adjudicative, and enforcement functions. The administrative record is maintained by agencies to ensure conformance with Congressional legislation. When conformance does not occur, a party may seek judicial review. The purpose and importance of each of these functions follows.

III.   RULEMAKING

A.   IN GENERAL

Rulemaking is the legislative function of agencies.[14] Before rulemaking begins, Congress passes legislation known as enabling acts to create new programs and designate agencies to implement them. Usually enabling acts give

---

[14]   APA § 553; 5 U.S.C.A. § 553.

agencies specific authority to draft rules and regulations. Final rules passed by agencies have the force and effect of law.

Procedures that govern the creation of rules are set out either in the APA, the agencies' enabling act, or by agencies' own regulations. The APA sets the minimum rulemaking standards agencies must follow. Congress may increase these standards through an agency's enabling act and in turn, agencies may further extend these standards through their own regulations. Each agency must follow its own regulations, especially when the regulations become more restrictive than the agency's enabling act or the APA. However, if an agency's rules or enabling acts fail to address a particular issue, then APA informal rulemaking procedures apply.[15]

Court cases that deal with rulemaking disputes often address whether agencies followed appropriate procedures or whether an agency allowed sufficient public participation. In addition, courts look at whether the rule is unreasonable, arbitrary, or not supported by substantial evidence in the administrative record. In administrative law, substantial evidence means only some evidence that an agency could find reasonable under the circumstances. It does not mean a preponderance of the evidence, which is a higher standard. Agencies need only show that their decision was one that a reasonable person could make, and it need not be the decision that most or all persons would make. Thus, courts will almost always uphold agency actions under the substantial evidence standard.[16] There are three rulemaking procedures: informal, hybrid, and formal; each of which follows different methods.[17]

---

[15]   *Id. See* Pierce, Richard J., Rulemaking and the Administrative Procedure Act, 32 Tulsa L.J. 185 (Winter 1996) APA § 553; 5 U.S.C.A. § 553.

[16]   O'Connor v. Heckler, 613 F.Supp. 1043, 1045 (S.D.N.Y.1985).

[17]   *See,* Bessemer Moutain, Rissler & McMurry Co. v. Council on Environmental Quality, 856 P.2d 450 (Wyo. 1993); *see, also* Weisz, Michael Gregory, Case note, Administrative Law - An Uncommonly Rare Decision - The Wyoming Supreme Court Orders Agency Rulemaking; Shwarts, Robert S., Administrative Law Delineation in the Exceptions to the Notice and Comment Provisions of the Administrative Procedures Act, 57 Geo. Wash. L. Rev. 1069 (1989).

B.   INFORMAL RULEMAKING

Informal rulemaking sets minimum procedures for agencies to follow in creating rules. This rulemaking is the least demanding on the agency. However, informal rulemaking is really a misnomer because formal procedures must still be followed in a timely fashion as required by the APA under Section 553. Informal rulemaking, also known as "notice and comment" rulemaking, requires agencies to publish a notice regarding the proposed rule in the Federal Register. This notice must give the time, place, and nature of the rulemaking proceedings and must refer to the legal authority under which the rule is made.[18] This notice must either provide the terms or substance of the proposed rule, or give a description of the subjects and issues involved.[19] Finally, the notice must include an opportunity for written, and sometimes oral comments by interested parties.[20] "A primary force compelling Congress to enact the APA was the lack of public participation in agency actions."[21] One of the major rulemaking goals is to encourage agencies to seek out and listen to as wide a spectrum of opinions and expertise as possible when contemplating a new rule.[22]

Under the APA, agencies must give interested persons an opportunity to participate in the rulemaking process by submitting written data, viewpoints or arguments.[23] Participation often begins when an agency publishes information as a public notice letter. This letter is mailed out to all interested parties and is often distributed through certain prearranged mailing lists. This notice letter offers the public an opportunity to respond. Agencies may also afford interested

---

[18]   APA § 553; 5 U.S.C.A. § 553.

[19]   APA § 553(b)(3); 5 U.S.C.A. § 553(b)(3).

[20]   APA § 553(c); 5 U.S.C.A. § 553(c); United States v. Chrysler Corporation, 995 F.Supp. 150, 155 (D.D.C. 1998).

[21]   Shwarts, Robert, Delineation in the Exceptions to the Notice and Comment Provisions of the Administrative Procedure Act, 57 Geo. Wash. L. Rev. 1069 (1989).

[22]   *See*, Johnson, Stephen M., The Internet Changes Everything: Revolutionizing Public Participation and Access to Government Information Through the Internet, 50 Admin. L. Rev. 277 (1998).

[23]   APA § 553(c); 5 U.S.C.A. § 553(c); *see*, Asiana Airlines v. Federal Aviation Administration, 134 F.3d 393, (D.C. Cir. 1998).

persons an opportunity for oral presentations. However, unless this opportunity is specifically established in an agency's enabling act, opportunities for oral presentation are discretionary and may not be permitted.

Once agencies consider all comments and determine what the final rule should be, they then publish the text of the rule and a general statement of its basis and purpose in the Federal Register at least 30 days before the rule's effective date.[24] This allows affected parties time to comply with the new rule. After the rule is published, interested persons may request that the rule be issued, amended, or repealed.[25] However, it is far more effective to participate in the rule's initial conception than to try to change the rule once it becomes published.

C.   HYBRID RULEMAKING

Hybrid rulemaking is the second rulemaking procedure. This type of rulemaking is not specifically addressed in the APA. The APA addresses only informal and formal rulemaking. Hybrid rulemaking is a recent concept recommended by administrative law scholars because it modifies and combines the beneficial functions of both informal and formal rulemaking.

Hybrid rulemaking includes all the requirements found in the APA under Section 553 (informal rulemaking), plus more. Thus, it is informally called "553+." Simply stated, hybrid rulemaking is "notice and comment" rulemaking with additional features. However, it is not as comprehensive as formal rulemaking. Hybrid rulemaking may be specifically called for by an agency's enabling act or regulations. However, if an agency's enabling act calls for only informal rulemaking, hybrid rulemaking will still be available at the option and discretion of the agency.

Hybrid rulemaking is popular because it allows for negotiated rulemaking and oral presentations. In addition, it offers a variety of participation options by interested persons, such as discovery, the right to have counsel present, the ability to testify, and limited cross-examination of other participants or government personnel. Two types of hybrid rulemaking exist as either negotiated rulemaking or public legislative hearings.

---

[24]   APA § 553(b), (c) and (d); 5 U.S.C.A. § 553(b) and (c); *see*, Public Citizen v. Carlin, 184 F.3d 900 (D.C.Cir. 1999).

[25]   APA § 553(e); 5 U.S.C.A. § 553(e).

1.   Negotiated Rulemaking

Negotiated rulemaking, also known as regulatory negotiation, is a form of hybrid rulemaking. It occurs prior to the legislative hearings stage and allows representatives from private and government groups to participate in the rule drafting process. An agency invites a limited number of representatives, called an advisory group, from all sides of a controversy to review the problem and suggest compromise regulations. "If [through this negotiated rulemaking process] a consensus is achieved, the resulting rule will be both improved in substance and more acceptable to the parties, thereby making it less likely that significant resources will be committed to the litigation of such rules."[26] After meetings with the advisory group, an agency publishes the proposed compromise rules in the Federal Register and requests written or oral comments from all interested parties.[27]

2.   Public Legislative Hearing

Another form of hybrid rulemaking occurs when an agency offers to hold public legislative hearings. Public legislative hearings allow for oral comments. These legislative hearings gather information and viewpoints. At these public hearings anyone, not just invited representatives, may present testimony for or against the proposed rules.[28] After considering all oral and written comments, an agency publishes its final rules in the Federal Register with an effective implementation date. Thereafter, the rules become law.

In summary, hybrid rulemaking is "notice and comment" rulemaking with additional features that allow an agency to implement negotiated rulemaking or legislative hearings where interested persons may give oral comments to reinforce their written ones. Hybrid rulemaking is often preferred over informal or formal rulemaking. It offers more opportunities for interested parties to participate than informal rulemaking, while costing far less than formal rulemaking. Hybrid rulemaking works well when an agency is proposing

---

[26]   McDonald, Derek R., Judicial Review of Negotiated Rulemaking, 12 Rev. Litig. 467, 468 (1993).

[27]   APA § 553; 5 U.S.C.A. § 553.

[28]   Administrative Resolution Dispute Act, 5 U.S.C.A. §§ 571-583.

regulations concerning highly controversial issues because it fosters more participation by adversely affected parties.

D.   FORMAL RULEMAKING

Formal rulemaking is the third type of rulemaking process. It requires more procedure, time, and resources than either informal or hybrid rulemaking. Here, agencies follow the informal rulemaking procedures of "notice and comment" as well as the additional full hearing requirements of the APA.[29] Congress may dictate which rulemaking procedures it wants an agency to use through the agency's enabling act. If the enabling act states that rules must be promulgated "on the record after opportunity for an agency hearing" then formal rulemaking must be used. This is "magic language" that triggers formal rulemaking.[30] On the other hand, if the enabling act merely states that an agency must promulgate rules without the specific language of "on the record after opportunity for an agency hearing," then an agency may promulgate rules by using the informal or hybrid procedures.

Once an agency determines that formal rulemaking applies, it must follow the full hearing requirements under Sections 556 and 557 of the APA.[31] These sections require that the hearing be an adversarial, trial-type proceeding with an ALJ presiding. The ALJ admits evidence and testimony under oath, allows direct and cross examinations of witnesses, rules on evidentiary objections, and ensures that a proper record is produced. Opposing counsel may object to the government's evidence and witnesses, and has a full opportunity to present its evidence and witnesses as well.

This process is very formal and ritualistic. First, the government presents its case and witnesses. This allows opposing counsel to cross-examine the witnesses, challenge the evidence, and object to any action it thinks is improper. Next, the opposing side presents its evidence and witnesses, allowing the government the opportunity to cross-examine and object to testimony and evidence it thinks is improper. The hearing ends after the parties present closing arguments. The resultant hearing record reflects the ALJ's ruling on each

---

[29]   APA §§ 553, 556 and 557; 5 U.S.C.A. §§ 553, 556 and 557.

[30]   APA § 553(c); 5 U.S.C.A. § 553(c).

[31]   APA §§ 556-557; 5 U.S.C.A. §§ 556-557.

finding of fact and conclusion of law and states the basis for the ruling. The ALJ must issue a decision on the proposed rules in the form of an "order."[32]

Formal rulemaking is more intensive, time-consuming, and expensive than informal or hybrid rulemaking. It is also more rigid, complex, and adversarial. However, formal rulemaking forces an agency to take a close look at the consequences of its proposed rules and promotes agency accountability. Any party not satisfied that an agency acted properly in rulemaking has a right to request judicial review of an agency's action by the courts.[33]

IV. ADJUDICATION

The objective of the three rulemaking procedures is to develop final rules to which the regulated community must comply with. Once rules have been developed, agencies then conduct adjudications to ensure that the regulated community maintains compliance.

A. IN GENERAL

Adjudication is the second major administrative function agencies perform. Adjudication helps determine whether the regulated community has complied with Congress or federal laws and agency rules or regulations. Adjudication refers to any agency process that determines the rights or duties of a member of the regulated community. This process may vary from the most informal communication to very formal, trial-like proceedings.

Although the adjudicatory process varies from agency to agency and certainly from federal agencies to state agencies, some aspects are common to all such actions. Constitutional law requires that the accused be given notice of the violation and an opportunity to explain, or if necessary, deny the charges against him before being penalized.[34] The opportunity to explain or deny the charges is a person's "hearing" and provides "due process" as required by the

---

[32]   APA § 557(c); 5 U.S.C.A. § 557(c).

[33]   APA § 702; 5 U.S.C.A. § 702.

[34]   Goss v. Lopez, 419 U.S. 565, 579; 95 S.Ct. 729, 738; 42 L.Ed.2d 725, 737 (1975).

Constitution.[35] Depending on the severity of the action, the "hearing" required under the law will vary from the most informal talk, conference, or letters, to the most formal administrative proceeding. This is a trial-like proceeding referred to as a "full hearing." An agency applies Constitutional law principles of due process in determining how much procedure is required to protect individuals from an arbitrary exercise of government power. Private and governmental interests are balanced in this determination.[36]

B. INFORMAL ADJUDICATIONS

As with rulemaking, an agency's enabling act may establish the type of hearing required in an administrative adjudication. If the statute merely asserts that an agency must provide a "hearing" without the specific language "on the record after opportunity for an agency hearing," an agency may handle the matter with an informal adjudication.

The most common informal adjudication is handled by mail. A letter notifies the party of the alleged wrongdoing. The party then has an opportunity to respond to the allegations only by writing the agency. In other instances, the letter of notification will state that the party may have a conference or oral communication with agency representatives to discuss the alleged wrongdoing and corrective measures. It may take several communications or conferences with an agency for the parties to agree on a solution. Once an agency allows the alleged wrongdoer a last opportunity to come to an agreement, it schedules a settlement conference. If the settlement conference is successful, a written agreement, called a consent agreement, will be entered. Consent agreements are discussed later in Section V(B) of this chapter, entitled, "Enforcement." If the settlement conference does not result in an agreement, then an agency refers the matter for "formal adjudication" or a "full hearing."

---

[35] U.S. CONST. amend. V.

[36] Mathews v. Eldridge, 424 U.S. 319, 335; 96 S.Ct. 893, 903; 47 L.Ed.2d 18, 33-34 (1976); *see also*, Barsotti, R., Administrative Law - Relief from Penalty Assessment Where Violator Had Inadequate Notice of Intended Meaning of Regulation – Rollins Environmental Services (NJ), Inc. v. United States EPA, 937 F.2d 649 (D.C. Cir.1991), 65 Temp. L. Rev. 931, 944 (1992).

C.   FORMAL ADJUDICATIONS

Formal adjudications are intensive, time-consuming, and expensive for all parties. Congress, through enabling acts, declares when a formal hearing is required. If an enabling act states that a decision must be rendered "on the record after opportunity for an agency hearing," then formal adjudicatory procedures must be used.[37]

Formal adjudications (administrative hearings) are governed by the APA under Sections 554, 555, 556, and 557.[38] The APA guarantees certain rights to all parties who are entitled to formal adjudication. For instance, parties are entitled to an ALJ who is a neutral decision maker. Section 554(d) of the APA emphasizes the importance of a neutral decision maker because it states that the decision maker may not have been involved in the investigation or prosecuting function of the case, or any factually related case.[39] Under Sections 556 and 557, the APA requires that the "hearing" be adjudicatory, meaning a trial-type proceeding with an ALJ presiding.[40] Parties are entitled to notice informing them of the time, place, nature of the hearing, the legal authority and jurisdiction under which the hearing is to be held, and the facts and laws asserted.[41]

Parties are also entitled to counsel of their choice, discovery, presentation of evidence, witnesses, cross-examination, and rebuttal. The ALJ admits evidence and testimony under oath, permits direct and cross-examinations of witnesses, promptly rules on evidentiary objections, and ensures that a proper hearing record is produced.[42] In this respect, the adjudicatory process is similar

---

[37]   United States Department of Justice, Attorney General's Manual on the Administrative Procedure Act 41-43 (1947); *see*, Penobscot Air Services, Ltd. v. Federal Aviation Administration, 164 F.3d 713, 720 (1st Cir. 1999).

[38]   APA §§ 554-557; 5 U.S.C.A. §§ 553.

[39]   APA § 554(d); 5 U.S.C.A. § 554(d); *see e.g.*, Grolier Inc. v. Federal Trade Commission, 615 F.2d 1215, 1220-1221 (9th Cir.1980).

[40]   APA §§ 556-557; 5 U.S.C.A. § 556-557.

[41]   APA § 554(b); 5 U.S.C.A. § 554(b).

[42]   Robbins v. Cyprus Cumberland Coal Company, 146 F.3d 425, 428 (6th Cir. 1998).

to formal rulemaking. Decisions must be based on the "hearing record." This record must reflect the ALJ's ruling on each finding of fact and conclusion of law and also state the reasons for the ruling.[43] The ALJ must issue an "order" giving his decision.[44] Such orders generally affect only the named parties.

V.   ENFORCEMENT

A.   IN GENERAL

The primary purpose of any enforcement program is to accomplish the mission and goals set forth in the enabling act. For example, an environmental statute's objective may be to protect human health, welfare, and the environment. To be effective, an enforcement program must be easy to implement, allow violators to correct their wrongful conduct, and prevent further destruction of the environment by deterring future misconduct.

As a primary focus, enforcement encourages the regulated community to voluntarily comply with laws and regulations. "Effective environmental enforcement restores and preserves environmental quality, deters violations and eliminates profits from non-compliance."[45] A stringent, visible, and effective enforcement program must motivate voluntary compliance and allow agencies to penalize the wrongdoer. Agencies have the enforcement authority to monitor entities. Monitoring may require the entity to maintain records of environmental activity, submit periodic reports on regulated activity and allow for agency inspections of regulated facilities. Furthermore, an agency can require entities to apply for licenses and permits. Once an agency implements these monitoring and licensing programs, it can closely supervise activities at a facility or plant.

When EPA finds that a rule, license or permit has been violated, it relies on administrative, civil, and criminal enforcement options. These measures provide sanctions that vary from small fines to large fines in the millions of

---

[43]   *See*, Milburn Colliery Company v. Hicks, 138 F.3d 524, 536 (4th Cir. 1998); Morehead Marine Services, Inc. v. Washnock, 135 F.3d 366, 375 (6th Cir. 1997).

[44]   APA § 557(c); 5 U.S.C.A. § 557(c).

[45]   Duval, Natalie M., Towards Fair and Effective Environmental Enforcement: Coordinating Investigations and Information Exchange In Parallel Proceedings, 16 Harv. Envtl. L. Rev. 535 (1992).

dollars depending on the risk posed to human health, welfare or the environment. Violations that pose a serious danger to society carry heavier penalties than those which do not.   In addition, those who commit serious violations either intentionally or with knowledge of the risk and danger to society are subject to criminal penalties including prison terms.

Each environmental act maintains its own sanctions and remedies. These are described in agency guidance documents called "penalty policies" that must be consulted to determine proper actions for each violation. In general, penalty policies look at many factors to determine the exact fine or sanction to impose against a wrongdoer. These factors include the seriousness of the violation, the intent to violate, the compliance history, and the need for deterrence.

> Penalties . . . can include administrative fines levied by the EPA or a state agency, civil fines levied by the courts, and criminal fines and/or imprisonment. Persons subject to these penalties include not only the individuals who actually perform the offending acts, but also their supervisors and responsible corporate officers. Corporations, as entities, are also liable for these penalties, and indeed several of the laws provide for particularly stiff fines for corporate defendants.[46]

Environmental laws authorize administrative, civil and criminal investigations, enforcement actions, and penalties. These actions are also known as remedies because they attempt to correct a violator's misconduct.[47]

B.   ADMINISTRATIVE REMEDIES

Agencies may impose administrative remedies for certain violations of federal law. These remedies are an intricate part of discussions that take place during informal adjudications and settlement conferences. Administrative remedies may also be assessed by the ALJ after a full hearing if the accused is found guilty. There are many remedies available to an agency. Some of the remedies available include: notice letters, consent agreements and decrees,

---

[46]   Kirsch, Lawrence S. & Moorman, James W., Environmental Compliance Assessments: Why Do Them, How To Do Them, and How Not To Do Them, 26 Wake Forest L. Rev. 97, 100 (1991).

[47]   Ray, Tom, An Interview with Martha Steincamp, Regional Counsel, U.S. Environmental Protection Agency, Region VII, 1 Mo. Envtl. L. & Pol'y Rev. 62 (1993).

modification or revocation of facility permits, administrative fines, injunctions, and administrative orders.

1. Notice Letters

To initiate enforcement actions, EPA issues warning letters known as either "Notice of Violations" (NOV) or "Notice of Deficiencies" (NOD). These notices list alleged violations; necessary, corrective or remedial measures that the violator must take; deadlines to meet, and opportunities to further discuss the violations with an agency. Many enforcement actions are resolved soon after receipt of the notice letter. The notice letter process is often resolved as an informal adjudication. It is wise to have a lawyer contact an agency as soon as possible after receipt of a notice letter. An environmental lawyer will know how best to approach an agency to allow his client the greatest opportunity to voice his concerns, objections, views, and any proposed solutions for settlement. In addition, legal counsel may also assist the client in determining whether it is in the client's best interest to request a full hearing.

2. Consent Agreements and Consent Decrees

As stated earlier, an agency may often give parties an opportunity to discuss the allegations and come to an agreed settlement by signing a consent agreement or decree. The consent agreement contains facts and conditions, conclusions of law, proposed fines or revocations, and suspensions of permits.

A "consent agreement" is a document, signed by all parties to the underlying agreement, that is the result of an informal adjudication. A "consent decree," on the other hand, is the result of a settlement reached during a formal agency adjudication or civil hearing. A "consent decree" is also a document, signed by all parties, but also approved by a judge. Its contents are similar to the "consent agreement." The key distinction is the requisite judicial approval. While neither admitting nor denying guilt, the parties to "consent agreements" and "consent decrees" agree to take certain corrective actions, pay administrative fines, and/or accept possible modifications or revocations of permits.[48]

---

[48] San Juan New Materials High Tech, Inc. v. International Trade Commission, 161 F.3d 1347, 1354 (D.C. Cir. 1998).

3.   Modifications or Revocations of Permits

An agency may modify, suspend, revoke or deny a facility's permit. Permits are required by enabling acts for highly regulated activities at a facility or plant. RCRA, the CAA and the CWA all require permits.[49] Because permits have the force of law, failure to comply with them can trigger any one of the administrative remedies.

A permit modification or revocation may initiate the right to a full hearing. An agency may seek to modify a permit. This can further restrict activity that was already monitored in the original permit. On the other hand, if an agency seeks to deny or revoke a permit, the consequences could be grave for the permit holder. A recommendation to deny or revoke a permit usually entitles the permit holder to a full hearing. If the ALJ denies or revokes a permit, a facility may cease to operate. Without a permit, a new facility will not be approved for construction.

4.   Administrative Fines

There is a difference between damages in private law suits and administrative fines. For example, private law suits compel defendants to compensate plaintiffs for harm caused by environmental damage. Under the administrative system, an agency not only has the discretion to impose a fine for violations, but may also impose specific conditions mandating cleanup. For example, discharging polluted wastewater from an industrial plant onto private property warrants administrative fines and an affirmative injunction (discussed below) forcing cleanup measures by the polluter.

Administrative fines are authorized in specific statutes. For example, RCRA and CAA allow fines of up to $25,000 per day per violation.[50] The CWA provides for fines that range from $10,000 per day but are not to exceed $125,000.[51] *In the Matter of Romero & Busot, Inc.*, the District Court held that EPA did not abuse its discretion in assessing a $29,500 administrative penalty.

---

[49]   RCRA § 3005; 42 U.S.C.A. § 6925; CAA § 129(e); 42 U.S.C.A. § 7429(e); CWA § 401(a); 33 U.S.C.A. § 1341(a).

[50]   RCRA § 3008; 42 U.S.C.A. § 6928; CAA § 205; 42 U.S.C.A. § 7524.

[51]   CWA § 309; 33 U.S.C.A. § 1319.

The penalty was properly based on the CWA penalty policy. The fine was based on the seriousness of the violation and the extent of the violator's deviation from the legal requirements. Mr. Romero allowed existing injection wells to overflow onto the ground, and improperly stored degreaser agents and motor wash solvents at the site.[52]

Sometimes fines fail to achieve their intended goals. For example, where they fail to hurt a company financially, the corporate polluter may perceive the fine simply as a cost of doing business. In these situations criminal penalties are more desirable. However, there may be some additional requirements before assessment of a penalty. For example, under the CWA, EPA is required to provide public notice and opportunity to comment on any proposed penalty.[53]

5.   Injunctions

An injunction is a court order that prohibits someone from doing some specified act or commands someone to act in a certain way, often to undo some wrong or injury. Because injunctions can only be issued by a court, not an agency, they are considered more of a civil remedy than an administrative remedy. For this reason, injunctions are discussed in more detail in the civil remedies section below.

6.   Administrative Orders

After a full hearing, an ALJ issues an administrative order. Such an order can require the facility to comply with regulations and permit provisions, conduct cleanup measures, and pay fines within specified time periods. For example, an order may require that certain activities stop because they were unauthorized, or it may require more restrictions upon the facility. It may demand that the facility take all necessary actions to clean up contamination and to take any mitigation and/or preventive measures, such as groundwater monitoring tests.

The order may also assess fines and require compliance by a specified date. For example, under the CWA, Sections 113 and 303 authorize the issuance

---

[52]   In the Matter of Romero & Busot, Inc., 785 F.Supp. 27, 28 (D.P.R.1992).

[53]   CWA § 309(a); 33 U.S.C.A. § 1319(a).

of administrative orders.[54] Failure to comply with these administrative orders can result in fines of up to $25,000 per day per violation and/or imprisonment of up to one year.[55] If enforcement problems are not resolved through administrative remedies, an agency may file suit in federal court and seek civil remedies.

C. CIVIL REMEDIES

1. In General

Civil remedies are sought in federal court unless the regulating agency is a state agency, then remedies are sought in state court. These remedies usually impose higher fines than those assessed through an administrative remedy. Civil remedies may be imposed for careless, inattentive or negligent violations. RCRA, CAA, and the CWA all impose civil penalties under a theory of "strict liability." This means penalties are imposed regardless of fault, intent or knowledge.[56] Civil remedies include a wide variety of actions such as modifications, suspensions or revocations of permits, fines, and injunctions.

Fines are assessed according to the penalty policy for the specific statute in question. However, in the civil context, the penalty policy gives the judge the discretion to increase the fine substantially. This encourages polluters to agree to pay the lesser agency imposed fines that would result in swift resolution of environmental matters. Imposing higher civil fines also allows the government to recover its litigation costs and helps discourage unnecessary suits.

If an administrative order is not complied with, an agency may seek enforcement of the order through the courts. An agency may also opt to forego administrative remedies and seek civil enforcement when it is authorized to do so by its enabling act. Congress allows civil enforcement actions that merit stricter penalties because of the serious nature of environmental violations.

---

[54] CAA § 113; 42 U.S.C.A. § 7413; CAA § 303; 42 U.S.C.A. § 7603.

[55] *Id.*

[56] Ferrey, S. & Last, Michael P., Officer and Director Liability For Environmental Law Violations, C414 ALI-ABA 207, 215 (1989).

2.   Injunctions

As discussed above, injunctions are a distinct enforcement tool and may only be issued by a court, not an agency. Injunctions are available to agencies filing suit against polluters, and to citizens filing suits against agencies or polluters. An injunction is a court order prohibiting someone from doing some specified act or commanding someone to undo some wrong or injury.

> There are essentially two types of injunctions: preventive and affirmative. Preventive injunctions stop identified conduct before harm is inflicted. Affirmative injunctions direct parties to undertake actions in a particular way. A party seeking a traditional preventive injunction must show that remedies at law are inadequate and that the challenged conduct will cause irreparable injury.[57]

For example, in environmental cases where a permit is at issue, courts will likely grant either a temporary or permanent injunction forbidding project construction until the dispute is resolved. In NEPA[58] cases, plaintiffs usually argue that either no environmental impact statement (EIS) was drafted or that an inadequate EIS was drafted, thus persuading the judge to issue an injunction halting further project construction until an adequate EIS is completed. These injunctions can delay major projects for many months and even years. In cases dealing with endangered species, the project may be permanently barred from construction.

> Injunctive relief is the most common form of remedy sought by citizens suing federal agencies in environmental cases . . . [C]ourts typically balance the potential harms to each party before deciding whether to enjoin challenged conduct.[59]

Injunctions are also effective tools for agencies to use against polluters. When a polluter commits repeated violations or if violations are considered to be serious (such as illegally operating a hazardous waste facility, harming a critical

---

[57]   Axline, Michael D., Constitutional Implications Of Injunctive Relief Against Federal Agencies In Environmental Cases, 12 Harv. Envtl. L. Rev. 1, 3-4 (1988).

[58]   Under NEPA, private parties may often seek an injunction to prevent a federal agency from proceeding with a project that is considered a "major federal action."

[59]   *Id.* at 2.

habitat for birds by destroying wetlands, or state violations of air quality standards), Congress may authorize an agency to forego administrative remedies and take immediate judicial action. This means an agency may go directly to court for civil sanctions and injunctions.

D. CRIMINAL REMEDIES

1. Policy and History

Despite the fact that, by 1972, the major federal environmental statutes contained criminal provisions, pursuit of civil remedies remained the norm for the next decade. However, by the late 1970s, under pressure from the Carter administration and an impatient Congress, EPA began to allocate more resources to enforcement, and in particular, to criminal enforcement.[60] Where repeat, flagrant, or willful violations occur making both administrative and civil remedies ineffective, an agency may also rely on criminal remedies to force compliance with the law.

No agency has independent authority to impose criminal penalties. Even though an agency itself cannot put the offender in jail, the violator may still go to jail if an agency's enabling act expressly provides for criminal penalties. An agency initiates criminal proceedings by referring criminal cases to the United States Department of Justice (DOJ). The DOJ then files criminal charges in federal court on behalf of the government (EPA).

In 1981, the DOJ created a joint program with the EPA to develop, refer, and prosecute environmental crimes cases. Within the DOJ, criminal cases were initially pursued by a small number of attorneys working in the environmental enforcement section of the Land and Natural Resources Division. In 1982, these attorneys were organized administratively into a unit of the environmental enforcement section of DOJ. This environmental crimes unit continued to grow and prosecute cases for several years, but it was not promoted to the status of a full department until May 1987.[61]

---

[60] Milne, Robert A., The Mens Rea Requirements of the Federal Environmental Statutes: Strict Criminal Liability In Substance But Not Form, 37 Buffalo L. Rev. 307, 316-317 (1989).

[61] Hogeland, Andrew S., Criminal Enforcement of Environmental Laws, 75 Mass. L. Rev. 112, 116-117 (1990).

In the late 1980s, because of increased pressure by Congress and the general public, EPA increased its use of criminal enforcement. In some cases, criminal enforcement has been preferable to administrative or civil enforcement. There are two general reasons. First, criminal sanctions deter future violations while most civil remedies only compensate for past ones. Second, even when the penalty imposed in a criminal action may not differ much from those in civil actions, prosecution imposes the great social and public stigma of being a "criminal" or "felon," a fate that all members of industry seek to avoid.[62] In today's society, a company's profit relies heavily on the public's perception; that the company operates cautiously when affecting the environment. A criminal record taints a company's public image and reputation.

2.   Historical Trends in Criminal Enforcement

National statistics indicate that from October 1983 to March 1986, nearly 180 indictments for environmental crimes were returned, and approximately 130 convictions were obtained. These cases resulted in more than $1.5 million in fines, and more than 10 years of cumulative time actually served in jail. By May 1989, indictments had grown to more than 520, resulting in more than 400 convictions, $22.5 million in assessed fines, and more than 248 years of imprisonment. In 1989 alone, the number of indictments and convictions or guilty pleas totaled more than 100 with fines of more than $12.7 million, and sentences totaling more than 53 years.[63] In 1990, the DOJ obtained 134 indictments; the most in any year since it began its campaign to vigorously prosecute environmental crimes. This was a 33 percent increase over the 1989 figure. Seventy eight percent of those indictments were returned against corporations and their top officers. In 1995, the DOJ obtained more than 250 indictments.[64] Since 1983, more than 800 individuals and 350 corporations have

---

[62]   Buchanan, Alfred L., Evolving RICO Issues For The Environmental/ Natural Resources Practitioner, 6 J. Min. L. & Pol'y 185, 192 (1990).

[63]   Hogeland, *supra* note 61, at 117.

[64]   Clifford, Mary, Environmental Crime: Enforcement, Policy, and Social Responsibility, p. 235 (Aspen Publishers, Inc., 1998) (citing P. Hutchens, Environmental Criminal Statistics FY 83 through FY 95, Department of Justice, Environmental Crimes Section, memo (December 13, 1995).

been convicted, and a total of 350 years of actual jail time has been served.[65] The DOJ has adopted a policy of conducting environmental criminal investigations with the goal of "identifying, prosecuting and convicting the highest-ranking, truly responsible corporate officials."[66] Federal officials view criminal sanctions as an effective method for assuring widespread compliance with environmental laws.[67]

3. Elements of Environmental Crimes

Criminal sanctions apply to willful acts, conducted with intent or knowledge, that pose an imminent danger to human health, welfare or the environment. Imminent danger is interpreted to be the high probability of serious bodily injury or death as a consequence of illegal environmental conduct.[68] Willful intent or knowledge in the environmental context has been determined not to require knowledge that one is violating the law, but merely requires an awareness of one's acts. For many non-environmental criminal acts, a defendant must have acted with specific intent to violate the law. By contrast, many environmental statutes only require the defendant to knowingly perform an act that was illegal, even though there was no intent to violate the law.[69]

---

[65]   *Id.*

[66]   Habituate, F. Henry, The Federal Perspective on Environmental Criminal Enforcement: How to Remain on the Civil Side, 17 Envtl. L. Representative. 10478, 10480 (1987).

[67]   Koppel, Brett G. & Marsala, Roger J., Nowhere to Run, Nowhere to Hide: Criminal Liability for Violations Of Environmental Statutes in the 1990s, 16 Calum. J. Envtl. L. 201, 202 (1991).

[68]   United States v. Villages, 784 F.Supp. 6, 11 (E.D.N.Y.1991), *aff'd* in part by United States v. Plaza Health Laboratories, Inc., 3 F.3d 643 (2nd Cir.1993).

[69]   Bartman, Thomas R., Gaynor, Kevin A., & Remer, Jodi C., Environmental Criminal Prosecutions: Simple Fixes For A Flawed System, 3 Vill. Envtl. L.J. 1, 11-12 (1992); *see also*, Capp, Barry, A Little Knowledge Can Be a Dangerous Thing – State of New Jersey v. Robertson & Mens Rea in the Freshwater Wetlands Protection Act of 1987, 15 Pace Envtl. L. Rev. 655 (1998).

4. Penalties and Sanctions

Many different penalties can be assessed against a violator. For example, in *United States v. Pozsgai*,[70] Pozsgai ignored repeated warnings by numerous parties, orders by EPA, and an order of a federal District Court not to fill forested wetlands without the proper permit. Pozsgai was charged $202,000 in fines and sentenced to three years in prison for his violations.[71]

One widely publicized example of criminal damage to natural resources occurred on March 24, 1989 when a supertanker, the Exxon Valdez, ran aground on Bligh Reef in Prince William Sound, Alaska. It is estimated that 10.8 million gallons of crude oil spilled, killing over 36,000 birds and 1,000 sea otters. In addition, hundreds of miles of previously pristine beaches were ruined. A criminal fine of $22 million, the highest ever imposed in an individual case, was assessed against Exxon.[72] From 1984 to 1993, $109.3 million in criminal fines were levied in EPA cases; of that, $62.9 million were imposed in 1992 alone.[73]

5. Burden of Proof

Administrative, civil, and criminal proceedings have significantly different burdens of proof. In criminal proceedings, the government must prove its case "beyond a reasonable doubt" as opposed to the lesser administrative and civil standard of a "preponderance of the evidence." "A preponderance of the evidence" means that one party's evidence is of greater weight than that of the opponent. "Beyond a reasonable doubt" means that the evidence proves, by its persuasive force, the near certainty of guilt. Thus, if EPA brings a civil action against someone for dumping hazardous wastes, EPA must show that the greater

---

[70] United States v. Pozsgai, 999 F.2d 719 (3d Cir.1993) *cert. denied*, 114 S.Ct. 1052 (1994) (good case regarding use of criminal remedies as a last resort).

[71] Adler, Robert W. & Lord, Charles, Environmental Crimes: Raising the Stakes, 59 Geo. Wash. L. Rev. 781, 784-786 (1991).

[72] *Id.* at 842, fn. 5 (citing, Alaska Oil Spill Commission, Spill: The Wreck of the Exxon Valdez III (1990); *see also*, Medical Waste News, Vol. 6, No. 1, ISSN:1048-4493 (January 11, 1994).

[73] Hunt, Terrell E. & Thompson, Steven E., Civil and Criminal Environmental Enforcement in Texas, Vol. 24 St. B. Tex. Envtl. L. J. 3, 20 (1993).

weight of the evidence indicates the defendant was responsible. On the other hand, if the DOJ prosecutes someone for violating a criminal environmental law, DOJ must prove that the act was committed beyond a reasonable doubt.

In environmental criminal actions, scientific facts demonstrating a polluter's guilt must be proven beyond a reasonable doubt. Although recent advancements in scientific technology alleviate many of the prosecutor's evidentiary problems in proving a case beyond a reasonable doubt, this is still a very difficult task to accomplish.[74] Thus, it is not easy to convince a prosecutor to pursue an environmental crimes case. For this reason, it may be more convenient for private parties to enforce the law directly through citizen suits.

E.   CITIZEN SUITS

1.   Purpose

In the environmental arena, the 1980s was the "decade of public participation." Congress increased the public's role in regulatory enforcement significantly with the intent that citizen action:

1)   replace inadequate administrative enforcement; and

2)   assist and supplement EPA enforcement actions.[75]

For instance, in crafting Section 505 of the CWA, the Senate authorized private actions by citizens in the form of citizen suits.[76]

The objective was, and still is, to empower the private sector to enforce environmental law. Citizens may sue the government or the polluter directly.[77]

---

[74]   Doerr, Barbara H., Prosecuting Corporate Polluters: The Sparing Use of Criminal Sanctions 62 U. Det. L. Rev. 659, 661-662 (1985).

[75]   Cross, Frank B., Rethinking Environmental Citizen Suits, 8 Temp. Envtl. L. & Tech. J. 55, 56 (1989).

[76]   CWA § 505(g); 33 U.S.C.A. § 1365(g).

[77]   Miller, Jeffrey G., Private Enforcement of Federal Pollution Control Laws: The Citizen Suit Provisions, 5D88 ALI-ABA 819 (1999).

Suits against the government encourage agencies to take enforcement actions against polluters. Suits against polluters induce compliance with the law and force cleanups of contaminated areas. In response to citizens' pleas, courts will not only impose sanctions but will also compel agencies to act and polluters to implement environmental protection measures.[78]

2.   Types of Citizen Suits

There are two types of citizen suits. First is the "enforcing" citizen suit. Here, a citizen files suit against a party who is alleged to have violated environmental laws or regulations. The second type is an "agency-forcing" citizen suit. Here, an individual sues a government agency that is alleged to have failed to aggressively pursue its non-discretionary duties.[79]

3.   Statutory Authority

Many environmental statutes provide for citizen suits. For example CERCLA, CAA, CWA and RCRA all have citizen suit provisions as follows:

1)   Section 310 of CERCLA provides that any person may bring suit on his own behalf for violations of CERCLA or for an agency's failure to implement required acts or duties.[80]

2)   Like CERCLA, Section 304 of the CAA also allows any person to bring suit against alleged violators. Furthermore, it offers injunctive relief by enforcing emission standards and limitations and through orders forcing the EPA administrator to perform compulsory obligations. The court may also impose civil penalties.[81]

---

[78]   Crawford, Colin, Pinning Gulliver Down: An Environmental Case Study on the Place of Decentralized Power in Federal Administrative Law Doctrine, 4 Fordham Envtl. L. Representative. 47, 61 (1992).

[79]   Cross, *supra* note 75, at 56.

[80]   CERCLA § 310; 42 U.S.C.A. § 9659.

[81]   CAA § 304; 42 U.S.C.A. § 7604.

3) Section 505 of the CWA grants citizen suits and enforcement measures similar to those offered under the CAA.[82]

4) Section 7002 of RCRA offers the same citizen suit and enforcement measures as the CAA and the CWA.[83]

Congress created these provisions to increase citizen participation in the enforcement and implementation of environmental laws. Citizen suits are effective when government agencies are slow to enforce environmental laws.

4. Citizens Suits

Most environmental statutes authorize two types of citizen suits. First, suits against the government authorize citizens to require the government to take any non-discretionary duty mandated by the appropriate statute. Second, Suits against polluters authorize citizens to sue private individuals or entities for violating their permits or other statutory requirements. The remedies available to citizens include judicial orders mandating action by an agency and modifications, suspensions, or revocations of permits, monetary fines, and injunctive relief from private entities. Monetary fines are deposited in a special government environmental fund.

5. Litigation Costs

In citizen suits, environmental statutes allow successful litigants to recover their court costs and attorneys' fees from the opposing party. Without such measures, most private citizens could not afford the high costs of environmental litigation. Thus, many potential litigants would be discouraged from bringing such suits in the public interest.

A court may also require that a party file a bond or other security when temporary restraining orders or preliminary injunctions are sought. Litigation costs are reimbursed under the authority of the following environmental statutes:

1) CERCLA Section 310(f); 42 U.S.C.A. Section 9659(f);

---

[82] CWA § 505; 33 U.S.C.A. § 1365.

[83] RCRA § 7002; 42 U.S.C.A. § 6972.

2)   CAA Section 304(d); 42 U.S.C.A. Section 7604(d);

3)   CWA Section 505(d); 33 U.S.C.A. Section 1365(d); and

4)   RCRA Section 7002(e); 42 U.S.C.A. Section 6972(e).

6.   Conclusion

Citizen suit provisions have not been ignored. On the contrary, citizens often file suits in both state and federal courts. Citizen suits effectively serve their legislative purpose of providing citizens an active role in enforcing environmental laws. Private citizens, environmental groups, and coalitions are truly the "watchdogs" who monitor the activity of potential defendants, the government, and regulated industry.

VI.   THE ADMINISTRATIVE RECORD

A.   POLICY

Public and judicial review are cornerstone concepts that allow close monitoring of agency actions. Judicial review of administrative action is based on an agency's administrative record. "The administrative record is filed with the reviewing court much like the record of proceedings before a trial court in the case of an appeal from a judgment in a plenary civil action."[84]

In agency proceedings, a record is kept of rulemaking and adjudicatory actions. This administrative record provides the court and the public an opportunity to examine the information and evidence upon which an agency decision or action is based. Agencies must document in the administrative record that their decisions are reasonable and not arbitrary or capricious. The factual basis of an agency's final decision should be reasonably apparent from the record. Public accessibility to the administrative record allows Congress, the public, and the courts an opportunity to satisfy themselves that an agency is operating effectively and fairly without abusing its authority or usurping undelegated powers.

---

[84]   *See* Cohen, William M., The Nature of the Administrative Record, 5D88 ALI-ABA 65 (1999), *see also*, Sive, David, The Problem of the "Record" in Judicial Review of Administrative Action, C534 ALI-ABA 451, 453 (1990).

B.   STATUTORY AUTHORITY

The APA discusses the administrative record in several sections as follows:

1)   Section 556(e) states that in rulemaking and administrative adjudications "the transcript of testimony and exhibits, together with all papers and requests filed in the proceeding, constitutes the exclusive record for a decision."[85]

2)   Section 557(c) states that, "The record shall show the ruling on each finding, conclusion, or exception [to the decision] presented. All decisions, including initial, recommended, and tentative decisions, are a part of the record and shall include a statement of:

(A)   findings and conclusions, and the reasons or basis therefore, on all the material issues of fact, law, or discretion presented on the record; and

(B)   the appropriate rule, order, sanction, relief, or denial thereof."[86]

3)   Section 706 limits a court's review of agency action to "the whole record or those parts of it cited by the party."[87]

C.   REGULATORY AUTHORITY

Regulations promulgated under the authority of a specific enabling act may require different or additional documentation in an administrative record than the APA requires. For instance, the regulations may delineate the contents required in a specific type of administrative record. In general, most regulations

---

[85]   APA § 556(e); 5 U.S.C.A. § 556(e).

[86]   APA § 557(c); 5 U.S.C.A. § 557(c).

[87]   APA § 706; 5 U.S.C.A. § 706.

enacted pursuant to Section 553 of the APA (informal rulemaking), require the record to:

    1)   state the decision;

    2)   identify documentation and evidence considered in making the decision; and

    3)   identify the legal authority for making the decision.[88]

D.   CONTENTS

Each agency determines what comprises its administrative record. It assembles the documents much as does the appellant in an appeal from a trial court, and submits what it denominates as the "record." The record is what an agency says it is.[89] Items or portions of items that are regarded as privileged may be excluded.[90] In *Goldberg v. Kelly*, the Supreme Court emphasized exclusive reliance on the record. The court could look to no evidence other than the administrative record to make its judicial determination, because to do otherwise would violate constitutional requirements.[91]

What comprises the administrative record may be disputed. In *Dopico v. Goldschmidt*, a federal District Court held that

    "the administrative record . . . is that upon which an agency acted and is adequate to enable the court to determine the path that an agency has

---

[88]   Administrative Conference of the United States (ACUS) Recommendation 74-4, Preinforcement Judicial Review of Rules of General Applicability, 1 C.F.R. § 305.74-4 (1994).

[89]   Harman Mining Company v. Layne, 161 F.3d 2 (4th Cir. 1998).

[90]   Sive, *supra* note 84, at 466-468.

[91]   Goldberg v. Kelly, 397 U.S. 254, 270-71; 90 S.Ct. 1011, 1022; 25 L.Ed.2d 287, 300 (1970); *see also*, Sive, David, The Problem of the "Record" in Judicial Review of Environmental Administrative Action, 5D88 ALI-ABA 81 (1999).

followed in making its decisions and the basis on which those decisions were made."[92]

Whether the record is adequate does not depend directly on the procedures employed; rather, it depends on whether an agency followed the APA or other relevant statutes.[93] The administrative record may include such items as:

1) a notice of proposed rulemaking or order;

2) public comments;

3) work product (unprivileged) created by or relied upon by an agency in promulgating its decision or implementing its action;

4) all notices, orders, motions, pleadings, evidence, official notice, oral and written statements, objections and hearing transcripts;

5) results of agency investigations;

6) information that an agency found useful in promulgating a rule or order;

7) intra- and inter-agency discussions;

8) statements of basis and purpose; and

9) the final rule or order.

E. JUDICIAL INTERPRETATIONS

When conflicts arise, courts interpret laws and regulations. Through legal analysis and reasoning, they provide clarity and meaning to the congressional purpose and intent of the statutes. Courts offer judicial opinions that serve an important function in fleshing out the significance of all laws.

---

[92] Dopico v. Goldschmidt, 518 F.Supp. 1161, 1180 (S.D.N.Y.1981), *rev'd in part*, 687 F.2d 644 (2d Cir.1981).

[93] Vermont Yankee Nuclear Power Corp. v. Natural Resources Defense Council, Inc., 435 U.S. 519, 547; 98 S.Ct. 1197, 1213; 55 L.Ed.2d 460, 482 (1978).

Below, are excerpts from three key cases that emphasize the use of the administrative record.

1) "[J]udicial review of agency action is limited to the administrative record . . . ."[94]

2) Review is limited to the "full administrative record" at the time a final agency decision is made.[95] In particular, the review is confined to the "full administrative record" before the secretary of an agency at the time a decision is made.[96]

3) What constitutes the administrative record may be contested.[97] The Supreme Court defines the administrative record as "that upon which an agency acted and is adequate to enable the Court to determine the path that an agency has followed in making its decisions and the basis on which those decisions were made. Whether the record is adequate is not dependent directly on the procedures employed, rather it depends on whether an agency followed the mandates of the APA or other relevant statutes."[98]

Thus, not only is a comprehensive administrative record paramount, but often it is the only evidence a court will review. Note however, a court does not have to rely solely on the administrative record where it is conducting a *de novo* review to examine certain questions of law.

---

[94] Animal Defense Fund v. Hodel, 840 F.2d 1432 (9th Cir.1988).

[95] Citizens to Preserve Overton Park, Inc. v. Volpe, 401 U.S. 402, 420; 91 S.Ct. 814, 825; 28 L.Ed.2d 136, 155 (1971).

[96] *Id.*

[97] Christopher Village Ltd. v. Cuomo, 1998 W.L. 422854, 29, 30 (U.S. Dist.Ct., S.D.Tex, 1998); Dopico v. Goldschmidt, 687 F.2d 644, 654 (2d Cir.1982).

[98] *Supra* note 95.

VII. JUDICIAL REVIEW

A. IN GENERAL

When a party to an adjudication or an interested person affected by a rule feels an agency action is not merited under the law, then the party or person may seek judicial review. Judicial review allows an administrative rule, order, or decision to be evaluated by an outside authority. This review takes place in the court system, not within an administrative agency. For example, EPA actions are reviewed by federal courts.[99]

For judicial review to take place, a court action must first be filed by "a [p]erson suffering legal wrong because of agency action, or adversely affected or aggrieved by agency action."[100] If the court has the power to hear the case, it is said to have jurisdiction, and it may determine the legality of the action. Most agency actions are subject to judicial review. However, the scope of the court's review is limited to an agency's administrative record. On the other hand, some actions may not be reviewed. This is known as unreviewability.

B. UNREVIEWABILITY

A disadvantage of judicial review is that it allows courts to direct agency action. Agencies sometimes consider court actions as interfering with an agency's policymaking functions. They argue that certain agency actions must be protected from judicial review to retain the sanctity of the expertise and discretion granted to an agency. Thus, Congress sometimes provides that specific actions be unreviewable.[101]

---

[99] Loug, Margaret L., Administrative Law - Reviewability of Agency Decisions – Davis Enterprises v. Environmental Protection Agency, 877 F.2d 1181 (3d Cir.1989), *cert. denied*, 58 U.S.L.W. 3521 (U.S. Feb. 20, 1990), 63 Temp. L. Rev. 117 (1990).

[100] APA § 702; 5 U.S.C.A. §.

[101] ICC v. Brotherhood of Locomotive Engineers, 482 U.S. 270, 107 S.Ct. 2360, 96 L.Ed.2d 222 (1987); Beehive Telephone Company v. Federal Communications Comm., 1999 W.L. 420441, *3 (D.C.Cir. 1999).

The policy behind unreviewability is to prevent excessive court intervention in issues involving agency discretion and expertise. There are two means by which an administrative decision may become unreviewable. They are:

1)   if an agency's enabling act expressly precludes review;[102] or

2)   if an agency's enabling act vests absolute discretion in an agency by operation of law.[103]

One must show clear and convincing evidence that Congress intended to expressly preclude judicial review or to vest absolute discretion in an agency without reviewability.[104] The best evidence of intent to disallow review is the specific words in the statute. For example, under CERCLA, Section 113(h) expressly precludes review through a statutory provision barring pre-enforcement review of administrative orders.[105] Under Section 307(e), the CAA contains a broad prohibition to judicial review where review has not been provided for in other sections of the statute.[106]

If unreviewability does not apply, then judicial review is presumably available. However, several procedural and constitutional elements must be established before a court may review the merits of a case. These elements include "jurisdiction," "standing" to sue an agency, the appropriate "timing," and the appropriate "forum" for review. Once these elements are established, the courts review the merits of the case, and then determine the proper scope of judicial review and the proper remedy.

---

[102]   Block v. Community Nutrition Institute, 467 U.S. 340, 345; 104 S.Ct. 2450; 81 L.Ed.2d 270 (1984).

[103]   APA § 701(a); *see, e.g.*, Bischoff v. Glickman, 54 F.Supp.2d 1226 (D.Wyo. 1999).

[104]   Dees v. California State University, Hayward, et al., 33 F.Supp.2d. 1190, 1197, (D.C.N.D.Ca. 1998).

[105]   CERCLA § 113(h); 42 U.S.C.A. § 9613(h).

[106]   CAA § 307(e); 42 U.S.C.A. § 7607(e); *see*, Moore, David M., Pre-Enforcement Review of Administrative Orders To Abate Environmental Hazards, 9 Pace Envtl. L. Rev. 675, 681-682 (1992).

C.   JURISDICTION

The APA does not create an independent ground for jurisdiction to bring suit, but rather, to the extent the APA creates a cause of action for the party aggrieved by agency action, jurisdiction exists under a general federal question statute, such as 28 U.S.C. § 1331, for example. The APA then serves as a waiver of sovereign immunity that allows a private party to sue the government.[107]

D.   STANDING

One must have standing to sue an agency.

Whether a party has a sufficient stake in an otherwise justiciable controversy to obtain judicial resolution of that controversy is what has traditionally been referred to as the question of standing to sue. Where the party does not rely on any specific statute authorizing invocation of the judicial process, the question of standing depends upon whether the party has alleged such a "personal stake in the outcome of the controversy."[108]

A plaintiff who fails to establish proper standing cannot have the case reviewed by a court. The easiest way to obtain standing is to show that an enabling act or regulation that empowers an agency to act, confers such a right to judicial review of such action. For example, under Section 113, CERCLA specifically provides for judicial review of any regulation promulgated under its authority.[109] If a relevant statute is vague or silent concerning judicial review, then courts generally examine two rules.

---

[107]   5 U.S.C.A. § 702, 28 U.S.C.A. § 1331; *see* Stockman v. Federal Election Commission, 138 F.3d 144, (5th Cir. 1998).

[108]   Sierra Club v. Morton, 405 U.S. 727, 731; 92 S.Ct. 1361, 1364; 31 L.Ed.2d 636, 641 (1972); *see also*, Cobell v. Babbitt, 30 F.Supp.2d 24 (U.S. Dist. Ct. D.C. Cir. 1998).

[109]   CERCLA § 113; 42 U.S.C.A. § 9613.

1.   Rule of Presumption of Judicial Review

First, is the rule of presumption of judicial review.[110]

Judicial review of a final agency action by an aggrieved person will not be cut off unless there is persuasive reason to believe that such was the purpose of Congress . . . . The [APA] provides specifically not only for review of agency action made reviewable by statute but also for review of 'final agency action for which there is no other adequate remedy in a court'.[111]

2.   Express Preclusion of Reviewability

The second rule is that Congress must expressly and unmistakenly disallow judicial review before access to the court will be forbidden.[112] "Mere silence in the statute should not be read as precluding judicial review under the APA. Such judicial review 'shall not be deemed foreclosed unless Congress has forbidden review in unmistakable terms.'"[113] For example under Section 113(h), CERCLA states, "No Federal court shall have jurisdiction under Federal law to review any challenges to removal or remedial action or to review any order issued."[114] In Section 307(e), the CAA states, "Nothing in this chapter shall be construed to authorize judicial review of regulations or orders of the Administrator under this chapter."[115]

---

[110]   Abbott Laboratories v. Gardner, 387 U.S. 136, 140; 87 S.Ct. 1507, 1511; 18 L.Ed.2d 681, 686-687 (1967).

[111]   APA § 704; *see*, Abbott Laboratories v. Gardner, 387 U.S. at 139-140; *see also* Hindes v. Federal Deposit Insurance Corp., 137 F.3d 148 (3d Cir. 1998).

[112]   Sierra Club v. Peterson, 705 F. 2d 1475, 1478 (9th Cir.1983).

[113]   *Id.*

[114]   CERCLA § 113(h); 42 U.S.C.A. § 9613(h).

[115]   CAA § 307(e); 42 U.S.C.A. § 7607(e).

3.   Standing Created by the APA

If the statute is silent on judicial review, then standing may be asserted pursuant to the APA. Section 702 of the APA grants the right to sue federal agencies, to any person "suffering legal wrong because of agency action, or adversely affected or aggrieved by agency action."[116] As long as the challenged agency action is final, imposes a legal obligation or right or involves the issuance of a permit or license from an agency, then it will likely be reviewable.[117]

Section 702 of the APA, as interpreted by the courts, requires that a plaintiff suffer personal injury brought about by the administrative action, and that the asserted injury arguably be protected or regulated by the statute in question.[118] The purpose of these requirements is to ensure that plaintiffs will be sufficiently involved or at risk to assure vigorous, adverse presentation of the issue. In addition, the requirement that a plaintiff suffer personal injury also operates to protect the courts from dealing with hypothetical or non-concrete issues.[119]

In *Sierra Club v. Morton*, the Sierra Club sued federal officials to prevent the approval and issuance of permits for construction of a ski resort in Mineral King and Sequoia National Park, California. The Supreme Court said that in absence of injury in fact of the Sierra Club or its members, standing did not exist. The Sierra Club failed to plead that it or its membership would:

> be affected in any of their activities or pastimes by the Disney development. No where in the pleadings or affidavits did the Club state that its members use Mineral King for any purpose, much less that they

---

[116]   APA § 702; 5 U.S.C.A. § 702; *see also* Hindes v. Federal Deposit Insurance Corp., 137 F.3d at 161.

[117]   APA § 704; 5 U.S.C.A. § 704.

[118]   *See*, Sierra Club v. Morton, 405 U.S. at 734-735; Association of Data Processing Service Organizations, Inc. v. Camp, 397 U.S. 150, 151-153; 90 S.Ct. 827, 829-830; 25 L.Ed.2d 184, 187-189 (1970).

[119]   Association of Data Processing Service Organizations, Inc. v. Camp, 397 U.S. at 151-153; 90 S.Ct. at 829-830; 25 L.Ed.2d at 187-189 (1970); *see also*, Barlow v. Collins, 397 U.S. 159, 164; 90 S.Ct. 832, 836; 25 L.Ed.2d 192, 197-198 (1970).

use it in any way that would be significantly affected . . . . [M]ere 'interest in a problem,' no matter how longstanding the interest and no matter how qualified the organization is in evaluating the problem, is not sufficient by itself to render the organization 'adversely affected' or 'aggrieved' within the meaning of the APA.[120]

E.   TIMING

Timing addresses the issue of when a lawsuit may be brought. Proper timing is required to avoid litigating issues where the plaintiff may no longer have a legal interest at stake. It also prevents premature judicial intervention into an agency's fact finding or adjudicatory functions. The elements of timing include the ripeness doctrine, the final order rule, the exhaustion doctrine and the Mootness doctrine.

1.   The Ripeness Doctrine

This doctrine ensures that the issue presented is sufficiently developed, concrete and adverse for judicial review. To determine the ripeness of a controversy for judicial review ordinarily requires the court to evaluate both the fitness of the issues for judicial determination and the hardship to the parties of withholding court consideration.[121] In *Abbott Laboratories v. Gardner*, the Supreme Court discussed several factors that the plaintiff must establish to meet the "ripeness" element. Those factors include:

1)   the agency fact-finding is complete and the issues presented by the case are purely legal in nature;

2)   the challenged agency action is final within the meaning of Section 704 of the APA;

3)   the challenged administrative conduct has or will have a direct and immediate impact upon the plaintiff; and

---

[120]   Sierra Club v. Morton, 405 U.S. at 734-738; *see also*, American Canoe Association v. United States EPA, 30 F.Supp.2d 908 (E.D.Va. 1998).

[121]   *See*, George E. Warren Corp. v. United States EPA, 159 F.3d 616 (D.C. Cir. 1998).

4)   judicial intervention will promote, rather than hinder, the effective regulatory functions of an agency.[122]

The U.S. Supreme Court has stated that a claim is not ripe for review if it rests upon "contingent future events that may not occur as anticipated, or indeed may not occur at all."[123]

2.   The Final Order Rule

This rule requires that the challenged agency action be final. Section 704 of the APA states that only "agency action made reviewable by statute and final agency action for which there is no other adequate remedy in a court are subject to judicial review."[124] Any agency action considered to be an interim decision or non-final action is not reviewable by the courts. The reason behind this rule is that an agency should be allowed to complete its decision making process prior to judicial intervention.[125]

3.   The Exhaustion Doctrine

Administrative efficiency requires that all administrative procedures be pursued and exhausted before judicial review is sought.[126] Thus, a potential plaintiff must seek resolution of the dispute at an agency level and pursue all available administrative remedies before going to court.

---

[122]   Abbott Laboratories v. Gardner, 387 U.S. at 148-154; *see also*, Tutein v. Daley, 43 F.Supp.2d 113, (D.Mass. 1999).

[123]   Texas v. United States of America, 523 U.S. 296; 118 S.Ct. 1257; 140 L.Ed.2d 406 (1998), quoting Thomas v. Union Carbide Agriculture Products Co., 473 U.S. 568; 105 S.Ct. 3325; 87 L.Ed.2d 409 (1985).

[124]   APA § 704; 5 U.S.C.A. § 704; Sierra Club v. Peterson, 1999 W.L. 618115 at 4 (5th Cir. 1999).

[125]   Pennzoil Co. v. Federal Energy Regulatory Commission, 742 F.2d 242 (5th Cir.1984).

[126]   McKart v. United States, 395 U.S. 185, 193; 89 S.Ct. 1657, 1662; 23 L.Ed.2d 194, 202 (1969); *see also*, Moncrief v. United States of America, 43 Fed.Cl. 276 (U.S. Ct. of Fed. Claims 1999).

If the plaintiff fails to pursue all available administrative remedies, then he has waived all rights of judicial review. The rationale is that an agency should be given an opportunity to correct its own mistakes. Thus, if an agency initially ruled against the complaining party and later alters its position at the administrative appellate level, an agency has had an opportunity to properly resolve the matter.

4.   The Mootness Doctrine

This doctrine mandates that federal courts hear only cases presenting an ongoing controversy capable of judicial resolution. A case will be found moot and excluded from judicial review if subsequent developments resolve the dispute. "The [Mootness] doctrine dictates that federal courts are empowered to decide cases only when the decision will affect the rights of the litigants. Thus, when the facts of a case change such that a judicial decision on the merits would be meaningless, courts are without power to decide the case."[127] For example, in *Natural Resources Defense Council v. United States Nuclear Regulatory Commission*, the plaintiffs challenged an agency rule as violating Section 553 of the APA. The Court of Appeals declared the case moot when it found that the agency had reissued the rule in compliance with Section 553.[128]

F.   THE PRIMARY JURISDICTION DOCTRINE

The primary jurisdiction doctrine (PJD) addresses whether a court or an agency should be the initial or primary forum for resolution of an issue or pursuit of a remedy. If a dispute raises matters that require the knowledge and discretion of an agency's experts or that require uniform regulatory procedures, then an agency is the proper forum for initial resolution. In these cases, the agency has primary jurisdiction and a party must subject himself to the agencies' processes and procedures before he gets his day in court.

The PJD allows a court to suspend consideration of a matter and refer the matter to an agency for an initial determination. This doctrine enforces the

---

[127]   Snider, Kipp D., The Vacatur Remedy For Cases Becoming Moot Upon Appeal: In Search Of A Workable Solution For The Federal Courts, 60 Geo. Wash. L. Rev. 1642, 1643 (1992).

[128]   Natural Resources Defense Council v. United States Nuclear Regulatory Commission, 680 F.2d 810, 813-814 (D.C. Cir.1982).

separation of powers between the executive and judicial branches of government guaranteed under the Constitution by promoting proper government relationships between agencies and courts. It also promotes an agency's right to exercise its discretionary powers and fact-finding functions prior to judicial intervention. Once the doctrine of primary jurisdiction is applied and an agency exercises its power, the court will then review the action.

Although no fixed formula exists for applying the doctrine of Primary Jurisdiction, the following factors help to guide a court's decision whether or not to refer a matter to an agency under such a doctrine, especially when such matters involve questions of fact:

      (1)   whether the agency determination lies at the heart of the task assigned to the agency by congress;

      (2)   whether agency expertise is required to unravel intricate, technical facts; and

      (3)   whether, though perhaps not determinative, the agency determination would materially aid the court.[129]

There are basically two reasons for requiring a private litigant to resort to the administrative process before pursuing court litigation. First, a referral to the agency may preserve needed uniformity in a regulatory program.[130] Second, the litigation may involve issues that go beyond the conventional experience of judges, and on which the expertise of the agency is helpful.[131]

The PJD is not a shield from judicial review because it encourages courts to review only those matters that fall within the court's jurisdiction. If, while

---

[129]   *See*, American Automobile Manufacturer's Assn. v. Massachusetts Dept. of Environmental Protection, 163 F.3d 74, 81 (1ˢᵗ Cir.1998).

[130]   Aman, Alfred C., Jr. & Mayton, William T., Administrative Law Hornbook Series, West Publishing Co., 442-447 (1993); *see also*, Texas & Pacific Railway v. Abilene Cotton Oil Co., 204 U.S. 426; 27 S.Ct. 350; 51 L.Ed. 553 (1907); Far East Conf. v. United States, 342 U.S. 570, 574; 72 S.Ct. 492; 96 L.Ed. 576 (1952).

[131]   *See*, United States v. Western Pacific Railroad Co., 352 U.S. 59, 65; 77 S.Ct. 161, 165-166; 1 L.Ed.2d 126, 132 (1956).

hearing a civil or criminal case, a court is presented with a dispute or issue it recognizes as falling comfortably within an agency's jurisdiction, the court may choose to postpone its decision until an agency resolves the issue. At this point, a court and an agency are said to have concurrent jurisdiction.[132] Concurrent jurisdiction will not apply when an agency resorts to the courts for enforcement nor if an issue raised is not exclusively within an agency's particular specialization or authority.[133]

Courts postpone their decisions when they recognize that the administrative issues are beyond the judges conventional experience and that uniform regulatory procedures should be preserved.[134] Thus, courts will allow agencies to exercise their own expertise with regard to administrative law matters before reviewing the agencies' action. Next, the court's role is to determine whether an agency acted within its legal authority and that it did not unreasonably or arbitrarily administer its programs. Once a plaintiff establishes standing and ripeness, meets the final order rule, exhausts all administrative remedies, and establishes a true case or controversy in the proper forum, a court will review the merits of the case. Once matters are properly before a court, it must then determine the appropriate scope and standard of review to apply to an agency action.

G.   SCOPE AND STANDARD OF REVIEW

Students of environmental law should keep in mind that the study of judicial standards of review is a very intricate and complex area more fully examined in an administrative law class. Many factors come into play in the review of agency actions. Questions of fact, law, or procedure are scrutinized in varying degrees. The type of agency action in review is also a factor in determining the standard to apply. The study of scope and standards of review is an intricate, complex area of the law which takes many hours of research and

---

[132]   Mountain States Corp. v. Petroleum Corp., 693 F.2d 1015, 1019 (10th Cir.1982).

[133]   Great Northern Railway v. Merchants Elevator Co., 259 U.S. 285; 42 S.Ct. 477; 66 L.Ed. 943 (1922).

[134]   Illinois v. Panhandle E., 730 F.Supp. 826, 939 (C.D.Ill.1990).

study to master. Our explanation is brief and simple and should only serve as a guide to the reader when reading the cases discussed in this book.[135]

The scope and standard of review are the extent and manner in which courts review agencies' conclusions on issues of fact, law or agency discretion. The standards are expressed by legal phrases or formulae. These standards include: *de novo* review, arbitrary and capricious, substantial evidence and strict scrutiny. The scope and standard of review differ depending upon the type of agency action being reviewed. Agency action can result from any one of five different categories of proceedings: informal rulemaking, hybrid rulemaking, formal rulemaking, informal adjudication, and formal adjudication.[136]

Upon review, the court examines an agency's administrative record in varying degrees depending on the issue and type of agency action. In some instances, the court need only consult an agency's enabling act. If an enabling act sets the scope and standard to be applied, the court must follow the mandates of the act. If an enabling act does not speak directly to the issue, then a court will consult the APA for direction.

In general terms, the court applies "de novo" review in rare instances where a jurisdictional or constitutional question of law is in dispute.[137] It applies an "arbitrary and capricious" standard to all informal rulemaking actions and to informal adjudicatory actions. It applies a "substantial evidence" standard to all questions of fact in formal rulemaking actions and formal adjudications. And finally it applies "strict scrutiny" to all questions of law.

---

[135]　*See*, Young, Gordon G., Judicial Review of Informal Agency Action on the Fiftieth Anniversary of the APA: The Alleged Demise and Actual Status of Overton's Park Requirement of Judicial Review "On The Record," 10 Admin.L.J. Am. Univ. 179 (1996).

[136]　Fletcher, Don. C, Holley, Richard F., & Wood, Steven G., Regulation, Deregulation and Re-Regulation: An American Perspective, 1987 B.Y.U. L. Rev. 381, 413 (1987).

[137]　Webster v. U.S. Department of Energy, 108 S.Ct. 2047; 100 L.Ed.2d 632 (1988); Ellison v. Connor, 153 F.3d 247, 253, (5th Cir. 1998).

1.   APA Provisions on Scope and Standard of Review

Section 706 of the APA addresses the scope of review. Below, we provide the exact language of Section 706, and we describe each of the standards in more detail. When necessary for decision making, a reviewing court shall decide all relevant questions of law, interpret constitutional and statutory provisions, and determine the meaning or applicability of the terms of an agency's action. To achieve this, a reviewing court shall:

1)   compel agency action unlawfully withheld or unreasonably delayed; and

2)   hold unlawful and set aside agency action, findings, and conclusions found to be --

A)   arbitrary, capricious, an abuse of discretion, or otherwise not in accordance with law;[138]

B)   contrary to constitutional right, power, privilege, or immunity;

C)   in excess of statutory jurisdiction, authority, or limitations, or short of statutory right;

D)   without observance of procedure required by law;

E)   unsupported by substantial evidence in a case subject to Sections 556 and 557 of this title [dealing with formal adjudications and formal rulemaking] or otherwise reviewed on the record of an agency hearing provided by statute;[139] or

---

[138]   Sierra Club v. Babbitt, 15 F.Supp.2d. 1274 (S.D.Ala. 1998).

[139]   Penobscot Air Services Ltd. v. Federal Aviation Administration, 164 F.3d 713 (1st Cir. 1999).

F)   unwarranted by the facts to the extent that the facts are subject to trial *de novo* by the reviewing court.[140]

2.   *De Novo* Review

De novo review means "review anew." It is conducted as if no agency decision had been previously rendered. The court literally begins from scratch and does not have to rely solely on the administrative record to base its review and decisions. *De novo* review is independent review in which the court may substitute its own judgment for that of an agency's. Section 706(2) of the APA allows *de novo* review where there are procedural, jurisdictional or constitutional questions of law.[141]

3.   Arbitrary and Capricious Standard

The arbitrary and capricious standard allows a court to determine whether an agency considered all relevant factors and whether an agency developed a rational connection between the evidence in the administrative record and an agency decision.[142] To help determine the arbitrary and capricious nature of agency actions, a court will make a searching and careful inquiry into the administrative record. However, a court will not examine the administrative record too strictly. When applying this standard, a court is not empowered to substitute its judgment for that of the agency's.[143]

The arbitrary and capricious standard is a liberal standard and easy to meet. In applying the arbitrary and capricious standard, a court will uphold an agency decision unless it is totally unreasonable. Thus, most agency decisions are not reversed.

---

[140]   APA § 706; 5 U.S.C.A. § 706.

[141]   APA § 706(2); 5 U.S.C.A. § 706(2); *see* Jicarilla Apache Tribe v. Federal Energy Regulatory Comm., 578 F.2d 289, 292-93 (10th Cir. 1978); Christopher Village Ltd. v. Cuomo, 1998 W.L. 422854 (S.D.Tex. 1998).

[142]   Citizens to Preserve Overton Park, Inc. v. Volpe, 401 U.S. at 416; 91 S.Ct. at 823-824; 28 L.Ed.2d at 155.

[143]   APA § 706(2)(A); 5 U.S.C.A. § 706(2)(A); *see*, Society Hill Towers Owners' Assn. v. Rendell, 20 F.Supp.2d 855 (E.D.Penn. 1998).

In applying the arbitrary and capricious standard, a court will set aside an agency's decision if, in the agency's decision making process it:

1)   relied on factors Congress had not intended;

2)   failed to consider an important aspect of the problem;

3)   offered an explanation that runs counter to the evidence before the agency; or

4)   offered an explanation so implausible it could not be ascribed to a difference in view or agency expertise.[144]

The APA establishes procedures that apply the arbitrary and capricious standard to informal agency proceedings.[145] In addition, the APA requires that "[t]he reviewing court shall hold unlawful and set aside agency action . . . unsupported by substantial evidence."[146]

4.   Substantial Evidence Standard

In administrative law, substantial evidence means the court looks for more than a mere scintilla of evidence to support the facts in a case.[147] The court applies the substantial evidence standard to all questions of fact in formal adjudications and formal rulemaking. To determine whether more than a mere scintilla of evidence exists, the court applies a reasonableness standard to the evidence in the administrative record. Reasonableness is measured by whether a reasonable person, looking at the evidence in the administrative record, could have come to the same conclusion as an agency. The United States Supreme

---

[144]   Motor Vehicle Manufacturers Association of the United States, Inc. v. State Farm Mutual Auto Insurance Co., 463 U.S. 29, 43; 103 S.Ct. 2856, 2867; 77 L.Ed.2d 443, 458 (1983).

[145]   APA § 706(2)(A); 5 U.S.C.A. § 706(2)(A).

[146]   APA § 706(2)(E); 5 U.S.C.A. § 706(2)(E).

[147]   Primeco Personal Communications L.P. v. Village of Fox Lake, 26 F.Supp.2d 1052 (N.D.Ill. 1998).

Court states that this standard requires "such relevant evidence as a reasonable mind might accept as adequate to support a conclusion."[148]

The substantial evidence standard allows the courts to rely on an agency's expert opinion, yet requires that the court be satisfied that an agency's decision was reasonable. While the substantial evidence standard applies to questions of fact, the strict scrutiny standard applies only to questions of law.

5.   Strict Scrutiny Standard

A strict scrutiny standard is applied to all questions of law. Questions of law arise as to the terms of the law by which the case is to be adjudicated and can be decided only by a court. The strict scrutiny standard allows the court to engage in a thorough and independent analysis of law with little or no deference to an agency. If the question of law involves procedure, then the court will look to see if an agency failed to abide by the procedural requirements of the Constitution, enabling act, APA, or agency's own rules, and it will not hesitate to overturn an agency's decision. If the question of law involves interpretation of substantive matters, then the court may again decide what the interpretation will be with little or no deference to agency expertise.

H.   REMEDIES

Once a court applies the appropriate standard of review and evaluates the merits of a case, it may find that an agency action was lawful, not arbitrary, or appropriately supported by substantial evidence. If so, the court affirms an agency decision. In other words, it agrees with an agency decision. On the contrary, if the court finds an agency indeed caused a party to suffer "legal wrong" or if it "adversely affected or aggrieved" a party, then the court determines the proper remedy.[149] Court remedies, like administrative remedies, are intended to correct wrongful conduct. Remedies available to the courts will differ depending on their findings.

---

[148]   Universal Camera Corp. v. National Labor Relations Board, 340 U.S. 474, 477; 71 S.Ct. 456, 459; 95 L.Ed. 456, 461-462 (1951)(citing Consolidated Edison Co. v. National Labor Relations Board, 305 U.S. 197, 229; 59 S.Ct. 206, 217; 83 L.Ed. 126, 140-141 (1938)).

[149]   APA § 702; 5 U.S.C.A. § 702.

1.   Actions Not Consistent with Prior Agency Policies

If the court concludes the administrative decision is not consistent with prior agency policies, it will return or "remand" the decision to the respective agency. This allows the agency an opportunity to reconsider why its decision was rational, reasonable, and not arbitrary and capricious. If an agency does not show the reasonableness of its actions, then the court will reverse the agency's decision. In other words, the court will "hold unlawful and set aside agency actions, findings, and conclusions."[150]

2.   Action is Unconstitutional, Outside Legal Authority or Procedurally Flawed

When an agency acts unconstitutionally or outside its legal authority, a court will likely deem the action unlawful. Here, the action is said to be "moot and void." If an agency fails to act in accordance with required procedure, a court will likely hold the action moot and void or remand it back to an agency to comply with procedure. Remand orders are not uncommon when an agency fails to follow rulemaking procedures set out in Section 553 of the APA.[151]

3.   Action is Not Supported by Substantial Evidence

When a plaintiff successfully argues that a final rule or order is not supported by substantial evidence, the court may hold the action moot and void. It may also choose to remand the decision back to an agency and allow it an opportunity to reconstruct the administrative record to show substantial evidence for an agency's decision.

In Section VI(D), we discussed how an agency initially determines what the administrative record will be. An agency assembles documents it feels demonstrates its process and action, and submits them to the court. Once a court remands the decision back to an agency because the record is not supported by substantial evidence, then an agency may add to the record, materials it had originally accumulated in the rulemaking or adjudicatory process. However, the agency may not seek out or add new documents or evidence to the record. As

---

[150]   APA § 706(2); 5 U.S.C.A. § 706(2).

[151]   APA § 553; 5 U.S.C.A. § 553.

with all court decisions, either party may appeal the decision to a higher court and continue doing so all the way to the United States Supreme Court.

VIII.   CONCLUSION

Administrative law is a body of law that establishes procedures that aid agencies in their decision making process. Agencies have the authority to exercise legislative, judicial, and executive powers when they formulate and implement their decisions and policies. Administrative law is a relatively new and continually expanding area of law that defines how agencies develop and implement their regulatory programs.

As you delve into each chapter on NEPA, RCRA, CERCLA, CAA and CWA, you will better understand the relationship between administrative law and environmental law. Each of these statutes declares national policy on environmental issues and addresses distinct problems. These statutes also authorize the use of some or all of the administrative functions discussed above, such as rulemaking, adjudication, administrative, civil and criminal enforcement, the administrative record, citizen suits, and judicial review.

Congress established EPA as the primary agency to implement these statutes. Administrative functions empower EPA, the states, and private citizens to take the responsibility to enforce the various authorized programs. These administrative functions not only shape environmental law, but also control the daily operations of both the regulated industry and agencies authorized to protect our environment.

CHAPTER 2

THE NATIONAL ENVIRONMENTAL POLICY ACT
(NEPA)

"Nature, to be commanded, must be obeyed."

- FRANCIS BACON, *Novum Organum*

CHAPTER 2: NATIONAL ENVIRONMENTAL POLICY ACT

I.   INTRODUCTION

The National Environmental Policy Act ("NEPA"),[1] was enacted in 1969 and signed into law by President Nixon on New Year's Day, 1970. It is a short, general statute designed to institutionalize, within the federal government, a concern for the "quality of the environment."[2] NEPA mandates environmental awareness among all federal agencies. Prior to 1970, most federal agencies acted within their delegated authority without considering the environmental impacts of their actions. However, in the 1960s, Congress seriously began to study pollution problems in this country. Because Congress found that the federal government is both a major cause of environmental harm as well as a major source of regulatory activity, almost all actions of the federal government are impacted by NEPA.

NEPA forces federal agencies, except Congress, the judiciary and the president, to consider the environmental consequences of their actions before implementing a proposal or recommendation. In addition, NEPA is designed to advise the President on the state of the nation's environment and to create an

---

[1]   Pub. L. No. 91-190, 83 Stat. 852 (1970), Codified at 42 U.S.C.A. §§ 4331 (1970); reprinted as amended 42 U.S.C.A. §§ 4321-4370.

[2]   Exec. Order No. 11,514, 3 C.F.R. § 902 (1966-1970).

advisory council called the Council on Environmental Quality (CEQ).[3] The CEQ provides NEPA compliance guidelines and also provides the President with consistent expert advice on national environmental policies and problems.[4]

Between 1970 and 1977, the CEQ served only as an advisory council to the president. However, in 1977, through an executive order, President Carter granted the CEQ binding authority to issue regulations.[5] These regulations set out details for matters that are broadly addressed by NEPA.

NEPA has been interpreted narrowly by the federal courts. As a result, many states have passed much stronger state environmental protection acts (SEPAs) as well. Today, NEPA analysis is undertaken as part of almost every recommendation or proposal for federal action. This not only includes actions by agencies of the federal government, but also states, local municipalities and private corporations whose projects either are respectively impacted by the federal government or are required by federal law to comply with NEPA. NEPA is Congress's mission statement that mandates the means by which the federal government, through the guidance of the CEQ, will achieve its national environmental policy.

II.   POLICY

Congress has declared its national environmental policy in Section 101 of NEPA. It recognized the profound impact of human activity on the natural environment, particularly with respect to population growth, urbanization, industrial expansion, resource exploitation and technological advances.[6]

---

[3]   40 C.F.R. §§ 1500-1517.7.

[4]   NEPA § 204; 42 U.S.C.A. § 4344.

[5]   Exec. Order No. 11,991; 3 C.F.R. § 123 (1977), reprinted in 42 U.S.C.A. § 4321 (1988).

[6]   NEPA § 101; 42 U.S.C.A. § 4331(a).

A.   STATUTORY APPROACH

1.   Congressional Declaration of Purpose

According to the United States Congress, the purpose of NEPA is to declare a national policy which will encourage productive and enjoyable harmony between man and his environment; to promote efforts which will prevent or eliminate damage to the environment and biosphere and stimulate the health and welfare of man; to enrich the understanding of the ecological systems and natural resources important to the Nation; and to establish a Council on Environmental Quality.[7]

According to the CEQ, "NEPA's purpose is not to generate paperwork . . . but to foster excellent action. The NEPA process is intended to help public officials make decisions that are based on an understanding of environmental consequences, and take actions that protect, restore and enhance the environment."[8]

2.   Congressional Declaration of National Environmental Policy

Congress has declared that it is the continuing policy of the federal government, in cooperation with State and local governments, and other concerned public and private organizations, to use all practicable means and measures, including financial and technical assistance, in a manner calculated to foster and promote the general welfare, to create and maintain conditions under which man and nature can exist in productive harmony, and fulfill the social, economic, and other requirements of present and future generations of Americans.[9]

---

[7]   NEPA § 2; 42 U.S.C.A. § 4321; *see also*, Andrean, William L., In Pursuit of NEPA's Promise: The Role of Executive Oversight in the Implementation of Environmental Policy, 64 Ind. L. J. 205 (1989).

[8]   40 C.F.R. § 1500.1(c).

[9]   NEPA § 101; 42 U.S.C.A. § 4331(a).

3.   Federal Government's Responsibility

Section 101 of NEPA sets out the federal government's responsibility for a national environmental policy. ". . . [I]t is the continuing responsibility of the Federal Government to use all practicable means . . . to improve and coordinate Federal plans, functions, programs, and resources to the end that the Nation may . . . achieve a balance between population and resource use which will permit high standards of living and a wide sharing of life's amenities."[10]

4.   Citizen's Responsibility

Congress "recognizes that each person should enjoy a healthful environment and that each person has a responsibility to contribute to the preservation and enhancement of the environment."[11]

Congress has routinely placed upon citizens a responsibility to take an active role in reporting environmental violations to the appropriate agency. Alternatively, citizens are empowered to enforce the law by bringing suit against a violator in state or federal courts.[12] These citizen suits can result in severe penalties against violators.

B.   JUDICIAL INTERPRETATION

Federal courts have interpreted NEPA as a requirement that agencies follow procedures, not that agencies obtain specific outcomes. For example, while NEPA mandates that alternative actions be considered, it does not

---

[10]   NEPA § 101(b)(5); 42 U.S.C.A. § 4331(b)(5). For a good explanation of the role of EPA and other Federal agencies involved in the implementation of NEPA, *see* Rogers, Jr., William H., Environmental Law (1994) [Section 9.2 (B-C), "EPA" and "Other Federal Agencies,"pgs. 824-831].

[11]   NEPA § 101(c); 42 U.S.C.A. § 4331(c). For additional information about the public's role in implementing NEPA, *see* Rogers, Jr., William H., Environmental Law (1994) [Section 9.1 (B)(4), "Public Participation" pg. 814].

[12]   Administrative Procedure Act § 702; 5 U.S.C.A. § 702; Solid Waste Disposal Act § 7002; 42 U.S.C.A. § 6972; Clean Air Act § 304; 42 U.S.C.A. § 7604; Water Pollution Prevention and Control Act § 505; 33 U.S.C.A. § 1365.

necessarily direct which specific alternatives to choose.[13] Despite federal courts' narrow interpretations, NEPA has had a tremendous impact on both government and private actions.

1.   Environmental Consequences Must be Considered

In *Calvert Cliffs' Coordinating Committee, Inc. v. United States Atomic Energy Commission*, the United States Atomic Energy Commission's procedural rules were challenged on the grounds that they failed to comply with the congressional policy of NEPA. The court held that NEPA makes environmental protection a mandate of every federal agency and department. The Appellate Court further stated that these agencies must consider environmental issues just as they consider other matters during their decision making process. Even projects with great economic value will be delayed or ended if insufficient planning is given to environmental concerns.[14]

2.   The Hard Look Doctrine

In *New York Natural Resources Defense Council, Inc. v. Kleppe*, the court held that NEPA requires that an agency take a "hard look" at its environmental consequences before it takes any action.[15] In this case, the State of New York, the Natural Resources Defense Council, and the counties of Suffolk and Nassau, sued Kleppe to prevent oil and gas exploration of submerged lands under the Mid-Atlantic Outer Continental Shelf. The sale of the rights to drill, remove, and dispose of off-shore oil and gas deposits did not comply with NEPA because the final environmental impact statement[16] was "materially deficient." The EIS inadequately analyzed state laws governing

---

[13]   For a good discussion about NEPA's requirement for alternatives, *see* Bear, Dinah, Who Defines the Purpose and Need for the Proposed Action and How are the "Reasonable" Alternatives Developed? SD25 ALI-ABA 199 (Dec. 10, 1998).

[14]   Calvert Cliffs' Coordinating Committee, Inc. v. United States Atomic Energy Commission, 449 F.2d 1109, 1113 (D.C. Cir.1971).

[15]   New York Natural Resources Defense Council, Inc. v. Kleppe, 429 U.S. 1307, 1310; 97 S.Ct. 4, 5-6; 50 L.Ed.2d 38, 41 (1976). Note that in 1976, Thomas E. Kleppe was the United States Secretary of the Interior.

[16]   For an explanation of an "environmental impact statement," see *infra* page 8.

shorelines but it failed to evaluate the extent of state cooperation or opposition to off-shore exploration.

The "hard look" doctrine also requires that courts examine closely the content and scope of an EIS to determine whether it is based on a consideration of relevant environmental factors and to make sure the agency followed the necessary procedural requirements.[17]

However, this scrutiny is balanced by a practical "rule of reasonableness" in which courts consider whether an EIS "has been compiled in good faith" and adequately sets forth sufficient information to allow a decision maker to consider alternatives and make a reasoned decision after balancing the risks of harm to the environment against the benefits of the proposed action."[18]

NEPA does not require an agency to favor an environmentally better course of action, only that it makes decisions to proceed with action after taking a "hard look at environmental consequences."[19] "NEPA does not prohibit the undertaking of federal projects patently destructive of the environment; it simply mandates that the agency gather, study and disseminate information concerning the projects' environmental consequences."[20] However, NEPA requires that agencies consider reasonable mitigation measures for alternatives.[21]

---

[17]   Natural Resources Defense Council, Inc. v. Morton, 458 F.2d 827, 838 (D.C. Cir.1972); Conservation Council of North Carolina v. Froehlke, 435 F.Supp. 775, 782 (M.D.N.C.1977); *see also*, King, Patricia S., Ph.D., Comment, Applying Daubert to the "Hard Look" Requirement of NEPA: Scientific Evidence Before the Forest Service in Sierra Club v. Marita, 2 Wis. Envtl. L. J. 147 (1995).

[18]   Friends of the Boundary Waters Wilderness v. Dombeck, 164 F.3d 1115, 1128 (8th Cir. 1999); City of Carmel by the Sea v. United States Department of Transportation, 123 F.3d 1142, 1155 (9th Cir. 1997); County of Suffolk v. Secretary of Interior, 562 F.2d 1368, 1375 (2d Cir. 1977).

[19]   Robertson v. Methow Valley Citizens Council, 490 U.S. 332, 350; 109 S.Ct. 1835, 1846; 104 L.Ed.2d 351, 370 (1989).

[20]   *Id.*

[21]   *Id.*

3.   Waiver of Sovereign Immunity

In *Citizens for Reid State Park v. Laird*, environmentalists tried to prevent the military from conducting amphibious training and landing exercises on the beaches of Reid State Park in Maine.[22] The District Court asserted that NEPA has a broad reach, applying to both private actions of citizens and to the United States military.[23] Although this is not a strict waiver of federal sovereign immunity, the effect of this decision provided a means for suing the federal government under NEPA, including the military to ensure that all federal agencies comply with NEPA. Ultimately, the District Court held that the Navy complied with NEPA because it considered various factors before conducting operations on the beach. These factors included: damage to the beaches from military vehicles and overnight training exercises, impact on local fishing, increased noise, damage to the ecological systems, and alternatives to the proposed operations.[24] Thus, the United States military, like all federal agencies, must comply with NEPA before making any proposal or recommendation for major federal action affecting the quality of the human environment.

4.   No Substitutes for an Environmental Assessment or an Environmental Impact Statement

The general rule is that there are no substitutes for an Environmental Assessment (EA) or an Environmental Impact Statement (EIS).[25] For example, in *Silva v. Romney*, the Department of Housing and Urban Development (HUD) guaranteed a mortgage to finance a housing project, and adjacent landowners sued to prevent its development.[26] The adjacent landowners claimed that HUD failed to comply with NEPA because no EIS was prepared. HUD presented a Special Environmental Clearance Worksheet in lieu of an EIS. As a result, the

---

[22] Citizens for Reid State Park v. Laird, 336 F.Supp. 783, 784, 788-789 (D.Me.1972); *see also*, Ichter, Cary, Note, "Beyond Judicial Scrutiny": Military Compliance with NEPA, 18 Ga. L. Rev. 639 (1984).

[23] *Id.*

[24] *Id.*

[25] For a detailed explanation defining an EA and an EIS, see *infra* p. 7-8.

[26] Silva v. Romney, 342 F.Supp. 783, 784-785 (D.Mass.1972).

District Court held that the Special Environmental Clearance Worksheet did not satisfy the requirement of Section 102(2)(C) of NEPA mandating an EIS wherever a major federal action was involved. Thus, the District Court ordered the defendants to "take no action to aid in the construction" of the project at that time.[27] Note however that there exists certain exceptions that allow substitutions for an EA or EIS where a "substantial equivalent" has been prepared.[28] However, where a substantial equivalent has been prepared, a thorough independent review must occur within a reasonable time to determine whether it complies with the standards set by NEPA.[29]

5.   NEPA Requires Alternatives

In *City of Boston v. Volpe*, the city of Boston sued to prevent the Massachusetts Port Authority from constructing an airport taxiway. The court held that NEPA requires government officials to consider the environment before a significant project is launched. In addition, alternatives to the proposed project should be considered when any irreversible effects are identified.[30]

III.   PRACTICAL APPLICATION

As NEPA is implemented, it usually begins with an EA which culminates into a Finding of No Significance (FONSI) or an EIS with a Record of Decision (ROD). Alternatively, an agency can decide to simply begin with an EIS which culminates into a ROD. Note that an EA, EIS, FONSI, and ROD are all analytical planning documents prepared as part of an agency's proposal for federal actions (projects). These documents are also prepared by private individuals and companies whose projects have some federal involvement that also may significantly affect the environment, or are required to comply with NEPA based on some federal guideline. After carefully reviewing the federal action, a decision is made to draft either an EA or document that the project falls

---

[27]   *Id.* at 785.

[28]   State of Wyoming v. Hathoway, 525 F.2d 66, 72 (10th Cir.1975) cert. denied, 426 U.S. 906; 96 S.Ct. 2226; 48 L.Ed.2d 830 (1976); *see*, 40 C.F.R. § 1500.4(n), (o) (authorizing adoption of other agencies' documents to eliminate duplication).

[29]   40 C.F.R. § 1500.5(e).

[30]   City of Boston v. Volpe, 464 F.2d 254, 255-57 (1st Cir.1972).

into one of several Categorical Exclusions ("CATXs"). The EA helps determine whether to issue an EIS or a FONSI.

A.   THE ENVIRONMENTAL ASSESSMENT (EA)

An EA is a public analytical document generally 10 to 15 pages long.[31] The EA provides evidence and analysis to help federal agencies determine whether to prepare an EIS or issue a FONSI.

Any one of several parties may prepare an EA during the early planning phase of a proposed project. For example, various lead agency or cooperating state and local agencies may take on the responsibility of drafting the EA. Private environmental consultants are often hired to prepare EAs, FONSIs and EISs for the government or for private companies engaging in projects that are subject to NEPA's regulatory requirements. In *Save Our Wetlands v. Sands*, the Court of Appeals stated, "[t]he agency is not required 'to do it alone' in reviewing the environmental impact of projects. The intent of the controlling regulations is that 'acceptable work [completed by the parties outside the agency] not be redone . . . .'"[32] The purpose of the EA is to evaluate whether proposed projects are "major federal actions significantly affecting the quality of the human environment."[33]

The EA is a useful tool because preparing an EIS is costly, time consuming, and involves input from numerous special interest groups, the public, and other federal agencies. The preparation of an EIS often delays and sometimes permanently ends proposed projects.

---

[31]   For a good discussions about Environmental Assessments and Programmatic Environmental Assessments, *see*, Mandeiker, Daniel R., Environmental Assessments and the Planning Process, SC56 ALI-ABA 519 (1998); *see also* Cooper, Jon C., Broad Programmatic Policy and Planning Assessments Under the National Environmental Policy Act and Similar Devices: A Quiet Revolution in an Approach to Environmental Considerations, 11 Pace Envtl. L. Rev. 89 (1993).

[32]   40 C.F.R. § 1506.5(a)(1979); Save Our Wetlands v. Sands, 711 F.2d 634, 642 (5th Cir.1983).

[33]   NEPA § 102(C); 42 U.S.C.A. § 4332(C).

An EA helps an agency comply with NEPA when no EIS is needed. However, if an EA leads to a decision to prepare an EIS, the EA serves as a foundation for its preparation. The EA includes a brief discussion of the need for the proposal, alternatives to the proposal, environmental impacts of both the proposal and alternatives, and a list of all who were consulted during its development.[34] The EA must also include analysis of other agencies and interested parties who are affected by the proposed action. This demonstrates a sincere effort to comply with NEPA and also provides a concise public document.[35] Many federal programs require preparation of an EA with similar information to an EIS. For example, an EA is required by the Energy Reorganization Act of 1974,[36] for private utility applicants to get a permit to construct nuclear power plants pursuant to mandates of the Nuclear Regulatory Commission.

B.   THE FINDING OF NO SIGNIFICANT IMPACT (FONSI)

The FONSI is a public document produced by a federal agency when it determines from the EA that an EIS is not necessary. It briefly sets out the reasons an action or project will not significantly affect the human environment.[37] A FONSI must include either the EA or a summary of the EA and any environmental documents related to it. If an EA is included, the FONSI may incorporate it by reference to avoid duplicating information.[38]

---

[34]   NEPA § 102(E); 42 U.S.C.A. § 4332(E).

[35]   40 C.F.R. § 1508.9.

[36]   42 U.S.C.A. § 5051.

[37]   40 C.F.R. § 1508.13; *see also*, Fogleman, Valerie M., Threshold Determinations Under the National Environmental Policy Act, 15 B.C. Envtl. Aff. L. Rev. 59 (1987); Garver, Geoffrey, Note, A New Approach to Review of NEPA Findings of No Significant Impact, 85 Mich. L. Rev. 191 (1988).

[38]   *See*, 40 C.F.R. §§ 1501.4(e), 1508.13.

C.   THE ENVIRONMENTAL IMPACT STATEMENT (EIS)[39]

Preparation of an EIS is extremely expensive, time consuming, and complex. Most are from 200 to 800 pages long, and like EAs, are public documents.[40] An EIS is not only a disclosure document, but it is also used by federal agencies to plan actions and make decisions. This process enables federal agencies, decision makers, and the public to make informed judgments regarding a proposed project's merits.[41] The CEQ outlines procedures for creating and implementing the EIS.[42] The responsibility for preparing the EIS rests with the lead federal agency in charge of the proposed action. An EIS must be prepared at an early stage in the planning process before final hearings on proposed projects are conducted.[43]

The EIS must contain enough technical information for scientists to identify significant environmental impacts. However, it must also be written clearly and in laymen's terms so that the general public can understand all the environmental consequences of the proposed action. It is crucial that in presenting this information, the EIS include all reasonable alternatives to the proposed action. These alternatives provide choices for developing a proposed action that do not significantly affect the environment. When alternatives are available, the lead agency is more able to choose the one that best balances the environmental impacts with the social needs of the proposed action. Note however, that the CEQ and NEPA do not require that the agency choose the alternative with the least environmental impacts. However, the EIS must take a hard look at the environmental consequences of the proposed action.

---

[39]   For an excellent discussion of the EIS, *see* Rogers, Jr., William H., Environmental Law (1994) [Section 9.3(B)(2)].

[40]   *See*, Frank, Robert P., Comment, Delegation of Environmental Impact Statement Preparation: A Critique of NEPA's Enforcement, 13 B.C. Envtl. Aff. L. Rev. 79 (1985).

[41]   Environmental Defense Fund, Inc. v. Corps of Engineers of U.S. Army, 348 F.Supp. 916, 993 (N.D.Miss.1972); *judgment aff'd by* Environmental Defense Fund, Inc. v. Corps of Engineers of U.S. Army, 492 F.2d 1123 (5th Cir. 1974).

[42]   40 C.F.R. § 1502.1-.25.

[43]   Greene County Planning Board v. Federal Power Commission, 455 F.2d 412, 418 (2nd Cir.1972) cert. denied, 409 U.S. 849 (1972).

Once the decision is made to prepare an EIS, the lead agency then publishes a Notice of Intent (NOI) in the Federal Register. The NOI should describe the proposed action and possible alternatives, the agency's intent to prepare an EIS, the agency's proposed project evaluation process (known as "scoping" under the CEQ), include any planned meetings, and the name and address of a contact person within the agency. This contact person is the recipient of all written comments and must be available for questions from the public.[44]

IV.   APPLICATION OF NEPA

A.   IS AN EIS REQUIRED?

1.   Federal Agency Review

NEPA requires that all federal agencies review their policies and procedures to ensure that they comply with the Act's purpose.[45] This forces agencies to factor environmental consequences into their regulatory and administrative actions and decisions. All agency policies and procedures must be reviewed unless they do not involve significant environmental impacts.[46] Once the review is complete, the agency must propose an EA and an EIS for those "major Federal actions" it determines are "significantly affecting the quality of the human environment."[47] Each of the elements in this provision have been the subject of extensive litigation and judicial interpretation.

2.   Conditions that Mandate an EIS

"[A]ll agencies of the federal government shall include [an EIS] in every recommendation or report on proposals for legislation and other major federal actions significantly affecting the quality of the human environment."[48] Section

---

[44]   40 C.F.R. §§ 1508.22(c).

[45]   NEPA § 103; 42 U.S.C.A. § 4333.

[46]   40 C.F.R. §§ 1501.4(a)(2), 1507.3(b)(2)(ii), and 1508.4.

[47]   NEPA § 102(C); 42 U.S.C.A. § 4332(C).

[48]   *Id.*

102(C) of NEPA determines whether an EIS should be produced. Thus, proper analysis of three critical components is essential. The action must be federal, must be major, and must significantly affect the quality of the human environment.

a. The Action Must be Federal

The CEQ defines federal action as projects potentially subject to federal control. Federal actions may also include instances when federal officials fail to act. Such inaction is judicially reviewable under the APA as agency action.[49] Generally, courts define federal action as direct or indirect financial assistance, federal approval, control, or responsibility. For example, a project is considered federal action if it cannot exist without a federal agency's approval or funding.[50]

In *Maryland Conservation Council, Inc. v. Gilchrist*, the Court of Appeals held that a state highway construction project was a major federal action because the highway would cross a state park established with a substantial federal grant.[51] It was also necessary to get approval from the Secretary of Interior to convert the parkland to a highway. In addition, construction of the highway would encroach on local wetlands, which would require permit approval by the Secretary of the Army Corp of Engineers. Moreover, to obtain additional federal funds, the Secretary of the Department of Transportation would have to approve the park land use for a transportation program. *Maryland Conservation Council, Inc. v. Gilchrist* exemplifies an instance of multi-federal agency involvement, hence, eliminating any doubt that this "action" is federal.

Where a project is local (city, county, or state), it is considered "federal action" where it is totally or partially funded with federal money. This could come in the form of a grant from such federal agencies as the Department of Interior (funding for a county park), or the Department of Transportation

---

[49]   40 C.F.R. § 1508.18; APA § 704.

[50]   For an in depth discussion of "federal actions," *see* Paget, David, NEPA's "Small Handle" Problem: The Scope of Analysis of Federal Action, SB64 ALI-ABA 175 (1997).

[51]   Maryland Conservation Council, Inc. v. Gilchrist, 808 F.2d 1039, 1042 (4th Cir.1986).

(funding for an intrastate road).[52] On the other hand, a project will not be classified as federal when the responsible federal agency neither gives direct financial aid nor is sufficiently involved.[53]

b.   The Action Must be Major

For an action to be "major," it must be more than merely routine. Projects must involve substantial expenditures of time, money, and resources.[54] The term "major" differentiates between projects that do not involve serious enough affects or are not of a magnitude to justify the costs of an EIS and those projects that are substantial enough to offset the high costs of preparing an EIS.[55] For example, cases which have found the existence of major federal action have ordinarily involved highway extensions, large structures which alter the neighborhood, major dams or river projects, and other projects which involve sizeable federal funding (typically more than $500,000, and usually far more than $1 million), large increments of time for the planning and construction stages, the displacement of many people or animals, or the reshaping of large areas of topography.[56] Courts have defined major federal actions to also include:

1)   construction of I-H 66, a six-lane interstate highway;[57]

---

[52]   Ely v. Velde, 363 F.Supp. 277, 285 (E.D.Va.1973).

[53]   Atlanta Coalition on Transportation Crisis, Inc. v. Atlanta Regional Commission, 599 F.2d 1333, 1347 (5th Cir.1979) (regional development plan was not "federal action" where state and local agencies were solely responsible for contents of the plan, projects proposed, and improvements recommended).

[54]   Julis v. City of Cedar Rapids, Iowa, 349 F.Supp. 88, 89 (N.D.Iowa 1972).

[55]   Township of Ridley v. Blanchette, 421 F.Supp. 435, 466 (E.D.Pa.1976); see also, Hanly v. Kleindiest (Hanly II), 471 F.2d 823 (2nd Cir.1972), cert. denied, 412 U.S. 908; 93 S.Ct. 2290; 36 L.Ed.2d 974 (1973).

[56]   Township of Ridley v. Blanchette, 421 F.Supp. at 466.

[57]   Arlington Coalition on Transportation v. Volpe, 458 F.2d 1323, 1330 (4th Cir.1972) cert. denied, 409 U.S. 1000; 93 S.Ct. 312; 34 L.Ed.2d 261 (1972).

2) $775,000.00 federal grant for construction of a correctional center;[58]

3)   licensing of a nuclear power plant;[59] and

4)   dispersal of $3,193,000 from federal loan funds to build a high-rise student dormitory;[60]

c.   The Action Must Significantly Affect the Human Environment

i.   The Human Environment

Although the legal concept of "human environment" originated within NEPA, NEPA's failure to specifically define "human environment" caused confusion among agencies trying to determine if an EIS was required for their projects. Ultimately, the CEQ defined "human environment" as follows:

"Human Environment" shall be interpreted comprehensively to include the natural and physical environment and the relationship of people with that environment. This means that economic or social effects are not intended by themselves to require preparation of an [EIS]. When an [EIS] is prepared and economic or social and natural or physical environmental effects are interrelated, then the [EIS] will discuss all of these effects on the human environment.[61]

---

[58]   Ely v. Velde, 451 F.2d 1130, 1132, 1139 (4th Cir.1971).

[59]   Izaak Walton League v. Schlesinger, 337 F.Supp. 287, 294 (D.D.C.1971).

[60]   Goose Hollow Foothills League v. Romney, 334 F.Supp. 877, 879 (D.Or.1971).

[61]   40 C.F.R. § 1508.14; *see also*, Robichaux, Jim H. & Shaw, Bill, Council on Environmental Quality: Defining Human Environment, 16 Cal. W. L. Rev. 201, 206, 207 (1980).

(A)   Impacts on the Human Environment

Section 101 of NEPA is very broad because it requires a consideration of the impact of proposed projects beyond the natural and physical environment to also include the "human environment" (e.g., social, health, ecological, aesthetic, historic, cultural, and economic effects).[62] This has led to conflicts among courts in statutory interpretation. As a result, a judicial trend has developed against looking solely toward impacts upon the social and economic environments.[63]

The determinative issue is whether the project's impact on the physical environment is sufficient to trigger NEPA, not whether the project affects only social and economic issues. Note, this physical impact need only be minimal, thereby broadening actions requiring NEPA analysis.[64] Note also, that once triggered, NEPA analysis is not limited solely to physical impacts. Thus if a project has impacts on the physical environment, cultural and historical environments must also be examined.

(B)   Impacts on the Physical Environment

The "physical environment" must be impacted before courts allow other effects to be considered. In *Metropolitan Edison v. People Against Nuclear Energy*, the Supreme Court defined the "physical environment" by looking to the Congressional Record.[65] The Congressional Record defines "physical environment" as impacts "on land, air, and water."[66]

---

[62]   40 C.F.R. §§ 1508.8, 1508.14.

[63]   Olmstead Citizens For A Better Community v. United States, 793 F.2d 201, 205 (8th Cir.1986).

[64]   Metropolitan Edison Co. v. People Against Nuclear Energy, 460 U.S. 766, 772-773; 103 S.Ct. 1556, 1560; 75 L.Ed.2d 534, 541 (1983).

[65]   *Id.*

[66]   115 Cong. Rec. 40416 (1969)(remarks of Sen. Henry Jackson, Washington, Dec. 20, 1969).

(C)   Historical Trends in Impact Analysis

In *Hanley v. Mitchell (Hanley I)*, residents of New York City successfully challenged the construction of a neighborhood jail purely on <u>social</u> and <u>economic</u> grounds and in upholding their challenge, the Second Circuit found that NEPA did not contain an exhaustive list of so-called "environmental considerations," but found that NEPA's aim should extend beyond sewage, garbage, water and air pollution to include the protection of the quality of life for city residents.[67] Noise, traffic, mass transit systems, crime, congestion, drugs, sewage and garbage are all profound influences of urbanization and should not be ignored under NEPA.[68]

However, by 1983, courts began to reexamine the broad language of NEPA when the Supreme Court in *Metropolitan Edison Co. v. People Against Nuclear Energy*, narrowed the language found in *Hanly I* and Section 101, and held that NEPA did not require agencies to assess every impact or social and economic effect of a proposed action but instead, NEPA requires assessment of only the impact on the physical environment.[69]

In a 1988 case, *Panhandle Producers & Royalty Owners Association v. Economic Regulatory Administration*, the Fifth Circuit clarified the dichotomy between the physical environment and the non-physical environment and held that when the only impact on the "human environment" is social and economic, an EIS would not be appropriate.[70] In this case, Panhandle Producers, unsuccessfully tried to stop a proposal to import Canadian natural gas by requiring EPA to complete an EIS in compliance with NEPA. Because the proposal involved using existing pipelines and did not involve construction of any new pipelines, the only effect would be social and economic. Because no

---

[67]   Hanly v. Mitchell (Hanly I), 460 F.2d 640, 647 (2d Cir.1972).

[68]   *Id.*

[69]   Metropolitan Edison Co. v. People Against Nuclear Energy, 460 U.S. at 772; 103 S.Ct. at 1560; 75 L.Ed.2d at 541 (1983) (potential psychological damage from the risk of nuclear disaster was not sufficient to trigger NEPA).

[70]   Panhandle Producers & Royalty Owners Association v. Economic Regulatory Administration, 847 F.2d 1168, 1179 (5th Cir.1988).

natural and physical environmental impacts were threatened, the Court of Appeals held that no EIS was necessary.

Thus, the interpretation of "human environment" can include both social and economic impacts but only after it is shown that natural and physical environmental impacts exist as well. Once "human environment" effects are identified, NEPA analysis requires one to assess whether those effects are "significant."

ii.   Effects Must Be Significant

(A)   Significant

"Significant" requires consideration of both context and intensity. In considering context, one looks at the setting or the interrelated conditions in which something exists or occurs. In considering intensity, one looks at the degree or magnitude of strength or force of impacts on the human environment.[71]

(1)   Context

The significance of an action must be analyzed in "context" including, but not limited to, both short-term and long-term effects on society, the affected region, the affected interests, and the affected locality. An action's significance will vary depending on the location and dynamics of the proposal. For example, local or site-specific projects should be analyzed in relation to "effects in the locale rather than in the world as a whole."[72] Conversely, if the project is regional or even national in scope then the context in which it should be analyzed would be proportionately larger.

(2)   Intensity

"Intensity" refers to the severity of the impact. Many factors should be considered when evaluating "intensity" such as:

1)   beneficial and adverse impact;

---

[71]   40 C.F.R. § 1508.27.

[72]   40 C.F.R. § 1508.27(a).

2)   public health and safety;

3)   unique characteristics of the geographic area such as proximity to historic or cultural resources, park lands, prime farmlands, wetlands, wild and scenic rivers (i.e. "ecologically critical areas");

4)   whether the effects on the quality of the human environment are highly controversial;

5)   whether the possible effects on the human environment are highly uncertain or involve unique or unknown risks;

6)   whether the action will establish precedent for future actions;

7)   whether, in relation to other actions, cumulative significant impacts exist;

8)   the effects on districts, sites, highways, structures, or objects listed or eligible for listing in the National Register of Historic Places or effects that will cause loss or destruction of significant scientific, cultural or historical resources;

9)   whether the action will affect any species or habitat determined to be critical under the Endangered Species Act of 1973; or

10)   whether the action would violate federal, state or local laws.[73]

B.   JUDICIAL INTERPRETATION OF "SIGNIFICANT"

When a conflict arises, courts are responsible for interpreting laws and regulations. Through legal analysis and reasoning, they provide additional clarity and meaning to the congressional purpose and intent of the statutes. Judicial opinions have served an important function in fleshing out when the effects on the human environment are "significant."

---

[73]   40 C.F.R. § 1508.27(b)(10).

1.   Significantly Affect

In *Hanly v. Kleindiest (Hanly II)*, the Second Circuit examined the decision by the General Services Administration (GSA) to build a jail in Manhattan, New York. To determine whether an EIS was necessary, the Court of Appeals had to interpret the term "significantly." The Court of Appeals was concerned that any major federal action, no matter how limited, would have some adverse effect on the human environment whether significant or not. Thus, in the absence of any solid guidelines, the Court of Appeals fashioned a two-part test to determine whether a proposal's effect was significant enough to warrant an EIS. Courts should examine:

1)   the extent to which the proposed action will cause adverse environmental effects in excess of those already in existence in the area; and

2)   the cumulative environmental effects of both the proposed action and the existing adverse conditions in the area.[74]

Meeting both parts of the test "constitutes an adequate consideration of cumulative impact[s] measured by the standard set forth in Hanly II."[75]

2.   Cumulative Effects May be Significant

The CEQ regulations define "cumulative impact" as the "incremental impact of the action when added to other past, present, and reasonably foreseeable future actions."[76] Cumulative impacts can result from individually minor, yet, collectively significant actions. "Cumulative impacts" may be significant enough to require an EIS.

In *Sierra Club v. Marsh*, the First Circuit held that not only should cumulative impact analysis include direct effects (e.g. in *Sierra Club v. Marsh*, the Appeals Court considered consequences to marine animals, waterfowl, water

---

[74]   Hanly v. Kleindienst (Hanly II), 471 F.2d 823, 830-831 (2d Cir.1972).

[75]   Trinity Episcopal School Corp. v. Romney, 387 F.Supp. 1033, 1082 (S.D.N.Y.1974), aff'd in part, rev'd in part, 523 F.2d 88 (2nd Cir.1975).

[76]   40 C.F.R. § 1508.7.

runoff, and land depletion), but it should also include indirect effects.[77] Indirect effects occur later in time or are further removed in distance, but are still reasonably foreseeable. Indirect effects can include changes to the physical and natural environment that will likely encourage industrial, commercial, or residential development in the area. Some examples consist of changes in the pattern of land use, changes in population density or growth rate, and their effect on air, water and other natural systems.[78]

In *City of Davis v. Coleman*, increased population, traffic, pollution, and increased demand for services, such as recreational facilities, utilities, education, and police and fire protection were all considered growth-inducing effects. However, because these effects were speculative, the Appellate Court held that they *did not have* to be considered.[79] *Emphasis added.* In preparing an EA or EIS, agencies should not consider highly speculative and/or indefinite impacts.[80]

C.   CATEGORICAL EXCLUSIONS (CATXs)

Agencies can identify actions in advance of project proposals, that do not significantly affect the human environment. For these actions, neither an EA nor an EIS is necessary even though they may be considered major federal actions.[81] Categorical exclusions (often referred to as "CATXs") are pre-designated activities that do not individually nor cumulatively have a significant effect on the environment.[82]

Agencies publish these CATXs and subsequently apply them to applicable proposals. If a CATX applies to a proposed action, usually no EA, FONSI nor EIS is required. However, sometimes an EIS may still be required,

---

[77]   Sierra Club v. Marsh, 769 F.2d 868, 877-878 (1st Cir.1985).

[78]   40 C.F.R. § 1508.8(b).

[79]   City of Davis v. Coleman, 521 F.2d 661, 665 (9th Cir.1975).

[80]   Kleppe v. Sierra Club, 427 U.S. 390, 404; 96 S.Ct. 2718, 2728; 49 L.Ed.2d 576, 587 (1976).

[81]   40 C.F.R. §§ 1501.4(a)(2), 1507.3(b)(2)(ii), 1508.4.

[82]   40 C.F.R. § 1508.4.

even if a CATX would apply. This occurs in extraordinary circumstances when a normally excluded action may still have significant environmental impacts. A CATX does not exempt a proposal from the NEPA process because the choice to use a CATX must still be documented, even though it helps reduce the necessity for an EA or EIS. One example of a federal agency developing its own CATXs is within the United States Department of Transportation (DOT). The DOT has established CATXs to be those certain actions that do not:

1)   involve significant environmental impact on planned growth or land use;

2)   require relocation of a populous;

3)   significantly impact natural, cultural, recreational, historic or other resources;

4)   significantly involve air, noise or water quality impacts;

5)   significantly impact traffic patterns; and

6)   otherwise significantly impact the environment, either individually or cumulatively.[83]

V.   NEPA'S PROCEDURAL STEPS

The process for implementing NEPA can be briefly summarized in four steps. First, conduct a preliminary environmental assessment to determine whether any CATXs apply. If no CATXs apply, or if there are extraordinary circumstances that make a CATX inapplicable, then prepare an EA. Second, determine whether to prepare a FONSI or an EIS. Third, follow the CEQ regulations throughout the NEPA process. Fourth, create a comprehensive administrative record of your actions.

---

[83]   23 C.F.R. § 771.117(a)(1999); *see also*, Jones v. Gorgon, 792 F.2d 821, 827-829 (9th Cir.1986).

A.   PREPARE AN EA

The main purpose for preparing an EA is to determine whether the lead agency should issue an EIS or a FONSI.[84] Agencies shall prepare an EA unless they have already decided to prepare an EIS.[85] If no CATXs apply and the lead agency has decided to prepare an EA, the lead agency shall involve other governmental agencies, interested private parties, and the public.[86]

Because the EA is a public document, agencies responsible for its preparation must involve the public through notice and hearings where required or applicable.[87] An agency shall hold public hearings whenever appropriate.[88] A public hearing should be held when there is:

1)   a substantial environmental controversy; or

2)   a request for a hearing is made by another agency with jurisdiction over the action.[89]

In addition, agencies shall provide notice to interested parties of the availability of environmental documents concerning the proceeding, and shall mail notice to those who have requested it.[90]

---

[84]   40 C.F.R. § 1508.9(a)(1).

[85]   40 C.F.R. § 1501.3(a).

[86]   40 C.F.R. § 1501.4(b).

[87]   For a good discussion of the role of public participation in NEPA, *see*, Tab, William Murray, The Role of Controversy in NEPA: Reconciling Public Veto with Public Participation in Environmental Decision Making, 21 Wm. & Mary Envtl. L. & Policy, Rev. 175 (1997).

[88]   40 C.F.R. § 1506.6(c).

[89]   Friends of Ompompanoosuc v. Federal Energy Regulatory Commission, 968 F.2d 1549, 1557 (2nd Cir.1992).

[90]   40 C.F.R. § 1506.6(b)(1).

B.   DETERMINE WHETHER TO PREPARE AN EIS OR FONSI

Once an EA has been prepared, the lead agency should study the results to determine whether the project will have a significant impact on the human environment. If so, then an EIS is required. If not, the agency should prepare a FONSI.[91]

1.   FONSI

If, after reviewing the EA, an agency recommends not to prepare an EIS, it shall issue a "finding of no significant impact" (commonly referred to as a "FONSI").[92] When the decision is made to prepare and issue a FONSI, the lead agency shall make diligent efforts to involve the public through notice and hearings where required.[93] Public notice and hearings are necessary to inform those interested persons and agencies of the proposed FONSI. Public notice and hearings allow interested parties an opportunity to voice their approval or opposition prior to a final decision to issue the FONSI.

In certain circumstances, public comment on a FONSI may reveal new information that subsequently necessitates creation of an EIS. When this occurs, an agency must make the FONSI publicly available for review for no less than 30 days before the agency makes its final determination to prepare an EIS and before any action may begin.[94] These circumstances apply when:

1)   the proposed action is, or is closely similar, to one that normally requires the preparation of an EIS; or

2)   the nature of the proposed action is unique and one without precedent.[95]

---

[91]   40 C.F.R. § 1501.4(c),(e).

[92]   40 C.F.R. §§ 1501.4(e), 1508.13.

[93]   40 C.F.R. § 1506.6.

[94]   40 C.F.R. § 1501.4(e)(2).

[95]   40 C.F.R. § 1501.4(e)(2)(I) and (ii).

"Precedent" occurs where similar actions have already been planned or commenced in the same area as the proposed actions. If this is the case, then the 30-day comment period is not necessary because interested parties have already had an opportunity to comment. However, when the action conflicts with other potential land uses in the same area, then the 30-day period is required.[96]

2.   Challenges to the FONSI

Once an agency issues a FONSI, the agency's decision is subject to judicial review. An aggrieved party may challenge the decision to issue a FONSI in federal court under the APA.[97] However, in the past, Appellate Courts were split on how review was to be conducted. As a result, Appellate Courts developed "divergent standards of review to assess an agency's failure to prepare an EIS."[98] These reviews were developed by applying either a "reasonableness" or an "arbitrary and capricious" standard. Historically, the circuits differed as follows:[99]

1)   The First, Second, Fourth and Seventh Circuits upheld the arbitrary and capricious standard.[100]

2)   The Third Circuit assumed but never really decided that a reasonableness standard was appropriate.[101]

---

[96]   Sabine River Authority v. United States Dept. of Interior, 745 F.Supp. 388, 400-01 (E.D.Tex.1990), Aff'd 951 F.2d 669 (5th Cir.1992).

[97]   APA § 706(2)(A).

[98]   Gee v. Boyd, 471 U.S. 1058, 1059; 105 S.Ct. 2123, 2124; 85 L.Ed.2d 487, 488 (1985).

[99]   Id.

[100]   Grazing Fields Farm v. Goldschmidt, 626 F.2d 1068, 1072 (1st Cir.1980); Hanly II, 471 F.2d at 828-29; Nucleus of Chicago Homeowners Assn. v. Lynn, 524 F.2d 225, 229 (7th Cir.1975), cert. denied, 424 U.S. 967; 96 S.Ct. 1462; 47 L.Ed.2d 734 (1976).

[101]   Township of Lower Alloways Creek v. Public Service Electric & Gas Co., 687 F.2d 732, 741-42 (3d Cir.1982).

3)   The Sixth Circuit refused to choose between the two standards.[102]

4)   The Court of Appeals for the District of Columbia developed a four-part test to determine whether agency action was arbitrary and capricious.[103]

5)   Five remaining circuits employed the "reasonableness" standard of review.[104]

In a 1973 case, *Save Our Ten Acres v. Kreger*, the Fifth Circuit employed the "reasonableness" test to scrutinize an agency's FONSI and determined that "the court should proceed to examine and weigh the evidence of both the plaintiff and the agency to determine whether the agency reasonably concluded that the particular project would have no effects which would significantly degrade our environmental quality."[105] This examination included administrative records, affidavits, depositions, and other proof concerning the project's environmental impact.[106] However, today, the reasonableness test is no longer the standard.

---

[102]   Boles v. Onton Dock, Inc., 659 F.2d 74, 75 (6th Cir.1981).

[103]   Sierra Club v. Peterson, 717 F.2d at 1413 (D.C. Cir.1983) Note: Cases in the D.C. Circuit have employed a four part test to scrutinize an agency's finding of no significant impact. The courts ascertained 1) whether the agency took a hard look at the problem; 1) whether the agency identified the relevant areas of environmental concern; 3) as to the problems studied and identified, whether the agency made a convincing case that the impact was insignificant; and 4) if there was an impact of true significance, whether the agency convincingly established that changes in the project sufficiently reduced it to a minimum.

[104]   Save Our Ten Acres v. Kreger, 472 F.2d 463, 466 (5th Cir.1973); Winnebago Tribe of Nebraska v. Ray, 621 F.2d 269, 271 (8th Cir.1980) cert. denied, 449 U.S. 836; 101 S.Ct. 110; 66 L.Ed.2d 43 (1980); Foundation for North American Wild Sheep v. United States Dept. of Agriculture, 681 F.2d 1172, 1177-78 (9th Cir.1982); Wyoming Outdoor Coordinating Council v. Butz, 484 F.2d 1244, 1248-49 (10th Cir.1973); Bonner v. City of Prichard, 661 F.2d 1206 (11th Cir.1981).

[105]   Save Our Ten Acres v. Kreger, 472 F.2d at 467.

[106]   *Id.*

In 1989, the United States Supreme Court abandoned the "reasonableness" standard of agency review, and held that an agency's decision is reviewable if it acted in an "arbitrary and capricious" manner.[107] In 1992, the Fifth Circuit followed the 1989 United States Supreme Court ruling in *Marsh v. Oregon Natural Resources Council*, by stating that "[t]he standard of review is limited, therefore, to the 'arbitrary and capricious' standard."[108]

In *Sierra Club v. Peterson*, the Court of Appeals for the District of Columbia held that the agency's action was "arbitrary and capricious" because the United States Department of Interior and the United States Forestry Service sanctioned activities, with the potential for disturbing the environment, without fully assessing the possible environmental consequences.[109] The agencies issued leases that allowed for drilling and road building on 28,000 acres of two national forests without an EIS. The Court of Appeals held that under the APA, the reviewing court should set aside agency actions, findings, and conclusions found to be arbitrary and capricious.[110]

C.   FOLLOW THE CEQ REGULATIONS THROUGHOUT THE NEPA PROCESS

The next step in NEPA compliance is to follow the CEQ regulations throughout the NEPA process. NEPA has declared one of its purposes the creation of the CEQ.[111] By executive order, President Carter gave the CEQ authority to issue binding regulations.[112] As such, CEQ regulations have the force of law and must be followed to implement NEPA.

---

[107]   Marsh v. Oregon Natural Resources Council, 490 U.S. 360; 109 S.Ct. 1851; 104 L.Ed.2d 377 (1989).

[108]   Sabine River Authority v. United States Dept. of Interior, 951 F.2d 669, 678 (5th Cir.1992).

[109]   Sierra Club v. Peterson, 717 F.2d at 1413.

[110]   APA § 706(2)(A); 5 U.S.C.A. § 706(2)(A).

[111]   NEPA §§ 2, 202; 42 U.S.C.A. §§ 4321, 4342.

[112]   Exec. Order No. 11,991, 42 Fed.Reg. 26,967 (1977).

1.   Issuing the EIS

An EIS serves two main purposes as well as others: (1) to provide decision makers with enough information to help decide whether to proceed with the project in light of its environmental consequences; and (2) to provide the public with information and an opportunity for oral and written participation. By doing so, NEPA guarantees that relevant information is made available to the public and ensures that the public also plays a role in the final decision.[113]

a.   Rule of Reason Test

Reasonable deliberation is called for in the final decision making process. The Appellate Court in *Trout Unlimited v. Morton*, phrased it simply: "A reasonably thorough discussion of the significant aspects of the probable environmental consequences is all that is required by an EIS."[114]

In 1975, the Fifth Circuit conveyed, "we are governed by the rule of reason, i.e., we must recognize 'on the one hand that [NEPA] mandates that no agency limit its environmental activity by the use of an artificial framework and on the other that the Act does not intend to impose an impossible standard on the agency.'"[115] In 1976, the Supreme Court followed suit by holding that the adequacy of an EIS should be determined through application of a practical "rule of reason."[116] This "rule of reason" must be applied throughout the EIS process, beginning with the preparation of an EIS.

b.   Timing

An agency must initiate an EIS at some point after a proposed action is deemed covered by NEPA. The timing is important. If the agency drafts the EIS after concluding which action to take, its locality, and which construction methods to use, then it would not be sincere in considering the environmental consequences, and it would be violating the spirit and objectives of NEPA. In

---

[113]   Citizens for a Better Henderson v. Hodel, 768 F.2d 1051, 1056 (9th Cir.1985).

[114]   Trout Unlimited v. Morton, 509 F.2d 1276, 1283 (9th Cir.1974).

[115]   Sierra Club v. Morton, 510 F.2d 813, 819 (5th Cir.1975).

[116]   New York Natural Resource Defense Council, Inc. v. Kleppe, 429 U.S. at 1311.

response, CEQ regulations provide guidance to agencies regarding the timing of an EIS. The EIS should contribute to the decision making process and not be used to rationalize or justify existing decisions. An agency shall prepare an EIS as closely as possible to the time the agency is itself developing a proposal or is presented with a proposal from an outside source. The EIS shall be prepared early enough to impact and contribute to the decision making process.[117] EIS timing has been the subject of much litigation. The EIS must be prepared before an irreversible commitment of resources is made.[118] Once large investments of time and money have been committed, it becomes more difficult to apply the principles of NEPA.[119] A federal agency may not advance a project by processing permit applications, issuing permits, or participating in interagency meetings to further the project's development before an EIS has been issued. With the exception of work and funding necessary to prepare the EIS, all federal participation must be suspended until the EIS is completed and filed.[120]

2.   Notice of Intent

As soon as practicable after its decision to prepare an EIS and before the proposed project evaluation process (scoping) begins, the lead agency must publish a notice of intent (NOI) in the Federal Register.[121] This notice announces that an EIS will be prepared for a specific project.[122]

3.   Scoping

Scoping is "an early and open process for determining the scope of issues to be addressed and for identifying the significant issues related to a proposed

---

[117]   *Id.*

[118]   Conner v. Burford, 848 F.2d 1441, 1446 (9th Cir.1988).

[119]   Environmental Defense Fund v. Andrus, Inc., 596 F.2d 848, 853 (9th Cir.1979).

[120]   Blue Ocean Preservation Society v. Watkins, 767 F.Supp. 1518, 1528 (D.Haw.1991).

[121]   40 C.F.R. § 1501.7.

[122]   40 C.F.R. § 1508.22.

action."[123]   At this point, various lead and cooperating agencies must be acknowledged to invite their participation.

a.   Lead Agency

When more than one federal agency is involved, the agencies designate a lead agency to supervise preparation of the EIS. When agencies disagree on which one should lead, they consider the following factors to determine who the lead agency should be:

1)   magnitude of an agency's involvement;

2)   project approval/disapproval authority;

3)   expertise concerning the action's environmental effects;

4)   duration of an agency's involvement; and

5)   the sequence of an agency's involvement.[124]

b.   The Scoping Process

The CEQ requires that once a lead agency is designated, it must complete the scoping process. As part of the process, the lead agency shall:

1)   invite the participation of affected federal, state, and local agencies and other interested persons;

2)   determine the significance and scope of issues to be analyzed in the EIS;

3)   identify and eliminate issues that are insignificant or that have been previously reviewed;[125]

---

[123]   40 C.F.R. § 1501.7.

[124]   40 C.F.R. § 1501.5(c)(1)-(5).

[125]   For example, under CEQ Section 1506.3, an agency may adopt another federal agency's draft or final EIS, narrowing the discussion of these issues to a brief presentation

4)   allocate assignments for EIS preparation among the lead and cooperating agencies, with the lead agency retaining responsibility for the statement;

5)   indicate any public EA and EIS that is being or will be prepared that is related to, but not a part of, the scope of the EIS under consideration;

6)   to prevent duplication of efforts, the lead agency shall identify other concurrent evaluation requirements and integrate them into the EIS; and

7)   to demonstrate consideration of environmental consequences prior to deciding final action, the agency must explain the timing of the EIS and its relationship to the planning and decision making schedule.[126]

c.   Implementing The Scoping Process

In drafting an EIS, the lead agency must conduct a scoping analysis to consider various actions, alternatives and impacts.[127]

i.   Actions

There are three types of actions the lead agency must examine during the scoping analysis: connected, cumulative, and similar actions.[128]

---

of why they will not have a significant effect on the human environment.

[126]   40 C.F.R. § 1501.7(a)(1)-(7).

[127]   40 C.F.R. § 1508.25.

[128]   *See*, Swartz, Lucinda L., Analyzing Cumulative Impacts Under NEPA, SB64 ALI-ABA 285 (1997).

(A)   Connected Actions

The CEQ requires that all "connected actions" be considered in a single EIS.[129] Actions are connected if they:

1)   automatically trigger other actions that may require an EIS;

2)   cannot proceed unless other actions are taken previously or simultaneously; or

3)   are interdependent parts of a larger action but depend on the larger action for their justification.[130]

For example, in *Thomas v. Peterson*, the Appellate Court held that because road construction and timber sales were connected actions, it was necessary to prepare an EIS analyzing their combined impact.[131] In this case, timber sales could not proceed without the roads and the roads would not be built but for the timber sales.

(B)   Cumulative Actions

The CEQ also requires that "cumulative actions" be considered together in a single EIS. Cumulative actions occur when environmental impacts increase because of the collective actions of past, present and reasonably foreseeable future events.[132] Results can be individually minor yet collectively significant over a period of time.[133]

---

[129]   *See*, Cohen, William M., Connected Actions and Cumulative and Synergistic Impacts Under NEPA, SB91 ALI-ABA 1361 (1997).

[130]   40 C.F.R. § 1508.25(a)(1)(I)-(iii).

[131]   Thomas v. Peterson, 753 F.2d 754, 757-759 (9th Cir.1985).

[132]   40 C.F.R. §§ 1508.7, 1508.25(a)(2).

[133]   For a good discussion of cumulative effects of actions, *see*, Randall, Gary B., Environmental Effects, SD25 ALI-ABA 223 (1998).

For example, the Ninth Circuit stated that there were situations in which an agency was required to consider several related actions in a single EIS and compelled the Forest Service to prepare an EIS analyzing the combined environmental impacts of both the road and timber sales.[134] The Fish and Wildlife Service made comments that were sufficient to raise substantial questions as to whether the proposed road and timber sales would have significant cumulative environmental effects. The Fish and Wildlife Service argued that, "separate documentation of related and cumulative potential impacts may be leading to aquatic habitat degradation unaccounted for in individual EAs. Lack of an overall effort to document cumulative impacts could be having present and future detrimental effects."[135]

(C)   Segmenting Cannot Evade Cumulative Impacts

When large projects are partitioned to avoid or minimize applications of the NEPA regulations, segmenting occurs. Substantial case law clearly prohibits segmenting for the purpose of avoiding the NEPA process.[136]

In *City of Rochester v. United States Postal Service*, the Rochester postal project involved construction of a new facility, abandonment of an older facility, and transfer of 1,400 employees. The EIS did not consider the effects of abandoning the older facility nor the transfer of 1,400 employees. The Court of Appeals held that while abandonment of the older facility and transfer of 1,400 employees were separable from a standpoint of construction, all activities combined and affected by the project required an EIS.

The Court of Appeals observed that the increase in commuter traffic, loss of jobs for residents who could not move or commute, and abandonment of the older facility would cause such urban decay that environmental repair would be difficult if not infeasible. The Court of Appeals further explained, "To permit non-comprehensive consideration of a project divisible into smaller parts, each

---

[134]   Thomas v. Peterson, 753 F.2d, at 758.

[135]   *Id.* at 759.

[136]   City of Rochester v. United States Postal Service, 541 F.2d 967 (2d Cir.1976); Alpine Lakes Protection Society v. Schlapfer, 518 F.2d 1089 (9th Cir.1975); Appalachian Mountain Club v. Brinegar, 394 F.Supp. 105 (D.N.H.1975).

of which taken alone does not have a significant impact but which taken as a whole has cumulative significant impacts would provide a clear loophole in NEPA."[137]

(D)   Similar Actions

Actions, when viewed with other foreseeable or proposed agency actions may have similarities that suggest a basis for evaluating their environmental consequences together, such as common timing or geography. The best way to assess the combined impact of similar actions is to treat them in a single EIS.[138] "The Supreme Court has read this provision to require that 'when several proposals that will have a cumulative or synergistic environmental impact upon a region are pending concurrently before an agency, their environmental consequences must be considered together.'"[139]

ii.   Alternatives

An agency must "study, develop and describe appropriate alternatives to recommended courses of action in any proposal, which involves conflicts concerning alternative uses of available resources."[140]

(A)   Regulatory Approach

According to the CEQ, alternatives are at the heart of an EIS. For example, federal agencies shall:

1)   rigorously explore and objectively evaluate all reasonable alternatives, and for alternatives which were eliminated from

---

[137]   City of Rochester v. United States Postal Service, 541 F.2d 967, 972 (2d Cir.1976).

[138]   40 C.F.R. § 1508.25(a)(3).

[139]   D'Agnillo v. United States Department of Housing and Urban Development, 738 F.Supp. 1443, 1447-1448 (S.D.N.Y.1990); Kleppe v. Sierra Club, 427 U.S. 390, 410; 96 S.Ct. 2718, 2730; 49 L.Ed.2d 576, 590 (1976).

[140]   NEPA § 102(E); 42 U.S.C.A. § 4332(E).

detailed study, briefly discuss the reasons for their having been eliminated;[141]

2)   devote substantial treatment to each alternative considered in detail including the proposed action so that reviewers may evaluate their comparative merits;[142]

3)   include reasonable alternatives not within the jurisdiction of the lead agency;[143]

4)   include the alternative of no action;[144]

5)   identify the agency's preferred alternative or alternatives, if one or more exists, in the draft statement and identify such alternative in the final statement unless another law prohibits the expression of such a preference;[145] and

6)   include appropriate mitigation measures not already included in the proposed action or alternatives.[146]

(B)   Judicial Approach

If an EIS is issued without considering alternatives, the EIS is inadequate.[147] NEPA's demand for alternative analysis requires that agencies

---

[141]   40 C.F.R. § 1502.14(a).

[142]   40 C.F.R. § 1502.14(b).

[143]   40 C.F.R. § 1502.14(c).

[144]   40 C.F.R. § 1502.14(d).

[145]   40 C.F.R. § 1502.14(e).

[146]   40 C.F.R. § 1502.14(f).

[147]   Idaho Conservation League v. Mumma, 956 F.2d 1508, 1519 (9th Cir.1992); *see also*, Citizens For A Better Henderson v. Hodel, 768 F.2d 1051, 1057 (9th Cir.1985).

take a "hard look" at the alternatives.[148] As a result, an agency must look at every reasonable alternative dictated by the nature and scope of the proposed action to permit a reasoned choice.[149]

It is important to note, however, that a federal agency does not have to address all alternatives, but only those that are reasonable.[150] For example, if a proposed highway could serve the community if constructed through a less environmentally fragile area, then the alternative route should be addressed. But if data suggests it is geologically unsound to construct through the alternative area, even though environmentally sound, it may not be reasonable and thus may not be included in the EIS. The EIS must discuss all reasonable alternatives the agency considered and why it either adopted or rejected each.

iii.   Impacts

Impacts are changes in the physical, natural and social environments that would be caused by proposed actions. They are categorized primarily as direct or indirect. Subcategories of these direct and indirect impacts are those that affect social, ecological, economic, and psychological environments.

(A)   Direct Impacts

Direct impacts are the reasonably foreseeable and immediate consequences of a proposed action. In *Sierra Club v. Marsh*, the Fifth Circuit held that impact analysis should include direct effects such as land depletion, water runoff, and repercussions on marine animals and waterfowl.[151] Some examples of direct impacts include:

---

[148]   Idaho Conservation League v. Mumma, 956 F.2d at 1519; *see also*, Robertson v. Methow Valley Citizens Council, 490 U.S. 332, 352; 109 S.Ct. 1835, 1847; 104 L.Ed.2d 351, 371 (1989).

[149]   Idaho Conservation League v. Mumma, 956 F.2d at 1520.

[150]   Natural Resources Defense Council, Inc. v. Morton, 458 F.2d 827, 836 (D.C. Cir.1972).

[151]   Sierra Club v. Marsh, 769 F.2d. 868 (1st Cir.1985).

1)   suspension of sediment and removal of organisms and vegetation caused by harbor dredging;[152]

2)   impacts of storing forest and food products at a cargo terminal development site on an undeveloped island;[153]

3)   the sacrifice of extensive aquatic habitat resulting from excavating a river bottom to widen a channel;[154]

4)   transfer of 7,500 people from an air force base in Missouri to one in Illinois;[155]

5)   population growth, urbanization and industrial expansion;[156]

6)   the destruction of wetlands by a housing developer to construct a canal system;[157] and

7)   coastal zone injury from the sale of off-shore oil and gas leases.[158]

(B)   Indirect Impacts

An EIS must also consider indirect impacts that may occur later in time and are reasonably foreseeable. Indirect impacts may include industrial or economic growth, changes in land use, population density and related effects on

---

[152]   Alison Rieser, Managing The Cumulative Effects of Coastal Land Development: Can Maine Law Meet The Challenge?, 39 Me.L.Rev. 321 (1987).

[153]   Sierra Club v. Marsh, 714 F.Supp. 539, 567 (D.Me.1989).

[154]   State of Mississippi v. Marsh, 710 F.Supp. 1488, 1511 (S.D.Miss.1989).

[155]   McDowell v. Schlesinger, 404 F.Supp. 221 (W.D.Mo.1975).

[156]   NEPA § 101(a); 42 U.S.C.A. § 4331(a).

[157]   Fritiofson v. Alexander, 772 F.2d 1225, 1246 (5th Cir.1985).

[158]   Secretary of the Interior v. California, 464 U.S. 312, 349; 104 S.Ct. 656, 675; 78 L.Ed.2d 496, 521 (1984).

air, water, and other natural ecosystems.[159] Agencies, however, should not consider highly speculative nor indefinite impacts.[160] For example, in *Warm Springs Task Force v. Gribble*, an injunction was sought challenging the validity of an EIS for a proposed dam.[161] The Court of Appeals said that the consequences of a dam failure as the result of an earthquake need not be discussed because "an impact statement need not discuss remote and highly speculative consequences."[162]

(C)   Mitigation

Mitigation offsets or compensates for adverse impacts caused by a proposed action. If adequate mitigation measures are incorporated into the design of a proposed action, the need for an EIS may be eliminated because the impacts may no longer be significant. For example, mitigation seeks to:

1)   avoid impacts altogether by not taking a certain action or parts of an action;

2)   minimize impacts by limiting the degree or magnitude of an action and its implementation;

3)   rectify impacts by repairing, rehabilitating or restoring an affected environment;

4)   reduce or eliminate impacts over time by preserving and maintaining operations during the life of an action; or

5)   compensate for impacts by replacing or providing substitute resources or environments.[163]

---

[159]   40 C.F.R. § 1508.8(b).

[160]   Sierra Club v. Marsh, 769 F.2d at 878; Kleppe v. Sierra Club, 427 U.S. at 402.

[161]   Warm Springs Dam Task Force v. Gribble, 621 F.2d 1017 (9th Cir.1980).

[162]   *Id*. at 1026.

[163]   Government Institutes, Inc., Environmental Regulatory Glossary, (William G. Frick & Thomas F.P. Sullivan eds., 5th Ed. 1990).

With mitigation, the overall adverse effects of a proposed project are minimized. Often, parties who seek to avoid an EIS will specify mitigating circumstances that downplay environmental concerns. While mitigating measures are an important ingredient of an EIS, NEPA does not require agencies to mitigate adverse environmental effects nor does it require a mitigation plan.[164] An example of a successful mitigation occurred in *Friends of the Payette v. Horseshoe Bend Hydroelectric Co.* Here, plaintiffs argued that the EA did not adequately consider the project's impact on the fishery in the bypass stretch. The Ninth Circuit held that because the United States Army Corps of Engineers (USACOE) included mitigation measures to compensate for fish killed and loss of diversity in the bypass stretch, no EIS was necessary and the EA was sufficient.[165] The measures sheltered wetlands against adverse effects and were designed to protect bald eagles and their habitat.

D.   CREATE AN ADMINISTRATIVE RECORD

A final step in complying with the NEPA process involves creating a comprehensive administrative record. Both public and judicial review are cornerstone concepts that allow close monitoring and scrutiny of agency actions. The most effective means of review is through the use of an agency's administrative record. Agencies must document in the administrative record that their decisions are reasonable and not arbitrary and capricious. Judicial review of administrative action is limited to an agency's administrative record.[166] As discussed in Chapter One, an agency determines what comprises the record by assembling the documents much as does the appellant in an appeal from a trial court to a Court of Appeals, and submits what it denominates as the record.

---

[164]   Robertson v. Methow Valley Citizens Council, 490 U.S. 332, 352; 109 S.Ct. 1835, 1847; 104 L.Ed.2d 351, 371 (1989).

[165]   Friends of the Payette v. Horseshoe Bend Hydroelectric Co., 988 F.2d 989, 993-994 (9th Cir.1993).

[166]   Sive, David, The Problem of the "Record" In Judicial Review of Administrative Action, C534 ALI-ABA 451, 453 (1990).

1.   Regulatory Authority

The CEQ requires that each agency prepare a concise public "record of decision (ROD)."[167] At a minimum, the ROD must: (1) state the decision; (2) identify alternatives considered; (3) specify alternatives found "environmentally preferable" based on economic and technical considerations, the agency's mission and the nation's policy influence on the decision; and (4) identify all mitigation measures adopted and/or rejected and give reasons for its choices.[168]

2.   Contents

The administrative record may include such items as:

1)   the notice of proposed rulemaking;

2)   public comments filed;

3)   work product (unprivileged) created by or relied upon by the agency in promulgating its decision or implementing its action;

4)   all notices, orders, motions, pleadings, evidence, official notice, oral and written statements, objections, and hearing transcripts;

5)   the results of agency investigations (EAs, EISs);

6)   information the agency found useful in promulgating the rule;

7)   intra- and inter-agency discussions;

8)   the statement of basis and purpose; and

9)   the final rule or order.

---

[167]   Note that other documents, such as the FONSI (if issued) must also be included in the administrative record.

[168]   40 C.F.R. § 1505.2(a)-(c).

3.   Judicial Review

Judicial review of agency actions is limited to the administrative record. This limitation is directly applicable to agency actions under NEPA.[169] The administrative record provides the court and public an opportunity to examine information (evidence) for which agency decisions are based. The factual basis of an agency's final decision is presumed reasonably apparent from the administrative record.

VI.   CONCLUSION

NEPA is the first federal mandate primarily focused on the whole environment, not just selected areas. It has forced private parties, as well as federal, state and local entities to take into account environmental consequences of proposed actions. As a result, NEPA is a uniquely effective planning tool. In practical terms, NEPA provides federal agencies with an opportunity to apply almost all environmental laws and certain sociological fields in its planning and decision making processes prior to taking actions that might impact the environment. Also, private citizens can take advantage of NEPA by utilizing it to force agencies and private companies to take environmental matters into consideration during their planning and decision making processes, so long as they qualify under the guidelines of NEPA.[170]

---

[169]   Cohen, William M., The Nature of the Administrative Record, SD47 ALI-ABA 307 (1999); *see also*, Animal Defense Council v. Hodel, 840 F.2d 1432 (9th Cir.1988).

[170]   Caldwell, Lynton K., Beyond NEPA: Future Significance of the National Environmental Policy Act, 22 Harv. Envtl. L. Rev. 203 (1998).

CHAPTER 3
RESOURCE CONSERVATION
AND
RECOVERY ACT
(RCRA)

"Conservation is a state of harmony between man and land."

- Aldo Leopold, *A Sand County Almanac, Part III, The Land Ethic*

CHAPTER 3: RESOURCE CONSERVATION AND RECOVERY ACT

I.   INTRODUCTION

The Resource Conservation and Recovery Act (RCRA)[1] is primarily designed to regulate five types of disposal activities: hazardous waste, solid waste, underground storage tanks, oil waste and medical waste. Under Subtitle C (hazardous waste), RCRA regulates both newly-generated solid waste that are hazardous and, under certain circumstances, the cleanup of abandoned hazardous waste sites. For newly-generated hazardous solid waste, RCRA sets up what is commonly referred to as a "cradle-to-grave" system that regulates hazardous waste from its generation point, through its transportation, and ultimately to its final disposal. RCRA is similar to the Comprehensive Environmental Response, Compensation and Liability Act ("CERCLA") in that both are designed to clean up hazardous waste sites. However, RCRA is limited to abandoned hazardous waste sites that have been categorized with a Hazardous Waste Index ("HWI") below 28.5 while CERCLA most often applies to all other abandoned hazardous waste sites with a HWI of 28.5 or above.[2]

---

[1]   42 U.S.C.A. §§ 6901-6992k; current through P.L. 106-38 (Jul. 22, 1999).

[2]   National Priorities List for Uncontrolled Hazardous Waste Sites, 56 Fed.Reg. 5598, 5599 (Feb. 11, 1991) (codified at 40 C.F.R. Part 300, App. B); 55 Fed.Reg. 51,532, 51,569 (Dec. 14, 1990) (codified at 40 C.F.R. Part 300); Laurent Hourcle, Professor of Law, Lecture at The National Law Center, George Washington University, Solid and Hazardous Waste Class (Oct. 31, 1994) ("The HWI of 28.5 was chosen by EPA

Under Subtitle D (solid waste), RCRA delegates authority to the states to manage and regulate municipal solid waste disposal facilities and programs. These facilities and programs are known as "sanitary landfills" and "solid waste disposal programs." Subtitle D also regulates various recycling programs. Under Subtitle I, RCRA maintains a regulatory program specifically designed to manage underground storage tanks (USTs). This program applies not only to hazardous substances, but many non-hazardous substances as well. UST regulations require storage tanks to be registered with the government, be periodically upgraded to meet minimum technology requirements, be properly closed when their use is completed, and meet certain cleanup regulations of contamination from leaks. RCRA also regulates used oil[3] and medical waste products[4] through a separate set of regulations.

This chapter begins with a focus on portions of RCRA that help define and clarify the complex definitions and management aspects of hazardous waste and solid waste. This chapter later examines various enforcement mechanisms under RCRA.

A.   BACKGROUND

Economic and industrial expansion during the early 1900's meant dramatic increases in the production of goods and their accompanying wastes. By the mid-1900's, the United States began to experience an environmental and health crisis caused by overcrowding, poor sanitation, and primitive methods of waste collection and disposal. By World War II, the sanitary landfill, a systematic layering of earth and waste, became the most widely-used disposal method in the United States. Landfills promised inexpensive and efficient disposal because of the abundance of cheap land.

Today, concern has arisen over a possible "garbage crisis" in America regarding waste volume, content, and availability of landfill space. In recent years, the volume of waste in the United States has increased dramatically. For

---

Administrator Gorsuch in a car on her way to a congressional hearing and represented a cutoff of sites being evaluated that would yield a total of 400 sites, or a proportional amount of sites for each congressional district."); Clark, Terry C., A Practitioner's View of the National Priorities List, 2 Envt'l L. 57 (1995).

[3]   RCRA § 3014; 42 U.S.C.A. § 6935.

[4]   RCRA §§ 11001 - 11012; 42 U.S.C.A §§ 6992 - 6992k.

example, between 1968 and 1988, municipal solid waste alone increased from 140 million tons to 180 million tons per year.[5] In addition, the composition of materials in the waste stream has also changed over the years, posing obstacles in collection as well as adding to the amount of toxic materials in the landfills.

In the 1880's, the most prevalent wastes posing difficult challenges to garbage collectors were coal and wood ash, seasonal food waste, and horse manure. While these wastes were not always pleasant to remove, they were not nearly as diverse, complex or dangerous as our waste streams today. Today such wastes include paper products, glass, plastics, rubbers, metals, leather goods, yard wastes, household chemicals and cleaners, as well as a host of other commercial chemicals and industrial byproducts that are dangerous to human health and the environment.[6] To assist with the concerns of public health and the environment from failed or improper land disposal practices, in 1965 Congress passed the Solid Waste Disposal Act (SWDA).[7]

B.   LEGISLATIVE HISTORY

In 1965, the original SWDA[8] initially failed to create a strong, enforceable federal solid waste program. Its purpose was only to encourage states to develop and implement solid waste management programs. In 1976, RCRA was enacted as Subtitle C and completely revised the SWDA.[9] When enacting RCRA, Congress' overriding concern was to establish the framework for a national system to ensure the safe management of hazardous waste.[10]

---

[5]   THE ENCYCLOPEDIA OF THE ENVIRONMENT, p. 792 (Ruth A. Eblen & William R. Eblen, eds., 1994).

[6]   *Id.*

[7]   *Id.* at 315.

[8]   42 U.S.C.A. §§ 3251-3254f; Pub.L. No. 89-272, 79 Stat. 992 (Oct. 20, 1965).

[9]   Pub.L. 89-272, Title II, § 1002; as amended, Pub.L. 94-580, § 2, Oct. 21, 1976.

[10]   American Mining Congress v. United States EPA, 824 F.2d 1177, 1179 (D.C. Cir.1987) citing to H.R. Representative. No. 1491, 94th Cong., 2d Sess. 3 (1976), U.S.Cong. & Admin.News 1976, 6238, 6240 and 6241.

One of the most significant amendments to RCRA was enactment of the Hazardous and Solid Waste Amendments (HSWA) which were passed in 1984.[11] HSWA increased RCRA's emphasis on recovery and recycling of hazardous wastes.[12] In those amendments, Congress sought to minimize the generation of hazardous waste and the land disposal of hazardous waste by encouraging process substitution, materials recovery, properly conducted recycling and reuse, and treatment.[13]

In 1986, additional amendments to RCRA were added as a result of the Superfund Amendments and Reauthorization Act of 1986 (SARA).[14] These amendments primarily regulated corrective actions for leaking Underground Storage Tanks (USTs).

RCRA was again amended on October 6, 1992 with the passage of the Federal Facility Compliance Act (FFCA).[15] The FFCA is an important act because its primary focus is to facilitate waivers of federal sovereign immunity from fines and penalties, and enforce federal compliance with applicable environmental laws. More specifically, it contains substantive regulations that keep federal facilities in compliance with RCRA.

C.   ORGANIZATION OF SWDA & RCRA

In 1976, RCRA was originally enacted as an amendment to the SWDA[16] and became a subsection of SWDA under Subtitle C. However, although the SWDA is composed of 10 separate subtitles including RCRA (Subtitle C), it is commonly referred to in its entirety as RCRA.

---

[11]   Pub.L. No. 98-616, 98 Stat. 3221 (H.R. 2867; Nov. 8, 1984), codified in various sections of 42 U.S.C.A.

[12]   Blue Circle Cement, Inc. v. Board of County Commissioner's of County of Rogers, 27 F.3d 1499, 1505 (10th Cir.1994).

[13]   *Id.*; 42 U.S.C. § 6902(a)(6).

[14]   Pub.L. No. 99-499, 100 Stat. 1613 (H.R. 2005; Oct. 17, 1986).

[15]   Pub.L. No. 102-386, 106 Stat. 1505 (H.R. 2194; Oct. 6, 1992), codified at 42 U.S.C.A §§ 6903, 6908, 6924, 6927, 6939c-6939e, 6961 and 6965 (1995).

[16]   Resource Conservation and Recovery Act of 1976, Pub.L. No. 89-272 (Codified at 42 U.S.C.A. §§ 6901 - 6992k (1976); Title II § 1002, as amended).

The 10 subtitles contained in RCRA include:

Subtitle A Subchapter I		General Provisions
Subtitle B Subchapter II		Office of Solid Waste; Authorities of the [EPA] Administrator
Subtitle C Subchapter III		Hazardous Waste Management
Subtitle D Subchapter IV		State or Regional Solid Waste Plans
Subtitle E Subchapter V		Duties of the Secretary of Commerce in Resource and Recovery
Subtitle F Subchapter VI		Federal Responsibilities
Subtitle G Subchapter VII		Miscellaneous Provisions
Subtitle H Subchapter VIII		Research, Development, Demonstration, and Information
Subtitle I Subchapter IX		Regulation of Underground Storage Tanks
Subtitle J Subchapter X		Demonstration Medical Waste Tracking

This chapter primarily focuses on Subtitles C, D, and G (listed above), which address some of the more visible areas of concern for waste disposal and waste management in the United States.[17] Subtitle C governs hazardous waste management, and directs EPA to develop, implement and enforce a comprehensive nationwide hazardous waste management system.[18] Subtitle D governs municipal solid waste management systems. Under this subtitle, the federal government has delegated power to the states to implement and regulate most of the municipal solid waste programs.[19] Subtitle G contains a number of subsections that include provisions for citizen suits, substantial endangerment actions, criminal enforcement and judicial review.[20]

---

[17]   This chapter does not address USTs because this is such a vast area of regulated activity. USTs would be better served in a subsequent edition with its own chapter.

[18]   RCRA §§ 3001-3011b; 42 U.S.C.A. §§ 6921-6931b.

[19]   RCRA §§ 4001-4009a; 42 U.S.C.A. §§ 6941-6949a.

[20]   RCRA §§ 7001-7009b; 42 U.S.C.A. §§ 6971-6979b.

The following diagram shows the dynamic relationship of three subtitles of SWDA, two of which (Subtitles C and D) are covered under this chapter:

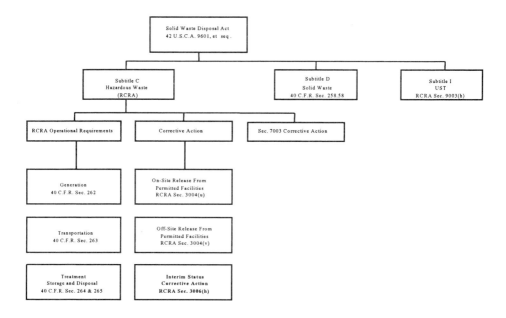

* Reprinted with permission from Mr. Bernie K. Schafer, Senior Counsel, Office of Assistant General Counsel (Installations and Environment), General Counsel of the Navy (December 2000).

II.   SUBTITLE C: HAZARDOUS WASTE

RCRA applies to all handlers of hazardous waste, including generators, transporters, and operators of treatment, storage, and disposal facilities (TSDF). Under RCRA, hazardous waste is a special kind of solid waste. To be a hazardous waste under RCRA, the substance must first be a solid waste.[21]

A.   SOLID WASTE DETERMINATION

RCRA broadly defines "solid waste" as any garbage, refuse, or sludge from a waste treatment plant, water supply treatment plant, or air pollution control facility, and other discarded material, including solid, liquid, semi-solid

---

[21]   Connecticut Coastal Fisherman's Assn v. Remington Arms, Co., Inc., 989 F.2d 1305, 1313 (2d Cir.1993).

or contained gaseous material from industrial, commercial, mining and agricultural operations, and from community activities.[22]

The term "solid waste" is very broad and includes both traditional non-hazardous solid waste, such as municipal garbage, and certain hazardous solid waste. Subtitle C regulates most solid waste that are hazardous. Subtitle D regulates traditional non-hazardous solid waste, and certain hazardous wastes excluded from regulation under Subtitle C, such as household hazardous wastes or hazardous wastes generated by small quantity generators.[23]

1.   Exemptions

Certain types of wastes are exempt by statute from the definition of solid waste.[24]   As a guide, EPA developed detailed regulations that list these exemptions.[25] The following materials are expressly exempt from the solid waste definition, and thus are not considered hazardous waste, even if they otherwise exhibit hazardous waste characteristics:[26]

1)   domestic sewage and any mixture of domestic sewage and other waste, including hazardous waste, that pass through a sewer system to a publicly owned treatment works (POTW);

2)   industrial wastewater discharges governed by National Pollution Discharge Elimination System (NPDES) permits;

3)   irrigation return flows;

---

[22]   RCRA § 1004(27); 42 U.S.C.A. § 6903(27); *see* e.g., American Mining Congress v. United States EPA, 824 F.2d at 1192; Connecticut Coastal Fisherman's Ass'n v. Remington Arms Co., Inc., 989 F.2d at 1314; Catellus Development Corp. v. United States, 34 F.3d 748 (9th Cir.1994).

[23]   United Technologies Corp. v. United States EPA, 821 F.2d 714, 717 (D.C. Cir.1987); Connecticut Coastal Fisherman's Ass'n v. Remington Arms Co., Inc., 989 F.2d at 1314; Steel Manufacturers Ass'n v. United States EPA, 27 F.3d 642, 644 (D.C. Cir.1994).

[24]   RCRA § 1004(27); 42 U.S.C.A. § 6903(27).

[25]   40 C.F.R. § 261.4(a).

[26]   40 C.F.R. § 261.4.

4)   certain specified nuclear and radioactive wastes;

5)   certain materials subject to in situ mining techniques which are not removed from the ground as part of the extraction process; and

6)   certain recycled or reused materials.

2.   Discarded Material

As noted above, the RCRA definition of solid waste specifically includes, other "discarded material." This "discarded material" portion of the solid waste definition has been a hotly contested area. Discarded material includes substances that have been abandoned, recycled, or considered inherently waste-like.[27] "Inherently waste-like" materials are substances normally disposed of, burned, or incinerated.[28]

3.   Recycled Material

Recycled materials have a unique status under RCRA and are exempt, subject to some specific regulations. Recycled materials, including any spent material, sludge, by-product, listed commercial chemical product, or scrap metal, are not considered exempt from the definition of a solid waste if they have been "discarded" by being recycled in one of four specific ways:[29]

1)   recycled in a manner constituting disposal;

2)   burned for energy recovery or used to produce fuel;

3)   reclaimed; or

4)   accumulated speculatively.

---

[27]   40 C.F.R. § 261.2(a)(2).

[28]   40 C.F.R. § 261.2(d).

[29]   40 C.F.R. § 261.2(c); *see*, American Mining Congress v. U. S. EPA, 824 F.2d at 1180.

However, recycled material is exempt from the definition of solid waste if:

1)   it is used or reused as an ingredient in an industrial process to make a product;

2)   used or reused as an effective substitute for a commercial product;

3)   returned to the original process that generated it without first being reclaimed; and

4)   reclaimed and returned to the original process, but only if tank storage is used and the reclamation process occurs in a closed loop system that does not involve controlled flame combustion.[30]

In 1987, the United States Court of Appeals for the District of Columbia rejected EPA's effort to include as a solid waste, material returned to an ongoing industrial process, and held that the material had not been discarded.[31] EPA proposed to interpret this decision narrowly by limiting it to material that is returned immediately to the same industrial process.[32] If a material is used in a different process, stored before reuse, or reclaimed before reuse, EPA will consider the material to be discarded as a solid waste, thus, subject to the solid waste regulations under RCRA.[33]

---

[30]   40 C.F.R. §§ 261.2(e) and 261.4(a)(8); *see*, American Mining Congress v. United States EPA, 824 F.2d at 1179.

[31]   *See* generally, American Mining Congress v. United States EPA, 824 F.2d 1177 (D.C. Cir.1987).

[32]   53 Fed. Reg. 519 (Jan. 8, 1988); *see also*, Owen Electric Steel Co. of South Carolina, Inc. v. Browner, 37 F.3d 146 (4th Cir.1994) (slag that was not immediately recycled for use within the same industry was treated by RCRA as a regulated hazardous waste.).

[33]   Owen Electric Steel Co. of South Carolina, Inc. v. Browner, 37 F.3d 146 (4th Cir.1994).

4.   Non-Solid, "Solid" Waste

A substance can be classified a solid waste even if it is not solid.[34] For example, solid waste can also include such materials as "liquid, semisolid, or contained gaseous material."[35]

B.   HAZARDOUS WASTE

After determining whether the material is a solid waste, the next step is to determine if it is a hazardous waste. RCRA defines hazardous waste as a solid waste, or combination of solid waste which, because of its quantity, concentration, or physical, chemical or infectious characteristics, may:

1)   cause, or significantly contribute to, an increase in mortality or an increase in a serious irreversible illness, or incapacitating, reversible illness; or

2)   pose a substantial present or potential hazard to human health or the environment when improperly treated, stored, transported, disposed of, or otherwise managed.[36]

The RCRA definition of hazardous waste does not provide much direction to the regulated community. It was intended only to be a guide for EPA. Through RCRA, Congress directed EPA to "develop and promulgate criteria for identifying the characteristics of hazardous waste, and for listing hazardous waste, . . . taking into account toxicity, persistence, and degradability in nature, potential for accumulation in tissue, and other related factors such as flammability, corrosiveness, and other hazardous characteristics."[37]

---

[34]   RCRA § 1004(27); 42 U.S.C.A. § 6903(27).

[35]   *Id.*

[36]   RCRA § 1004(5); 42 U.S.C.A. § 6903(5); *see*, Shell Oil Co. v. United States EPA, 950 F.2d 741, 747 (D.C. Cir.1991).

[37]   RCRA § 3001(a); 42 U.S.C.A. § 6921(a).

1.   Types of Hazardous Waste

EPA regulations define what constitutes a hazardous waste.[38] EPA has divided hazardous waste into two general categories: listed hazardous wastes and characteristic hazardous wastes.[39] Listed hazardous wastes are specific substances that have been indexed in the C.F.R. Characteristic hazardous wastes are substances that exhibit specific characteristics that are identified in the C.F.R.

a.   Listed Hazardous Waste

Listed hazardous waste is divided into three groups:[40]

1)   **F WASTE**: hazardous waste from non-specific sources;

2)   **K WASTE**: hazardous waste from specific sources; and

3)   **U & P WASTE**: discarded commercial chemical products.

Any substance in any of these groups is a hazardous waste regardless of its nature, unless it is the subject of a successful delisting petition. If any F or K Waste contain any of the compounds listed under 40 C.F.R. § 261.31, then such waste is regulated under RCRA.[41]

U & P Wastes are hazardous wastes if they are discarded as outlined in the C.F.R.[42] For example, RCRA applies when a responsible party discards a listed chemical, or when a listed commercial chemical is present in an accidental spill.[43] Note, that each listed hazardous waste is accompanied by a Hazard Code that identifies it as either:

---

[38]   40 C.F.R. § 261.

[39]   40 C.F.R. § 261 © & D); United States v. ILCO, Inc., 996 F.2d 1126, 1131 (11th Cir.1993).

[40]   40 C.F.R. § 261.30(a).

[41]   40 C.F.R. § 261.31.

[42]   40 C.F.R. § 261.2(a)(2)(i).

[43]   40 C.F.R. § 261.33.

Waste	Code
Ignitable Waste	Code I
Corrosive Waste	Code C
Reactive Waste	Code R
Toxic Waste	Code E
Acutely Hazardous Waste	Code H
Toxic Waste	Code T [44]

Each hazardous waste listed by a Hazard Code is assigned an EPA Hazardous Waste Number which precedes the name of the waste.[45]

i.   F WASTES

F Wastes are hazardous waste derived from non-specific sources such as various types of spent solvents, metal baths, waste and wastewater from industrial processes, and leachate from landfills containing one or more listed hazardous wastes.[46] The C.F.R. provides a detailed table that outlines numerous categories of F Wastes and identifies each category with an industry number, an EPA hazardous waste number, a brief description of the substance and a corresponding hazard code.[47]

ii.   K WASTES

K Wastes are hazardous wastes derived from specific sources such as waste generated by wood preserving, organic and inorganic chemical manufacturing, pesticide manufacturing, explosives manufacturing, petroleum manufacturing, primary metals, pharmaceutical, ink formulation, and coking processes.[48] The C.F.R. provides a detailed table that outlines numerous categories of K Wastes and identifies each category with an industry number, an

---

[44]   40 C.F.R. § 261.30(b).

[45]   40 C.F.R. § 261.30(c); *see also*, 40 C.F.R. § 261.30; United States v. Recticel Foam Corp., 858 F.Supp. 726, 729 (E.D.Tenn.1993).

[46]   40 C.F.R. § 261.31.

[47]   *Id.*

[48]   40 C.F.R. § 261.32.

EPA hazardous waste number, brief description of the substance, and a corresponding hazard code.[49]

iii.   U & P WASTES

U & P Wastes are listed hazardous wastes that include discarded commercial chemical products. These types of commercial chemical products are hazardous when they are made of pure grades, commercial grades, or when the designated chemical is the sole active ingredient in the product.[50] The difference between U Wastes and P Wastes is that P Wastes are acutely hazardous wastes, and U Wastes are toxic hazardous wastes.

Acutely hazardous wastes are specific wastes listed under 40 C.F.R. § 261.33 (e). Toxic hazardous wastes are specific wastes listed under 40 C.F.R. § 33(f). Note that wastes in each category may be listed under other hazard codes as well. The C.F.R. provides a detailed table that outlines numerous types of P Wastes and their corresponding EPA Hazardous Waste Numbers,[51] and provides a detailed table that outlines numerous types of U Wastes and their corresponding EPA Hazardous Waste Numbers.[52]

iv.   Delisting a Listed Hazardous Waste

Under a successful petition, a listed hazardous waste can be delisted and reclassified as a non-hazardous waste. To delist a hazardous waste, the petitioner must demonstrate to EPA that the waste produced by a particular generating facility does not meet any of the criteria under which the waste was listed as a hazardous or acutely hazardous waste.[53] The burden is on the petitioner to convince EPA that the particular waste, although initially listed as a hazardous waste, is in fact a non-hazardous waste.

---

[49]   *Id.*

[50]   40 C.F.R. § 261.33.

[51]   40 C.F.R. § 261.33.

[52]   40 C.F.R. § 261.33.

[53]   40 C.F.R. § 260.22; Shell Oil Co. v. United States EPA, 950 F.2d at 748.

For the delisting petition to be approved, EPA must provide public notice and an opportunity for comment.[54] To the maximum extent practical, EPA shall publish the petition in the Federal Register within 12 months from receipt of the petition, and shall grant or deny the petition within 24 months after receiving the delisting application.[55] The decision to approve a delisting petition is purely discretionary and is effective only on a case-by-case basis.[56] In addition, a delisting petition is site-specific. If EPA grants a petition, then only that particular petitioner, substance and related site are delisted.[57]

b.   Characteristic Hazardous Wastes

The second general category of hazardous waste is characteristic hazardous waste. Because it would be virtually impossible to list every possible waste that could pose a danger to human health or the environment, EPA also has authority to list characteristics which, if possessed by a solid waste, would allow EPA to regulate the waste as a hazardous waste. Under Subpart C (Characteristics of Hazardous Waste), EPA has identified four characteristics of hazardous waste: ignitability, corrosivity, reactivity, and toxicity.[58]

i.   Ignitability

A hazardous waste is considered ignitable if it is either:[59]

1)   a liquid with a flash-point of less than 60° centigrade (140° F), except aqueous solutions containing less than 24% alcohol;[60]

---

[54]   RCRA § 3001(f)(1); 42 U.S.C.A. § 6921(f)(1).

[55]   RCRA § 3001(f)(2)(A); 42 U.S.C.A. § 6921(f)(2)(A).

[56]   Shell Oil Co. v. United States EPA, 950 F.2d at 749.

[57]   See, Hazardous Waste Treatment Council v. United States EPA, 886 F.2d 355 (D.C. Cir.1989).

[58]   40 C.F.R. § 261.20.

[59]   40 C.F.R. § 261.21.

[60]   This class includes many common organic liquids, such as cleaning solvents and petrochemicals.

2)   a non-liquid, capable under normal conditions of spontaneous and sustained combustion through friction or absorption of moisture;

3)   an ignitable compressed gas according to United States Department of Transportation (DOT) regulations; or

4)   an oxidizer as defined by DOT regulations under 49 C.F.R. § 173.151.

ii.   Corrosivity

EPA has established the corrosivity characteristic because certain hazardous wastes are capable of corroding metal and could subsequently eat through containers containing hazardous waste. A substance is corrosive if it is either:[61]

1)   an aqueous material with a pH less than or equal to two (2), or greater than or equal to 12.5; or

2)   a liquid that corrodes steel at a rate greater than 6.35 mm (.25 inches) per year at a temperature of 55° C (130° F).

iii.   Reactivity

Reactivity applies to wastes that are extremely unstable and may explode. A solid waste that is "reactive" exhibits any one (or more) of the following characteristics:[62]

1)   normally unstable and reacts violently without detonating;

2)   reacts violently with water;

3)   forms an explosive mixture with water;

4)   generates toxic gases, vapors or fumes when mixed with water;

---

[61]   40 C.F.R. § 261.22.

[62]   40 C.F.R. § 261.23.

5)   contains cyanide or sulfide and generates toxic gases, vapors or fumes at a pH level of between 2 and 12.5;

6)   capable of detonation if heated under confinement or subjected to a strong initiating source;

7)   capable of detonation at a standard temperature and pressure; or

8)   listed by DOT as Class A or B explosive.

iv.   Toxicity

Toxicity characteristics identify wastes that are likely to leak hazardous elements into groundwater. To determine the toxicity characteristic, EPA established a testing protocol that simulates the flow of toxins into the groundwater.[63] A solid waste exhibits toxicity characteristics if it contains any contaminant listed in the C.F.R. identified as Maximum Concentration of Contaminants for the Toxicity Characteristic.[64]

2.   Mixtures of Hazardous and Non-Hazardous Waste

EPA regulates mixtures of hazardous and non-hazardous wastes. For example, a generator of hazardous waste "X" may combine it with a non-hazardous waste "Z" so as to "water down" the amount of hazardous material present. However, EPA regulations were created to prevent generators from eluding reporting requirements by commingling hazardous and non-hazardous wastes in an attempt to create a substance that no longer demonstrates hazardous characteristics.[65]

a.   Two Types of Mixtures Regulated

There are two types of mixtures of hazardous and non-hazardous wastes regulated under RCRA: substances that are mixed with hazardous waste and

---

[63]   40 C.F.R. at Part 261, Appendix II.

[64]   40 C.F.R. § 261.24 (Table 1).

[65]   Shell Oil Co. v. United States EPA, 950 F.2d 741 (D.C. Cir.1991).

substances that are derived from hazardous waste. Often, mixing hazardous and non-hazardous wastes in any form makes the entire mixture a hazardous waste.[66]

i.   Mixture Rule

RCRA applies different regulations for mixtures of hazardous and non-hazardous waste depending on whether the waste is a "listed" hazardous waste or "characteristic" hazardous waste. If a "listed" hazardous waste is mixed with a non-hazardous solid waste, the entire resulting mixture is regulated as a hazardous waste, even if the resulting mixture is not hazardous.[67] If a "characteristic" hazardous waste is mixed with a non-hazardous solid waste, the entire resulting mixture is only hazardous if the final mixture itself exhibits a particular hazardous waste "characteristic."[68]

ii.   Derived From Rule

The "derived from" rule applies to the residual compounds found after treatment of certain hazardous wastes .[69] This rule is very similar to the mixture rule, in that it sets different standards for "listed" and "characteristic" hazardous waste. Generally, this rule states that wastes derived from a listed hazardous waste are themselves hazardous waste, and waste derived from characteristic hazardous wastes are only hazardous if they exhibit a hazardous waste characteristic. For example, solid waste generated from treatment, storage, or disposal of a listed hazardous waste, including any sludge, spill residue, ash, emission control dust, or leachate, is a hazardous waste.[70] The following chart helps explain the difference between the mixture rule and the derived from rule.

---

[66]   40 C.F.R. § 261.3; City of Chicago v. Environmental Defense Fund, 511 U.S. 328; 114 S.Ct. 1588; 128 L.Ed.2d 302 (1994); United States v. McDonald & Watson Waste Oil Co., 933 F.2d 35 (1st Cir.1991); *see also*, 40 C.F.R. § 261.3(a)(2)(iv)(A-E) (there are five exemptions for mixtures involving certain waste waters).

[67]   40 C.F.R. § 261.3(a)(2)(iv).

[68]   40 C.F.R. § 261.3(a)(2)(iii).

[69]   40 C.F.R. § 261.3(c).

[70]   40 C.F.R. § 261.4(c) and (d); Mobil Oil Corp. v. United States EPA, 35 F.3d 579, 581 (D.C. Cir.1994).

RULE	LISTED HAZARDOUS WASTE	CHARACTERISTIC HAZARDOUS WASTE
MIXTURE RULE[71]	With solid, non-hazardous waste = hazardous waste	With solid non-hazardous waste = hazardous, only if it exhibits hazardous waste characteristics
DERIVED FROM RULE[72]	All are hazardous	These are hazardous only if they exhibit hazardous waste characteristics

Both the "mixture" and "derived from" rules were originally EPA guidelines for determining whether a waste was hazardous. However, in 1991, the D.C. Circuit struck down both rules because EPA did not allow adequate notice and opportunity for comment as required by the Administrative Procedure Act.[73] The court granted a grace period so that both rules remained effective until April 28, 1993. Since that time, both rules have remained in effect as interim final rules.[74]

On November 19, 1999, EPA proposed to amend its regulations governing solid wastes that are designated as hazardous, because they have been mixed with, or derived from listed hazardous wastes.[75] These regulations are called the 1999 Hazardous Waste Identification Rule (HWIR). This proposal retains the mixture and derived from rules listed in 40 C.F.R. §§ 261.3(a)(2)(iii), 261.3(a)(2)(iv) and 261.3(c)(2)(i) as "in effect" on an emergency basis and the HWIR formally proposed their retention.[76]

---

[71]   This includes mixtures of hazardous and non-hazardous materials.

[72]   These include residual compounds found after treatment of certain hazardous wastes.

[73]   Shell Oil v. United States EPA, 950 F.2d 741 (D.C. Cir.1991).

[74]   *See* 57 Fed. Reg. 49280 (Oct. 30, 1992). Note however, these rules have been reproposed as the 1999 Hazardous Waste Identification Rule (HWIR), see 64 Fed. Reg. 63381 (Nov. 19, 1999).

[75]   64 Fed. Reg. 63,382 (Nov. 19, 1999).

[76]   U.S. EPA, Hazardous Waste Identification Rule, Frequently Asked Questions (FAQ), Internet Website: www.epa.gov/epaoswere/hazwaste/id/hwirwste/faq.htm.

HWIR also proposed two revisions to the mixture and derived from rules. One exempts wastes and their residuals listed solely for the ignitability, corrosivity, and/or reactivity characteristics. The other will be a separate proposal for a conditional exemption from the mixture and derived from rules for "mixed wastes" (wastes that are both hazardous and radioactive).[77]

Also included in this HWIR proposal is the "HWIR Exemption." This exempts from hazardous waste management wastes that meet chemical-specific exemption levels. Possible changes to the Land Disposal Restriction (LDR) treatment standards are also discussed.[78]

The public comment period for the mixture and derived from rules ended on Feb. 17, 2000. The public comment period for the "HWIR Exemption" and the LDR treatment standards ended on May 17, 2000.[79] EPA is scheduled to take final action on revisions to the mixture and derived from rules by April 30, 2001, after public comments have been considered.[80]

3.   Hazardous Waste Exclusions

RCRA regulations contain several statutory exclusions to the definition of hazardous waste. Although these excluded substances constitute solid waste and may exhibit hazardous waste characteristics, they are not considered hazardous under Subtitle C. They may, however, still be regulated by RCRA as solid, non-hazardous waste.

Under 40 C.F.R. § 261.4(b), the following materials are excluded from the definition of hazardous waste and therefore are not considered hazardous even if they otherwise exhibit a hazardous waste characteristic. These substances are listed below and include:[81]

---

[77]   *Id.*

[78]   *Id.*

[79]   64 Fed. Reg.63,382 (Nov. 19, 1999).

[80]   *Supra* note 76.

[81]   40 C.F.R. § 261.4(b); *see*, United States v. Iron Mountain Mines, Inc., 812 F.Supp. 1528, 1538 (E.D.Cal.1992).

1)   household wastes;[82]

2)   agricultural wastes which are returned to the soil as fertilizers;

3)   mining overburden[83] returned to the mine site;[84]

4)   fly ash, bottom ash, slag, and flue gas emission control waste, generated primarily from combustion of coal or other fossil fuels;[85]

5)   drilling fluids, produced waters and other wastes associated with the exploration, development or production of crude oil, natural gas or geothermal energy;

6)   wastes that fail the test for the Toxicity Characteristic because chromium is present, or are listed under Subpart D due to the presence of chromium and otherwise do not fail the Toxicity Characteristic test for any other substance;[86]

7)   certain solid wastes from the extraction, beneficiation, and processing of ores and minerals, including coal;

8)   cement kiln dust waste;

---

[82]   Household waste may include, garbage, trash and sanitary septic tank waste. *See* City of Chicago v. Environmental Defense Fund, 114 S.Ct. 1588; 128 L.Ed.2d 302; 62 U.S.L.W. 4283 (1994); Environmental Defense Fund, Inc. v. Wheelabrator Technologies, Inc., 725 F.Supp 758, 769 (S.D.N.Y.1989); Aff'd on appeal in 931 F.2d 211 (2d Cir.1991), cert. denied, 502 U.S. 974; 112 S.Ct. 453; 116 L.Ed.2d 471 (1991).

[83]   40 C.F.R. § 260.10 (1986); Haz. Waste L. & Prac. § 6.36 (1986) ("any material overlying an economic mineral deposit which is removed to gain access to that deposit and is then used for reclamation of a surface mine").

[84]   Horsehead Resource Development Co., Inc., v. Browner, 16 F.3d 1246, 1255 (D.C. Cir.1994).

[85]   Solite Corp. v. United States EPA, 952 F.2d 473 (D.C. Cir.1991).

[86]   Note, this exception only applies if chromium is generated from an industrial process which uses chromium exclusively in a trivalent as opposed to a hexavalent state.

9)   certain discarded arsenic-treated wood or wood products;

10)   petroleum-contaminated media and debris that fail the test for the Toxicity Characteristic of Hazardous Waste Codes D018 - D043;

11)   injected groundwater that is hazardous only because it exhibits the Toxicity Characteristic in 40 C.F.R. § 261.24, and is reinjected as part of the recovery process at petroleum refineries, petroleum marketing terminals, petroleum bulk plants, petroleum pipelines, and petroleum transportation spill sites until January 25, 1993;

12)   used chlorofluorocarbon refrigerants from totally enclosed heat transfer equipment, provided the refrigerant is reclaimed for further use;

13)   non-terne plated used oil filters that have been gravity hot-drained; and

14)   used oil re-refining distillation bottoms that are used as feedstock to manufacture asphalt products.

RCRA can still regulate these substances as solid waste rather than as hazardous waste. Of course, the regulatory requirements for solid and hazardous waste are different.

4.   Residue From Empty Containers

For the most part, hazardous residues that remain after a substance or mixture is removed from "empty containers" are not regulated under RCRA.[87] If the container is to be reused as part of an ongoing container recycling process, then residues in the container are not considered "wastes." On the other hand, if the container is not reused, whether the residue is regulated depends on what substances were held in the container and how much residue remained. For example, any hazardous waste remaining in either an empty container or an inner liner removed from an empty container, is not subject to most hazardous waste regulations. A container or liner is considered empty if all wastes have been

---

[87]   40 C.F.R. § 261.7(a).

removed that can be removed by using the practices commonly employed to remove materials from that type of container and:[88]

1)   no more than 2.5 centimeters (one inch) of residue remains in the bottom of the container; or

2)   no more than 3.0% of the container's total capacity remains in the container or liner if the container holds 110 gallons or less; or

3)   no more than 0.3% of the container's total capacity remains in the container or liner if the container holds more than 110 gallons.

C.   HAZARDOUS WASTE REGULATION

1.   Overview

a.   Cradle-to-Grave System of Regulation

RCRA establishes a "cradle-to-grave" system of managing hazardous waste. This system imposes requirements on both generators and transporters of hazardous waste, as well as on treatment, storage and disposal facilities (TSDFs).[89] The cradle-to-grave system maintains two elements central to its regulatory scheme:

(1) the manifest requirement; and

(2) the TSDF permit requirement.

RCRA requires that a shipping document (manifest) accompany shipments of hazardous waste.[90] This manifest is initially signed by a generator, carried and signed by a transporter (or numerous transporters if the

---

[88]   40 C.F.R. § 261.7(b); *see*, Crockett v. Uniroyal, Inc., 772 F.2d 1524, 1533-34 (11th Cir.1985).

[89]   City of Chicago v. Environmental Defense Fund, 114 S.Ct. 1588, 1590; 128 L.Ed.2d 302, 307 (1994).

[90]   RCRA § 3002(a)(5); 42 U.S.C.A. § 6922(a)(5).

circumstances warrant), and then received and signed by a TSDF operator who is the last handler of the hazardous material and who then returns the completed manifest to the original generator. Generators who are at the beginning of the cradle-to-grave system, are primarily responsible for preparing the original manifest. TSDFs are the caretakers of the "grave" in this cradle-to-grave system and must comply with specific regulations described later in this chapter.

b.   State Authorization to Regulate Hazardous Waste

Under RCRA, EPA assists states in developing, implementing and enforcing the cradle-to-grave program.[91] Upon federal delegation to a state, the state program becomes effective in lieu of the federal program.[92] The federal RCRA program sets minimum requirements for the substitute state program and can be used as a convenient model for the state program, but RCRA authorizes the state programs to be more stringent than the federal program.[93] The federal government delegates such authority to the states through two steps: interim authorization; and final authorization.[94] Interim authorization allows states to go forward with their own hazardous waste programs in lieu of a federal program so long as the states' programs are "substantially equivalent" to the federal programs.[95] Final authorization allows states to go forward with their own hazardous waste programs that are "equivalent" and "consistent" with the federal program and provide for "adequate enforcement."[96]

2.   Generators of Hazardous Waste

Although RCRA does not have a statutory definition of "generator," it does describe hazardous waste generation as "the act or process of producing

---

[91]   RCRA § 3006; 42 U.S.C.A. § 6926.

[92]   *Id.*

[93]   RCRA § 3009; 42 U.S.C.A. § 6929.

[94]   *See*, United States v. T & S Brass and Bronze Works, Inc., 681 F.Supp. at 315.

[95]   RCRA § 3006(c); 42 U.S.C.A. § 6926(c).

[96]   RCRA § 3006(b); 42 U.S.C.A. § 6926(b).

hazardous waste."[97] Supplementing this RCRA provision, EPA has developed regulations that more fully define generators.[98] A generator is:[99]

> [a]ny person, by site, whose act or process produces hazardous waste identified or listed in Part 261 of this chapter or whose act first causes a hazardous waste to become subject to regulation.

Generators do not have to be owners or operators of industrial activities that produce hazardous waste. In fact, generators can be anyone who produces hazardous waste intermittently, infrequently, or accidentally as a result of such incidents as hazardous material spills, hazardous materials stored in excess of their shelf life, and the failure to comply with RCRA transportation or treatment, storage, and disposal requirements.

a.   Types of Generators

Generators are divided into large quantity, small quantity, and conditionally-exempt small quantity generators. Regulations impose different requirements on large quantity generators who create hazardous waste of more than 1,000 kg/mo;[100] small quantity generators of between 100 and 1000 kg/mo; and conditionally exempt small quantity generators of less than 100 kg/mo.

i.   Large Quantity Generators (LQGs)

A generator who creates more than 1,000 kg/mo of hazardous waste is considered a large quantity generator. Such generators are required to follow a long list of steps, including preparation of biennial reports, and procedures for handling hazardous waste. These steps are described in detail in a subsequent section of this chapter titled, "Formal Generator Responsibilities."

---

[97]   RCRA § 1004(6); 42 U.S.C.A. § 6903(6).

[98]   40 C.F.R. § 260.10.

[99]   *Id.*

[100]   "Kg/mo" indicates the amount of kilograms of material that is produced per month.

ii.   Small Quantity Generators (SQGs)

A generator who creates more than 100 kg/mo but less than 1,000 kg/mo of hazardous waste is generally subject to most of the requirements for large quantity generators. However, they are not required to prepare biennial reports, and they are subject to less stringent reporting requirements than generators of more than 1,000 kg/mo.[101] In addition, because these generators do not produce such large quantities of hazardous waste, they are allowed special interim storage privileges not available to large quantity generators who exceed 1,000 kg/mo. These generators may also accumulate hazardous waste on site for up to 180 days as long as the quantity accumulated does not exceed 6,000 kg, and the generator meets certain emergency preparedness requirements.[102] Finally, these generators may store hazardous waste on site for up to 270 days if they must transport their waste more than 200 miles for disposal.[103]

iii.   Conditionally Exempt Small Quantity Generators

A generator who creates less than 100 kg/mo of non-acutely hazardous waste and/or less than 1 kg/mo of acutely hazardous waste, is called a "conditionally exempt small quantity generator."[104] These generators are not required to comply with many of the RCRA generator requirements so long as:[105]

1)   For acute hazardous waste:[106]

    a)   the waste tests positive for acutely hazardous waste qualities pursuant to 40 C.F.R. § 262.11;

---

[101]   40 C.F.R. § 262.44.

[102]   40 C.F.R. § 262.34(d).

[103]   40 C.F.R. § 262.34(e).

[104]   40 C.F.R. § 261.5.

[105]   Environmental Defense Fund, Inc. v. Wheelabrator Technologies, Inc., 725 F.Supp at 769.

[106]   40 C.F.R. § 261.5(f).

b)   is not accumulated on site in amounts greater than 1 kg, pursuant to 40 C.F.R. § 261.5(e); and

c)   is disposed of onsite or offsite only in an interim status or a permitted hazardous waste disposal facility, a licensed municipal or industrial landfill, or any other licensed disposal facility.[107]

2)   For non-acute hazardous waste:[108]

a)   the waste tests positive for hazardous waste qualities pursuant to 40 C.F.R. § 262.11;

b)   is not accumulated onsite in amounts greater than 1,000 kg pursuant to 40 C.F.R. § 261.5(g)(2);[109] and

c)   is disposed of onsite or offsite only in an interim status or a permitted hazardous waste disposal facility, a licensed municipal or industrial landfill, or any other licensed disposal facility.[110]

3.   Formal Generator Responsibilities

In order to protect human health and the environment, generators must carry out specific responsibilities.[111] These responsibilities are found in 40 C.F.R. Sections 262.10 - 262.44. Such responsibilities require generators to identify whether their waste is hazardous, obtain an EPA identification number, prepare a manifest, package and label the waste as hazardous waste, avoid

---

[107]   40 C.F.R. § 261.5(f).

[108]   40 C.F.R. § 261.5(g).

[109]   Because these conditionally-exempt small quantity generators are still generating less than 100 kg per month, they are allowed to accumulate up to 1000 kg per month on-site, at which point they must dispose of the hazardous waste or be treated like an SQG, instead of a conditionally exempt SQG.

[110]   40 C.F.R. § 261.5(g)(3).

[111]   RCRA § 3002; 42 U.S.C.A. § 6922.

accumulating or storing hazardous waste onsite for longer than 90 days without a storage permit, and prepare Biennial Reports and exception reports to EPA describing the waste generation. The following requirements were developed by EPA and authorized under RCRA because they "may be necessary to protect human health and the environment."[112]

a.   Hazardous Waste Identification

Generators must continually determine whether the waste they create is hazardous.   This is done either by testing the substances or by using the generator's knowledge of the waste's character.[113] Waste generators are allowed to rely on actual knowledge they have acquired only if such knowledge enables them to certify that their waste complies with applicable treatment standards.[114] Generators are also required to keep detailed records of all data that goes into their certifications.[115] In addition, generators are subject to penalties for making erroneous certifications.[116]

b.   EPA Generator Identification Number

A generator must not treat, store, dispose of, transport, or offer for transportation, a hazardous waste without having received an EPA identification number.[117]   In addition, a generator must not offer his hazardous waste to transporters or to TSDFs that have not received an EPA identification number.[118] Thus, each separate facility that generates or handles a hazardous waste must

---

[112]   RCRA § 3002; 42 U.S.C.A. § 6922.

[113]   40 C.F.R. § 262.11; Hazardous Waste Treatment Council v. United States EPA, 886 F.2d at 369.

[114]   40 C.F.R. § 268.7(a)(2).

[115]   40 C.F.R. § 268.7(a)(4).

[116]   40 C.F.R. § 268.7.

[117]   40 C.F.R. § 262.12(a).

[118]   40 C.F.R. § 262.12(c).

apply for and receive a separate identification number.[119] The purpose of maintaining identification numbers is to document which parties handled the substances from "cradle-to-grave."

c.   Prepare a Manifest

A generator who transports hazardous waste for offsite treatment, storage, or disposal, must prepare a manifest.[120] EPA has established a uniform manifest form.[121] In this manifest, generators must designate a facility that is permitted to handle the waste described in the manifest.[122] The generator may designate an alternative facility permitted to handle waste in the event of an emergency.[123] A generator must:[124]

1)   sign the manifest certification;

2)   obtain a signature of the initial transporter and date of acceptance on the manifest; and

3)   retain a copy of the manifest in accordance with 40 C.F.R. § 262.40(a) for at least three years, or until he/she receives a signed copy from the final, designated facility that received the waste.

---

[119]   40 C.F.R. § 262.12(b); Old Bridge Chemicals, Inc. v. New Jersey Dept. of Environmental Protection, 965 F.2d 1287 (3d Cir.1992).

[120]   40 C.F.R. § 262.20(a).

[121]   *Id.* (Manifest OMB control number 2050-0039 on EPA Form 8700-22). Note that many states also have their own manifest forms, in compliance with EPA's standards and as authorized by EPA's delegating authority. Currently, EPA is proposing to amend its manifest system to include implementation of an electronic manifest system.

[122]   40 C.F.R. § 262.20(b).

[123]   40 C.F.R. § 262.20(c).

[124]   40 C.F.R. § 262.23(a).

A generator must give the transporter copies of the manifest.[125] Before leaving with the hazardous waste, the transporter should sign the manifest and leave a signed copy with the generator. The generator should also receive a copy of the manifest with a signature of the owner or operator of the designated TSDF within 35 days of the date the waste was accepted by the initial transporter.

If the generator fails to receive a completed or finalized manifest, he must contact the transporter and/or owner or operator of the facility to determine the status of the hazardous waste.[126] If the generator still cannot obtain a copy of the manifest with the appropriate signatures from the owner or operator of the designated facility within 45 days of the date the waste was accepted by the initial transporter, the generator must file an "exception report" with EPA.[127] An "exception report" must include:

1)   a legible copy of the manifest for which the generator does not have confirmation of delivery; and

2)   a cover letter signed by the generator or his authorized representative explaining the efforts taken to locate the hazardous waste and the results of those efforts.[128]

d.   Packaging and Labeling Hazardous Waste

Before transporting hazardous waste or offering hazardous waste for transportation offsite, a generator must package the waste in accordance with applicable DOT regulations on packaging, labeling, marking, and placarding of hazardous materials.[129]

---

[125]   40 C.F.R. § 262.23(b).

[126]   40 C.F.R. § 262.42(a)(1).

[127]   40 C.F.R. § 262.42(a)(2); Environmental Defense Fund, Inc. v. Wheelabrator Technologies, Inc., 725 F.Supp 758 (S.D.N.Y.1989); Old Bridge Chemicals, Inc. v. New Jersey Dept. of Environmental Protection, 965 F.2d 1287 (3d Cir.1992).

[128]   40 C.F.R. § 262.42.

[129]   40 C.F.R. §§ 262.30-33; *see also*, Environmental Defense Fund, Inc. v. Wheelabrator Technologies, Inc., 725 F.Supp. at 762.

e.   Accumulating or Storing Hazardous Waste

A generator may accumulate or store hazardous waste onsite without a permit under two circumstances referred to as the "90 Day Rule" and the "Satellite Accumulation Rule."

i.   90 Day Rule

The general rule is that a large quantity generator can accumulate and store hazardous wastes on-site for up to 90 days without obtaining a hazardous waste storage permit.[130] Each hazardous waste storage container must be marked with a hazardous waste label that contains a date the hazardous waste was placed in the container.[131] The 90 day storage is only allowed in tanks or special containers.[132] A 30 day extension, in addition to the 90 day storage period, may be granted by EPA for unforeseen, temporary and uncontrollable circumstances.[133]

If hazardous waste is stored in excess of 90 days, the generator is then considered an operator of a hazardous waste storage facility, and thus is subject to additional regulations.[134] Under storage facility regulations, tanks must be managed to ensure that they are emptied at least every 90 days and a record of verification must be kept. Generators must also comply with the "emergency preparedness and contingency planning requirements" of Part 265, Subpart C and D of the C.F.R.[135]

---

[130]   40 C.F.R. § 262.34(a).

[131]   40 C.F.R. § 262.34(a)(2) and (3).

[132]   40 C.F.R. § 262.34(a)(1).

[133]   40 C.F.R. § 262.34(b); *see, e.g.,* Hazardous Waste Treatment Council v. United States EPA, 886 F.2d at 359.

[134]   40 C.F.R. §§ 262.34(b) and 268.50(a)(1).

[135]   40 C.F.R. § 262.34(a)(4).

ii.   Satellite Accumulation Rule

The "satellite accumulation rule" allows a generator to accumulate up to 55 gallons of hazardous waste or up to one quart of acutely hazardous waste in containers at or near the point of generation without obtaining a permit or interim status, for an indefinite period of time, so long as:[136]

1) the hazardous substances are stored in containers that are in good condition;[137]

2) containers are made of or lined with materials that will not react with the hazardous substances being stored so that the ability of the container to contain the waste is not impaired;[138] and

3) the container holding the hazardous waste is always closed during storage, except when it is necessary to add or remove the waste.[139]

f.   Prepare Reports

A generator must prepare and submit to EPA a biennial report by March 1 of each even numbered year.[140] This report must cover generator activities during the previous year and include such information as:

1) the EPA identification number;

2) the calendar years covered by the report;

3) the name, address, and EPA identification number of each offsite TSDF in the United States to which the generator's waste was shipped;

---

[136]   40 C.F.R. § 262.34(c)(1).

[137]   40 C.F.R. § 265.171.

[138]   40 C.F.R. § 265.172.

[139]   40 C.F.R. § 265.173(a).

[140]   40 C.F.R. § 262.41(a).

4)   the name, address, and EPA identification number of each transporter used during the reporting period;

5)   a description, EPA hazardous waste number, DOT hazard class, and quantity of each hazardous waste shipment off-site;

6)   a description of efforts made during the reporting period to reduce the volume and toxicity of waste generated; and

7)   a description of the changes in volume and toxicity of waste actually achieved during the reporting period in comparison to previous years.[141]

g.   Recordkeeping

A generator must keep a copy of each manifest he initiated for at least three years or until he receives a signed copy from the designated facility that received the waste.[142] A generator must keep a copy of each biennial report and exception report for a period of at least three years from the due date of the report.[143] A generator must also keep and maintain records of any test results, waste analysis, and other determinations for at least three years from the date the waste was last sent to a TSDF.[144]

h.   Generator Liability

Section 107(a)(3) of CERCLA makes generators strictly liable without regard to fault for cleanup costs at TSDFs where the generator's waste was treated, stored, or disposed of.[145]

---

[141]   40 C.F.R. § 262.41(a)(1)-(8).

[142]   40 C.F.R. § 262.40(a).

[143]   40 C.F.R. § 262.40(b).

[144]   40 C.F.R. § 262.40(c).

[145]   CERCLA § 107(a)(3); 42 U.S.C.A. § 9607(a)(3).

4.   Transporters of Hazardous Waste

Although a "transporter" of hazardous waste is not defined under RCRA, EPA has created specific definitions for both "transporters" and "transportation." A "transporter" of hazardous waste is "a person engaged in the offsite transportation of hazardous waste by air, rail, highway, or water."[146] "Transportation means the movement of hazardous waste by air, rail, highway, or water."[147]   RCRA does not have many specific regulations that monitor transporters.[148]

5.   Formal Transporter Responsibilities

a.   EPA Identification Number

A transporter must not transport hazardous waste without having obtained an EPA identification number.[149]

b.   Manifesting

A transporter may not accept hazardous waste from a generator unless it is accompanied by a manifest signed by the generator.[150] The transporter must sign and date the manifest acknowledging acceptance of the hazardous waste from the generator, and return a signed copy to the generator before leaving the generator's property.[151]   The transporter must deliver the manifest to any subsequent transporter or to the final destination at the disposal facility.[152]

---

[146]   40 C.F.R. § 260.10.

[147]   *Id.*

[148]   However, transporters are highly regulated by the Department of Transportation ("DOT") under 49 C.F.R. Subtitle B, Chapter I and Subchapter C, Parts 171-177.

[149]   40 C.F.R. § 263.11; *see e.g.*, Old Bridge Chemicals, Inc. v. New Jersey Dept. of Environmental Protection, 965 F.2d 1287 (3d Cir.1992).

[150]   40 C.F.R. § 263(20)(a).

[151]   40 C.F.R. § 263(20)(b).

[152]   40 C.F.R. § 262.20(d); *see*, Crockett v. Uniroyal, Inc., 772 F.2d at 1533.

c.   Handling

A transporter must comply with DOT requirements for transportation of hazardous materials under 49 C.F.R. Subtitle B, Chapter I and Subchapter C (Parts 171-177). These DOT regulations are incorporated by reference in the hazardous waste regulations.[153]

d.   Recordkeeping

The transporter must keep a copy of the manifest signed by both the generator, and the next designated transporter or the owner or operator of the designated facility, for a period of three years from the date the hazardous waste was accepted by the initial transporter.[154] There are additional record keeping requirements for transporters who ship hazardous waste by rail, water, and outside the United States.[155]

e.   Spill Response Requirements

In the event of a discharge of hazardous waste during transportation, the transporter must take appropriate immediate action to protect human health and the environment (e.g. notify local authorities, contain the discharge, etc.).[156] A transporter must cleanup any discharge of hazardous waste that occurs during transportation or take such action as may be required or approved by federal, state, or local officials so that the hazardous waste no longer poses a threat to human health or the environment.[157]

f.   Transporter Becomes a Generator

Transporters are subject to the same regulations that are applied to generators of hazardous waste if they:

---

[153]   40 C.F.R. § 263.10.

[154]   40 C.F.R. § 263.22(a).

[155]   40 C.F.R. § 263.22(c), (d).

[156]   40 C.F.R. § 263.30(a).

[157]   40 C.F.R. § 263.31.

1)   transport hazardous waste into the United States from abroad; or

2)   mix hazardous waste of different DOT shipping descriptions by placing them into a single container.[158]

6.   Treatment, Storage and Disposal Facilities (TSDFs)

A TSDF is generally a facility that treats, stores, or disposes of hazardous waste. Once again, RCRA does not have one generalized definition for what constitutes a TSDF. However, federal regulations provide guidance that help define a TSDF's components.[159] "Treatment" is defined as:

> any method, technique, or process, including neutralization, designed to change the physical, chemical, or biological character or composition of any hazardous waste so as to neutralize such waste, or so as to recover energy or material resources from the waste, or so as to render such waste non-hazardous, or less hazardous; safer to transport, store, or dispose of; or amenable for recovery, amenable for storage, or reduced in volume.[160]

"Storage" is defined as:

> the holding of hazardous waste for a temporary period, at the end of which the hazardous waste is treated, disposed of, or stored elsewhere.[161]

"Disposal" is defined as:

> the discharge, deposit, injection, dumping, spilling, leaking, or placing of any solid waste or hazardous waste into or on any land or water so that such solid waste or hazardous waste or any constituent thereof may

---

[158]   40 C.F.R. § 263.10(c).

[159]   40 C.F.R. § 260.10.

[160]   40 C.F.R. § 260.10; *see,* American Petroleum Institute v. United States EPA, 906 F.2d 729 (D.C. Cir.1990).

[161]   Edison Electric Institute v. United States EPA, 996 F.2d 326 (D.C. Cir.1993).

enter the environment or be emitted into the air or discharged into any waters, including ground waters.[162]

Under RCRA Section 1004(3), disposal takes on a more broad definition and includes the unintentional as well as intentional placement of hazardous waste into or on any land or water so that the waste enters the environment.[163]

"Facility" is defined as:

> all contiguous land, and structures, other appurtenances, and improvements on the land that are used for treating, storing, or disposing of hazardous waste.[164]

A facility may consist of several treatment, storage, or disposal operational units (e.g. one or more landfills, surface impoundments, or combinations of them). Owners and operators may be held liable for activities that occur at their facilities. An "owner" is defined as a person who owns a facility or part of a facility.[165] An "operator" is defined as a person responsible for the overall operation of a facility.[166]

7.   Permitting Procedures for TSDFs

In addition to manifest requirements, the TSDF permit program is the second requirement of the RCRA system of managing hazardous waste. All facilities that treat, store, or dispose of hazardous waste must obtain a RCRA permit, unless they operate under authorization referred to as "interim status."[167] A RCRA permit may be issued for a period of up to ten years. However, land

---

[162]   United States v. MacDonald and Watson Waste Oil Co., 933 F.2d 35 (1st. Cir.1991).

[163]   RCRA § 1004(3); 42 U.S.C.A. § 6903(3).

[164]   RCRA § 1004(3); 42 U.S.C.A. § 6903(3); *see also*, Chemical Manufacturer's Association v. United States EPA, 919 F.2d 158 (D.C. Cir.1990).

[165]   RCRA § 1004(3); 42 U.S.C.A. § 6903(3); FMC Corp. v. Northern Pump Co., 668 F.Supp. 1285 (D.Minn.1987).

[166]   RCRA § 1004(3); 42 U.S.C.A. § 6903(3).

[167]   RCRA § 3005(a), (e); 42 U.S.C.A. § 6925(a), (e).

disposal permits must be reviewed after five years and be updated to reflect current requirements.[168] Except for certain PCB incinerators, new facilities must obtain permits before construction and operations begin.[169]

a.   Hazardous Waste Permit

All TSDFs must obtain a hazardous waste permit from either EPA or a respective state, where applicable.[170]

b.   Applicable Permit Standards

All RCRA hazardous waste permits incorporate standards set by 40 C.F.R. Part 264, as well as such additional conditions that EPA finds necessary to protect human health and the environment.[171]

c.   Permit by Incorporation

Certain TSDFs are not required to obtain RCRA permits as long as they comply with other requirements contained in the hazardous waste regulations. For example, hazardous waste injection wells with permits issued under the Underground Injection Control program (UIC), and publicly owned treatment works (POTWs) with NPDES permits are authorized to treat or dispose of hazardous waste without a RCRA permit if they comply with their own applicable permits and the requirements set out in 40 C.F.R. Section 270.60. Thus, even though a TSDF may handle hazardous wastes, it isn't automatically regulated through RCRA.

d.   Additional Requirements

Each TSDF permit should include a number of general conditions analogous to those contained in NPDES permits under the Clean Water Act.

---

[168]   RCRA § 3005(c)(3); 42 U.S.C.A. § 6925(c)(3).

[169]   RCRA § 3005(a); 42 U.S.C.A. § 6925(a); 40 C.F.R. § 270.10(f)(3).

[170]   RCRA § 3005(a); 42 U.S.C.A. § 6925(a).

[171]   RCRA § 3005(c)(3); 42 U.S.C.A. § 6925(c)(3); 40 C.F.R. § 264.1(b); *see e.g.*, Mardan Corp v. C.G.C. Music, Ltd., 600 F.Supp. 1049, 1112 (D.Ariz.1984); Aff'd, 804 F.2d 1454 (9th Cir.1986).

These conditions include the duty to comply with all permit requirements; operate and maintain the facility properly; provide information requested by EPA; give notice of planned changes to the facility; and report noncompliance.[172]

e.   Permit Application Form and Procedures

A RCRA permit application consists of two parts. Part A consists of a limited amount of general facility information, which is submitted on a brief form. Part B is similar to a lengthy report that explains how the detailed regulatory requirements applicable to the facility will be satisfied.[173] Procedures for processing, finalizing, and appealing RCRA permits are found in 40 C.F.R. Part 124.

f.   Permit Modifications

Once a permit is issued, it may be modified either at the request of the permittee or by EPA. A permit may be modified to account for significant changes to the facility, new information, new requirements, or events beyond a permittee's control.

The federal regulations establish three classes of permit modifications, ranging from Class 1, for relatively minor or ministerial changes, to Class 3, for significant changes in the operation of the facility or significant departures from typical permit requirements.[174] Class 1 modifications may be made without EPA approval. However, a permittee must notify EPA and the public of the changes. In addition, EPA may reject the modification and require the permittee to comply with the original permit conditions.[175] Class 2 and 3 modifications must receive prior EPA approval and are subject to public notice and comment procedures.[176]

---

[172]   40 C.F.R. § 270.30; United States EPA v. Environmental Waste Control, Inc., 917 F.2d at 330.

[173]   40 C.F.R. § 270.10(e).

[174]   40 C.F.R. § 270.42 Appendix I.

[175]   40 C.F.R. § 270.42(a).

[176]   40 C.F.R. § 270.42(b), (c).

8.   Facilities Operating under Interim Status

TSDFs do not need a RCRA permit while they operate under interim status. However, TSDFs that do operate under interim status must comply with standards outlined in 40 C.F.R. Part 265 which contain regulations regarding preparedness and prevention, emergency procedures, manifests, record keeping and reporting, groundwater monitoring, closure and post-closure care, financial responsibility, and specific types of hazardous waste management units. These requirements are similar to the requirements for permitted facilities.[177]

a.   Submission of Part A and Interim Status

Facilities in existence on November 19, 1980, that notified EPA of their existence and applied for a RCRA permit by filing Part A of the permit application, have qualified to receive interim status.[178]   Note also, that a facility that filed Part A of its permit application late or failed to comply with the notification requirement could still be authorized to continue operations under an EPA compliance order or an interim status compliance letter.[179] In addition, an existing facility that becomes subject to the requirement for a RCRA permit must submit Part A of their permit application no later than six months after the date of the publication that requires them to have a permit; or within 30 days after the date that the facility first becomes subject to the permit regulation, which ever comes first.[180] Failure to comply with the requirements of a Part A application may result in termination of interim status.[181]

b.   Submission of Part B

Anytime after promulgating Phase II,[182] the owner or operator of an existing hazardous waste facility may be required to submit Part B of their permit

---

[177]   United States EPA v. Environmental Waste Control, Inc. 698 F.Supp. at 1427.

[178]   *Id.* at 1426.

[179]   40 C.F.R. § 270.10(e).

[180]   40 C.F.R. §§ 270.10, 270.70.

[181]   40 C.F.R. § 270.13.

[182]   40 C.F.R. § 270.2.

application.[183] The State Director may also require submission of Part B if the State in which the facility is located has received interim authorization for Phase II or final authorization; if not, EPA's regional administrator may require submission of Part B. Any owner or operator of a TSDF shall be allowed at least 6 months from the date of the request to submit Part B of the application.[184] Note, a facility does not have to await EPA's request and can voluntarily submit its Part B application earlier.[185]

c.   Changes During Interim Status

An interim status facility may make changes to its operations by submitting a revised Part A application to EPA.[186] Most of the changes must be approved before implementation, and the cost of the changes generally may not exceed 50 percent of the capital cost of a comparable entirely new facility.[187] The federal regulations do not provide an opportunity for public comment on changes to an interim status facility. Facility changes that are not allowed under interim status are subject to the same permitting requirements governing a newly-constructed facility.

d.   Loss of Interim Status

A facility may lose interim status for a variety of reasons, including failure to submit a timely Part B permit application or failure to certify compliance with applicable groundwater monitoring requirements.[188]

---

[183]   40 C.F.R. § 270.10(e)(4).

[184]   *Id.*

[185]   *Id.*

[186]   40 C.F.R. § 270.72(a).

[187]   40 C.F.R. § 270.72(b).

[188]   40 C.F.R. § 270.73 (interim status terminates when, "(a) Final administrative disposition of a permit application is made; or (b) Interim status is terminated as provided in § 270.10(e)(5); (c) for owners or operators of each land disposal facility which has been granted interim status prior to November 8, 1984, on November 8, 1985, unless: (1) The owner or operator submits a Part B application for a permit for such facility prior to that date; and (2) The owner or operator certifies that such a facility is in compliance with all applicable groundwater monitoring and financial responsibility requirements . .

9.   Formal TSDF Responsibilities

TSDFs are subject to a vast array of strict federal, state, and municipal regulations. In accordance with RCRA Section 3004, EPA has promulgated regulations establishing performance standards for owners and operators of TSDFs. Such standards include, but are not limited to:

1) maintaining records of hazardous waste treated, stored or disposed of at the TSDF;

2) reporting, monitoring, inspecting and complying with the manifest system;

3) treatment, storage or disposal practices that are satisfactory to EPA;

4) regulating the location, design, and construction of such hazardous waste TSDFs;

5) contingency plans for any unexpected damage from any treatment, storage or disposal of hazardous waste;

6) proper maintenance and operations of TSDFs, including financial responsibility for corrective action; and

7) requirements for permits under RCRA Section 3005.[189]

a.   EPA Identification Number

Just like generators and transporters, every TSDF owner or operator must apply for an EPA identification number.[190]

.); *see also*, United States v. Production Plated Plastics, Inc., 742 F.Supp. 956 (W.D.Mich.1990); 955 F.2d 45 (6th Cir.1992); cert denied, 506 U.S. 820; 113 S.Ct. 67; 121 L.Ed.2d 34 (1992).

[189]   RCRA § 3005; 42 U.S.C.A. § 6925.

[190]   40 C.F.R. § 264.11.

b.   Required Notices

The owner or operator of a TSDF who receives hazardous waste (except where the TSDF is also the generator), must inform the generator in writing that he has the appropriate permit for, and will accept, the waste the generator is shipping. The owner or operator must keep a copy of this written notice as part of the operating record.[191]

c.   Waste Analysis

An owner or operator of a TSDF must obtain a detailed chemical and physical analysis of the wastes it receives. This analysis must be repeated as often as necessary to ensure it is always accurate and up to date.[192] At a minimum, the analysis must be repeated:

1)   when the owner or operator of a TSDF is notified, or has reason to believe, that the process or operation generating the hazardous waste has changed; and

2)   for off-site facilities, when the results of applicable inspections[193] indicate that the hazardous waste received at the TSDF does not match the waste designated on the manifest.

d.   Security

An owner or operator of a TSDF must prevent the unknowing or unauthorized entry of people, animals, or equipment onto an active or potentially hazardous portion of the facility.[194] Such a facility must have a 24-hour surveillance system, or an artificial or natural barrier system that completely surrounds the active portion of the facility, as well as a means to control access

---

[191]   40 C.F.R. § 264.12.

[192]   40 C.F.R. § 264.13; *see*, Solite Corp. v. United States EPA, 952 F.2d at 481.

[193]   Certain inspections are required under 40 C.F.R. § 264.13(a)(4).

[194]   40 C.F.R. § 264.14; *see*, United States v. Indiana Woodtreating Corp., 686 F.Supp. 218, 223 (S.D.Ind.1988).

to the facility at the gate or other entrance.[195] In addition, a sign must be clearly posted at each entry stating "**DANGER UNAUTHORIZED PERSONNEL KEEP OUT.**"[196]

e.   Inspections

The owner or operator of a TSDF must inspect his facility for malfunctions and deterioration, operator errors, and discharges that may cause a release of hazardous waste, or create a threat to humans.[197] These inspections must be done often enough to identify and correct problems before human health or the environment is harmed.[198] Owners and operators must keep a written schedule of inspections and record inspection dates and results in a log book.[199]

f. .   Personnel Training

All TSDF personnel must complete a training program that teaches them to perform their duties in a way that ensures the facility's compliance with RCRA and the applicable regulations.[200] At a minimum, the training must be designed to teach personnel how to respond to hazardous waste emergencies.[201] In addition, personnel must undergo annual follow-up training.[202] Note, however, these regulations have been superseded by more rigorous OSHA requirements

---

[195]   *Id.*

[196]   *Id.*

[197]   40 C.F.R. § 264.15; *see*, United States v. Indiana Woodtreating Corp., 686 F.Supp. at 223.

[198]   *Id.*

[199]   *Id.*

[200]   40 C.F.R. § 264.16.

[201]   *Id.*

[202]   *Id.*

that mandate an initial 24 to 40 - hour training program and an eight hour annual refresher course.[203]

g.   Manifesting, Record keeping and Reporting

A TSDF must process each manifest that accompanies a shipment of waste delivered from an off-site location.[204]   The facility must attempt to reconcile any discrepancy between the amount or type of waste described on the manifest and the amount or type of waste received. If the discrepancy cannot be resolved within 15 days of receiving the waste, the facility must submit a letter to EPA describing the discrepancy. A facility must keep records of each waste received, and methods and locations for its treatment, storage, or disposal. Furthermore, the facility must submit a biennial report to EPA by March 1 of each even-numbered year describing certain TSDF activities conducted during the previous year.

h.   TSDF Preparedness and Prevention

A TSDF must be designed, constructed, maintained, and operated to minimize possibilities of fire, explosion, or unplanned release of hazardous waste.[205]   In addition, a facility must also be equipped with an alarm system; equipment to contact local fire departments, police departments, or emergency response teams; portable fire extinguisher; and firefighting water.[206]   This equipment must be periodically tested and maintained as necessary to ensure its proper operation in time of emergency.[207]   Sufficient aisle space must be maintained to allow unobstructed movement by personnel in case of an

---

[203]   29 C.F.R. § 1910.120(e); *see*, Gade v. National Solid Wastes Management Ass'n, 505 U.S. 88; 112 S.Ct. 2374; 120 L.Ed.2d 73 (1992).

[204]   40 C.F.R. § 264(E) (if the facility accepts hazardous waste without a manifest, the facility must prepare and submit to EPA an Unmanifested Waste Report within 15 days of receiving the waste).

[205]   40 C.F.R. Part 264 Subpart C; *see*, United States v. Indiana Woodtreating Corp., 686 F.Supp. at 223.

[206]   *Id.*

[207]   *Id.*

emergency.[208] Local police, fire departments, and emergency response teams must be trained to be familiar with the TSDF's layout, types of hazardous waste handled and places where facility personnel would normally work, including entrances, and evacuation routes.[209]

In addition, each owner or operator of a TSDF must design a contingency plan to minimize hazards to human health and the environment from fires, explosions, or unplanned releases of hazardous waste.[210] Copies of the contingency plans must be submitted to local police departments, fire departments, hospitals, and state and local emergency response teams. The plans must be revised to reflect facility changes. A designated emergency coordinator must be onsite or on call at all times.

i.   Groundwater Monitoring Requirements

Each surface impoundment, waste pile, land treatment unit, or landfill at a TSDF that received hazardous waste after July 26, 1982, must be equipped with a groundwater monitoring system.[211] This monitoring system must be equipped with a sufficient number of wells to determine the impact of waste disposal on the groundwater.[212] The groundwater monitoring program is divided into three phases:

1)   detection monitoring, designed to detect hazardous waste;[213]

2)   compliance monitoring, designed to identify the extent of groundwater contamination;[214] and

---

[208]   40 C.F.R. § 264.35.

[209]   40 C.F.R. § 264.37.

[210]   40 C.F.R. Part 264 Subpart D; *see*, United States v. Indiana Woodtreating Corp., 686 F.Supp. at 223.

[211]   40 C.F.R. § 264.97.

[212]   United States v. Indiana Woodtreating Corp., 686 F.Supp. at 223.

[213]   40 C.F.R. § 264.98.

[214]   40 C.F.R. § 264.99.

3)   corrective actions, designed to remove and treat contamination.[215]

Whenever a monitoring system reveals a significant increase in hazardous waste that exceed the limitations outlined in the permit, compliance monitoring must be conducted. Whenever the groundwater protection standard is exceeded, corrective action is required. The groundwater protection standard is exceeded if hazardous waste in the groundwater exceeds the National Interim Primary Drinking Water Standards (NIPDWS), or so-called alternative concentration limits specified in the permit. Variances from groundwater monitoring requirements may be obtained if the TSDF:[216]

1)   meets certain engineering, operating and performance requirements, such as not receiving liquid waste and is equipped with a double liner and leak detection system; or

2)   exhibits no potential for migration of hazardous waste constituents.

However, if no variance is obtained and concentrations of hazardous waste exceed permissible limits, then actions must be taken to correct and subsequently monitor the problem.

j.   Closure and Post-Closure Requirements

A TSDF must have a plan that describes how each hazardous waste management unit at its facility will be closed when it stops receiving hazardous waste.[217] This plan must describe how and when the unit will be closed; how closure will be conducted; the maximum inventory of hazardous waste that the unit will contain at closure; methods for removing, transporting, storing or disposing of hazardous waste; methods for decontaminating equipment; the schedule for achieving closure; and the estimated closure costs.

Within 90 days after closure, the TSDF must submit a survey plat to the local zoning authority and to EPA that identifies the location and size of the

---

[215]   40 C.F.R. § 264.100.

[216]   40 C.F.R. Part 264 Subpart G.

[217]   United States EPA v. Environmental Waste Control, Inc., 698 F.Supp. at 1427.

disposal area. The facility also must record a notice in the deed records that the property has been used to manage hazardous waste; that its future use is restricted; and that a survey plat identifying the waste disposal areas has been filed with the local zoning authority. If the unit has been closed clean, the permittee may request EPA to eliminate the deed notice requirement.[218] Post-closure operations are conducted, when necessary, under the terms of a separate post-closure permit. During post-closure, the unit generally must be maintained to prevent any releases.[219]

k.   Financial Responsibility Requirements Under Closure Operations

In addition to demonstrating that closure plans exist, a TSDF must also demonstrate its financial ability to comply with all closure requirements. An owner or operator of a disposal facility must demonstrate his financial ability to comply with all post-closure care requirements.[220] As part of the closure and post-closure care plans submitted with Part B of the permit application, the facility must include a written estimate of the costs required to close the facility.

Moreover, some type of financial assurances must be provided with closure and post-closure care. Financial assurances may include a trust fund, a surety bond, a letter of credit, insurance, a financial test (provided certain requirements are met, including a tangible net worth of at least $10 million) and a corporate guarantee, or a combination of the above.[221]

l.   Liability Coverage Requirements

A TSDF must demonstrate liability coverage of at least one million dollars per occurrence at an annual aggregate of two million dollars for third

---

[218]   40 C.F.R. Part 264 Subpart G.

[219]   United States EPA v. Environmental Waste Control, Inc., 710 F.Supp. at 1229.

[220]   40 C.F.R. Part 264 Subpart H; see, e.g., United States v. EKCO Housewares, Inc., 853 F.Supp. 975 (N.D.Ohio 1994).

[221]   United States v. Indiana Woodtreating Corp., 686 F.Supp. at 223.

party bodily injury and property damage claims.[222] In addition, a facility with a hazardous waste surface impoundment, landfill, or land treatment unit must demonstrate liability coverage of at least three million dollars per occurrence at an annual aggregate of six million dollars for non-sudden, accidental occurrences.[223] Liability coverage may be demonstrated through liability insurance, a written guarantee, a letter of credit, a surety bond, a trust fund, or a financial test.[224] The limited availability of insurance to cover pollution incidents makes it hard for a poorly capitalized company to demonstrate the necessary liability coverage.

m.   Corrective Action

Corrective action is the remedial response to releases of hazardous waste from a TSDF.[225] In July 1990, EPA proposed a far ranging corrective action program modeled after the remedial approach developed under CERCLA.[226] This program was later codified in the C.F.R.[227] In its corrective action rule, EPA announced two general goals:[228]

1) to achieve consistency between RCRA and CERCLA so that the regulated community cannot exploit any inconsistency in conducting cleanups; and

2) to incorporate flexibility into the remedy and final cleanup standards selection.

---

[222] 40 C.F.R. § 264.147; United States v. EKCO Housewares, Inc., 853 F.Supp. at 987.

[223] United States EPA v. Environmental Waste Control, Inc., 917 F.2d at 333.

[224] United States v. EKCO Housewares, Inc., 853 F.Supp. at 987.

[225] United States v. Indiana Woodtreating Corp., 686 F.Supp. at 223.

[226] See, 55 Fed. Reg. 30,798 (July 29, 1990).

[227] 40 C.F.R. § 264.100 (1987).

[228] 55 Fed. Reg. 30,852, 30,802 (July 27, 1990).

EPA also announced five basic principles it would utilize in selecting corrective actions for a facility.[229] These principles are that:

1) the highest priority will be given to the most environmentally significant facilities and the most environmentally significant problems at each facility;

2) "conditional remedies" will be incorporated to reduce risks to levels acceptable for a facility's current use or where complete cleanup is impractical;

3) voluntary cleanups will be encouraged by removing the regulatory disincentives for such cleanups;

4) the site analysis must focus on the most plausible concerns and most likely remedies to expedite cleanup; and that

5) it will emphasize early action and expeditious remedial decisions.

EPA requires that any permit issued after November 8, 1984, mandate that the permittee perform corrective actions for all releases of hazardous waste from any unit at a facility where solid waste was managed regardless of when the unit ceased to operate.[230] These permits must also include a schedule for performing corrective action and financial assurances.[231] EPA's corrective action authority extends to releases beyond a facility's boundary.[232] Procedures for imposing corrective action requirements must comply with the same general regulations and standards applicable to TSDF permits.[233] RCRA also authorizes

---

[229]   55 Fed. Reg. 30,582, 30,802-03 (July 27, 1990).

[230]   RCRA § 3004(u); 42 U.S.C.A. § 6924(u).

[231]   *Id.*

[232]   *Id.*; RCRA § 3004(v); 42 U.S.C.A. § 6924(v).

[233]   40 C.F.R. Part 124.

EPA to impose corrective action requirements on interim status facilities.[234] This authority extends to generators that treat, store, or dispose of hazardous waste without authorization. The procedures for issuing interim status corrective action orders are governed by specific regulations that provide only limited opportunity for a hearing and review by EPA.[235] This corrective action program contains four steps:[236]

1) RCRA Facility Assessment (RFA)
    EPA assesses available information and may conduct sampling to determine whether a hazardous waste has been released into the environment. This is similar to the preliminary assessment/site investigation under CERCLA.

2) RCRA Facility Investigation (RFI)
    If the RFA identifies a release, the permittee must characterize the nature, extent, and rate of migration of the hazardous waste. This is similar to a remedial investigation under CERCLA.

3) Corrective Measures Study (CMS)
    The permittee must then identify and recommend remedial measures to address the releases. This is similar to the feasibility study under CERCLA.

4) Corrective Measures Implementation (CMI)
    After EPA selects the desired remedy, the permittee must design, construct, and implement the remedy. This is similar to the remedial design and final remedial action under CERCLA.

The following chart shows the RCRA corrective action process utilizing the four RCRA corrective steps.

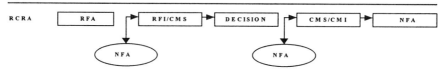

Reprinted with permission from Mr. Bernie K. Schafer, Senior Counsel, Office of Assistant General Counsel (Installations and Environment), General Counsel of the Navy (December 2000).

---

[234] RCRA § 3008(h); 42 U.S.C.A. § 6928(h); *see* e.g., Apache Powder Co. v. United States, 968 F.2d 66, 69 (D.C. Cir.1992).

[235] 40 C.F.R. § 24.

[236] RCRA Corrective Action Plan, EPA Office of Solid Waste and Emergency Response (June 1988).

At the conclusion of the RFI, the permittee may apply for a "no further action" determination (NFA) based on a demonstration that the release or presence of hazardous wastes do not exist or pose a threat to human health or the environment. The NFA determination is implemented through a modification of a permit that terminates the corrective action compliance schedule.[237] However, EPA's "no further action" determination does not limit its authority to take future actions.[238]

If, at the onset, the RFA indicates that specified "action levels" have been exceeded and the permittee does not qualify for a "no further action" determination, then the permittee must immediately conduct a CMS.[239] EPA will select a remedy based on the CMS. The remedy must:[240]

1)   protect human health and the environment;

2)   attain the specified cleanup standards;

3)   control the source of contamination; and

4)   comply with applicable waste management standards.

In implementing a remedy, the treatment, storage, and disposal of hazardous waste must comply with all applicable requirements. However, the corrective action rule may authorize treatment or storage in temporary units that do not have to meet the strict requirements found in 40 C.F.R. Part 264. The corrective action rule also authorizes EPA to waive certain closure requirements for units used to manage the corrective action waste.[241] When the remedy selected cannot meet cleanup standards, EPA may determine that the remedy is technically impractical and require the permittee to take alternative measures.[242]

---

[237]   55 Fed. Reg. at 30,875.

[238]   *Id.*

[239]   *Id.*

[240]   Apache Powder Co. v. United States, 968 F.2d at 70.

[241]   55 Fed. Reg. 30,798, 30880, 30882 (July 27, 1990).

[242]   55 Fed. Reg. at 30,880.

The remedy is complete when cleanup standards have been achieved, source control actions have been completed, and the necessary closure and post-closure requirements have been met. At any point during the corrective action process, EPA may require the permittee to undertake interim measures to abate a release that poses an immediate threat to human health or the environment.[243] These measures may include controlling contamination sources, installing security fencing, and providing alternative water supplies to affected persons.[244]

10.   The Land Ban

Generally, hazardous waste is prohibited from land disposal unless it has been treated to meet specific standards or it qualifies under a narrow set of variances or exceptions.[245] Land disposal includes any placement of hazardous waste in a landfill, surface impoundment, waste pile, injection well, land treatment facility, salt dome or salt bed formation, or underground mine or cave.[246] The land ban's purpose is to prevent the migration of hazardous waste that may endanger human health or the environment. However, the land ban restrictions do not apply to SQGs.[247] Thus, many SQGs who produce less than 100 kg/mo may still dispose of their waste in a landfill.[248]

a.   Schedule For Land Disposal Restrictions

Under RCRA, Congress divided all hazardous waste into five basic categories and specified when EPA must promulgate land ban rules for each category. These five categories include: solvents, dioxin wastes and the three listed groups of hazardous wastes referred to as the first, second and third

---

[243]   *Id.*

[244]   55 Fed. Reg. at 30,839.

[245]   *See*, e.g., National Solid Wastes Management Ass'n v. Alabama Dept. of Environmental Management, 910 F.2d 713 (11th Cir.1990).

[246]   RCRA § 3004(k); 42 U.S.C.A. § 6924(k); *see*, Chemical Waste Management, Inc. v. United States EPA, 976 F.2d 2, 20 (D.C. Cir.1992).

[247]   40 C.F.R. § 268.1(e)(1); Environmental Defense Fund, Inc. v. Wheelabrator Technologies, Inc., 725 F.Supp at 772.

[248]   40 C.F.R. § 268.1(e)(1).

"thirds."[249] The "third" category also includes all characteristic hazardous waste.[250] Congress further provided that if EPA failed to act by a specified date, each waste in the category for which the deadline was missed could be land disposed of only in a unit that satisfied the minimum technical requirements (such as double lining, etc.), and only if the generator was able to certify there was no practical alternative to the land disposal.[251] In addition, Congress has provided that if EPA failed to act by May 5, 1990, for promulgating the last set of regulations, each hazardous waste in the category for which the deadline was missed would be banned automatically from land disposal, regardless of whether it had been treated.[252] For the most part, EPA has met all required deadlines.[253]

b.   Treatment Standards

For each land-banned waste, EPA has specified the best demonstrated available technology (BDAT) be used as a guide for handling and treatment of hazardous waste. The BDAT standard either specifies a treatment technology or a concentration for each hazardous waste constituent that a treatment technology must attain before the waste can be disposed of in a land facility.[254] Alternatively, for some wastes, EPA has not specified a BDAT and has instead banned the land disposal of the waste altogether.[255] Satisfying the treatment standard through some other means, such as dilution or evaporation, is not allowed.[256]

---

[249]   RCRA § 3004(d), (e), (f), (g); 42 U.S.C.A. § 6924(d), (e), (f), (g).

[250]   RCRA § 3004(g)(4)(C); 42 U.S.C.A. § 6924(g)(4)(C).

[251]   RCRA § 3004(g)(5); 42 U.S.C.A. § 6924(g)(5).

[252]   RCRA § 3004(g)(6)(C); 42 U.S.C.A. § 6924(g)(6)(C); *see*, Steel Manufacturers Ass'n v. United States EPA, 27 F.3d at 644.

[253]   Steel Manufacturers Ass'n v. United States EPA, 27 F.3d at 644.

[254]   RCRA § 3004(m); 42 U.S.C.A. § 6924(m).

[255]   40 C.F.R. § 268.42 (Table 1); *see*, e.g., Steel Manufacturers Ass'n v. United States EPA, 27 F.3d at 644.

[256]   40 C.F.R. §§ 268.3, 268.4(b); Chemical Waste Management, Inc. v. United States EPA, 976 F.2d at 19.

c.   Variances and Exceptions

EPA has granted a number of two-year variances from the effective date of the land disposal prohibition because there was an inadequate national capacity for waste treatment.[257] The Hazardous and Solid Waste Amendments (HSWA) have also authorized EPA to grant up to two additional one-year extensions on a case-by-case basis where a treatment or alternative disposal facility is being constructed under a binding contract, but is not yet available.[258]

EPA is also authorized to exempt from the land ban a disposal unit when the owner or operator demonstrates that there will be "no migration of hazardous constituents from the disposal unit or injection zone for as long as the wastes remain hazardous."[259] EPA has granted a series of "no migration petitions" to injection wells, but the requirements for obtaining such exemptions are so stringent that surface disposal facilities are unlikely to qualify.

In addition, a generator or TSDF may petition EPA requesting permission to use an alternative treatment method. To be successful, a petitioner must demonstrate that the treatment method is equally effective in reducing the toxicity and/or mobility of the hazardous waste constituents as treatment methods already in existence under BDAT.[260]

d.   Effect of the Land Ban on Storage

Extended storage of land-banned waste is prohibited unless it is necessary to accumulate enough waste to allow proper recovery, treatment, or disposal. Storage for up to one year is presumptively proper, but the facility must demonstrate that storage of the waste for more than one year is necessary.[261]

---

[257]   RCRA § 3004(d)(1); 42 U.S.C.A. § 6924(h)(2).

[258]   RCRA § 3004(h)(3); 42 U.S.C.A. § 6924(h)(3); *see*, Mobil Oil Corp. v. United States EPA, 871 F.2d 149, 151 (D.C. Cir.1989).

[259]   RCRA § 3004(d)(1); 42 U.S.C.A. § 6924(d)(1).

[260]   40 C.F.R. § 268.42(b).

[261]   40 C.F.R. § 268.50.

III.   SUBTITLE D: SOLID WASTE MANAGEMENT

A.   INTRODUCTION

Congress enacted the initial Solid Waste Disposal Act (SWDA, hereinafter referred to as RCRA) in 1965[262] to establish grant programs to develop solid waste management plans by States and interstate agencies. RCRA establishes a federal program for the comprehensive management of "solid waste."[263] Subtitle D of RCRA is the principal regulatory section that controls solid waste management.[264] Under Subtitle D, "solid wastes" are almost exclusively defined as non-hazardous substances.[265] Management and disposal of solid (non-hazardous) waste have traditionally been regulated by state and local governments.[266] The primary objectives of Subtitle D under RCRA Section 4001, "are to assist in developing and encouraging methods for the disposal of solid waste that are environmentally sound and that maximize the use of valuable resources including energy and materials, that are recoverable from solid waste and to encourage resource conservation."[267] Therefore, RCRA requires states to create state plans that address all aspects of solid waste management, from collection to disposal and resource recovery.

States with approved solid waste management plans can receive federal assistance for planning, studies, source-separation projects and similar activities, but not for other types of construction, land purchase, or subsidies for recovered materials.[268] The state must also provide for public participation.[269] Minimum

---

[262]   42 U.S.C.A. §§ 3251-3259 (1965).

[263]   RCRA §§ 4001-4009; 42 U.S.C.A. §§ 6941-6949.

[264]   *Id.*

[265]   RCRA § 1004(27); 42 U.S.C.A. § 6903(27).

[266]   Central Vermont Quality Services, Inc. v. City of Rutland, Vt., 780 F.Supp. 218, 219 (D.Vt.1991).

[267]   RCRA § 4001; 42 U.S.C.A. § 6941; C & A Carbone, Inc. v. Town of Clarkstown, N.Y., 511 U.S. 383; 114 S.Ct. 1677, 1691; 128 L.Ed.2d. 399 (1994).

[268]   RCRA §§ 4007, 4008; 42 U.S.C.A. §§ 6947, 6948.

[269]   40 C.F.R. Part 256.

requirements for state plans are set out in 40 C.F.R. Part 256. As of May 11, 1995, 16 states[270] had approved solid waste landfill permit programs and 6 states[271] plus two Indian tribes received tentative adequacy determinations for their landfill programs.[272]

B.   DISPOSAL FACILITIES

RCRA requires that EPA develop criteria to classify solid waste disposal facilities and practices.[273] EPA has created regulations that contain criteria known as "Subtitle D Criteria" to determine which facilities pose a reasonable probability of adverse effects on health and the environment. Facilities that meet the criteria are sanitary landfills. Facilities that fail to meet the criteria are considered open dumps for purposes of state solid waste management planning.

1.   Sanitary Landfill

A sanitary landfill is a solid waste disposal facility for which there is "no reasonable probability of adverse effects on health or the environment from disposal of solid waste at such facility."[274] A sanitary landfill generally must:[275]

---

[270]   59 Fed. Reg. 9979 (1994) (Alabama); 59 Fed. Reg. 65,334 (1994) (Arizona); 59 Fed. Reg. 10,382 (1994) (Delaware); 59 Fed. Reg. 35,340 (1994) (Florida); 59 Fed. Reg. 28,523 (1994) (Hawaii); 59 Fed. Reg. 86 (1994) (Illinois); 59 Fed. Reg. 11,268 (1994) (Michigan); 59 Fed. Reg. 17,526 (1994) (Missouri); 59 Fed. Reg. 10,645 (1994) (Nevada); 59 Fed. Reg. 66,306 (1994) (New Mexico); 59 Fed. Reg. 30,353 (1994) (Ohio); 59 Fed. Reg. 42,045 (1994) (Oklahoma); 59 Fed. Reg. 29,804 (1994) (Pennsylvania); 59 Fed. Reg. 44,144 (1994) (Puerto Rico); 59 Fed. Reg. 15,201 (1994) (Virginia); 59 Fed. Reg. 15,203 (1994) (Washington).

[271]   59 Fed. Reg. 23,202 (1994), 59 Fed. Reg. 48,427 (1994) (Massachusetts); 59 Fed. Reg. 52,299 (1994) (New Hampshire); 59 Fed. Reg. 54,190 (1994) (New Jersey); 59 Fed. Reg. 38,463 (1994) (New York); 59 Fed. Reg. 60,631 (1994) (North Dakota); 59 Fed. Reg. 16,647 (1994) (South Dakota).

[272]   59 Fed. Reg. 24,422 (1994) (Campo Band of Mission Indians); 59 Fed. Reg. 16,642 (1994) (Cheyenne River Sioux Tribe).

[273]   RCRA § 4004; 42 U.S.C.A. § 6944.

[274]   RCRA § 4004(a); 42 U.S.C.A. § 6944(a); see e.g., City of Gallatin v. Cherokee County, 563 F.Supp. 940, 944 (E.D.Tex.1983); superseded by statute in Blue Legs v. United States EPA, 668 F.Supp. 1329 (D.S.D.1987); Middlesex County Board of Chosen

1)   not affect or be affected by 100-year floods;[276]

2)   not contribute to a "taking" of an endangered species or the destruction or adverse modification of critical habitat;[277]

3)   not discharge pollutants into surface waters;[278]

4)   not contaminate groundwater beyond the waste boundary or specified alternate boundary;[279]

5)   not result in the application of specified chemicals to land used for food-chain crops above specified rates;[280]

6)   minimize the population of onsite disease vectors through application of cover or other mechanisms;[281]

7)   control application of sewage sludge and septic tank waste within specified parameters;[282]

8)   not engage in open burning;[283] and

Freeholders v. State of New Jersey, Dept. of Environmental Protection, 645 F.Supp. 715 (D.N.J.1986).

[275]   40 C.F.R. § 257.3.

[276]   40 C.F.R. § 257.3-1.

[277]   40 C.F.R. § 257.3-2.

[278]   40 C.F.R. § 257.3-3.

[279]   40 C.F.R. § 257.3-4.

[280]   40 C.F.R. § 257.3-5.

[281]   40 C.F.R. § 257.3-6.

[282]   *Id.*

[283]   40 C.F.R. § 257.3-7.

9)   limit explosive gas accumulation, bird hazards to aircraft, and public access.[284]

2.   Open Dump

An open dump is any facility or site where solid waste is disposed of which is not a sanitary landfill and not a facility for disposal of hazardous waste.[285] RCRA prohibits open dumping except as provided in a state solid waste management plan.[286] Citizens are authorized to enforce a ban on open dumping through citizen suits. However, because penalties are not available, prevailing plaintiffs may only recover their costs and attorneys fees.[287]

IV.   ENFORCEMENT REMEDIES

Like most major federal environmental statutes, RCRA authorizes the government to take enforcement action in any of the available forums: administrative, civil, or criminal. In addition, citizens are authorized to initiate enforcement actions to obtain civil penalties and injunctive relief.

A.   ADMINISTRATIVE REMEDIES

Administrative remedies are available where failure to comply with RCRA or its applicable regulations has been discovered. Administrative remedies include such actions as: administrative compliance orders, corrective action orders, and monitoring, testing and analysis orders.

1.   Administrative Compliance Orders

EPA may issue administrative compliance orders that require a violator to comply with RCRA immediately or within a specified time period.[288] In

---

[284]   40 C.F.R. § 257.3-8.

[285]   RCRA § 1004(14); 42 U.S.C.A. § 6903(14).

[286]   RCRA § 4005(a); 42 U.S.C.A. § 6945 (a).

[287]   RCRA § 7002; 42 U.S.C.A. § 6972; *See*, 40 C.F.R. Part 254; *see also*, Blue Legs v. United States Bureau of Indian Affairs, 867 F.2d 1094 (8th Cir.1989).

[288]   RCRA § 3008(a); 42 U.S.C.A. § 6928(a).

conjunction with the order, EPA may assess an administrative penalty of up to $25,000 per day per violation.[289] If the violation occurs in a state where RCRA authority has been delegated, EPA must provide notice to the state before issuing the order, but EPA is not required to obtain the state's permission to proceed.[290] The procedures governing the assessment of RCRA administrative penalties and the issuance of orders are set out in RCRA Section 3008(b) and 40 C.F.R. Part 22. Failure to comply with the orders subjects the respondent to penalties of $25,000 per day of noncompliance and revocation of its permit.[291]

2.   Interim Status Corrective Action Orders

EPA may issue administrative orders requiring the operators of interim status facilities to take corrective action to address any hazardous waste release from their respective facility.[292] EPA has interpreted this authority to extend to facilities that have lost interim status or never qualified for interim status because they failed to submit the required notification or Part A of the permit application. A corrective action order also may revoke a facility's interim status. Failure to comply with a corrective action order also subjects the violator to civil penalties of up to $25,000 per day of noncompliance.[293]

3.   Monitoring, Analysis and Testing Orders

EPA can also issue an administrative order requiring the current or previous owner or operator of any TSDF, or where a release of hazardous waste may present a substantial hazard to human health or the environment, to conduct any monitoring, testing, analysis, or reporting deemed reasonable by EPA.[294]

---

[289] *Id.*

[290] *Id.*

[291] RCRA § 3008(c); 42 U.S.C.A. § 6928(c).

[292] RCRA § 3008(h); 42 U.S.C.A. § 6928(h).

[293] RCRA § 3008(h)(2); 42 U.S.C.A. § 6928(h)(2).

[294] RCRA § 3013(a); 42 U.S.C.A. § 6934(a).

Failure to comply with such an order subjects the violator to civil penalties of up to $5,000 per day of noncompliance.[295]

B.   CIVIL REMEDIES

As an alternative to its administrative authority, EPA may initiate a civil action for RCRA violations.[296] Penalties of up to $25,000 per day per violation and injunctive relief are available.[297] Under RCRA, EPA may initiate a civil action against any person who has contributed or is contributing to the handling, storage, treatment, transportation, or disposal of any solid or hazardous waste that may present an imminent and substantial endangerment to human health or the environment.[298] Upon a proper showing of endangerment, the court may order the defendant to take any action "as may be necessary," and EPA may issue an administrative order that requires specific remedial action.[299] This provision was virtually the sole remedy available to the government to address abandoned waste sites before CERCLA was enacted.

Section 7003 of RCRA is potentially a powerful tool because it reaches solid as well as hazardous waste, and the available relief is subject to few statutory constraints. The requirement that EPA demonstrate that "imminent and substantial endangerment" may be present has not proven to be a major barrier because the courts have construed the terms "imminent," "substantial" and "endangerment" broadly. Since the passage of CERCLA, however, EPA typically uses that statute instead of Section 7003, because it provides more favorable procedural advantages to the government and allows the government to recover its costs.

C.   CRIMINAL ENFORCEMENT AUTHORITY

Criminal violations under RCRA can be prosecuted in either federal or state criminal courts. Such violations can result in fines, imprisonment, or both.

---

[295]   RCRA § 3013(e); 42 U.S.C.A. § 6934(e).

[296]   RCRA § 3008(a); 42 U.S.C.A. § 6928(a).

[297]   *Id.*

[298]   RCRA § 7003; 42 U.S.C.A. § 6973.

[299]   *Id.*

Prison terms for environmental crimes are determined by the federal sentencing guidelines. "There are seven acts identified in section 3008 of RCRA that carry criminal penalties ranging from a fine of $50,000 per day to a possible total fine of $ 1,000,000, or a prison sentence of up to 5 years. Six of the seven criminal acts carry a penalty of up to $50,000 per day or from 2 to 5 years in jail. Stated briefly, these acts are "knowingly:"

1)   transporting waste to a non-permitted facility;

2)   treating, storing, or disposing of waste without a permit or in violation of a material condition of a permit or interim status standard;

3)   omitting important information from, or making a false statement in a label, manifest, report, permit, or compliance document;

4)   generating, storing, treating, or disposing of waste without complying with RCRA's record keeping and reporting requirements;

5)   transporting waste without a manifest; or

6)   exporting a waste without the consent of the receiving country.

The seventh criminal act is the "knowing endangerment" violation. A separate criminal penalty of $250,000 and/or imprisonment of up to 15 years is provided for those who knowingly transport, treat, store, dispose of, or export any hazardous waste or used oil with the knowledge that he is placing another person in imminent danger of death or serious bodily injury.[300] Corporate violators of this provision are subject to a $1 million fine.

The courts generally construe the requirement that the violation be "knowing" to mean only that "a defendant was aware that he was performing the proscribed acts; [and that] knowledge of regulatory requirements is not necessary."[301] The defendant may be criminally liable for his actions even if he

---

[300]   RCRA § 3008(e); 42 U.S.C.A. § 6928(e).

[301]   United States v. Laughlin, 10 F.3d 961, 965 (2d Cir.1993); *see also*, United States v. International Minerals & Chem. Corp., 402 U.S. 558; 563-65; 91 S.Ct. 1697,

was unaware that the wastes were classified for regulatory purposes as hazardous or that his actions were governed by a regulatory requirement. The knowledge requirement may be demonstrated through circumstantial evidence, such as the fact that the waste disposal arranged for by the defendant cost far less than a reasonable person would have expected.[302] In addition, a defendant can be held criminally liable even though he did not know any permit requirements existed. Courts have consistently held that knowledge of RCRA's permit requirements is not an element of any violation.[303]

D.   CITIZEN SUITS

RCRA authorizes citizens to bring enforcement actions against both potential RCRA violators and EPA in federal court.[304] Citizens may sue EPA requiring it to take any non-discretionary duty mandated by RCRA.[305] Citizen suits filed because of EPA's failure to comply with non-discretionary duties may be brought in the district court for the district in which the alleged violation occurred or in the District Court for the District of Columbia.[306]

1.   Scope of Citizen Suit Authority

RCRA authorizes citizens to bring enforcement actions against potential violators in federal court. Citizens may seek civil penalties of up to $25,000 per day per violation as well as injunctive relief.[307] Prevailing citizen plaintiffs may also recover attorney fees and costs.[308] Note that the Court of Appeals in *Furrer*

1700-1701; 29 L.Ed.2d 178 (1971) (in prosecuting for knowing violation of hazardous materials regulation, government was not required to prove that defendant was aware of the regulation, but only that he was aware of shipment of the hazardous material).

302   United States v. Haves Int'l Corp., 786 F.2d 1499 (11th Cir.1986).

303   United States v. Wagner, 29 F.3d 264, 265 (7th Cir.1994).

304   RCRA § 7002(a)(2); 42 U.S.C.A. § 6972(a)(2).

305   RCRA § 7002(a); 42 U.S.C.A. § 6972(a).

306   RCRA § 7002; 42 U.S.C.A. § 6972.

307   RCRA § 7002(a); 42 U.S.C.A. § 6972(a).

308   RCRA § 7002(e); 42 U.S.C.A. § 6972(e).

v. Brown, specifically held that the authorization for the court to Order "other citizen action as may be necessary" in the citizen suit provision of RCRA did not authorize a money judgement to recover costs of remediation of contaminated property. The court states that "RCRA specifically authorizes citizen suits only for injunctive relief. . . . The overriding purpose of RCRA is to prevent creation of hazardous waste sites."[309] Note that remediation cost recovery actions are allowed under CERCLA.[310]

2.   Notice Requirements

Citizens must give 60 days notice to EPA, the state in which the violation occurred and the alleged violator before bringing suit, and they may not sue a defendant in an ongoing governmental enforcement action concerning the same violation.[311] Note, any person may intervene as a matter of right in an ongoing governmental enforcement action against any party who is alleged to be in violation of any permit, standard, regulation, condition, requirement, prohibition, or order.[312]

V.   JUDICIAL REVIEW

Under RCRA, there are three types of government (EPA) activities that may be reviewed by the courts: promulgation of RCRA regulations, permit decisions, and other final agency actions that do not involve permits. A fourth type of judicial review is initiated by individuals through the use of "citizen suits."

A.   PROMULGATOIN OF REGULATIONS

Judicial review of RCRA regulations that have national applicability (verses regional or local) may only be obtained in the United States Court of

---

[309]   RCRA § 1002(a) ; 42 U.S.C.A. § 6902(a); Furrer v. Brown, 62 F.3d 1092, 1097 (8th Cir. 1995).

[310]   *See* CERCLA chapter in this book.

[311]   RCRA § 7002(b); 42 U.S.C.A. § 6972(b); *see also*, Hallstrom v. Tillamook County, 493 U.S. 20; 110 S.Ct. 304; 107 L.Ed.2d 237 (1989).

[312]   RCRA § 7002(a)(1)(A); 42 U.S.C.A. § 6972(a)(1)(A).

Appeals for the District of Columbia.[313] National applicability may include actions of the EPA administrator in promulgating any regulation, or requirement under RCRA, or denying any petition to promulgate, amend or repeal any regulation under RCRA.[314]

B.   PERMIT DECISIONS

Judicial review of RCRA decisions to issue or deny a permit lies in the United States Court of Appeals for the federal circuit where the facility is located.[315] However, actions to challenge a permit requirement must be initiated in federal District Court. In addition, permits issued by a state which has been delegated RCRA authority, must be filed in state court.[316]

C.   OTHER FINAL AGENCY ACTIONS

All requests for judicial review of RCRA related EPA decisions that do not involve a permit, such as requests for variances or appeals of Section 3008(h) orders,[317] generally must be brought in federal district court.[318]

VI.   CONCLUSION

RCRA is the nation's response to the ever-growing concern regarding solid and hazardous waste disposal practices. It establishes several important programs to help manage our solid and hazardous waste. Two such programs have been discussed in this chapter and include RCRA's solid waste management program and hazardous waste management program. RCRA applies to solid wastes that are potentially dangerous to human health and the environment if improperly transported, treated, stored or disposed of.

---

[313]   RCRA § 7006(a); 42 U.S.C.A. § 6976(a).

[314]   *Id.*

[315]   RCRA § 7006(b); 42 U.S.C.A. § 6976(b).

[316]   RCRA § 3006; 42 U.S.C.A. § 6926; *see also*, United States v. T & S Brass and Bronze Works, Inc., 865 F.2d 1261 (4th Cir.1988).

[317]   RCRA § 3008(h); 42 U.S.C.A. § 6928(h).

[318]   RCRA § 3008(h)(1)(A); 42 U.S.C.A. § 6928(h)(1)(A).

Solid waste is defined as waste solids, liquids, sludges, and contained gases.   Hazardous waste includes "solid waste" that meets certain specific characteristics, such as ignitability, corrosivity, toxicity, and reactivity.   Under Subtitle D, open dumping of solid waste is prohibited and landfills must meet strict regulatory requirements in order to be considered "sanitary."   Under Subtitle C, hazardous waste must be monitored from "cradle-to-grave" with the use of such measures as a manifest.   In addition, safety standards must be met from the moment the waste is generated, through all phases of transportation, treatment, storage and disposal.   In addition to the manifest requirements, owners and operators must also obtain operating permits for their hazardous waste facilities.

To assist in implementing effective solid and hazardous waste management programs, RCRA authorizes EPA (and certain authorized states) to administer various levels of enforcement ranging from administrative actions to both civil and criminal actions.   As a result, effective solid and hazardous waste management programs allow for and encourage protection and conservation of our natural resources while at the same time, balance our needs to dispose of our ever-increasing waste.

CHAPTER 4

THE COMPREHENSIVE ENVIRONMENTAL RESPONSE, COMPENSATION AND LIABILITY ACT (CERCLA)

"The lands [of the planet] wait for those who can discern their rhythms . . . each continent, each river valley, the rugged mountains, the placid lakes, all call for relief from the constant burden of exploitation."

- Vine Victor Deloria, Jr., *God is Red*

CHAPTER 4: COMPREHENSIVE ENVIRONMENTAL RESPONSE, COMPENSATION, AND LIABILITY ACT

I.   INTRODUCTION

The Comprehensive Environmental Response, Compensation, and Liability Act (CERCLA)[1] is designed to protect the public health and environment from exposure to hazardous substances.[2] CERCLA identifies abandoned and inactive waste sites where hazardous substances could be released into the environment. It also sets up a funding and liability program to ensure such sites are cleaned. The funding program is called the Hazardous Substance Superfund or "Superfund." Superfund allows the federal government to help

---

[1]   Pub.L.No. 96-510, 94 Stat. 2767, amended by Pub.L.No 99-499, 100 Stat. 1613 (1986), Codified at 42 U.S.C.A. §§ 9601-9675.

[2]   Dedham Water Co. v. Cumberland Farms Dairy, Inc., 805 F.2d 1074, 1081 (1st Cir.1986).

finance cleanups of some of the worst hazardous waste sites in the country.[3] Superfund also provides financial incentives for private parties to swiftly and safely clean these sites. Before 1980, Congress' environmental agenda focused primarily on air and water pollutants. However, after 1980, new environmental concerns emerged once Congress became aware of the large number of abandoned hazardous waste sites in the United States. Existing laws were deemed inadequate to handle the magnitude of the hazardous waste problems facing the nation.[4] Thus, CERCLA was enacted in 1980 partially as a result of the Love Canal disaster in New York.

A.   LOVE CANAL

Between 1942 and 1953, Hooker Chemicals, a chemical and plastics company, used a 16-acre site in Niagara Falls, N.Y. to bury 22,000 tons of industrial wastes. Once buried, the company covered the wastes with a layer of clay, an accepted industry custom at that time. The land was later sold to the Niagara Falls Board of Education for $1 and subdivided for residential use and neighborhood schools.[5] By 1970, toxic chemicals had broken through the clay barrier and seeped into household basements. Residents reported "foul odors, and suffered higher than normal rates of miscarriages, birth defects, epilepsy, and liver ailments."[6] In 1978, the New York Commissioner of Health declared the area an emergency, and in 1979, he ordered the relocation of all families with children under two years old and pregnant women. Congress enacted CERCLA the following year.

---

[3]   55 Fed.Reg. 6,157 (1990).

[4]   H.R. Representative. No. 1016, Part I, 96th Cong., 2d Sess. 17, reprinted in 1980 U.S. Code Cong. & Ad. News, 6119, 6120.

[5]   United States v. Hooker Chemicals and Plastic Corp., 850 F.Supp. 993, 1026 (W.D.N.Y.1994).

[6]   Fisher, The Toxic Waste Dump Problem and a Suggested Insurance Program, 8 B.C. Envtl. Aff. L. Rev. 421, 428-33 (1980).

B. CONGRESS ENACTS CERCLA

Although the Resource Conservation and Recovery Act of 1976 (RCRA),[7] and the Clean Water Act of 1972 (CWA)[8] dealt with improper disposal of hazardous wastes and contamination of navigable waters, neither act addressed the type of environmental problems associated with the Love Canal disaster. For example, RCRA applies to the transfer, storage, and disposal of hazardous wastes by facilities currently in operation. However, in the Love Canal incident, the chemical plant was no longer in operation. Furthermore, the CWA, which applies only to navigable waters, failed to address previously contaminated groundwater. Thus, prior to CERCLA's enactment, there was no legal avenue available to hold Hooker Chemicals responsible for the environmental damages it caused.[9]

In 1980, the enactment of CERCLA filled a void in the existing environmental laws. It confronted hazardous waste disposal problems by providing for investigation, identification, and cleanup of abandoned sites by establishing funds for such actions, and by imposing liability on responsible parties.[10] Under CERCLA, either the government or private parties can clean up hazardous waste sites. First, the federal government may either:

1) clean the site using funds from the Superfund and later sue the "potentially responsible parties" (PRPs) for reimbursement, hence replenishing the Superfund;[11] or

---

[7] RCRA §§ 1002-11012; 42 U.S.C.A. §§ 6901-6992k.

[8] CWA §§ 101-607; 33 U.S.C.A. §§ 1251-1387.

[9] For discussion, *see*, Green, Michael D., Successors and CERCLA: The Imperfect Analogy to Products Liability and an Alternative Proposal, 87 NW. U. L. Rev. 897, 900 (1993).

[10] *Id.* at 900, 901.

[11] CERCLA § 107; 42 U.S.C.A. § 9607.

2)   issue administrative orders requiring the PRPs to clean the sites themselves.[12]

Second, private citizens may clean up sites themselves and then later sue PRPs for reimbursement.[13]

C.   SUPERFUND AMENDMENTS AND REAUTHORIZATION ACT (SARA)

Although CERCLA has been amended repeatedly, the most significant changes occurred in the 1986 Superfund Amendments and Reauthorization Act (SARA).[14] SARA increased the initial fund of $1.6 billion to $8.5 billion and required EPA to become more aggressive in investigating potential sites, cleaning sites, and collecting cleanup costs from PRPs. The increase in funding was in response to the extremely high costs associated with cleaning contaminated sites. For example, when the Love Canal cleanup was finally completed in 1988, a Federal District Court found Occidental Chemical Corporation, a successor to Hooker Chemicals, the company who created the landfill, liable for an estimated $250 million. This figure was far more than originally anticipated.[15] Like Love Canal, most CERCLA sites cost millions of dollars to clean and often require several years to complete. With the enactment of SARA, additional money became available to help clean these sites.

In spite of the many amendments to CERCLA, time and experience has shown that cleaning up abandoned hazardous waste sites is far more difficult than CERCLA's creators anticipated. As a result, litigation has flourished over its interpretation, application, and implementation.

---

[12]   CERCLA § 106; 42 U.S.C.A. § 9606.

[13]   CERCLA § 107(a)(4)(B); 42 U.S.C.A. § 9607(a)(4)(B); CERCLA § 113(f); 42 U.S.C.A. § 9613(f) (where PRP incurred response costs associated with a cleanup, that PRP may seek contribution from other PRPs for some or all of the costs it incurred).

[14]   SARA, Pub. L. No. 99-499, 100 Stat. 1613 (1986); 42 U.S.C.A. § 9611 (1988).

[15]   Wald, Patricia M., The Role of the Judiciary in Environmental Protection, 19 B.C. Envt. Aff. L. Rev. 519, 544 (1992).

II.   POLICY

Congress has implemented CERCLA's goal of quickly cleaning up hazardous waste sites by providing EPA with Superfund money to establish a system that:

1)   provides a national inventory of inactive hazardous waste sites;

2)   establishes a program for appropriate environmental response to protect public health and the environment;

3)   authorizes emergency assistance and containment actions at sites posing an immediate threat;

4)   establishes a Hazardous Waste Response Fund to finance emergency responses;

5)   establishes a federal cause of action in strict liability enabling rapid recovery of response costs for containment and emergency actions against persons responsible for spills and releases; and

6)   encourages private parties to voluntarily pursue environmental cleanup actions at inactive waste sites.[16]

Congress also set out specific factors to consider when setting priorities for Superfund response actions. These include:

1)   the population at risk;

2)   potential hazards at facilities;

3)   the potential for contamination of drinking water;

4)   the potential for direct human contact;

5)   the potential for destruction of sensitive ecosystems;

---

[16]   H.R. Representative. No. 1016, Part I, 96th Cong., 2d Sess. 17, reprinted in 1980 U.S. Code Cong. & Ad. News, 6119, 6120.

6)   the damage to natural resources, contamination of the ambient air,

7)   as well as other appropriate factors.[17]

III.   THE SUPERFUND PROCESS

EPA has implemented five primary phases to the Superfund process. These include: identification, assessment, placement on the National Priorities List (NPL), investigation, and remedy selection.

A.   IDENTIFYING ABANDONED SITES

Before EPA places sites on its National Priorities List (NPL), it must identify the location and gravity of risk to both human health and the environment at each site. Contaminated sites are often initially brought to the attention of EPA by the media, private citizens, and local and state agencies. In addition, CERCLA imposes statutory obligations on certain parties to disclose vital information to EPA.[18]

Section 103(c) of CERCLA assists EPA in developing a inventory of hazardous waste sites.[19] It requires owners, operators of inactive hazardous waste sites, and persons who transported hazardous substances to these sites, to notify EPA of the existence of these facilities. As a result of compliance with this notification requirement, EPA has identified over 33,000 potentially

---

[17]   Henrichs, Ragna, Superfund's NPL: The Listing Process, 63 St. John's L. Rev. 717, 722-23 (1989); CERCLA § 105(a)(8)(A); 42 U.S.C.A. § 9605(a)(8)(A).

[18]   CERCLA § 103; 42 U.S.C.A. § 9603.

[19]   CERCLA § 103(c); 42 U.S.C.A. § 9603(c) (Any person who owns or operates or who at the time of disposal owned or operated, or who accepted hazardous substances for transport, and selected a facility at which hazardous substances . . . are or have been stored, treated, or disposed of shall . . . notify the Administrator of the Environmental Protection Agency of the existence of such facility, specifying the amount and type of any hazardous substance to be found there, and any known, suspected, or likely releases of such substances from such facility).

hazardous waste sites for evaluation and possible response.[20] In addition, over 1,200 sites have been included on the NPL for remediation,[21] and hundreds of other sites have been the subject of emergency-type removal actions.[22] The NPL is expected to grow to about 2,100 sites by the year 2,000.[23]

1.   Hazardous Substances Under CERCLA

Under CERCLA, section 101(14) designates as hazardous, all substances listed or regulated under other federal environmental laws, and additional substances specifically listed under CERCLA Section 102.[24] In summary, CERCLA regulates almost any substance identified under the following statutes as hazardous:

1)   CERCLA Section 102; 42 U.S.C.A. § 9609;

2)   CWA Section 311; 33 U.S.C.A. § 1321;

3)   CWA Section 307; 33 U.S.C.A. § 1317;

4)   RCRA Section 3001; 42 U.S.C.A. § 6921;

5)   CAA Section 112; 42 U.S.C.A. § 7412; and

---

[20]   Mugdan, Walter E., Environmental Due Diligence and Liability Under Superfund for Lenders and Fiduciaries, CA51 ALI-ABA 31, 33 (Oct. 26, 1995).

[21]   *Id.* at 34.

[22]   *Id.*

[23]   *Id.*

[24]   CERCLA § 101(14); 42 U.S.C.A. § 9601(14) ("The term 'hazardous substance' means (A) any substance designated pursuant to section 1321(b)(2)(A) of Title 33, (B) any element, compound, mixture, solution, or substance designated pursuant to section 9602 of this title, (C) any hazardous waste having the characteristics identified under or listed pursuant to section 3001 of the Solid Waste Disposal Act [42 U.S.C.A. § 6901 et seq.], (D) any toxic pollutant listed under section 1317(a) of Title 33, (E) any hazardous air pollutant listed under section 112 of the Clean Air Act [42 U.S.C.A. § 7412], and (F) any imminently hazardous chemical substance or mixture with respect to which the Administrator has taken action pursuant to section 2606 of Title 15).

6)   Any other imminently hazardous chemical substance listed under 15 U.S.C.A. Section 2606.

As a general rule, most hazardous substances that are harmful to human health are both regulated and reportable under CERCLA.[25]

2.   Notification of Releases at Active Sites

Parties who manage a vessel or facility must notify the National Response Center (NRC) when they become aware of a release of a hazardous substance.[26]   Notice of a release is the essential first step that enables the government to respond quickly should the responsible party fail to do so.[27] Once notice is given, the NRC must then notify "all appropriate Government agencies, including the Governor of any affected State."[28]

This notification requirement attaches potential liability to owners, operators, and persons of relatively low rank within a company, if they were in a position to detect, prevent, or abate the hazardous release.[29] Keep in mind, there are several hundred hazardous substances that must be reported,[30] and that failure to report a release of a hazardous substance to EPA or the submission of false or misleading information may result in fines and/or imprisonment.[31]

---

[25]   40 C.F.R. § 302.4; *see also*, Mininberg, Mark, Hazardous Substance Spills: What and When to Tell the Government (and Others), 63 Conn. B.J. 69, 75 (1989).

[26]   CERCLA § 103(a); 42 U.S.C.A. § 9603(a).

[27]   United States v. Carr, 880 F.2d 1550, 1553 (2d Cir.1989); NL Industries, Inc. v. Kaplan, 792 F.2d 896, 899 (9th Cir.1986).

[28]   CERCLA § 103(a); 42 U.S.C.A. § 9603(a).

[29]   United States v. Carr, 880 F.2d at 1554.

[30]   CERCLA § 103(b); 42 U.S.C.A. § 9603(b).

[31]   CERCLA § 103(a); 42 U.S.C.A. § 9603(a); SWDA §§ 1004 (5), (5)(B); 42 U.S.C.A. §§ 6903(5), (5)(B); United States v. Laughlin, 10 F.3d 961 (2d Cir.1993) (provision of CERCLA requiring person in charge of facility to inform the National Response Center of any release of a hazardous substance did not require the defendant, who dumped the waste have knowledge of CERCLA's regulatory requirements, but only

3. CERCLIS

When a site is first reported it is entered into the Comprehensive Environmental Response, Compensation, and Liability Information System (CERCLIS).[32] CERCLIS is EPA's database that inventories and monitors sites to be addressed by Superfund. This is the official inventory of CERCLA sites and provides Superfund planning data. CERCLIS information is available to the public under the Freedom of Information Act.[33]

B. PRELIMINARY ASSESSMENT (PA)

Once identified, CERCLIS sites receive a preliminary assessment (PA) also known as a remedial evaluation. The PA helps determine whether a response action is necessary. If the site requires remediation, it will ultimately be listed on the NPL. If no response action is necessary, the site is removed from the remedial evaluation process and will not appear on the NPL.[34]

If the PA indicates a threat of contamination to human health or the environment from a site, additional physical inspections of the site should occur. EPA employs a two-stage approach to site inspections. During the first stage, EPA looks for obvious danger signs such as leaking drums or dead and discolored vegetation. During the second stage, EPA takes samples of soil, air, and water. In addition, investigators determine whether the general public or more specifically, if children have access to the site. If so, barriers are placed and signs are posted that warn of the potential dangers. Following the PA, samples and data are analyzed. This analysis determines a site's "score" (risk of actual or threatened release), as measured by the Hazard Ranking System (HRS).

---

that he be aware of his acts. Defendant received a three year prison sentence and a $607,868 fine.).

[32] *See* generally, Reilly, Bernard J., Minimizing Your Company's Superfund Liabilities, PLI Order No. N4-4497 (1988).

[33] Freedom of Information Act (FOIA), 5 U.S.C.A. § 552, as amended by Pub. L. No. 99-570, §§ 1801-1804 (1986).

[34] Curry, J. Stanton, Hamula, James J. & Rallison, The Tug-Of-War Between RCRA and CERCLA at Contaminated Hazardous Waste Facilities, 23 Ariz. St. L.J. 359, 373 (1991).

The HRS is a site evaluation strategy "designed to estimate the potential hazard presented by releases or threatened releases of hazardous substances, pollutants and contaminants."[35] As a result of the site evaluation, a site is assigned a Hazardous Waste Index (HWI). The HWI is calculated by analyzing various pathways of human or environmental exposure through contaminated groundwater, surface water, soils, and air. Also, the HWI takes into account three factors designed to encompass the probability of exposure to hazards through releases, and the possible magnitude or degree of harm from exposure. These factors include:[36]

1) the existence or likelihood of a release;

2) the characteristics of the hazardous substances; and

3) the population or environment that is threatened.

Once the PA is complete, sites attaining an HWI score of 28.50 or higher, out of a possible 100, are proposed for placement on the National Priorities List (NPL).[37] After public notice and an opportunity for comment, EPA considers all comments received and makes its final determination of sites to be placed on the NPL.[38]

Some of the better known NPL sites and their HWI score ranges include:[39]

1) Love Canal, Niagara Falls, N.Y. (52.05 - 55.28);

2) Times Beach, Mo. (38.29 - 40.36);

---

[35] Eagle-Picher Industries, Inc. v. United States EPA, 759 F.2d 905, 910 (D.C. Cir.1982).

[36] *Id.*

[37] 40 C.F.R. Part 300, Appendix A.

[38] 40 C.F.R. § 300.425.

[39] Rodgers, William H., Jr., Environmental Law, Hazardous Wastes & Substances, Vol. 4. (West, 1992).

3)   Valley of the Drums, Shepherdsville, Ky. (55.71 - 58.30);

4)   Stringfellow Acid Pits, Riverside, Calif. (58.41 - 75.60);

5)   Picillo Pig Farm, Coventry, R.I. (55.71 - 58.30);

6)   Lipari Landfill, Pitman, N.J. (58.41 - 75.60);

7)   Odessa Chromium #2, Odessa, TX (40.37 - 42.24).

C.   THE NATIONAL PRIORITIES LIST (NPL)

CERCLA requires that the President (who has delegated this responsibility to EPA) establish a national priorities list (NPL).[40] The NPL is EPA's catalog of the most serious uncontrolled or abandoned hazardous waste sites in need of long-term remedial action. As of 1995, there were over 1,200 sites on the NPL. This number rapidly increases each year. The NPL is expected to reach a total of about 2,100 sites by the year 2,000.[41]

There are three mechanisms for placing sites on the NPL:[42]

1)   As described above, if the HRS rates a site at a HWI of 28.50 or greater, the site is eligible for the NPL.[43]

2)   The top one hundred of the highest priority facilities should include sites designated by each state as presenting the greatest danger to public health, welfare, or the environment.[44]

---

[40]   CERCLA § 105(a)(8)(A); 42 U.S.C.A. § 9605(a)(8)(A).

[41]   Mugdan, *supra* note 20 at 33.

[42]   55 Fed. Reg. 6157 (1990); *See*, Borland, Lorelei J., Superfund: An Overview, PLI Order No. H4-5152 (1993).

[43]   40 C.F.R. § 300, App. B.

[44]   CERCLA § 105(a)(8)(B); 42 U.S.C.A. § 9605(a)(8)(B); *See also*, 40 C.F.R. Part 300, App. B (1990) (31 of the top 100 sites are state designated).

3)   Even with an HWI below 28.50, CERCLA may still apply if (a) the Agency for Toxic Substances and Disease Registry has issued a health advisory recommending that individuals stay away from the release, and (b) EPA determines that the release poses a significant threat to the public health and remediation under CERCLA would be more cost effective than removal under RCRA.[45]

Inclusion on the NPL does not automatically create CERCLA liability nor require remedial response. The NPL only gives EPA authority to conduct long term and expensive clean-up activities with Superfund money if necessary.[46]

D.   INVESTIGATION

Once listed on the NPL, a site must undergo a two part investigation process known as the remedial investigation/feasibility study (RI/FS).[47] During the RI/FS process, the lead agency[48] defines the nature and threat of the hazardous substances at the site with respect to human health and the environment. The RI/FS helps EPA officials select the most efficient cleanup measures available to eliminate, reduce, or control risks to human health and the environment. Each part of the RI/FS is both expensive and time-consuming. It is estimated that the average cost of a RI/FS is approximately one million dollars.[49] RI/FS activities include: project scoping, data collection, risk assessment, treatability studies, and available alternative analysis.[50]

---

[45] 40 C.F.R. § 300.425(c)(3)(iii).

[46] 40 C.F.R. 300.425(b)(2) (1990); *see also*, Gaba, Jeffrey M., Recovering Hazardous Waste Cleanup Costs: The Private Cause of Action Under CERCLA, 13 Ecology L.Q. 181, 191 and 232 (1986).

[47] 40 C.F.R. § 300.430.

[48] 40 C.F.R. § 300.5.

[49] Lorelei Joy Borland, Superfund: An Overview, PLI Order N. N4-4542 (1990).

[50] For a good discussion of these activities, *see* e.g., Steincamp, Charles C., Toeing The Line: Compliance with the National Contingency Plan for Private Party Cost Recovery Under CERCLA, 32 Washburn L.J. 190 (1993).

The RI/FS develops many remedial alternatives and helps select an appropriate remedy. CERCLA requires that certain criteria be considered in assessing alternative remedial actions. These include:[51]

1)   long-term uncertainties associated with land disposal of contaminants from the site;

2)   goals, objectives, and requirements of RCRA;

3)   persistence, toxicity, mobility, and propensity of bio-accumulation of hazardous substances and their constituents;

4)   short and long term adverse health effects;

5)   long term maintenance costs;

6)   future remedial action costs if alternatives fail; and

7)   threat to human health and the environment associated with excavation, transportation, re-disposal, or containment of contaminants from the site.

Once alternative remedies are developed, a more detailed analysis is conducted by the lead agency. The costs of implementation as well as state and community acceptance of the alternatives are all considerations in the analysis process.[52] The RI/FS balances the benefits, effectiveness, and costs of each remedy.

E.   REMEDIAL ACTIONS

Once the RI/FS is complete, EPA selects a preferred cleanup remedy. EPA then notifies the public of its choice in the Federal Register, and allows interested persons an opportunity to comment.[53] After EPA considers all comments, it selects a final remedy for the site. This final remedy is published

---

[51]   CERCLA § 121(b)(1); 42 U.S.C.A. § 9621(b)(1).

[52]   Steincamp, *supra* note 50 at 216.

[53]   CERCLA § 117; 42 U.S.C.A. § 9617.

in a written document called a "record of decision" (ROD) which is also published in the Federal Register.[54] After selecting a final remedy, EPA and the PRPs design and implement the remedy as well as a cost allocation plan. If an agreement cannot be reached between EPA and the PRPs, EPA conducts the final remedy on its own. The EPA may later attempt to recover response costs from the PRPs under the liability provisions of Section 107. It is often more advantageous for a PRP to negotiate the final remedy with EPA. Although a PRP cannot escape liability, it may be able to reduce its expenditures by offering to pay EPA up front or by offering to assist in the cleanup itself. Such negotiations are important because once the government implements its remedy, it will vigorously pursue PRPs for reimbursement of the Superfund costs associated with the cleanup.

IV.   SECTION 107 LIABILITY AND COST RECOVERY ACTIONS

A.   INTRODUCTION TO COST RECOVERY ACTIONS

A cost recovery action under CERCLA is a lawsuit brought either by the government under Section 107 or private parties under Section 113 to recover response costs incurred while cleaning up a site.[55] One of CERCLA's primary objectives is to motivate quick cleanups. To do this the government often uses the Superfund to finance its cleanups and then seeks reimbursement of the Superfund through a cost recovery action. Where a PRP incurs response costs, it can then attempt to sue other PRPs for contribution.[56]

1.   Causation

In order to recover expenses from PRPs, a plaintiff must show causation, a causal connection between contamination and a PRP. For liability to be initially triggered, it must be shown that a release occurred, and that the release

---

[54]   The ROD is more fully discussed under Section IV(H)(3)(b)(ii)(c) in this chapter.

[55]   CERCLA § 107; 42 U.S.C.A. § 9607.

[56]   Sevack, Joseph A., Passing The Big Bucks: Contractual Transfers of Liability Between Potentially Responsible Parties Under CERCLA, 75 Minn. L. Rev. 1571, 1591 (1991).

created response costs.[57] Federal courts have liberally construed CERCLA as imposing sweeping liability on PRPs by adopting "substantially diluted causation requirements."[58]

No formal inquiry is necessary to determine whether a hazardous substance found at a facility specifically came from a defendant's site in order to assess liability. For example, in *Dedham Water Co. v. Cumberland Farms Dairy, Inc.*, a water utility company sued a truck maintenance facility owner for chemical discharges that caused groundwater contamination.[59] The facility owner was found liable even though it was not necessary for the plaintiff to prove defendant's waste actually contaminated plaintiff's property. The only requirement was that the defendant's waste was present and caused the plaintiff to incur response costs.[60] In *Violet v. Picillo*, the District Court stated, "Section 107(a) is a strict liability scheme which requires only a minimum showing of causation."[61] The defendant need not have chosen the disposal site, nor must the plaintiff prove that the defendant's waste actually caused the ecological harm at the site.[62] Thus, traditional legal notions such as proximate cause do not apply.

Despite the minimum showing of causation, CERCLA does provide sufficient assurances that defendants will not be held liable for costs unrelated to response actions.[63]

---

[57]   United States v. Alcan Aluminum Corp., 964 F.2d 252 (3rd Cir.1992); *see also*, Mendel, Julie, CERCLA Section 107: An Examination of Causation, 40 Wash. U.J. Urb. & Contemp. L. 83, 103 (1991).

[58]   Wolf, Sidney M., Up In The Air: Recovery Of Attorney Fees In A CERCLA § 107(A)(4)(B) Suit, 69 N.D. L. Rev. 275 (1993).

[59]   Dedham Water Co. v. Cumberland Farms Dairy, Inc., 889 F.2d 1146 (1st Cir.1989).

[60]   *Id.* at 1152.

[61]   Violet v. Picillo, 648 F.Supp. 1283, 1290, 1295 (D.R.I.1986).

[62]   *Id.*

[63]   Kocher, Kim, Recovery of Response Costs Under CERCLA: A Question Of Causation Under Dedham Water Co. v. Cumberland Farms Dairy, Inc. 3 Vill. Envtl. L.J. 225, 235 (1992).

2.   Elements

In addition to a causal connection, the following five elements must be present for a plaintiff to succeed in a cost recovery action:[64]

1)   the contaminated property must be a vessel or facility;

2)   the party being pursued must be a potentially responsible party (PRP);

3)   the substance found at the facility must be a hazardous substance;

4)   there must be a release or threatened release of a hazardous substance that causes response costs; and

5)   the response costs incurred must be necessary and consistent with CERCLA's National Contingency Plan (NCP).

Once these elements have been met and causation has been established, a plaintiff has the opportunity to succeed in a cost recovery action against a PRP.

B.   PROPERTY MUST BE A VESSEL OR FACILITY

1.   Vessel

A "vessel" includes all categories or classes of water craft. It is broadly defined by Congress as any conceivable device used for transportation on water.[65]   This definition is intentionally broad because Congress created CERCLA to help clean up all hazardous substance spills occurring in United States waters. Vessels may include the following:

1)   naval vessels;[66]

---

[64]   CERCLA § 107(a); 42 U.S.C.A. § 9607(a).

[65]   CERCLA § 101(28); 42 U.S.C.A. § 9601(28).

[66]   FMC Corporation v. United States Department Of Commerce, Brown (Ronald), Secretary of Commerce, 29 F.3d 833 (3rd Cir.1993).

2) incineration vessels;[67] and

3) charter vessels.[68]

2. Facility

CERCLA imposes liability where there is a release or threatened release of a hazardous substance from a "facility."[69] CERCLA broadly defines a facility to include every place, all structures, and all areas where hazardous substances are found. CERCLA's definition of a facility includes far more than conventional dumpsites. The following are examples of buildings, structures, sites, or areas that are considered "facilities":

1) buildings, pillars, and the undersides of those pillars coated with asbestos;[70]

2) a hotel building containing asbestos products;[71]

3) a truck from which waste paint was released;[72]

---

[67] CERCLA § 107(a)(3); 42 U.S.C.A. § 9607(a)(3).

[68] CERCLA § 101(20)(A); 42 U.S.C.A. § 9601(20)(A).

[69] CERCLA § 101(9); 42 U.S.C.A. § 9601(9) ("facility" means (a) any building, structure, installation, equipment, pipe or pipeline (including any pipe into a sewer or publicly owned treatment works), well, pit, pond, lagoon, impoundment, ditch, landfill, storage container, motor vehicle, rolling stock, or aircraft, or (b) any site or area where a hazardous substance has been deposited, stored, disposed of, or placed, or otherwise come to be located).

[70] National Railroad Passenger Corp. v. New York City Housing Authority, 819 F.Supp. 1271, 1276 (S.D.N.Y.1993).

[71] CP Holdings, Inc. v. Goldberg-Zoino & Associates, Inc., 769 F.Supp. 432, 439 (D.N.H.1991).

[72] United States v. Carr, 880 F.2d at 1551.

4)   containers from which hazardous substances are released;[73]

5)   drums of hazardous substances themselves;[74]

6)   the site where mine tailings containing hazardous substances are deposited after migration in surface water;[75]

7)   a real estate subdivision with asbestos fibers on the surface of the ground;[76] and

8)   North Carolina roadside where PCB-contaminated oil was sprayed.[77]

When creating CERCLA, Congress discussed many other sites as justification for such strict regulations: Valley of the Drums in Kentucky;[78] dirt roads in Texas contaminated with nitrobenzene and cyanide;[79] radium waste sites under restaurants in Denver, Co.,[80]; abandoned toxic chemical tanks near the Nanticoke River in Maryland;[81] the Hudson River sites in New Jersey where

---

[73]   United States v. Bliss, 667 F.Supp. 1298, 1305 (E.D.Mo.1987).

[74]   In re T.P. Long Chemical, Inc., 45 B.R. 278, 284 (N.D.Ohio 1985).

[75]   State of Colorado v. Idarado Mineral Co., 707 F. Supp. 1227 (D.Colo.1989), rev'd on other grounds at 916 F.2d 1486 (10th Cir.1990).

[76]   United States v. Metate Asbestos Corp., 584 F.Supp. 1143, 1148 (D.Ariz.1984).

[77]   United States v. Ward, 618 F.Supp. 884, 895 (E.D.N.C.1985).

[78]   A & P Health, 103 Comm. Print 60 (1983).

[79]   A & P Health, 103 Comm. Print 12 (1979).

[80]   *Id.*

[81]   *Id.*

PCB dumping occurred;[82] and spills of hazardous substances on the George Washington Bridge in New York.

C.   POTENTIALLY RESPONSIBLE PARTIES

Congress has determined that polluters should pay for the dangerous conditions they create. Potentially responsible parties ("PRPs") are individuals or entities who are regarded as those who should be liable for the contamination they cause. Because PRPs are liable parties, they are responsible for either financing cleanups, cleaning up sites themselves, or reimbursing the government or other PRPs for their respective cleanup costs.[83]

Under CERCLA, four categories of "covered" persons may be PRPs and held liable for cleanup costs.[84] "Covered persons" include:

1)   the owner and operator of a vessel or a facility;

2)   any person who at the time of disposal of any hazardous substance owned or operated any facility at which such hazardous substances were disposed of;

3)   any person who by contract, agreement, or otherwise arranged for disposal or treatment, or arranged with a transporter for transport for disposal or treatment, of hazardous substances owned or possessed by such person, by any other party or entity, at any facility or incineration vessel owned or operated by another party or entity and containing such hazardous substances; and

4)   any person who accepts or accepted any hazardous substances for transport to disposal or treatment facilities, incineration vessels or sites selected by such person, from which there is a

---

[82]   *Id.*

[83]   Pennsylvania v. Union Gas Co., 491 U.S. 1, 3; 109 S.Ct. 2273; 105 L.Ed.2d 1 (1989).

[84]   CERCLA § 107(a); 42 U.S.C.A. § 9607(a).

release, or a threatened release [of a hazardous substance] which causes the incurrence of response costs . . ."[85]

The term "person" as used above is broadly defined as, "[a]n individual, firm, corporation, association, partnership, consortium, joint venture, commercial entity, United States Government, state, municipality, commission, political subdivision of a state or any interstate body."[86]

1.   Current Owners and Operators

CERCLA imposes liability on current owners and operators of vessels or facilities from which there is a release or a threatened release of a hazardous substance.[87] A current owner or operator is defined as:

1)   any person owning, operating or chartering a vessel; and

2)   any person owning or operating an onshore or offshore facility.[88]

Current owners and operators do not include such PRPs who hold an "indicia of ownership" in the form of a security interest and who do not participate in the management of the vessel or facility.[89] Also excluded are common carriers, and units of state and local governments. For example, an "owner or operator" does not include state or local governments that acquire title to or control of a site involuntarily through bankruptcy, tax delinquency, abandonment, or other circumstances by virtue of their function as sovereign.[90]

---

[85]   *Id.*

[86]   CERCLA § 101(21); 42 U.S.C.A. § 9601(21).

[87]   CERCLA § 107(a)(1); 42 U.S.C.A. § 9607(a)(1).

[88]   CERCLA § 101(20)(A); 42 U.S.C.A. § 9601(20)(A).

[89]   *Id.*

[90]   CERCLA § 101(20)(D); 42 U.S.C.A. § 9601(20)(D).

a.   Owner

An "owner" is any owner named in the most recent deed of title to the vessel or facility. Generally, current owners are in the best position to manage the potential hazardous waste at their sites. They are presumed to have more knowledge about the risks inherent in the wastes located on their property and how to best avoid adverse consequences. Current owners are also presumed to be in the best position to determine how to dispose of their wastes.[91]

Current owners may incur liability even if they did not own the facility when disposal of hazardous substances on the property occurred. In other words, they are not considered to be innocent landowners and automatically exempt from liability (though such a defense is allowed under limited circumstances). As current owners, they are connected to the site and in control of ensuring that public health and the environment are not threatened by activities on the property.

In 1985, the Second Circuit held that Section 107(a)(1) imposes liability on current owners of property where hazardous substances are deposited, regardless of whether they owned the site at the time of disposal, whether they caused the presence of toxic wastes, or whether they caused the release of toxic wastes.[92] In *State of New York v. Shore Realty*, the Appellate Court reasoned that if the current owner of a site could avoid liability merely by having purchased the site after chemical dumping ceased, waste sites would certainly be sold to new owners who could avoid liability under CERCLA.[93] Current owners are also held strictly liable for cleanup costs caused by hazardous waste activities of a lessee, even when the owners were not actively involved in the lessee's activities.[94]

---

[91]   Senate Comm. On Environmental and Public Works, Environmental Emergency Response Act, S. Representative. No. 848, 96th Cong., 2d Sess. 15 (1980).

[92]   State of New York v. Shore Realty Corp., 759 F.2d 1032 (2d Cir.1985).

[93]   *Id.* at 1045.

[94]   Barnard, Kathryn A., EPA's Policy Of Corporate Successor Liability Under CERCLA, 6 Stan. Envtl. L.J. 78, 81 (1987).

b. Operator

"Operators" usually manage and control the day-to-day activities of vessels or facilities. The rationale for operators liability is similar to that of owners; they are also presumed to be in the best position to do something about the contamination. Because of their authority, current operators are liable even though they were not the operators when previous disposal activities took place. [CITE].

In 1989, a Delaware district court identified several factors to consider when identifying whether a person is an "operator" under CERCLA.[95] In determining "operator" liability, the court assessed whether the operator:

1) controls the finances of the facility;

2) manages employees of the facility;

3) manages the daily business operations of the facility;

4) is responsible for maintenance of environmental control at the facility; and

5) confers or receives any commercial or economic benefit from the facility other than payment or receipt of taxes.[96]

In 1990, a California court identified thirteen factors to consider in determining whether a person exercised enough control to be held liable under CERCLA. "This control need not be day-to-day, but rather depends on various factors weighed as a whole."[97] These factors include the following:

1) expertise and knowledge of dangers of hazardous waste;

2) site suitability;

---

[95] United States v. New Castle County, 727 F.Supp. 854 (D.Del.1989).

[96] *Id.* at 869.

[97] United States v. Stringfellow, 20 Envtl. L. Representative. 20656, 20658 (C.D.Cal.1990).

3)   site design;

4)   supervision;

5)   inspections;

6)   receipt of site reports;

7)   employee hiring;

8)   determining operational responsibilities;

9)   disposal control;

10)   ability to discover and abate harm;

11)   public declarations of responsibility;

12)   participation in opening and closing of a site; and

13)   benefitting from the existence of the site.[98]

Some examples of operators may include:

1)   a sublessor where the lessor exercised control over the property;[99]

2)   a parent corporation that is familiar with hazardous waste disposal at a facility, had the capacity to control such disposals and had the capacity to make decisions and implement actions to prevent damage caused by such disposals;[100]

---

[98]   *Id.*

[99]   United States v. A & N Cleaners and Launderers, Inc., 788 F.Supp. 1317 (S.D.N.Y.1992).

[100]   State of Idaho v. Bunker Hill Co., 635 F.Supp. 665, 672 (D.Idaho 1986).

3)　　　an operator who operated the site after the hazardous waste was placed on the land and knew nothing about the hazardous waste at the time the site was acquired;[101]

4)　　　individual shareholders of corporations and corporate officers and directors;[102]

5)　　　a person who owns an interest in a facility and is actively participating in its management;[103]

6)　　　a holder of a pipeline easement if hazardous substances are released from the pipeline;[104]

7)　　　a lending institution as a result of action taken by the lender in administering or enforcing a loan on contaminated property;[105] and

8)　　　a developer that moved contaminated soil from one part of a construction site to another.[106]

---

[101]　　United States v. Peterson Sand and Gravel, Inc., 806 F.Supp. 1346 (N.D.Ill.1992).

[102]　　*See* generally, United States v. Mottolo, 695 F.Supp. 615, 624 (D.N.H.1988).

[103]　　State of Idaho v. Bunker Hill Co., 635 F.Supp. at 671.

[104]　　Long Beach Unified School District v. Dorothy B. Godwin California Living Trust, 32 F.3d 1364 (9th Cir.1994) (merely standing by and failing to prevent contamination without doing anything more active is insufficient to raise the easement holder's status to that of an operator).

[105]　　Schworer, Philip J. & White, Catherine M., Environmental Problems and the Effect on Lending Institutions, 18 N. Ky. L. Rev. 175 (1990).

[106]　　Kaiser Aluminum and Chemical Corp. v. Catellus Development Corp., 976 F.2d 1338 (9th Cir.1992).

c. Special Conditions and Exemptions From Liability

CERCLA expressly excludes certain individuals or groups from liability if they fall under one of the statutory exemptions such as the state and local government exemption, the security interest owner exemption, or the non-independent common or contract carriers exemption.

i. State and Local Governments

State and local governments are exempt from liability where they acquired the contaminated property because of bankruptcy, foreclosures, tax delinquencies, or abandonment. Under these conditions, any person who owned, operated, or controlled activities at the facility immediately before the transfer of ownership to the state or local government is held liable as a PRP.[107]

Note, this exemption does not apply to state or local governments that cause or contribute to the release or threatened release of hazardous substances.[108] For example, where a state or local government takes title to property through bankruptcy, and then moves contaminated soils that cause a release of a hazardous substance, it may become liable as a "nongovernmental entity."[109] However, state and local governments are liable as owners and operators in all other situations where they own or operate property that contains hazardous waste.[110] "Congress intended that States be liable along with everyone else for cleanup costs recoverable under CERCLA."[111]

---

[107] CERCLA §§ 101(20)(A)(iii), (D); 42 U.S.C.A. §§ 9601(20)(A)(iii), (D).

[108] CERCLA § 101(20)(D); 42 U.S.C.A. § 9601(20)(D).

[109] *Id.*

[110] CERCLA § 101(21); 42 U.S.C.A. § 9601(21).

[111] Pennsylvania v. Union Gas Co., 491 U.S. 1, 8; 109 S.Ct. 2273, 2278; 105 L.Ed.2d 1, 12 (1989).

ii. Security Interest Owners

Security interest owners are creditors who have an ownership interest in property as the result of a security agreement. Security agreements provide a claim or stake in property in exchange for guaranteeing payment or performance of an obligation. The most common example is a mortgage contract or loan agreement granting a security interest in real estate.

Security interest owners are exempt from CERCLA liability if they do not participate in the management of a vessel or facility.[112] They are exempt from liability because generally security interest owners are not in control of the day-to-day operational activities at a facility nor of the hazardous substances found on the property. This exemption to liability is also known as the "lender defense" which is discussed later in Section IV(K)(5) of this chapter.[113]

There is, however, an exception to this exemption. For example, a security interest owner may still be held liable even though he was not an actual facility operator by virtue of participation in the financial management of the facility to a degree that influences the facility's treatment of hazardous waste. The critical issue is whether the security interest owner sufficiently participated in management to incur liability.

iii. Common or Contract Carriers

Common or contract carriers, who are not independent contractors, will not be held liable as owners and operators.[114] This exemption exists because carriers who are not independent contractors do not hold themselves out as being in sole control of the product they transport. They merely act as a representative or agent for the true owners of the product. Note, however, they may still be liable as generators or transporters if they happen to fall under Sections 107(a)(3)

---

[112]   CERCLA § 101(20)(A); 42 U.S.C.A § 9601(20)(A).

[113]   United States v. Fleet Factors Corp., 901 F.2d 1550 (11th Cir.1990); *see also*, Kelly v. United States EPA, 1994 WL 27881 (D.C. Cir.1994).

[114]   CERCLA § 101(20)(C); 42 U.S.C.A. § 9601(20)(C).

or (4).[115] For example, carriers that act as independent contractors and transport hazardous substances may be liable as owners and operators.[116]

Carriers who are independent contractors are liable as owners and operators where they hold themselves out as being in sole control of the product they transport. In addition, if a carrier selected the site to which it transported a hazardous substance, it would be liable regardless of its carrier status.[117]

2. Prior Owners and Operators: CERCLA's Retroactive Provision

CERCLA imposes liability on "any person who at the time of disposal of any hazardous substance owned or operated any facility at which such hazardous substances were disposed of."[118] In short, prior owners and operators are liable for releases or threatened releases of hazardous substances. They may be held liable only if they owned or operated the site at the time of disposal.[119]

A prior owner is any owner named in the deed of title to a vessel or facility. Generally, prior operators are parties that actively engaged in managing the property for all prior owners. Prior operators controlled day-to-day activities at the site. For that reason, they are presumed to have been in the best position to safely manage and dispose of hazardous substances. The law considers prior operators to be directly responsible for the dangerous conditions posed to human health and the environment by the past contamination. In addition, because prior owners and operators reaped the benefits of conducting an operation, public policy demands that the polluter, not the taxpayer, pay.

Prior lessees or sublessors of property are also held liable as prior owners and operators. Lessees of property, while retaining less than a complete

---

[115]   CERCLA §§ 107(a)(3), (4); 42 U.S.C.A. §§ 9607(a)(3), (4).

[116]   CERCLA § 101(20)(B); 42 U.S.C.A. § 9601(20)(B).

[117]   United States v. Hardage, 761 F.Supp. 1501, 1517 (W.D.Okla.1990).

[118]   CERCLA § 107(a)(2); 42 U.S.C.A. § 9607(a)(2).

[119]   *Id.*; *see also*, State of N.Y. v. Shore Realty Corp., 759 F.2d 1032, 1044 (2d Cir.1985).

ownership interest in property, do have a limited interest which gives the lessee "ownership" status. The following are examples of other persons held to be prior owners or operators:

1) secured creditors;[120]

2) all prior owners named in any deeds of title;[121]

3) prior owners despite their efforts to cleanup;[122]

4) a parent company liable for subsidiary's past activities;[123] and

5) a reorganized debtor liable for his pre-bankruptcy activities.[124]

3. Generators

CERCLA imposes liability on any person who either arranged for disposal, treatment, or transport for disposal or treatment of hazardous substances at a facility owned or operated by any other party.[125] This provision is known as the "generator" provision. Generators of hazardous substances often arrange for its off-site disposal. If a generator arranged for off-site disposal at a site that was later found to be contaminated, the generator would be held liable for the cleanup.

For example, in *United States v. South Carolina Recycling and Disposal, Inc.*, the government sued for response costs against both an absent owner of a waste disposal company that leased the site and disposed of 7,200 drums of

---

[120] United States v. Fleet Factors Corp., 901 F.2d 1550 (11th Cir.1990).

[121] CERCLA § 107(a)(2); 42 U.S.C.A. § 9607(a)(2).

[122] United States v. Ottati & Goss, Inc., 630 F.Supp. 1361 (D.N.H.1985).

[123] United States v. Nicolet, Inc., 712 F.Supp. 1193, 1204 (E.D.Pa.1989).

[124] In the Matter of Penn Central Transportation Co., 944 F.2d 164, 165 (3rd Cir.1991).

[125] CERCLA § 107(a)(3); 42 U.S.C.A. § 9607(a)(3).

hazardous waste, and against generators of hazardous waste that arranged for disposal at the site.[126] The District Court determined that CERCLA presumed "contributory causal relationships" between hazardous substances disposed of at the site and the generators who had dumped waste at the sites. The court reasoned that "the only required nexus between the defendant and the site is that the defendant have dumped his waste there and that the hazardous substances found in the defendant's waste are also found at the site."[127] The causation is presumed because the interaction of hazardous substances at the site often creates a greater danger than would each substance by itself.

In *United States v. South Carolina Recycling & Disposal, Inc.*, the District Court established four elements to help identify generator liability:

1)   the generator's hazardous substances were shipped to a facility;

2)   the generator's hazardous substances or similar hazardous substances were present at the site;

3)   there was a release or threatened release of hazardous substances at the site; and

4)   the release or threatened release caused the incurrence of response costs.[128]

Following *United States v. South Carolina Recycling and Disposal, Inc.*, the District Court in *United States v. Ottati and Goss, Inc.*, emphasized that the government need not "fingerprint" wastes found at the site to each defendant.[129] As long as a generator defendant shipped wastes to a facility and those types of wastes are found at the site, then the defendant can be held liable for response costs. The *Ottati* court refused to require that causation be proven by a plaintiff. In other words, the plaintiff need not draw a direct causal link between a

---

[126]   United States v. South Carolina Recycling and Disposal, Inc., 653 F.Supp. 984 (D.S.C.1986).

[127]   *Id.* at 992.

[128]   *Id.* at 991-992.

[129]   United States v. Ottati and Goss, 630 F.Supp. at 1402.

generator's particular waste and the cleanup performed; an indirect link that meets the four part test described above is enough. Courts have held generators liable:

1)   for participation in disposal decisions;[130]

2)   regardless of the generator's knowledge of intended disposal sites;[131]

3)   regardless of minimal amounts of wastes sent to the site;[132]

4)   regardless of trans-shipping of hazardous wastes from one site to another;[133]

---

[130]   United States v. Ward, 618 F.Supp. 884, 894 (E.D.N.C.1985) (an officer of a company who exercises authority for the company's operations and participates in arranging for the disposal of hazardous wastes is liable as a generator).

[131]   *Id.* Note that the District Court in *United States v. Ward* rejected the defendants' argument that they could not be held liable unless the plaintiff demonstrated that the generator defendants knew that their disposal contractor planned to deposit the PCB oil at various locations. The District Court held that a generator's knowledge of the intended disposal site is not a prerequisite to CERCLA liability.

[132]   United States v. Conservation Chemical Co., 619 F.Supp. 162 (W.D.Mo. 1985) (several generators argued that they were not liable because they only sent minimal amounts of wastes to a site. The District Court rejected this argument and stated that the principal of *de minimis* participation does not apply to CERCLA liability); *see also*, United States v. Stringfellow, 14 Env'tl L.Rep. 20385 (C.D.Cal.1984) (definition of "hazardous substance" under CERCLA does not distinguish hazardous substances on the basis of quantity of concentration. To help de minimis contributors, CERCLA provides joint and several liability under the Gore Amendment to allow apportionment of liability as appropriate on equitable grounds).

[133]   State of Missouri v. Independent Petrochemical Corp., 610 F.Supp. 4 (E.D.MO.1985) (a state may seek to recover response costs from parties who deposited hazardous wastes at one site and subsequently transported them to another site that was the cause of a release or threatened release); *see also*, United States v. Conservation Chemical Co., 619 F.Supp. at 233-234 (a generator whose waste is transshipped from its original disposal site to a second site can be held liable under CERCLA for response costs at the second site).

5)   regardless of whether the wastes sent are used to neutralize or treat other hazardous wastes;[134] and

6)   even if the generator did not select the disposal site.[135]

4.   Transporters

Transporters are the fourth category of parties liable under CERCLA Section 107(a). CERCLA imposes liability on:

> any person who accepts or accepted any hazardous substances for transport to disposal or treatment facilities, incineration vessels or sites selected by such person, from which there is a release, or threatened release . . . of hazardous substances . . . .[136]

The terms "transport" and "transportation" are defined under Section 101(26). The terms mean movement of a hazardous substance by any mode, including pipeline.[137] Thus, transportation by land, air, or water by any method is regulated. Judicial decisions involving transporters have held that:

1)   off-site transporters who select the disposal site are strictly liable;[138]

2)   transporter liability is retroactive;[139] and that

---

[134]   United States v. Conservation Chemical Co., 619 F.Supp. at 239.

[135]   State of Missouri v. Independent Petrochemical Corp. 610 F.Supp. 4 (E.D.Mo.1985) (a generator's selection of the disposal site is not a prerequisite to his liability).

[136]   CERCLA § 107(a)(4); 42 U.S.C.A. § 9607(a)(4).

[137]   CERCLA § 101(26); 42 U.S.C.A. § 9601(26).

[138]   United States v. Northeastern Pharmaceutical & Chemical Co., Inc., 810 F.2d 726 (8th Cir.1986).

[139]   State ex. rel. Brown v. Georgeoff, 562 F.Supp. 1300, 1314 (N.D.Ohio 1983).

3)   a transporter corporation may be liable.[140]

D.   THERE MUST BE A HAZARDOUS SUBSTANCE

In order for Section 107 liability to attach, there must be a release or threatened release of a hazardous substance. Under CERCLA, the definition of a hazardous substance is very broad. A hazardous substance is defined under Section 101(14) of CERCLA as follows:[141]

1)   any substance designated pursuant to Section 311(b)(2)(A) of the Clean Water Act; [142]

2)   any element, compound, mixture, or substance designated as a CERCLA hazardous substance under Section 102 of CERCLA;[143]

3)   any hazardous waste having the characteristics (ignitability, corrosivity, reactivity, or toxicity) as identified or listed pursuant to the Solid Waste Disposal Act under Section 3001 of the SWDA/RCRA;[144]

4)   any toxic pollutant listed under Section 307(a) of the Clean Water Act;[145]

---

[140]   United States v. Conservation Chemical Co., 619 F.Supp. at 191 (a corporation who admitted that it accepted cyanide-containing wastes for transport, arranged for the transport of the wastes to a disposal site, and then selected the site, was liable as a transporter for response costs where the substances were disposed).

[141]   CERCLA § 101(14); 42 U.S.C.A. § 9601(14).

[142]   CWA § 311(b)(2)(A); 33 U.S.C.A. § 1321(b)(2)(A).

[143]   CERCLA § 102; 42 U.S.C.A § 9602.

[144]   RCRA § 3001; 42 U.S.C.A § 6921.

[145]   CWA § 307; 33 U.S.C.A. § 1317.

5)   any hazardous air pollutant listed under Section 112 of the Clean Air Act[146]; and

6)   any imminently hazardous substance or mixture to which EPA has taken action pursuant to Section 7 of the Toxic Substances Control Act.[147]

In addition, the amount of hazardous substances found at a site does not determine whether CERCLA applies. The mere fact that a hazardous substance is present and may be released, or is released, is enough. In *United States v. Carolawn Co.*, the District Court stated that:

> A waste is defined as a "hazardous substance" under CERCLA if it contains substances listed as hazardous under any of the statutes referenced in CERCLA Section 101(14) regardless of volumes or concentrations of those substances . . . .[148]

Because CERCLA refers to five environmental statutes to define "hazardous substances," each statute requires independent examination in order to determine if a specific substance is covered.

E.   THE PETROLEUM EXCLUSION

Several substances are excluded from CERCLA's definition of hazardous substances, even though their release may cause environmental harm. CERCLA states that a "hazardous substance" does not include petroleum, crude oil, natural gas, natural gas liquids, liquefied natural gas, or synthetic gas usable for fuel (or mixtures of natural gas and such synthetic gas).[149]

While this exclusion is limited in its application, the scope of the exclusion is unclear. The term "petroleum" is not defined in the statute and there

---

[146]   CAA § 112; 42 U.S.C.A. § 7412.

[147]   TSCA § 7; 15 U.S.C.A. § 2606.

[148]   CERCLA § 101(14); 42 U.S.C.A. § 9601(14); United States v. Carolawn Co., 14 Envtl. L. Representative. 20696 (D.S.C.1984).

[149]   CERCLA § 101(14); 42 U.S.C.A. § 9601(14).

is little legislative history to offer clarification on the purpose or scope of the exclusion. Thus, disagreement exists regarding the breadth of the petroleum exclusion. EPA's general counsel has stated that the petroleum exclusion applies to:

1)   crude oil and crude oil fractions;

2)   hazardous substances, indigenous to petroleum products, such as benzene; and

3)   hazardous substances normally added to crude oil or oil fractions during the refining process.[150]

Many petroleum products such as gasoline, diesel fuel, jet fuel, soil mixed with petroleum, and waste cutting oils have also been found by the courts to be excluded from CERCLA.[151] Yet, in some cases, courts have found that certain petroleum products such as petroleum wastes are not protected under the exclusion and are hazardous substances even where no commingling existed. For example, EPA has stated that the petroleum exclusion does not extend oil that has had hazardous substances added.[152] Some examples of petroleum products that are not covered by the petroleum exclusion include:

---

[150]   *See*, memorandum from Blake, Francis S., EPA General Counsel, to J. Winston Porter, Assistant Administrator for Solid Waste and Emergency Response, Scope of the CERCLA Petroleum Exclusion Under §§ 101(14) and 104(a)(2) (July 31, 1987), reprinted in 14 Chem. Waste Lit. Representative. 842 (1987); *see also*, Bacher, Leo O., Jr., When Oil Is Not Oil: An Analysis of CERCLA's Petroleum Exclusion In The Context Of A Mixed Oil Spill, 45 Baylor L. Rev. 233, 234-235 (1993).

[151]   Wilshire Westwood Associates v. Atlantic Richfield Corp., 881 F.2d 801, 810 (9th Cir.1989); Equitable Life Assurance Society v. Greyhound Corp., 31 Env. Representative. Cas. (BNA) 1079 (E.D.Pa.1990); New York v. United States, 620 F.Supp. 374 (E.D.N.Y.1985); Southern Pacific Transportation Co. v. California, 790 F.Supp. 983 (C.D.Cal.1991); The Marmon Group, Inc. v. Rexnord, Inc., No. 85-C-7838, 1986 W.L. 9746 (N.D.Ill. June 16, 1986), rev'd other grounds, 822 F.2d 31 (7th Cir.1987); *see also*, Gibson, Michael M. & Young, David P., Oil And Gas Exemptions Under RCRA and CERCLA: Are They Still "Safe Harbors" Eleven Years Later?, 32 S. Tex. L. Rev. 361, 390 (1991).

[152]   *Id*. at 388-390.

1)   contaminated waste oil used to cool and lubricate rolls of aluminum during manufacturing;[153]

2)   gasoline waste sludge containing hazardous metal contaminants, such as lead, chromium and nickel from the walls of gasoline storage tanks;[154] and

3)   waste oil contaminated with hazardous substances not naturally found in oil.[155]

Although the petroleum exclusion has been broadly interpreted to include substances other than petroleum products, courts narrowly construe the petroleum exclusion which is designed to encourage oil and gas exploration and refining. For example, in *United States v. Western Processing Co.*, the District Court held that the primary purpose for the exclusion was to remove oil spills or other oil releases from the scope of CERCLA response and liability.[156] The District Court went on to say that the exclusion was not intended to embrace petroleum waste transported to treatment, storage, or disposal facilities. Because the petroleum exclusion is not a total exclusion to liability, regulations, judicial opinions, and EPA guidance documents should be consulted to determine specific applicability in each situation.

F.   RELEASE, OR THREAT OF RELEASE AND THE INCURRENCE OF RESPONSE COSTS

1.   Release

The word "release" is defined broadly to include almost every conceivable way a substance could make contact with the environment. This includes spilling, leaking, discharging, disposing and even migration.[157]

---

[153]   City of New York v. Exxon Corp., 744 F.Supp. 474 (S.D.N.Y.1990).

[154]   United States v. Western Processing Co., 761 F.Supp. 713 (W.D.Wash.1991).

[155]   United States v. Alcan Aluminum Corp., 755 F.Supp. 531 (N.D.N.Y.1991).

[156]   United States v. Western Processing Co., 761 F.Supp. at 713.

[157]   CERCLA § 101 (22); 42 U.S.C.A. § 9601(22).

2.   Threat of a Release

CERCLA does not require an actual release for liability to attach. Though many other environmental statutes only make parties liable for actual releases, CERCLA "expressly expanded liability to also cover threatened releases."[158] The threat of a release has been interpreted to require only a reasonable probability that a release will occur. For example, in *Voluntary Purchasing Groups, Inc. v. Reilly*, potential flood conditions threatened to release hazardous substances from a site.[159] As a result, EPA executed emergency response actions at the site where pesticides, herbicides, and other hazardous substances were processed and stored. Other examples of threatened releases include:

1)   the presence of corroding and deteriorating hazardous waste tanks at a site;[160] and

2)   the storage of hazardous substances in deteriorating drums and unlined lagoons.[161]

3.   Incurrence of Response Costs

a.   Response Costs

Response costs are the result of removal or remedial actions associated with cleaning contaminated sites. Response costs are not considered assessments of actual environmental damage. Instead, they are the costs of preventing or correcting harm to human health and the environment.[162] Response costs are

---

[158]   Dedham Water Co. v. Cumberland Farms Dairy, Inc., 889 F.2d 1146, 1152 (1st Cir.1989).

[159]   Voluntary Purchasing Groups, Inc. v. Reilly, 889 F.2d 1380 (5th Cir.1989).

[160]   State of New York v. Shore Realty Corp., 759 F.2d at 1045.

[161]   United States v. Medly, 13 Chem. Waste Lit.Rep. 143, 146 (D.S.C.1986).

[162]   Mraz v. Canadian Universal Insurance Co., Ltd., 804 F.2d 1325 (4th Cir.1986).

justified if a release or threatened release is likely to violate, or does violate, any federal or state environmental statute.[163]

Although the technical term "response costs" is not expressly defined under CERCLA, the language of CERCLA provides the government with broad cost recovery rights. By way of definition, CERCLA states that the terms "respond" or "response" means "remove, removal, remedy, and remedial action; all such terms include enforcement activities related thereto."[164] More succinctly, response costs are:

1)   all costs of removal or remedial action incurred by the government not inconsistent with the national contingency plan (NCP);

2)   any other necessary costs of response incurred by any other person consistent with the national contingency plan (NCP);

3)   damages for injury to, destruction of, or loss of natural resources including costs of assessing such damage;

4)   costs of any health assessment or health effects study; and

5)   interest on those sums at the rate specified for investments of the Hazardous Substance Superfund.[165]

In addition, EPA regulations indicate that courts possess discretion to decide, on a case-by-case basis, what response costs may be recovered by private parties.[166] For example, courts have ruled that attorney's fees (under certain

---

[163]   Amoco Oil Co. v. Borden, Inc., 889 F.2d 664, 671 (5th Cir.1989).

[164]   CERCLA § 101(25); 42 U.S.C.A. § 9601(25).

[165]   CERCLA §§ 107(4)(A)-(D); 42 U.S.C.A. §§ 9607(4)(A)-(D).

[166]   55 Fed. Reg. 8794 (1990).

circumstances) may be recoverable as response costs where they are a necessary expense to CERCLA enforcement actions.[167]

b. All Costs of Removal or Remedial Actions

i. Removal Actions

Removal actions are short term solutions sometimes associated with "emergency" conditions that require swift cleanup measures. These cleanups are identified as short term because they are necessary to remove an immediate threat.[168] Removal actions do not require that a site be listed on the NPL, nor do they require a RI/FS.[169]

CERCLA identifies removal actions as those cleanups with expenditures limited to two million dollars and that take no longer than 12 months to complete.[170] Not only do removal actions encompass cleanups, they also include such activities as erecting security fencing, bringing in alternative water supplies, conducting in-depth site analysis, removing hazardous substances from sites, and even temporarily evacuating and housing threatened individuals.[171]

In *United States v. Rohm & Hass Co.*, the 3rd Circuit Court of Appeals outlined removal actions as follows:[172]

1) cleanup or removal of released hazardous substances from the environment;

---

[167] General Electric Co. v. Litton Industrial Automation Systems, Inc., 920 F.2d 1415, 1421-22 (8th Cir.1990), *cert. denied*, 499 U.S. 937; 113 L.Ed.2d 446; 111 S.Ct. 1390 (1991); Pease & Curren Refining, Inc. v. Spectrolab, Inc., 744 F.Supp. 945 (C.D. Cal. 1990) (this case is more often cited as authority because it offers a more detailed discussion of the issue surrounding recovery of attorney's fees in CERCLA actions).

[168] CERCLA § 101(23); 42 U.S.C.A. § 9601(23).

[169] 40 C.F.R. § 300.425.

[170] CERCLA § 104(c)(1); 42 U.S.C.A. § 9604(c)(1).

[171] CERCLA § 101(23); 42 U.S.C.A.§ 9601(23).

[172] *Id.*; United States v. Rohm & Hass Co., 2 F.3d 1265, 1271 (3d. Cir.1993).

2)   actions necessarily taken in the event of a threat of release of hazardous substances into the environment;

3)   actions necessary to monitor, assess, and evaluate the release or threatened release of hazardous substances;

4)   disposal of removed material; or

5)   other actions taken, necessary to prevent, minimize, or mitigate damage to the public health, welfare, or environment, which may otherwise result from a release or threat of a release, without being limited to actions taken under CERCLA Section 104, and emergency assistance provided under the Disaster Relief and Emergency Assistance Act.[173]

ii.   Remedial Actions

(a)   Generally

Remedial actions attempt to create a permanent remedy to prevent the release of hazardous substances. These actions include, but are not limited to: storage; confinement; perimeter protection using dikes, trenches, or ditches; clay cover; neutralization; and cleanup of released hazardous substances.

Remedial actions are massive and complex legal, scientific, engineering and construction cleanup projects. They address numerous hazardous substances, contaminants, and pollutants in a "variety of media" such as soil, ground and surface water, and air. Often, remedial actions take several years to complete. For this reason, the remedial process is regulated by a set of rigid EPA regulations governing investigations, studies (RI/FS), plans, and reports to ensure the remedial action selected will achieve the objectives of CERCLA. Strict compliance with such regulations is required before costs can be recovered from a PRP. Remedial actions may be financed by Superfund only for sites listed on the NPL.[174]

---

[173]   42 U.S.C.A. § 5121 et. seq. (1995).

[174]   CERCLA § 101(24); 42 U.S.C.A. § 9601(24).

Before EPA can launch a remedial action, it must enter into a "contract or cooperative agreement" with the state in which the remedial action is needed, and ensure that the site is on the NPL. In the contract, states must agree to:[175]

1)   ensure future maintenance of the remedial action until its conclusion;

2)   assure availability of acceptable treatment, storage, and disposal facilities for off-site storage, destruction, treatment, or secure disposition of hazardous substances generated by the remedial action; and

3)   pay or guarantee payment of ten percent of the remedial action costs or 50% of the cost if the state or a political subdivision of the state is responsible for the release.

(b)   CERCLA Requirements

Once it is determined that a remedial action is necessary, CERCLA requires the remedy to be:

1)   consistent with the National Contingency Plan;[176]

2)   cost-effective;[177]

3)   a permanent solution to the problem;[178]

4)   protective of human health and the environment;[179] and

---

[175]   CERCLA § 104(d); 42 U.S.C.A. § 9604(d).

[176]   CERCLA § 104(a)(1); 42 U.S.C.A. § 9604(a)(1); CERCLA §§ 107(a)(4)(A), (B); 42 U.S.C.A. §§ 9607(a)(4)(A), (B).

[177]   CERCLA §§ 121(a), (b); 42 U.S.C.A. §§ 9621(a), (b).

[178]   CERCLA § 121(b); 42 U.S.C.A. § 9621(b).

[179]   CERCLA § 104(a)(1); 42 U.S.C.A. § 9604(a)(1).

5)   compatible with applicable or relevant and appropriate requirements (ARARs).[180]

(c)   Record of Decision

The record of decision (ROD) is a document that outlines and describes the remedy selected for a particular hazardous waste site. Once a remedy has been selected, all facts, analysis of facts, and site-specific policy determinations are documented in the ROD.[181] The ROD should include the following information:[182]

1)   the ARARS applicable to the site-specific plan;

2)   indicate the remediation goals that the remedy is expected to achieve;

3)   discuss significant changes and responses to comments from public notices of the proposed action; and

4)   provide a commitment for further analysis and selection of long-term response measures within an appropriate time-frame.

The ROD should also discuss:

1)   how the selected remedy protects human health and the environment;

2)   how the remedy is cost-effective;

---

[180]   CERCLA §§ 121(d)(1), (2)(A); 42 U.S.C.A. §§ 9621(d)(1), (2)(A) (ARARs are designed to help determine just how clean a site should be. ARARS require that all legally applicable or relevant and appropriate federal standards and all of the more stringent state standards be applied as guidelines to CERCLA site cleanups. ARARs are commonly outlined and discussed in the ROD).

[181]   40 C.F.R. § 300.430(f)(5).

[182]   *Id.*

3)   how the remedy utilizes permanent solutions and alternative treatment or resource recovery technologies to the maximum extent practicable;

4)   whether a preference for a remedy is satisfied by the selected remedy and an explanation as to why it is not, if necessary; and

5)   describe whether hazardous substances, pollutants, or contaminants will remain at the site such that a review of the site, less than every five years, would be necessary.

After the ROD is approved and signed, the lead agency[183] publishes a notice of the ROD in a major newspaper of general circulation, and makes the ROD available for public inspection and copying prior to any remedial action.[184]

c.   Any Other Necessary Costs of Response

CERCLA recognizes response costs incurred by persons other than the federal government.[185] As such, CERCLA creates a cause of action for private parties to recover response costs from other PRPs.[186] In order for private parties to recover their expenses for response costs, such response costs must be necessary and consistent with the NCP.[187]

---

[183]   40 C.F.R. § 300.5.

[184]   40 C.F.R. § 300.430(6) (community relations when the ROD is signed).

[185]   CERCLA § 107(a)(4)(B); 42 U.S.C.A. § 9607(a)(4)(B).

[186]   Southland Corp. v. Ashland Oil, Inc., 696 F. Supp. 994, 998 (D.N.J.1988); see also, Shilton, David C., Groundwater Pollution Litigation in the Federal Courts: An Evaluation of Three New Private Remedies, 3 J. Envtl. L. & Litig. 91, 95 (1988).

[187]   See U.S. v. Northeastern Pharmaceutical and Chemical Corp., 810 F.2d 726 (8th Cir.1986); Prisco v. A&D Carting Corp., 168 F.3d 593, 602-03 (2d Cir.1999); Redwing Carriers, Inc. v. Saraland Apartments, 94 F.3d 1489, 1496 (11th Cir. 1996).

d. Damages for Loss of Natural Resources

CERCLA authorizes both federal and state governments to act as public trustees in assessing damages to natural resources.[188] The government or appointed public trustee "may bring a cause of action to recover for injury to natural resources."[189] CERCLA defines natural resources as:[190]

> land, fish, wildlife, biota, air, water, groundwater, drinking water supplies, and other such resources belonging to, managed by, held in trust by, appertaining to, or otherwise controlled by the United States . . . [and] any State or local government.

The government may seek recovery for damages if natural resources cannot be restored to their original state.[191] The costs of damage to natural resources include restoration, rehabilitation, replacement or acquisition of equivalent damaged resources, and the diminished value of real property.[192] However, CERCLA does not create a private right of recovery for such costs. Furthermore, private parties may still recover under such common law tort theories as negligence, nuisance, or strict liability.[193]

PRPs can defend against suits to recover damages to natural resources if they demonstrate that:

1) damages complained of were previously and specifically identified as an irreversible commitment of natural resources in an environmental impact statement (EIS);

---

[188] CERCLA § 107(f)(1); 42 U.S.C.A. § 9607(f)(1).

[189] Michael, Patrick T., III, Natural Resource Damages Under CERCLA: The Emerging Champion of Environmental Enforcement, 20 Pepp. L. Rev. 185, 190 (1992).

[190] CERCLA § 101(16); 42 U.S.C.A. § 9601(16).

[191] Hyson, John M. & Judge, John P., A Comparative Analysis of the Federal and Pennsylvania Superfund Acts, 1 Vill. Envtl. L.J. 1, 68 (1990).

[192] Michael, *supra* note 189 at 201.

[193] Ward, Kevin M., Recovery Of Natural Resource Damages Under CERCLA, 25 Tort & Ins. L.J. 559, 576 (1990).

2)   the decision granting a permit or license authorized a commitment of such natural resources; and

3)   the facility or project operated within the terms of its permit or license.[194]

e.   Health Assessments

Health assessments are also considered forms of response costs recoverable under CERCLA.   Such assessments are often complex, time consuming, and expensive.   Each assessment must include the six following steps:

1)   evaluation of information on the site including physical, geographical, historical, geological, and operational information;

2)   identification of community health concerns;

3)   a determination of contaminants associated with the site;

4)   identification and evaluation of exposure pathways;

5)   a determination of public health implications based on medical and toxicological information; and

6)   conclusions and recommendations concerning the health threat posed.[195]

Although health assessments are generally recoverable as response costs under CERCLA, courts are divided on whether medical screening and future medical monitoring are necessary response costs as well.[196]   The judicial trend

---

[194]   *Id.* at 582.

[195]   Boston, Gerald W., A Mass-Exposure Model of Toxic Causation: The Content Of Scientific Proof And The Regulatory Experience, 18 Colum.J.Envtl.L. 181 (1993).

[196]   Steincamp, *supra* note 50 at 199.

is to deny costs of such medical monitoring.[197] Yet, some courts hold that these costs fall within the definition of "remove" and should still be recoverable as response costs.[198]

G.   NECESSARY AND CONSISTENT WITH THE NATIONAL CONTINGENCY PLAN (NCP)

1.   The NCP

The NCP establishes procedures and standards for investigating hazardous waste sites, sets criteria for determining the priority of site response actions, and establishes standards for proper site cleanup for both government and private actions.[199] It is periodically revised and republished in the Federal Register. CERCLA provides:

> Whenever (A) any hazardous substance is released or there is a substantial threat of such release into the environment, or (B) there is a release or substantial threat of release into the environment of any pollutant or contaminant which may present an imminent and substantial danger to the public health or welfare . . . [EPA] is authorized to act, consistent with the national contingency plan, to remove or arrange for the removal of, and provide for remedial action . . . or take any other response measure consistent with the national contingency plan . . . necessary to protect the public health or welfare or the environment.[200]

The NCP establishes minimum standards to evaluate and remedy releases or threatened releases. It also establishes criteria to determine the appropriate

---

[197]   Coburn v. Sund Chemical Corp., 28 Env't Rep.Cas. (BNA) 1665, 1671 (E.D.Pa.1988) (medical screening costs and medical monitoring are not necessary response costs); Brewer v. Raven, 680 F.Supp. 1176, 1179-80 (M.D.Tenn.1988) (medical monitoring costs are not allowed under CERCLA as personal damages).

[198]   Cook v. Rockwell Intern, 755 F.Supp. 1468, 1474 (D.Colo.1991).

[199]   CERCLA § 105; 42 U.S.C.A. § 9605.

[200]   CERCLA § 104(a)(1); 42 U.S.C.A. § 9604(a)(1).

extent of response.[201] In addition, the NCP delineates the roles and responsibilities of federal, state and local governments, as well as non-governmental entities in response actions.[202]

Response costs must be necessary and consistent with the NCP in order for the government or other private parties to be reimbursed for their cleanup costs.[203] Government response costs are presumed to be consistent with the NCP but may be proven otherwise. The burden of proof lies on the defendant PRP to show that the costs incurred by the government were not consistent with the NCP.[204] In contrast however, private parties must affirmatively show that their response costs are necessary and consistent with the NCP.[205] Because two different burdens are present, many commentators requested EPA to address the confusion regarding the meaning of "consistent with the national contingency plan."[206] As a result, EPA explained that "response costs are consistent with the NCP if the response, evaluated in its entirety, substantially complies with applicable regulations and results in a CERCLA-quality cleanup."[207]

---

[201]   Green, Larry V., Sifting Through The Ambiguity: A Critical Overview Of The Comprehensive Environmental Response Compensation and Liability Act As Amended By The Superfund Amendments And Reauthorization Act, 17 T. Marshall L. Rev. 191, 210 (1991).

[202]   *Id.*

[203]   CERCLA § 107(a); 42 U.S.C.A. § 9607(a).

[204]   Philadelphia v. Stepan Chemical Co., 713 F.Supp. 1484 (E.D.Pa.1989).

[205]   Patterson, Geoffrey D., A Buyer's Catalogue Of Pre-purchase Precautions To Minimize CERCLA Liability In Commercial Real Estate Transactions, 15 U. Puget Sound L. Rev. 469, 475 (1992); *see also*, Amland Properties Corp. v. Aluminum Co. of America, 711 F.Supp. 784, 794 (D.N.J.1989); Artesian Water Co. v. New Castle County, 659 F.Supp. 1269, 1291 (D.Del.1987).

[206]   For discussion, *see*, Kaplan, Eric D., Attorney Fee Recovery Pursuant to CERCLA § 107(a)(4)(B), 42 Wash. U.J. Urb. & Contmp. L. 251, 263 (1992).

[207]   *Id.*; 40 C.F.R. § 300.700(c)(3)(i); NL Industries, Inc. v. Kaplan, 792 F.2d 896, 888-889 (9th Cir.1986); *see also*, Anderson, Jerry L., Removal Or Remedial? The Myth of CERCLA's Two-Response System, 18 Colum J. Envtl. L. 103, 107 (1993).

2.   CERCLA-Quality Cleanup

Though CERCLA does not clearly define what a "CERCLA-quality cleanup (CQC)" is, its preamble does provide some guidance. For example, to achieve CQC status, a cleanup must:[208]

1)   protect human health and the environment;

2)   utilize permanent solutions and alternative treatment technologies to the maximum extent practicable;

3)   be cost-effective;[209]

4)   must attain "applicable or relevant and appropriate requirements" (ARARs) from other environmental laws;[210] and

5)   ensure that meaningful public participation is provided.[211]

H.   EXTENT OF LIABILITY

Once a contaminated site and its PRPs are identified, and cleanup costs are anticipated or incurred, there must be a method to determine the extent of each PRP's liability. Those who clean a site may be able to collect their costs from other PRPs connected to the site. At some sites, hundreds of PRPs are identified.

---

[208]   CERCLA § 121(b)(1); 42 U.S.C.A. § 9621(b)(1).

[209]   Harrison, Andrew J., Jr., Palko, Monica J. & Reitz, Arnold W., Cost Recovery by Private Parties Under CERCLA: Planning A Response Action For Maximum Recovery, 27 Tulsa L.J. 365, 397 (1992) (consistency with the NCP does not mandate cost-effectiveness for a removal action, but does require such a finding for remedial actions).

[210]   CERCLA § 121(d)(4); 42 U.S.C.A. § 9621(d)(4); 55 Fed. Reg. 8793 (March 8, 1990).

[211]   CERCLA § 117; 42 U.S.C.A. § 9617.

The "extent of liability" determines whether a party will be held responsible for all or only a portion of the cleanup expenses. Section 107(a), CERCLA's liability provision, specifically states that "covered persons" shall be liable.[212] The term "person" as used above is defined as:

> An individual, firm, corporation, association, partnership, consortium, joint venture, commercial entity, United States Government, State, municipality, commission, political subdivision of a State or any interstate body.[213]

CERCLA identifies four categories of "covered persons" who are PRPs: current owners and operators, past owners and operators, generators, and transporters.[214] The liability provision includes any party that falls under the definition of "person," and who also meets the elements of one of the four categories of "covered persons." The parties covered under the liability provision (the PRPs) are liable for:

1) all costs of removal or remedial actions incurred by the government that are not inconsistent with the NCP;

2) any other necessary costs of response incurred by any other person consistent with the NCP;

3) damages for injury, destruction or loss of natural resources including costs of assessing any injury, destruction, or loss resulting from a release;

4) costs of health assessments or health effects studies; and

5) interest on the above amounts.[215]

---

[212] CERCLA § 107(a); 42 U.S.C.A. § 9607(a).

[213] CERCLA § 101(21); 42 U.S.C.A. § 9601(21).

[214] CERCLA § 107(a); 42 U.S.C.A. § 9607(a).

[215] *Id.*

PRPs must understand that the financial burden of liability may be huge, and may bear no relationship to the size or assets of the individual or entity, nor to the value or size of the property.[216] A "covered person" may be held liable "individually" or as an "organization."[217] In addition, this liability can be "retroactive," "strict," and either "joint and several," or "divisible and apportionable."

1.   Individual Liability

Individual liability means a person must personally pay for amounts assessed against him as a PRP. Individual liability often attaches to persons that have supervisory authority over generating or handling (treating, storing, or disposing of) hazardous substances. For example, courts have found corporate officers and directors individually liable under CERCLA because they were either personally involved in the release, or had the ability to prevent the release.[218] In addition, such corporate officers may have had the capacity to control events leading up to the release.

Courts may also find an individual liable based on actual or imputed knowledge of a release. A corporate official cannot escape liability by "looking the other way."[219] However, the greater the liability imposed, the stronger the nexus needs to be when connecting an individual to a release.

For example, in *New York v. Shore Realty Corp.*, a corporate officer was found individually liable as a CERCLA operator because he was "in charge of the operation of the facility in question."[220] In addition, the Appellate Court

---

[216]   Robb, Kathryn E. B., Environmental Considerations In Project Financing, PLI Order No. A4-4433 (1993).

[217]   CERCLA § 101(21); 42 U.S.C.A. § 9601(21).

[218]   *See*, Kelley v. Thomas Solvent Company, 727 F.Supp. 1532, 1544 (W.D.Mich.1989); *see also*, Bick, Alan N., Hatch, Josiah O., III & Olson, John F., Liability of Corporate Directors and Officers Under CERCLA And RCRA, PLI Order No. A4-4383, 623 PLI/COMM 377 (1992).

[219]   State of New York v. Shore Realty Corp., 759 F.2d at 1052.

[220]   *Id.*

found all the corporate defendant's shareholders and officers individually liable under Section 107(a)(1) as owners and operators of the waste site. The Appellate Court also held all defendants jointly and severally liable. The Appellate Court stated that Section 101(20)(A), which defines owner and operator, implies that a shareholder who manages the corporation may be individually liable as an owner or operator.[221] Other cases have held that:

1) Parties can be held individually liable as operators under CERCLA if they "exercise control over the company immediately responsible for the [release]."[222]

2) The president of a company can be held individually liable if he "possessed ultimate authority to control the disposal of the hazardous substance."[223]

3) Corporate officers who assert managerial responsibility and control over the disposal of hazardous waste may be individually liable under CERCLA.[224]

4) Individual liability may flow to persons who are officers, directors, shareholders, and employees of a corporation who have direct control and supervision of the wrongful activity.[225]

5) A former president and director of a company, who supervised day-to-day operations, can be individually liable as an operator

---

[221] *Id.*

[222] Levin Metals v. Parr-Richmond Terminal Company, 781 F.Supp. 1454, 1457 (N.D.Cal.1991).

[223] United States v. Mexico Feed and Seed Co., 764 F.Supp. 565, 571 (E.D.Mo.1991).

[224] Conductron Corp. v. Gladys P. Williams, 785 F.Supp. 271, 274 (D.N.H.1991).

[225] Columbia River Service Corp. v. Gilman, 751 F.Supp. 1448, 1454 (W.D.Wash.1990).

under CERCLA even though he did not personally participate in the wrongful acts.[226]

2.   Organizational Liability

The definition of a person under CERCLA Section 101(21) specifically names all types of entities and organizations the statute intends to regulate as "covered persons." If an organization is a named PRP and is held liable, then it must pay all costs assessed against it. It is not uncommon for such a PRP to declare bankruptcy and close operations.

Courts have also extended liability to successor corporations. Although many of the states' corporate laws have resisted successor corporate liability, federal courts look to whether a successor corporation continues the prior business practices under a new name. To this end, federal courts look to whether the successor corporation "uses the same employees, equipment or methodology, engages in the same business practice and with knowledge of the predecessor's problems, operates under the same name, produces the same products, serves the same customers, and continues the same hazardous waste disposal practices" as its predecessor, the parent corporation.[227]

3.   Retroactive Liability

CERCLA is a uniquely severe law because its liability provisions apply retroactively. This means that a PRP who, before CERCLA was enacted, acted in such a way as to have caused a threat to the environment, may be held liable for response costs of the contamination. This is true even if the past action was customary and legal at the time it was done. Retroactive laws attach new obligations to past actions.

CERCLA's legislative history indicates that Congress intended the statute to be "backward-looking." CERCLA is a remedial statute to be applied against

---

[226]   United States v. Carolina Transformer Co., Inc., 739 F.Supp. 1030, 1037-38 (E.D.N.C.1989).

[227]   Robb, *supra* note 216 at 46.

past conduct.[228] During its passage, the Honorable Jennings Randolph, Chairman, Committee on Environment and Public Works, United States Senate, stated:

> Society should not bear the costs of protecting the public from hazards produced in the past by a generator, transporter, consumer, or dumpsite owner or operator who has profited or otherwise benefitted from commerce involving these substances.[229]

Because of the tremendous costs associated with cleanups, retroactive application has been a source of much controversy and litigation. The most common controversy is that retroactive application disregards constitutional due process. However, because of strong public policy and governmental interests in cleaning up sites posing a threat to human health and the environment, CERCLA's retroactive application has been held not to be unconstitutional. Key judicial decisions support CERCLA's retroactive application and have held that:

1) The statute's explicit limit on recovery of certain damages and its failure to limit retroactive recovery of response costs indicate that CERCLA authorizes recovery of costs incurred before and after enactment. Further, "Congress, in CERCLA, has overridden the presumption against retroactive application of statutes."[230]

2) "Although CERCLA does not expressly provide for retroactivity, it is manifestly clear that Congress intended CERCLA to have retroactive effect. The language used in the key liability provision, CERCLA Section 107, . . . refers to actions and conditions in the past tense: any person who at the time of disposal of any hazardous substances owned or operated, . . . any person . . . who arranged with a transporter for

---

[228] Resila, James A., The Retroactive Application of CERCLA: Preenactment Response Costs, 1 Fordham Envtl. L. Representative. 69, 75 (1989).

[229] S.Rep. No. 848, 96th Cong., 2d Sess. at 98 (1980).

[230] CERCLA § 302(a); 42 U.S.C.A. § 9652(a); United States v. Hooker Chemicals & Plastics Corp., 680 F. Supp. 546, 557 (W.D.N.Y.1988).

disposal' . . . and any person who . . . accepted any hazardous substances for transport to . . . sites selected by such person."[231]

3) Congress' burden in enacting retroactive legislation is met by showing that a rational legislative purpose exists. CERCLA is justified by the rational legislative purpose of protecting human health and the environment from the high risks posed by contaminated sites.[232]

4. Strict Liability

Strict liability means "no fault" or "absolute" liability. It is liability without fault or intent to release hazardous substances. A "person" is automatically considered to be "strictly liable" if they fall within one of the categories of responsible persons.[233] Courts have held that CERCLA imposes strict liability;[234] without regard to causation, fault, or state of mind. "Congress intended that responsible parties be held strictly liable even though an explicit provision for strict liability was not included [in CERCLA]."[235]

---

[231] United States v. Northeastern Pharmaceutical & Chemical Co., Inc., 810 F.2d 726, 732-733 (8th Cir.1986); United States v. R.W. Meyer, Inc., 889 F.2d 1497 (6th Cir.1989).

[232] United States v. Conservation Chemical Co., 619 F.Supp 162, 221 (W.D.Mo.1985); United States v Northeastern Pharmaceutical & Chemical Co., Inc., 810 F.2d at 734; United States v. Ottati and Goss, Inc., 630 F.Supp. 1361, 1399 (D.N.H.1985); United States v. Shell Oil Co., 605 F. Supp. 1064 (D.Colo.1985) (CERCLA is unavoidably retroactive because Congress intended to impose cleanup costs on responsible parties rather than on taxpayers); Town of Boonton v. Drew Chemical Corp., 15 Envtl. L. Representative. 20,962 (D.N.J.1985) (municipality could recover response costs incurred before CERCLA was enacted).

[233] Craig J. Reece, Trustees And Secured Lenders As Owners Or Operators Under CERCLA, PLI Order No. H4-5162 (1993).

[234] United States v. Buckley, 934 F.2d 84, 88 (6th Cir.1991); United States v. Monsanto Co., 858 F.2d 160, 169 (4th Cir.1988).

[235] State of New York v. Shore Realty Corp., 759 F.2d at 1042, 1044; United States v. Ward, 618 F.Supp. at 893.

5.   Joint and Several Liability

CERCLA provides joint and several liability among the responsible parties for hazardous waste cleanup costs.[236] This means that each PRP is presumed liable for the entire cleanup bill where divisibility of the harm cannot be determined. The driving force behind CERCLA cleanup actions is the government's power to threaten individual defendants with overwhelming liability.[237] In other words, the government or private party who attempted to clean up a site and incurred response costs, may seek reimbursement in full from any one, or all of the PRPs.[238]

The joint and several liability scheme is controversial because the party who incurred costs is likely to go after the defendant PRP with the most money, regardless of the extent of the defendant's actual contamination. For example, a PRP may have only owned contaminated property for a short period where there was little or no disposal of hazardous waste, and may be held 100% liable for the entire cost of cleanup. At the same time, another PRP who owned the same property for a long period of time in which most of the hazardous wastes were disposed of is likely not to be sued if the party is insolvent.

Although harsh, joint and several liability is justified because:

1)   it shifts cleanup costs from victims of contamination to the parties responsible for creating the hazard;

2)   it creates incentives for safer handling and disposal by placing cleanup costs on the waste-generating business ensuring internalization of these costs; and

---

[236]   Sand Springs Home v. Interplastic Corp., 670 F.Supp. 913, 915-916 (N.D.Okla.1987).

[237]   Harvard Law Review Association, Liability Issues In CERCLA Cleanup Actions, 99 Harv. L. Rev. 1151 (1986).

[238]   McDavid, Diana L., Liabilities of the Innocent Current Owner Of Toxic Property Under CERCLA, 23 U. Rich. L. Rev. 403, 406 (1989); *see also*, Steinzor, Rena, Local Governments And Superfund: Who Will Pay The Tab?, 22 Urb. Law. 79, 80 (1990).

3)   it relieves the strain on the government's limited budget by encouraging defendants to locate and implead other responsible parties.[239]

a.   Contribution

Any party held to be jointly and severally liable has a right to file a contribution suit against other liable parties. Contribution evolved as a result of strict, joint and several liability allowing the courts to find any one PRP liable for 100% of costs. Contribution allows a party who has incurred response costs, to seek other PRPs who can share the liability. Section 113(f) governs the equitable allocation of obligations among joint and severally liable parties.[240] In apportioning damages among liable parties, courts may consider among other factors, the following:[241]

1)   the ability of the parties to demonstrate that their contribution to a discharge, release, or disposal of a hazardous waste can be distinguished;

2)   the amount of hazardous waste involved;

3)   the degree of toxicity of the hazardous waste involved;

4)   the degree of involvement by the parties in the generation, transportation, treatment, storage, or disposal of the hazardous waste;

---

[239]   McDavid, *supra* note 238 at 420.

[240]   CERCLA § 113(f)(1); 42 U.S.C.A. § 9613(f)(1) (Any person may seek contribution from any other person who is liable or potentially liable under section [107(a)] . . . during or following any civil action . . . . In resolving contribution claims, the court may allocate response costs among liable parties using such equitable factors as the court determines are appropriate).

[241]   H.R. 7020, § 3071(a)(3)(B) in Senate Committee on Environment & Public Works, 2 Legis.Hist. of CERCLA, 97th Cong.2d Sess. 439 (1983); *see also*, United States v. A & F Materials Co., 578 F.Supp. 1249, 1256 (S.D.Ill.1984).

5) the degree of care exercised by the parties with respect to the hazardous waste concerned, taking into account the hazardous characteristics of such waste; and

6) the degree of cooperation by the parties with Federal, State, or local officials to prevent any harm to the public health or the environment.

Contribution suits may arise out of three contexts:

1) when the government sues less than all PRPs and a subsequent action for contribution is brought by the parties named in the government action against the remaining unnamed PRPs;

2) when a private party incurring response costs does not name all PRPs in its reimbursement action and subsequent actions for contribution are brought by the named PRPs against remaining unnamed PRPs; and

3) when one PRP brings a private action to recover response costs against another PRP.[242]

There are exceptions to joint and several liability under CERCLA. Congress did not intend to hold local governments or individual citizens to a standard of strict, joint and several liability with respect to disposal of household wastes.[243]   Also, the courts have held that joint and several liability is inappropriate where the harm is divisible and capable of reasonable apportionment.[244]

---

[242]   Russo, Tricia R., casenote, FMC Corp. v. United States Department of Commerce: An Over-Expansion of "Operator" Liability under CERCLA, 7 Vill. Envtl. L.J. 157, 161 (1996).

[243]   Reinders, Lynne A., Municipal Liability Under Superfund As Generators Of Municipal Solid Waste: Addressing The Plight Of Local Governments, 43 Wash. U. J. Urb. & Contemp. L. 419, 425 (1993) (waste collected from cleaning products used in homes is not what Congress intended to regulate when it created CERCLA).

[244]   United States v. Alcan Aluminum Corp., 964 F.2d at 271.

b.   Divisibility

Today, technology gives parties the ability to demonstrate divisibility of each party's responsibility for their respective environmental harm and thus prove each party's limited liability. If PRPs can demonstrate that their liability is divisible, the government cannot impose joint and several liability.[245]

I.   DEFENSES

There are several defenses available to CERCLA liability. For example, a number of formal elements are often required for various actions under CERCLA, and failure to establish these elements present mirror-image defenses for the opposition. Although several defenses to CERCLA liability exist, they are limited in scope.[246] Some of these defenses to Section 107 actions include showing a lack of a hazardous substance, the absence of a facility, lack of a release, or that the damages sought were not response costs, or were not consistent with the NCP.[247]

Some unique defenses are statutorily created, such as the "act of God," "act of war," "act of a third party," "innocent landowner," "lender," "bankruptcy," and "inheritance" defenses. CERCLA provides:[248]

---

[245] Sand Springs Home v. Interplastic Corp., 670 F. Supp. 913, 915-916 (N.D.Okla. 1987) (because the injury was indivisible, liability was joint and several); United States v. Chem-Dyne Corp., 572 F.Supp. 802 (S.D.Ohio 1983) (defendants must provide "substantial and persuasive proof" of an individual PRP's contamination for divisibility of the allocation of response costs to apply); O'Neil v. Picillo, 883 F.2d 176, 179 (1st Cir.1989) cert. denied, 490 U.S. 1160 (1990) (joint and several liability frequently affects defendants who pay more than their share of costs. Recognizing the unrealistic prospect of finding solvent defendants in an action for contribution the court considered divisibility as a basis for mitigation).

[246] Taub, Theodore C., Pre-Transaction And Transactional Issues Involving Hazardous Materials Waste, C851 ALI-ABA 251, 254 (1993).

[247] In addition, there are also frequently used tactical defenses such as statutes of limitations, right to jury trials and third party initiatives such as joinder and intervention as well as discovery sanctions and procedural disclosure laws under Rule 26 of the Federal Rules of Civil Procedure.

[248] CERCLA § 107(b); 42 U.S.C.A. § 9607(b).

There shall be no liability . . . [for] the release or threat of release of a hazardous substance and the damages resulting therefrom caused solely by--

(1) an act of God;

(2) an act of war; [or]

(3) an act or omission of a third party.

1.   Act of God: Force Majeure

CERCLA excuses releases caused by an "act of God."[249] CERCLA states that an "act of God" means "unanticipated grave natural disaster or other natural phenomenon of exceptional, inevitable, and irresistible character, the effects of which could not . . . [be] prevented or avoided by the exercise of due care or foresight."[250]

Because events such as heavy rains, high floodwaters, tornados, hurricanes, earthquakes, and lightning are foreseeable and anticipated, the defense will only be successful to relieve a PRP from liability if he shows that he took all reasonable steps to prevent the damage caused by such a foreseeable event.[251] The "act of God" defense usually relieves responsible parties from CERCLA liability in only "drastic and rare circumstances."[252]

---

[249]   CERCLA § 107(b)(1); 42 U.S.C.A. § 9607(b)(1).

[250]   CERCLA § 101(1); 42 U.S.C.A. § 9601(1).

[251]   Lumbermens Mutual Casualty Co. v. Belleville Industries Inc., 938 F.2d 1423 (1st Cir.1991) (insurance coverage for sudden and accidental polluting events does not reach continuous polluting activity punctuated by a tropical rainstorm, fire and sporadic spills); United States v. Stringfellow, 661 F.Supp. at 1061 (rains were foreseeable based on normal climatic conditions and any harm caused by the rain could have been prevented through design of proper drainage channels); State of Colorado v. Idarado Mining Co., 707 F.Supp. at 1236.

[252]   Norris, Debra Baker, CERCLA and Real Estate Transactions: A Game of Chance, 25 Apr., Hous.Law. 20, 22 (1988).

2.   Act of War

CERCLA provides that there shall be no liability for a person who can establish that the release or threat of release of a hazardous substance and the damages resulting therefrom were caused solely by an "act of war."[253]

An "act of war" is not defined in American law and appears to have been borrowed from international law that defines "act of war" as "use of force or other action by one state against another" which "the state acted against, recognizes . . . as an act of war, either by use of retaliatory force or a declaration of war."[254]

In *United States v. Shell Oil*, defendants asserted the act of war defense where the United States sought to recover response costs from Shell Oil's McColl site in Fullerton, California.[255] The wastes at the site included acid sludge byproducts of alkylation processes used by the oil company during World War II to produce high octane aviation fuel. This fuel was produced in large quantities at the demand of the federal government as part of the war effort. At the time, government regulations required all industries to cooperate with the government in providing supplies to military forces. During the war, the petroleum industry was subject to continuous government oversight and the threat of being taken over by the government should they refuse to cooperate.

The court, unable to find judicial precedent defining the term "act of war" in the context of CERCLA or environmental law, determined that the term "act of war" cannot be reasonably construed to cover government wartime contracts for the regulation of oil companies' production of aviation fuel and denied use of the defense.[256]

---

[253]   CERCLA § 107(b)(2); 42 U.S.C.A. § 9607(b)(2).

[254]   United States v. Shell Oil Co., 841 F.Supp 962, 970 (C.D.Cal.1993); *see*, Fox, James R., Dictionary of International and Comparative Law 6 (1992); Union Academique Internationale, Dictionnaire de la Terminologie du Droit Internationale 12-13 (1960).

[255]   *Id.*

[256]   *Id.*

Since the enactment of CERCLA, the "act of war" defense like the "act of God" defense has proven to be extremely difficult to prevail upon.[257] The best example of environmental damage from an act of war is the "environmental terrorism" inflicted upon the air, land and water of the Persian Gulf by Saddam Hussein during the Gulf War in 1991.[258]

3. Act of a Third Party

CERCLA provides:[259]

> There shall be no liability . . . for a person who can establish . . . that the release or threat of release of a hazardous substance and the damages resulting therefrom were caused solely by . . . an act or omission of a third party other than an employee or agent of the defendant, or than one whose act or omission occurs in connection with a contractual relationship . . . with the defendant . . . if the defendant establishes by a preponderance of the evidence that (a) he exercised due care . . . in light of all relevant facts and circumstances, and (b) he took precautions against foreseeable acts or omissions of any such third party and the consequences that could foreseeably result from such acts or omissions . . . .

The term "contractual relationship" is defined by CERCLA to include, but not be limited to:[260]

> . . . land contracts, deeds or other instruments transferring title or possession unless the real property on which the facility concerned is located was acquired by the defendant after the disposal or placement of the hazardous substance on, in or at the facility, and . . . .[a]t the time

---

[257] Quinn, Paul C., The EPA Guidance on Landowner Liability and the Innocent Landowner Defense: The All Appropriate Inquiry Standard: Fact or Fiction?, 2 Vill. Envtl. L.J. 143, 150, n.47 (1991).

[258] Korodudui-Fubara, Oil in the Persian Gulf War: Legal Appraisal of an Environmental Warfare, 23 St.Mary's L.J. 123 (1991).

[259] CERCLA § 107(b)(3); 42 U.S.C.A. § 9607(b)(3).

[260] CERCLA § 101(35)(A); 42 U.S.C.A. § 9601(35)(A).

the defendant acquired the facility the defendant did not know and had no reason to know that any hazardous substance . . . was disposed of on, in, or at the facility . . . . [or the] defendant is a government entity who acquired the facility by . . . involuntary transfer . . . . [or the] defendant acquired the facility by inheritance or bequest.

The third party defense is appropriately applied if the contamination did not occur in connection with a "contractual relationship," such as where a third party dumps waste in the middle of the night on the defendant's property.[261] If a "contractual relationship" does exist, the defense shifts the burden of proof of causation to the defendants.[262] The defendant must prove by a preponderance of the evidence that although a contractual relationship existed with a third party, who solely caused the release, the defendant exercised due care and took actions against any foreseeable acts and omissions by the third party.[263]

4.   Innocent Landowner

CERCLA originally imposed strict liability on all owners of contaminated property regardless of ownership.[264] However, controversy arose as a result of several cases where "innocent" landowners were held liable for response costs that exceeded the value of the land.[265] As a result, Congress provided the innocent landowner defense to unknowing purchasers of property on which hazardous substances may have already been released.

This defense hinges on whether the landowner can prove by a preponderance of the evidence that "[a]t the time the defendant acquired the facility the defendant did not know and had no reason to know that any

---

[261]   Baker, Debra L. & Baroody, Theodore G., What Price Innocence? A Realistic View Of The Innocent Landowner Defense Under CERCLA, 22 St. Mary's L.J. 115, 120 (1990).

[262]   *Id.*; *see also*, Violet v. Picillo, 648 F.Supp. at 1293.

[263]   *Id.*

[264]   United States v. Shell Oil, 841 F.Supp. at 970.

[265]   *Id.*; *see also*, United States v. Maryland Bank & Trust Co., 632 F.Supp. 573 (D.Md.1986).

hazardous substance . . . was disposed of on, in or at the facility."[266] In addition, to establish that the defendant had no reason to know, " . . . the defendant must have undertaken, at the time of acquisition, all appropriate inquiry into the previous ownership and uses of the property . . . ."[267]

Furthermore, the court must take into account "any specialized knowledge or experience on the part of the defendant, the relationship between the purchase price and the value of the property if uncontaminated, commonly known or reasonably ascertainable information about the property, the obviousness of the presence or likely presence of contamination at the property, and the ability to detect such contamination by appropriate inspection."[268]

In *United States v. Shell*, the defendants asserted the "innocent landowner" defense. In this case, the court held that for a defendant to successfully avoid CERCLA liability by such a defense, he must establish that:

1)   at the time the property was acquired by the defendant the defendant did not know and had no reason to know that the property was contaminated;

2)   no hazardous substances were disposed of on the property during the defendant's ownership of the site;

3)   the defendant exercised due care with respect to the hazardous substances once it acquired the property; and

4)   the defendant did not by any act or omission cause or contribute to the release or threatened release of hazardous substances at the site.[269]

---

[266]   CERCLA § 101(35)(A)(i); 42 U.S.C.A. § 9601(35)(A)(i).

[267]   CERCLA § 101(35)(b); 42 U.S.C.A. § 9601(35)(B).

[268]   *Id.*

[269]   United States v. Shell Oil, 841 F.Supp. at 973.

5.   Lender

Under certain circumstances, a "lender" may be exempt from CERCLA liability as a security interest owner. Security interest owners are creditors or "lenders" who have an ownership interest in property as the result of a security agreement. Security agreements provide a claim or stake in property in exchange for guaranteeing payment or performance of an obligation. The most common example is a mortgage contract or loan agreement granting a security interest in real estate in return for a loan of money. CERCLA provides:

> The term "owner or operator" . . . does not include a person, who, without participating in the management of a vessel or facility, holds indicia of ownership primarily to protect his security interest in the vessel or facility."[270]

Security interest owners are exempt from CERCLA liability if they do not participate in the management of a vessel or facility.[271] They are exempt because generally they are not in control of the day-to-day operations nor the hazardous substances of a facility. The rationale is that their connection to the property is too small to trigger CERCLA liability.[272]

However, this exemption may not always apply. For example, a security interest owner may still be liable even though he was not in control of the day-to-day operations of the facility. Liability can attach if the security interest owner participated in the financial management of the facility to a degree that could influence the facility's treatment of hazardous substances. The critical issue is whether the security interest owner sufficiently participated in management to incur liability.[273]

---

[270]   CERCLA § 101(20)(A); 42 U.S.C.A. § 9601(20)(A).

[271]   *Id.*

[272]   Wilson, Scott, When A Security Becomes A Liability: Claims Against Lenders In Hazardous Waste Cleanup, 38 Hastings L.J. 1261, 1287 (1987).

[273]   United States v. Fleet Factors Corp., 901 F.2d 1550 (11th Cir.1990); *see also*, Zinnecker, Timothy R., Lender Liability Under CERCLA and the Fleeting Protection of the Secured Creditor Exemption, 44 SW.L.J 1449 (1991).

For example in *United States v. Fleet Factors Corp.*, the government sued the creditor of a bankrupt cloth printing facility who held a security interest in the facility, its equipment, inventories, and fixtures.[274] The court held that the secured creditor may be liable as an owner and operator, even though it did not actually influence the facility's treatment of hazardous waste.[275] "[A] secured creditor will be liable if its involvement with the management of the facility is sufficiently broad to support the inference that it could affect hazardous waste disposal decisions if it so chose."[276] Under the *Fleet Factors* standard a lender could incur CERCLA liability simply by having been in the position to control the borrower's hazardous waste decisions, regardless if the lender actually exercised that control.[277]

The *Fleet Factors* decision caused considerable discomfort in financial circles and even prompted some lenders to abandon properties rather than foreclose for fear of liability.[278] As a result, in 1992, EPA established new regulations defining the security interest holder exemption.[279] Under this new regulation, EPA's rule indicated that a lender would be considered to be participating in the management of its borrower only if it either (1) exercised decision making control over the borrower's environmental compliance such that it had "undertaken responsibility for the borrower's hazardous substance handling or disposal practices," or (2) exercised control "at a level comparable to that of a manager of the borrower's enterprise, such that the holder had assumed or manifested responsibility for the overall management of the enterprise encompassing the day-to-day decision making of the enterprise" with respect to environmental compliance or all, or substantially all, of the operational

---

[274]   *Id.*

[275]   *Id.* at 1555.

[276]   *Id.* at 1558.

[277]   Greenberg, Michael I. & Shaw, David M., To Lend Or Not To Lend -- That Should Not Be The Question: The Uncertainties Of Lender Liability Under CERCLA, 41 Duke L.J. 1211, 1217 (1992).

[278]   Kelly v. United States EPA, 1994 WL 27881 (D.C. Cir.1994).

[279]   National Oil and Hazardous Substances Pollution Contingency Plan, 57 Fed. Reg. 18,344, 18382 (1992).

(as opposed to financial or administrative) aspects of the enterprise other than environmental compliance.[280]

6.   Inheritance or Bequest

A person may avoid CERCLA liability where property containing hazardous waste was acquired by inheritance or bequest. CERCLA excludes from the definition of "contractual relationship," transfers of title or possession of property containing hazardous substances if the defendant can prove that the property was acquired by inheritance or bequest.[281] However, a defendant must still make a reasonable inquiry into the environmental conditions of the property in order to avoid CERCLA liability. This reasonable inquiry helps a defendant meet the "due care" requirements of the third party "innocent landowner" defense.[282] After a reasonable inquiry, if no contamination is discovered, then this exception could also insulate executors, guardians, custodians and trustees from liability as owners. However, this defense will not apply to fiduciaries of an estate who have held property for a long period of time after acquiring control through inheritance or bequest.[283]

J.   SETTLEMENTS

The purpose of CERCLA settlements is to determine allocation of PRP responsibility without resorting to costly and time-consuming litigation. By settling, PRPs may agree to undertake cleanup work, knowing in advance the

---

[280]   40 C.F.R. § 300.1100(c)(1); for an excellent discussion of EPA's Lender Liability Rule, *see* Miller, Jeffrey G. and Johnston, Craig N., The Law of Hazardous Waste Disposal and Remediation (West Publishing Co. 1996)

[281]   CERCLA § 101(35)(A)(iii); 42 U.S.C.A. § 9601(35)(A)(iii); *see also*, McReynolds, H. Lewis, The Unsuspecting Fiduciary and Beneficiary as "Owner Or Operator" of a Hazardous Waste Facility Under CERCLA, 44 Baylor L. Rev. 71, 89 (1992).

[282]   Rodosevich, Denise, The Expansive Reach of CERCLA Liability: Potential Liability of Executors of Wills and Inter Vivos and Testamentary Trustees, 55 Alb. L. Rev. 143, 178, n.132 (1991).

[283]   McReynolds, *supra* note 281 at 91.

percentage of the costs they will each be responsible for.[284] Formal settlement negotiation is initiated when EPA sends "notice letters" to PRPs that contain the names and addresses of other PRPs, the volume and nature of substances contributed by each PRP, and a ranking by volume of the substances at the site.[285] In addition, EPA must provide notice to the public of any settlement agreement, publish the proposed settlement in the Federal Register, and then provide 30 days for the public to comment in response.[286] There are several types of settlements authorized under Section 122 of CERCLA: mixed-work settlements, mixed-funding settlements, non-binding preliminary allocation of responsibility settlements (NBARs), and de minimis settlements. EPA also allows for cash settlements, cash-out settlements, and covenants not to sue.

1.   Mixed-Work Settlements

A mixed-work settlement is one in which the actual cleanup is a cooperative effort between EPA and the PRPs.[287] It is totally within EPA's discretion to determine whether they wish to enter into a mixed-work settlement.[288] In making this decision, EPA considers the strength of the case against the PRPs, the amount offered by the PRPs, the good faith of the PRPs, whether a mixed-work settlement will achieve the goal of a quick cleanup, and EPA's options should negotiations fail.[289]

2.   Mixed-Fund Settlements

A mixed-fund settlement is one in which EPA and PRPs agree to both clean up a site using both PRP resources and funds from the Superfund. For

---

[284]   Boomgaarden, Lynnette & Breer, Charles, Surveying The Superfund Settlement Dilemma, 27 Land & Water L. Rev. 83, 87-88 (1992).

[285]   *Id.* at 89.

[286]   *Id.*

[287]   CERCLA § 122(d)(1)(A); 42 U.S.C.A. § 9622(d)(1)(A); *See also*, Boomgaarden, *supra* note 284 at 92.

[288]   *Id.*

[289]   *Id.*

example, mixed-funding is used when EPA finds that one group of PRPs is willing to settle while another group of PRPs is not.[290]

CERCLA provides:[291]

> An agreement . . . may provide that the President [EPA] will reimburse the parties to the agreement from the Fund . . . for certain costs of actions . . . the parties have agreed to perform but which the President [EPA] has agreed to finance. In any case . . . [of such] reimbursement, the President [EPA] shall make all reasonable efforts to recover the amount of such reimbursement under section [107] . . . .

Section 122(b)(1) enables EPA to settle with willing PRPs and pay for the costs attributable to the non-settlors from the Superfund, and later, sue the non-settling parties for the remainder of the response and remediation costs.[292] The result is a combination of Superfund and PRP resources working together to remediate hazardous substance contamination.[293]

3. Non-Binding Preliminary Allocation of Responsibility (NBAR)

The NBAR process allows EPA to allocate a percentage of a site's response costs among PRPs.[294] NBARs reduce costs by apportioning 100% of

---

[290] Crable, Stephen, ADR: A Solution For Environmental Disputes, 48 Arb. J. 24, 28 (March 1993).

[291] CERCLA § 122(b)(1); 42 U.S.C.A. § 9622(b)(1).

[292] CERCLA § 122(b)(1); 42 U.S.C.A. § 9622(b)(1).

[293] Feldman, Stephen M., CERCLA Liability, Where it is and Where it Should Not be Going: The Possibility of Liability Release For Environmentally Beneficial Land Transfers, 23 Envtl. L. 295, 315 (1993).

[294] CERCLA § 122(e)(3)(A); 42 U.S.C.A. § 9622(e)(3)(A) ("When it would expedite settlement the President [EPA] may provide a non-binding preliminary allocation of responsibility [NBAR] which allocates percentages of the total cost of response among potentially responsible parties at the facility."); see also, Reardon, James J., Jr., Limiting Municipal Solid Waste Liability Under CERCLA: Towards the Toxic Cleanup Equity & Acceleration Act of 1993, 20 B.C. Envtl. Aff. L. Rev. 533, 545 (1993).

the liability at an early stage, administratively instead of judicially.[295] The NBAR is not binding on either the government nor PRPs. It is a preliminary process in that PRPs are free to agree to different allocations of percentages set by EPA. For example, if an NBAR alleged Company A was 20% liable and Company B 80% liable; these PRPs could counter offer to EPA that each company be 50% liable. Regardless of how PRPs allocate percentages of liability among themselves, the counter offer must account for 100% of the total liability.

Under Section 122, EPA may issue an NBAR to expedite settlement.[296] EPA rarely uses this authority because the NBAR acts as an offer for settlement that, if rejected, requires EPA to provide a written explanation for the rejection. An NBAR may be used for cleanup allocations, response costs, recovery actions, or de minimis cash-out settlements. A brief outline of the NBAR process follows:

1)   First, EPA notifies all PRPs and offers the NBAR process. Alternatively, EPA may prepare an NBAR at the request of a group of PRPs, to assist the parties in apportioning the cleanup costs among themselves.[297]

2)   Within 60 days of notification by EPA, PRPs must negotiate allocations and responsibilities among themselves and make an offer to settle in good faith to EPA.[298]

3)   Next, EPA either accepts the offer or, if requested by the PRPs, provides an additional 60 days for negotiation. 120 days is the

---

[295]   *Id.*

[296]   *Id.*

[297]   Littell, David, Consent And Disclosure In Superfund Negotiations: Identifying And Avoiding Conflicts of Interest Arising From Multiple Client Representation, 17 Harv. Envtl. L. Rev. 225 (1993).

[298]   CERCLA § 122(e)(4); 42 U.S.C.A. § 9622(e)(4).

maximum time period allowed under CERCLA for PRPs to consider an NBAR settlement.[299]

4)   If settlement does not occur within 120 days, the NBAR becomes void and EPA may then sue the PRPs.[300]

In order to protect settling PRPs, NBARs are not admissible as evidence in court.[301]   In addition, no court has jurisdiction to review an NBAR.[302] Furthermore, an NBAR is not a legal apportionment or statement of divisibility of harm, and all costs of performing an NBAR are response costs recoverable under CERCLA Section 107.[303]   Note that the NBAR process is not binding on future settlement negotiations nor on litigation involving the PRPs.[304]

4.   De Minimis Settlements

Whenever practicable and when in the public interest, EPA may enter into a final settlement with a PRP if such a settlement involves only a minor portion of the response costs at the site and, in the judgement of EPA, either of the following two conditions are met:[305]

1)   the amount of hazardous substances contributed by a PRP to the facility are minimal in comparison to other hazardous substances found at the facility; or the level of toxicity or other hazardous effects of the substances contributed by the PRP to the facility is minimal in

---

[299]   *Id.*

[300]   *Id.*

[301]   CERCLA § 122(e)(3)(C); 42 U.S.C.A. § 9622(e)(3)(C).

[302]   *Id.*

[303]   CERCLA § 122(e)(3)(D); 42 U.S.C.A. § 9622(e)(3)(D).

[304]   Dinkins, Carol E. & Nutt, C. David, Settlement Issues In Superfund Cases, C757 ALI-ABA 777 (1992).

[305]   CERCLA § 122(g)(1); 42 U.S.C.A. § 9622(g)(1).

comparison to other hazardous substances found at the facility; or

2)   the PRP qualifies as a true "innocent landowner."

De minimis parties who are innocent landowners are "those landowners who, in the [j]udgement of the [a]gency . . . during the term of ownership did not conduct or permit the generation, transportation, storage, treatment, or disposal of any hazardous substances at the facility."[306] For innocent landowners to qualify as de minimis settlors, they must show that they:[307]

1)   are the owners of the real property where the facility is located;

2)   did not conduct or permit the generation, transportation, storage, treatment, or disposal of any hazardous substance at the facility; and

3)   did not contribute to the release or threat of release of a hazardous substance at the facility through any action or omission.

A de minimis settlement is not allowed if a PRP purchased property knowing it was used for either generation, transport, storage, treatment, or disposal of any hazardous substance.[308]

The goal of de minimis settlements is to encourage qualifying parties to resolve their potential liability as quickly as possible. This results in minimal litigation costs and allows the government to focus resources on other areas such as negotiations and litigation with major hazardous substance contributors.[309]

---

[306]   54 Fed. Reg. 34235 (Aug. 18, 1989).

[307]   CERCLA § 122(g)(1); 42 U.S.C.A. § 9622(g)(1).

[308]   *Id.*

[309]   54 Fed. Reg. at 34239.

The de minimis settlement is entered through either a judicial consent decree or administrative order.[310] In return for a de minimis settlement, a landowner is required to provide EPA access to the site, and cooperate in all response activities.[311] In addition, EPA may also require that the landowner provide assurances that it will continue to exercise due care.[312] A PRP who is an innocent landowner is required to file in the local deed records a notice stating that hazardous substances were disposed on-site and that EPA has made no representation as to the appropriate use of the property.[313] In return, a *de minimis* settler will be insulated from contribution actions from other PRPs.

5.   Cash-Out Settlements

A cash-out settlement is a cash payment made to the Superfund or a site-specific fund in lieu of performing cleanup work at the site.[314] In a "cash-out" settlement, a premium is paid up front for the right to assume title without fear of future liability.[315] Once the PRP has paid the settlement, it cannot be sued by other PRPs for contribution.   Most de minimis PRPs prefer cash-out settlements.[316] Prior to 1986, many de minimis PRPs refused to participate in settlement negotiations because the costs of negotiations often exceeded the costs of liability.[317] However, Section 122 resolved this dilemma by authorizing EPA

---

[310]   CERCLA § 122(g)(4); 42 U.S.C.A. § 9622(g)(4).

[311]   54 Fed. Reg. 34,240.

[312]   *Id.*

[313]   *Id.*

[314]   Mays, Richard H., EPA Enforcement Policies Under SARA: An Analysis Of Guidelines, On Releases, De Minimis Settlements, NBARS, and Mixed Funding, PLI Order No. H4-5046, 349/Lit 327 (1988).

[315]   CERCLA §§ 122(f), (g)(2); 42 U.S.C.A. §§ 9622(f), (g)(2); *see also*, Feldman, Stephen M., CERCLA Liability, Where It Is And Where It Should Not Be Going: The Possibility Of Liability Release For Environmentally Beneficial Land Transfers, 23 Envtl. L. 295, 319 (1993).

[316]   Feldman, *supra* note 316 at 319.

[317]   Dinkins and Nutt, *supra* note 305 at 6.

to reach cash-out settlements with PRPs who were considered de minimis, and to site owners who were unaware of or had no reason to be aware of contamination upon acquisition of the property.[318]

6. Covenants Not To Sue

A covenant not to sue is a promise not to sue. "Covenants not to sue" provisions are usually offered in settlement consent agreements. EPA may offer a PRP a covenant not to sue as long as the following conditions are met:[319]

1) the covenant not to sue is in the public interest;

2) the covenant not to sue would expedite response action consistent with the NCP;

3) the person is in full compliance with a consent decree under Section 106 for response to the release or threatened release concerned; and

4) the response action has been approved by EPA.

Note, once a covenant not to sue is established, EPA must except any liability related to a release or threatened release which arises from conditions at the site that are unknown at the time the remedial action is complete.[320]

V. GOVERNMENT CLEANUP OPTIONS

The federal government has two options it can use to clean up a hazardous waste site. First, the government can clean up the site itself under the authority of Section 104. This type of cleanup is funded from the Hazardous Waste Superfund. Once the government uses Superfund money to clean up a site, it can then initiate a cost recovery action against those who polluted the site

---

[318] CERCLA §§ 122(f), (g)(2); 42 U.S.C.A. §§ 9622(f), (g)(2).

[319] CERCLA § 122(f); 42 U.S.C.A. § 9622(f).

[320] CERCLA § 122(f)(6)(A); 42 U.S.C.A. § 9622(f)(6)(A); *see also*, Addison, Frederick W., III, Reopener Liability Under Section 122 Or CERCLA: "From Here To Eternity," 45 S.W.L.J. 1081 (1991).

by establishing their liability under Section 107.[321] Second, EPA can issue a unilateral administrative order under Section 106 requiring site cleanup by those parties it believes are responsible.[322] Such administrative orders are called "Section 106 Orders."[323]

Under Sections 104 and 106, CERCLA requires that the contamination at a site "present an imminent and substantial danger to the public health or welfare." The term "imminent and substantial danger" is not specifically defined in CERCLA. However, in *United States v. Conservation Chemical*, the District Court held that EPA need only show that there "is a reasonable cause for concern that someone or something may be exposed to a risk of harm" to satisfy the endangerment requirement.[324] EPA does not have to prove that an "imminent and substantial danger" actually exists because the statute clearly authorizes EPA to obtain relief when there may be an "imminent and substantial danger."[325]

---

[321] CERCLA § 107; 42 U.S.C.A. § 9607.

[322] CERCLA § 106; 42 U.S.C.A. § 9606.

[323] CERCLA § 106(a); 42 U.S.C.A. § 9606(a) ("When the [EPA] determines that there may be an imminent and substantial endangerment to the public health or welfare or the environment because of an actual or threatened release of a hazardous substance from a facility, [EPA] may . . . secure such relief as may be necessary to abate such danger or threat . . . . including but not limited to, issuing such orders as may be necessary to protect public health, welfare and the environment").

[324] United States v. Conservation Chemical, 619 F.Supp. at 194, ("the quantities of dioxin and other compounds found at the Deny farm site were highly toxic at low dosage levels and given the conditions of the soil and bedrock beneath the site, there was a substantial likelihood of human and environmental exposure").

[325] J.V. Peters & Co., Inc. v. Ruckelshaus, 584 F.Supp. at 1010; *see also*, United States v. Northeastern Pharmaceutical and Chemical Co., 810 F.2d at 734, (because of the region's soil conditions, there was a substantial likelihood that hazardous waste in a trench could enter the environment and migrate into groundwater. Thus, without considering the concentration of the hazardous substances, the point of exposure, nor the number of persons or organisms that might be exposed, the court found that the conditions of the site presented an imminent and substantial danger); United States v. Seymour Recycling Corp., 618 F.Supp. 1 (S.D.Ind.1984) (although studies did not show an immediate danger to people using water wells in the subdivision, the District Court found that because the groundwater flowed toward the subdivision and contaminants could be expected to reach those residences, an imminent and substantial endangerment

For example, in *United States v. Dickerson*, EPA filed suit seeking immediate access to a CERCLA site under Section 106 to clean a creosote release.[326] The District Court granted the request and set forth the following standard:[327]

> In order to establish its right to conduct a [Section 104] response action . . . EPA must establish that it has a reasonable basis to believe that there has been or may be a release of a hazardous substance into the environment, or that there has been or there is a substantial threat of release into the environment of a pollutant or contaminant which may present an imminent and substantial danger to the public health or welfare. It must further demonstrate that this conclusion is not arbitrary and capricious, an abuse of discretion, or otherwise not in accordance with law . . . . Congress has already determined that the substances classified as being hazardous . . . meet that criterion as a matter of law . . . since the EPA contends that hazardous substances have been and continue to be released . . . the EPA need only demonstrate that there has been a release or may be a release of a hazardous substance.

A. SECTION 104 CLEANUP ACTIONS

Section 104 provides EPA with the authority to actually go onto and clean contaminated sites[328] that "present an imminent and substantial danger to the public health or welfare."[329] Under Section 104(a)(1), EPA is authorized to

---

was present. Because hazardous substances are capable of causing serious harm, a substantial endangerment may exist when a release or threatened release of a hazardous substance places the environment or the public at risk).

[326] United States v. Dickerson, 660 F.Supp. 227 (M.D.Ga.1987).

[327] *Id.* at 231.

[328] CERCLA § 104(a); 42 U.S.C.A. § 9604(a).

[329] CERCLA § 104(a)(1); 42 U.S.C.A. 9604(a)(1) (Whenever (A) any hazardous substance is released or there is a substantial threat of such release into the environment, or (B) there is a release or substantial threat of release into the environment of any pollutant or contaminant which may present an imminent and substantial danger to the public health or welfare . . . the [EPA] is authorized to act, consistent with the national contingency plan, to remove or arrange for the removal of, and provide for remedial

respond to a release or threatened release of both hazardous substances and pollutants or contaminants.[330] In *Dickerson v. United States EPA*, the Appellate Court held that a demonstration of "imminent and substantial" danger must be present for EPA to remove pollutants and contaminants, not only hazardous substances.[331]

Under CERCLA, the statutory definition of "pollutants or contaminants" is so broad that it refers to basically any substance that may reasonably be anticipated to cause harm to the environment.[332] The rationale is that "[t]he `pollutant or contaminant' provision is designed to cover dangerous substances that have not been captured by the `hazardous substance' provisions of CERCLA."[333]

There are important consequences that result when labeling a material either a "pollutant or contaminant" or a "hazardous substance." While response authority and funding under CERCLA apply to releases of hazardous substances and pollutants or contaminants, the government cannot bring a cost recovery

---

action . . . or take any other response measure consistent with the national contingency plan . . . necessary to protect the public health or welfare or the environment").

[330]   Eagle Picher Industries v. United States EPA, 759 F.2d at 931.

[331]   CERCLA § 104(a)(1)(B); 42 U.S.C.A. § 9604(a)(1)(B); Dickerson v. United States EPA, 834 F.2d 974, 977 (11th Cir.1987).

[332]   CERCLA § 101(33); 42 U.S.C.A. § 9601(33) (The term "pollutant or contaminant" shall include, but not be limited to, any element, substance, compound, or mixture, including disease causing agents which after release into the environment and upon exposure, ingestion, inhalation, or assimilation into any organism either directly from the environment or indirectly by ingestion through food chains, will or may reasonably be anticipated to cause death, disease, behavioral abnormalities, cancer, genetic mutation, physiological malfunctions, or physical deformations, in such organisms or their offspring; except that the term "pollutant or contaminant" shall not include petroleum, including crude oil or any fraction thereof which is not otherwise specifically listed or designated as a hazardous substance . . . and shall not include natural gas, liquefied natural gas, or synthetic gas of pipeline quality).

[333]   Eagle Picher Industries v. United States EPA, 759 F.2d at 931.

action for a "pollutant or contaminant" like it can for a "hazardous substance."[334] For example, under Section 107, the owner of a facility may be liable for cleanup of a release or threatened release of a 'hazardous substance,' but not for the cleanup of a release of a 'pollutant or contaminant.'[335] Note however, that under Section 104(a)(1), EPA is authorized to respond to a release or threatened release of both hazardous substances and pollutants or contaminants.[336]

B.   SECTION 106 ORDERS

EPA can also issue a unilateral administrative order under Section 106 to require cleanup by those parties it believes are responsible.[337] Such administrative orders are called "Section 106 Orders."[338] These types of orders are far more appealing to the federal government than Section 104 actions because they do not require the government to spend any money on cleanup efforts. EPA may file a Section 106 Order to "secure such relief as may be necessary to abate such danger or threat" and issue "such orders as may be necessary to protect public health and welfare and the environment."[339]

1.   Enforcement Remedies

Under Section 106, EPA may issue administrative orders or seek injunctive relief through the courts to mandate that PRPs clean up a site

---

[334]   Crough, Maureen M. & Ramsey, Stephen D., The Superfund Amendments And Reauthorization Act of 1986, C266 ALI-ABA 27, 29 (1988).

[335]   CERCLA § 107, 42 U.S.C.A. § 9607; Eagle Picher Industries v. United States EPA, 759 F.2d at 932.

[336]   Eagle Picher Industries v. United States EPA, 759 F.2d at 931.

[337]   CERCLA § 106; 42 U.S.C.A. § 9606.

[338]   CERCLA § 106(a); 42 U.S.C.A. § 9606(a) ("When the [EPA] determines that there may be an imminent and substantial endangerment to the public health or welfare or the environment because of an actual or threatened release of a hazardous substance from a facility, [EPA] may . . . secure such relief as may be necessary to abate such danger or threat . . . . including but not limited to, issuing such orders as may be necessary to protect public health and welfare and the environment").

[339]   *Id.*

themselves.[340] Section 106(a) authorizes EPA to go to federal court and obtain a court order compelling persons to clean up a site.[341]

2.   Violations of Section 106 Orders

Persons who fail to comply with a Section 106 order may be subject to penalties of up to $25,000 per day for each day of noncompliance if the violation was "without sufficient cause."[342] Note that SARA gives a party the option of complying with the order and then seeking reimbursement from the Superfund if they can show that "the response action ordered was arbitrary and capricious or was otherwise not in accordance with the law."[343]

VI.   CONCLUSION

CERCLA was enacted to help clean the dangerous conditions at abandoned hazardous waste sites. One of its mechanisms to motivate such cleanup efforts is through the use of the hazardous waste Superfund. This fund was created to help assist in the enormous costs associated with cleaning up hazardous waste sites. CERCLA confronts contamination by providing for investigation, identification and cleanup standards of abandoned hazardous waste sites, funds for such actions and the imposition of liability upon potentially responsible parties. Specifically, CERCLA provides both the government and private citizens the necessary legal mechanisms to clean up sites themselves (with rights for reimbursement) or to compel such responsible parties to clean up polluted sites at their own expense.

CERCLA is a very controversial law because it forces those who caused environmental contamination in the past (before regulations and pollution prevention laws were enacted) to pay for today's cleanups of polluted sites. However, because of strong public policy and governmental interests in cleaning up these hazardous waste sites, CERCLA's retroactive provision has withstood constitutional challenge and review. In an ideal world of pollution prevention

---

[340]   *See* Boomgaarden, *supra* note 284 at 86-87.

[341]   CERCLA § 106(a); 42 U.S.C.A. § 9606(a).

[342]   CERCLA § 106(b)(1); 42 U.S.C.A. § 9606(b)(1).

[343]   *Id.*

and minimization, with adequate natural resource management programs, laws like CERCLA would not be necessary. However, in a growing, industrialized society, dependent upon the use and enjoyment of natural resources, it is imperative that threats posing serious danger to human health and the environment be cleaned up. CERCLA provides Americans with the necessary legal tools to clean up such environmental threats.

CHAPTER 5

THE CLEAN AIR ACT
(CAA)

*"The use of the sea and air is common to all;
. . . neither nature nor public use and custom
permit any possession thereof."*

- Elizabeth I

CHAPTER 5: THE CLEAN AIR ACT

I.   INTRODUCTION

The Clean Air Act (CAA) is the primary federal statute regulating the emission of air pollutants.[1] The act's intent is to protect and enhance the quality of the nation's air, public health and welfare.[2] The current CAA has evolved through a series of acts passed by Congress between 1955 and 1990.[3]

The primary objective of the CAA is to regulate emissions of air pollutants in order to protect human health and the environment.[4] In general, the CAA delegates responsibility to state and local governments to prevent and control air pollution. It does this by requesting states to submit state implementation plans (SIPs) to EPA for program approval and delegation of

---

[1]   Air Pollution Control Act, Pub.L. No. 84-145, 69 Stat. 322 (1955).

[2]   CAA § 101; 42 U.S.C.A. § 7401.

[3]   Air Pollution Control Act, Pub.L. No. 84-145, 69 Stat. 322 (1955); Clean Air Act, Pub.L. No. 88-206, 77 Stat. 392 (1963); Air Quality Act, 42 U.S.C.A. § 76, Pub. L. No. 90-148, 81 Stat. 485 (1967); 1990 Clean Air Act.

[4]   *See* generally, Manewitz, Mark L., Clean Air Act Overview, 459 PLI/LIT 99 (1993).

implementation responsibilities. SIPs are written plans that states develop to provide for attainment and maintenance of the National Ambient Air Quality Standards (NAAQS). This gives states the authority to regulate air pollution activities within their own boundaries. If a state fails to create and implement an adequate SIP, EPA must create and implement its own SIP for that state.[5]

The post 1990 CAA contains many programs. Three of the more recent programs require EPA to draft regulations and create programs to control pollutants emitted by mobile sources, to control pollutants considered to cause or contribute to acid rain, and to establish a schedule for phasing out the production and use of substances which cause or contribute to stratospheric ozone depletion.

A.   NEW PROGRAMS

1.   Mobile Source Regulations

The CAA regulates mobile sources.[6] Mobile sources include automobiles, aircraft, buses, off-road vehicles and certain engines. For example, the CAA has implemented new restrictive tailpipe emission standards for automobiles.[7] These standards include requirements to produce clean alternative fuels such as methanol, ethanol and reformulated gasoline.[8] The act also implements a fleet vehicle program for large employers that requires the use of clean fuels in many nonattainment areas, and in some cities, requires large employers to create carpool programs to reduce the number of commuters to job sites.[9] The CAA has also implemented new on-board vapor recovery and

---

[5]   CAA § 110; 42 U.S.C.A. § 7410.

[6]   CAA §§ 202-250; 42 U.S.C.A. §§ 7521-7590; see, Arnold W. Reitze, Jr., Mobile Source Air Pollution Control, 6 Envtl. Law 309 (2000).

[7]   CAA § 177; 42 U.S.C.A. § 7507; CAA § 202(m); 42 U.S.C.A. § 7521(m).

[8]   CAA § 182(e)(3); 42 U.S.C.A. § 7511a(e)(3); 40 C.F.R. Part 88; 57 Fed. Reg. 60,046 (Dec. 17, 1992); 58 Fed. Reg. 11,901 (Mar. 1, 1993).

[9]   CAA §§ 241-249; 42 U.S.C.A. §§ 7581-7589.

evaporative emission controls on all new combustible fuel engines.[10] In addition, the CAA authorizes EPA to propose emission standards for aircraft engines which cause or contribute to air pollution which may endanger public health or welfare.[11]

2.   Acid Rain Regulations

Acid rain deposits airborne acids, not just in rain, but also in snow, fog, and dry acidic particles.[12] The primary source of acid rain is burning of coal and oil in electrical power plants, industrial boilers, and internal combustion engines. Burning fossil fuel produces sulfur dioxide and oxides of nitrogen. In the atmosphere, these compounds react chemically with ozone and other compounds to form sulfuric and nitric acids - the acids in acid rain. There is clear evidence that acid rain causes biological damage in acid-sensitive lakes and streams. Small changes in acid loading, and thus lake acidity, may make lakes uninhabitable for many species.[13]

The CAA authorizes EPA to promulgate regulations to control and dramatically cut acid rain precursors.[14] This includes a 10 million ton reduction in sulfur dioxide (SO_2) emissions and a two million ton reduction in nitrogen

---

[10]   CAA § 202(a)(6); 42 U.S.C.A. § 7521(a)(6); *see*, The Movement Against Destruction v. Trainor, 400 F.Supp. 533 (D.Md. 1975) (discussion of potential implementation problems involving the mobile source regulations).

[11]   CAA § 231; 42 U.S.C.A. § 7571.

[12]   THE ENCYCLOPEDIA OF THE ENVIRONMENT, pg. 1, (Ruth A. Eblen & William R. Eblen, eds. 1994).

[13]   *Id.* at 2; *see also*, Indianapolis Power & Light Company v. United States EPA, 58 F.3d 643 (D.C. Cir.1995) (excellent explanation of the acid rain program); *see also*, May, James R., The Real Acid Test of Title IV of the Clean Air Act Amendments of 1990: External Cost Justifications Not Related to Acid Deposition Control, 3 Fordham Envtl. L. Representative. 97 (1992) (for a discussion of some of the problems and costs associated with the acid rain program).

[14]   CAA §§ 401-416(o); 42 U.S.C.A. §§ 7651-7651(o); *see,* State of New York v. Browner, 1999 WL 364277, (N.D.N.Y. 1999); *see also*, Dallas Burtraw & Byron Swift, A New Standard of Performance: An Analysis of the Clean Air Act's Acid Rain Program, 26 ELR 10411 (1996).

oxide (NOx) emissions. Phase I controls for 111 coal-fired power plants began in 1995.[15] Phase II controls on most power plants are to be in effect by the year 2000.[16]

To comply with the acid deposition control regulations, electric utilities face difficult choices for electric utilities on whether and how to use high or low sulfur coal, oil, or nuclear fuels, and whether to incur the cost of new capital equipment to control emissions.[17] These choices have become more difficult in recent years by government mandated programs requiring utilities to purchase power from cogeneration plants and to run power through their lines and facilities for the benefit of customers who wish to purchase power from distant sources.[18]

3.   Stratospheric Ozone Protection

In order to comply with certain international treaties designed to protect stratospheric ozone, the CAA authorizes EPA to regulate substances which cause or contribute significantly to harmful effects upon the earth's ozone shield. The ozone shield serves to protect the earth from harmful ultraviolet rays.

The CAA lists several categories of chlorofluorocarbons, halons, hydrochlorofluorocarbons, carbon tetrachlorides, and methyl chloroforms as ozone depleting substances.[19] CAA regulations affect many appliances or devices which contain the listed substances. Most of the ozone depleting substances are refrigerants used in air conditioners, refrigerators, and freezers.[20] These

---

[15]   CAA § 404(c); 42 U.S.C.A. § 7651(c).

[16]   CAA § 405(d); 42 U.S.C.A. § 7651(d).

[17]   Shea, Edward E., Introduction to U.S. Environmental Laws, Oceana Publications, p. 16 (1995); *see also, Appalachian Power Company v. Environmental Protection Agency*, 135 F.3d 791(D.C.Cir. 1998).

[18]   Shea *supra* note 17 at 17.

[19]   CAA § 602; 42 U.S.C.A. § 7671a.

[20]   CAA § 601; 42 U.S.C.A. § 7671.

regulations have pushed industry to research and develop alternative substances that do not harm the earth's ozone shield.

B. MAJOR PROGRAMS

In addition to mobile source, acid rain and stratospheric ozone protection regulations, the CAA contains five major programs. These programs include: new source performance standards (NSPS), national ambient air quality standards (NAAQS), non-attainment areas program (NA), prevention of significant deterioration program (PSD), and national emission standards for hazardous air pollutants program (NESHAPs).

1. New Source Performance Standards (NSPS)

NSPS are emission standards for new or modified stationary sources. These sources include categories or classes of facilities that EPA determines cause or contribute significantly to air pollution.[21] New and modified sources are targeted by this program because incorporation of pollution controls and technologies is easier and less expensive for sources about to be built or modified (as compared to the even more costly expense of forcing pre-existing sources to upgrade their equipment or technology).

NSPS are technology-based emission limits that restrict the quantities or concentrations of air pollutants a source may emit. These performance standards are established by EPA to reflect the degree of emission limitations achievable through the application of the best technological system of continuous emission reduction that EPA determines has been adequately demonstrated by similar sources in industry. EPA must weigh factors such as costs, environmental risks, and the ability of technology to provide the necessary equipment, designs or methods of operation for compliance with NSPS.

2. National Ambient Air Quality Standards (NAAQS)

National Ambient Air Quality Standards (NAAQS) are air quality standards that EPA sets as a goal for acquiring high levels of clean air. NAAQS set standards for maximum allowable concentrations of air pollutants in the ambient air, measured at various locations set in the standards. Thus, the

---

[21]   CAA § 111(b)(1)(A); 42 U.S.C.A. § 7411(b)(1)(A).

NAAQS are not emissions limitations for the maximum allowable releases from stationary or mobile sources. Instead, they are the goal of cleanliness for the entire nation.

To date, EPA has only targeted six pollutants under this program. The pollutants are known as "criteria pollutants." These six pollutants include: carbon monoxide, lead, nitrogen oxides, ozone, particulate matter and sulfur dioxide. The decision to regulate these pollutants is based on criteria documents created by EPA. Criteria documents show the health and environmental effects of each pollutant, and determine whether the pollutant is a known hazard to human health and the environment. Upon studying the criteria documents, EPA determines the safe, allowable levels or amounts of these pollutants that should have no adverse effects on humans or the environment.

NAAQS have been divided into two standards, primary and secondary. Both standards are applied to the six criteria pollutants. Primary standards protect human health. Secondary standards protect the public welfare, which "includes, but is not limited to, effects on soils, water, crops, vegetation, manmade materials, animals, wildlife, weather, visibility, climate, and damage to and deterioration of property."[22]

3. Nonattainment Areas (NA) Program

A nonattainment area (NA) is an area that fails to meet the NAAQS.[23] Emission limitation standards for stationary sources are much stricter in areas that have not met goals set by the NAAQS. The purpose is to bring the NA region into compliance so the state's emissions are maintained at acceptable levels once they have met the NAAQS. The emission standards are set by nonattainment regulations and apply to new major sources and major modifications of existing sources. A major source is one that "emits or has the potential to emit, one hundred tons per year or more of any air pollutant."[24] In addition, each new or modified source must be constructed using the lowest achievable emission rate technology (LAER) available. This means that any new

---

[22] CAA § 302(h); 42 U.S.C.A. § 7602(h).

[23] CAA § 171(2); 42 U.S.C.A. § 7501(2).

[24] CAA § 302(j); 42 U.S.C.A. § 7602(j).

or modified source must install the most stringent pollution control technology available.[25]

4. Prevention of Significant Deterioration (PSD)

The Prevention of Significant Deterioration (PSD) program preserves air quality in areas that already meet or exceed the NAAQS for clean air. This program primarily applies to industrial projects that build new facilities or increase emissions through the expansion and modification of existing facilities. New or modified facilities that create significant increases of regulated pollutants must employ strict technology-based controls (Best Available Control Technology, or BACT) to ensure the NAAQS are maintained. In other words, the goal is to prevent the significant deterioration of the air in an unpolluted area by mandating that pollution sources install strict pollution control technology.[26]

5. National Emission Standards for Hazardous Air Pollutants (NESHAPs) Program

Though the CAA establishes the NAAQS to regulate six criteria pollutants, it also provides for regulation of 189 hazardous air pollutants (HAPs) from various stationary sources. All of the pollutants listed in the National Emission Standards for Hazardous Air Pollutants (NESHAPs) are known to cause cancer, leukemia, reproductive problems, birth defects, problems with the human nervous system, lung diseases and other major disorders.[27] Under the CAA, "major" sources of HAPs must implement maximum achievable control technology (MACT) and other non-major sources, "area sources," must implement generally available control technology (GACT).

II. NEW SOURCE PERFORMANCE STANDARDS (NSPS)

A. INTRODUCTION

The NSPS program was created to regulate non-NAAQS pollutants emitted by stationary sources that are none the less found to be "harmful." This

---

[25] CAA §§ 171, 173, and 302; 42 U.S.C.A. §§ 7501, 7503, and 7602.

[26] CAA § 160; 42 U.S.C.A. § 7470.

[27] CAA § 112; 42 U.S.C.A. § 7412.

program serves as a "base" or foundation of initial environmental protection measures. The NSPS goal is to control all harmful emissions, not just NAAQS pollutants, from major new, existing, and modified sources regardless of their location. New and modified sources are held to high standards of clean air technology. The new source performance standards (NSPS) are technology-based emission limits that apply to specific pollutants on an industry-wide basis.[28] These standards have been established for more than 70 categories of sources. These standards are imposed on new and modified sources because they are in a better position economically to install newer, less polluting technology than existing sources. In fact, new sources give industry an opportunity to implement processes far superior to emission control techniques in current operation.

B.   STATUTORY SCHEME

1.   Relevant Statutory Section

Section 111 is the NSPS section.[29] This section applies to major new and existing sources of any air pollutant. The pollutants covered by this program are emitted by a specific category of sources that cause or contribute significantly to, "air pollution which may reasonably be anticipated to endanger public health or welfare."[30]

Several key terms are important to understand which pollution sources are regulated under NSPS. "Major" sources are defined as those sources that directly emit, or have the potential to emit, one hundred tons per year or more of any air pollutant.[31] The term "new" source means any stationary source, the construction or modification of which is commenced after the publication of regulations under this program.[32] "Modification" means any physical change in

---

[28]   CAA § 111; 42 U.S.C.A. § 7411.

[29]   CAA § 111; 42 U.S.C.A. § 7411; *see*, e.g., Friedman, Frank B. & Rosenberg, Ernest S., Outline of Some Major Stationary Source Issues under the Clean Air Act, as amended, L795 ALI-ABA 315 (1993).

[30]   CAA § 111(b); 42 U.S.C.A. § 7411(b).

[31]   CAA § 302(j); 42 U.S.C.A. § 7602(j).

[32]   CAA § 111(a)(2); 42 U.S.C.A. § 7411(a)(2).

the method of operation for a stationary source that increases the amount of any air pollutant emitted or which results in the emission of any air pollutant not previously emitted.[33] "Existing" sources are any stationary source other than a new source.[34]

2.   The Federal Role

a.   List of Categories

The first step in establishing NSPS is for EPA to publish a list of categories of stationary sources. EPA shall include a category of sources on the list if it causes, or contributes significantly to air pollution that may reasonably be anticipated to endanger public health or welfare.[35] EPA "may distinguish among classes, types, and sizes within categories of new sources for the purpose of establishing such standards."[36]

b.   Standards of Performance

i.   New and Modified Sources

After listing categories of stationary sources, EPA then publishes proposed regulations establishing federal standards of performance for new/modified sources within such categories.[37] The standards of performance apply to any pollutant emitted from sources in a listed category, and must reflect "the degree of emission limitation and the percentage of reduction achievable through application of the best technological system of continuous emission

---

[33]   CAA § 111(a)(4); 42 U.S.C.A. § 7411(a)(4); *see,* Wisconsin Electric Power v. Reilly, 893 F.2d 901 (7th Cir.1990).

[34]   CAA § 111(a)(2),(4); 42 U.S.C.A. § 7411(a)(2),(4).

[35]   CAA § 111(b)(1)(A); 42 U.S.C.A. § 7411(b)(1)(A).

[36]   CAA § 111(b)(2); 42 U.S.C.A. § 7411(b)(2).

[37]   CAA § 111(b)(1)(B); 42 U.S.C.A. § 7411(b)(1)(B); *see,* Central Wayne Energy Recovery, L.P. v. United States EPA , 173 F.3d 428 (6th Cir. 1999).

reduction which EPA determines has been adequately demonstrated."[38] Simply phrased, the standard of performance for major new and modified sources is the best demonstrated technology (BDT).

Standards of performance vary from one categorical source to another. EPA's role is to identify emission levels that are achievable with adequately demonstrated technology, and, after making such a determination, EPA must exercise its discretion to choose an achievable emission level that represents the best balance of economic and environmental considerations.[39]

ii.   Existing Sources

Although the NSPS program primarily targets new and modified sources, the CAA requires EPA to enact regulations asking each state to submit a plan establishing performance standards for existing sources. The plan must "take into consideration, among other factors, the remaining useful life of the existing source to which such standard applies."[40]

c.   Program Delegation

Once a state creates procedures for implementing and enforcing standards of performance for its new sources, EPA reviews the program. Upon approval, EPA delegates to the state any authority it has to implement and enforce the program.[41] If EPA does not approve the program, than EPA must create and implement its own program for the state.[42]

---

[38]   CAA § 111(a)(1); 42 U.S.C.A. § 7411(a)(1).

[39]   CAA § 111; 42 U.S.C.A. § 7411; *see also*, Sierra Club v. Costle, 657 F.2d 298 (D.C. Cir.1981).

[40]   CAA § 111(d); 42 U.S.C.A. § 7411(d); *see also*, United States v. Atlantic Richfield Co., 478 F.Supp. 1215 (D.Mont.1979).

[41]   CAA § 111(c); 42 U.S.C.A. § 7411(c).

[42]   *Id.*

3.   The State Role

a.   Program Delegation

The state develops and submits to EPA a procedure for implementing and enforcing NSPS standards of performance on new sources. If EPA delegates the program to the state, the state must implement and enforce the delegated program.[43]

b.   Permit Requirements

States translate standards of performance into source-specific emissions limitations found as conditions in a state-issued CAA permit.[44] If EPA finds it is not feasible to prescribe or enforce a standard of performance under a state issued permit, it may instead promulgate a design, equipment, work practice, or operational standard, or combination thereof, that reflects the best technological system of continuous emission reduction that has been adequately demonstrated (BDT).[45] Also, as part of the permit, Section 504 requires monitoring, testing, and periodic reporting of information to the enforcing state or federal agency.[46]

c.   Waivers

A facility may apply for a waiver of the NSPS requirements waiver if the facility proposes to use an innovative technological system that reduces emissions. The waiver allows a facility to develop, test, and demonstrate new clean air technology to be used in lieu of the technology recommended by the regulations. After a public hearing, and with the consent of the state governor, EPA may grant such a waiver.[47]

---

[43]   40 C.F.R. §§ 51.166, 52.21.

[44]   CAA § 111(c); 42 U.S.C.A. § 7411(c).

[45]   CAA § 111(h); 42 U.S.C.A. § 7411(h).

[46]   CAA § 504; 42 U.S.C.A. § 7661c.

[47]   CAA § 111(j); 42 U.S.C.A. § 7411(j).

C.   JUDICIAL INTERPRETATIONS

The following cases represent two key decisions involving the NSPS program.

1.   Arbitrary and Capricious Standards of Review

In *Sierra Club v. Costle*, the Appellate Court upheld EPA's NSPS for coal-burning power plants.[48]   The Appellate Court examined EPA's methodology, uses, models and justifications for setting performance standards for coal-burning power plants and found that EPA acted legally, within reason and not arbitrarily and capriciously.[49]

2.   NSPS and the Bubble Policy

In *Asarco, Inc. v. United States EPA,* the Appellate Court struck down EPA's NSPS standards which sought to implement the bubble policy.[50] The bubble policy allows some modifications to take place without the need for a "new source review" and the required permit prior to modification. The court interpreted the plain meaning of Section 111 to disallow the bubble policy in the NSPS program.[51] However, application of the bubble policy has been allowed in NA regions and under PSD programs.

The NSPS program was created to regulate non-NAAQS pollutants that are nonetheless found to be "harmful" and that are emitted by stationary sources. This program serves as a "base" or foundation of initial environmental protection measures. New businesses must demonstrate compliance with the NSPS before they are allowed to construct and operate any facility that would add any air

---

[48]   Sierra Club v. Costle, 657 F.2d 298 (D.C. Cir.1981).

[49]   *Id.*

[50]   The bubble policy classifies an entire plant as a single stationary source. Thus, a source "modification" for NSPS does not occur unless the change results in a net increase of pollutants emitted from the whole plant around which the bubble is drawn, instead of just a net increase from a specific pollution source within the facility. *See* e.g., Asarco, Inc. v. United States EPA, 578 F.2d 319 (D.C. Cir.1978).

[51]   *Id.*

pollutants. NSPS requires major new and modified sources to install strict pollution control technology known as "best system adequately demonstrated" for harmful pollutants emitted by specific categories of sources regardless of the facility's location. If the new source of pollution will also be emitting criteria (NAAQS) pollutants, then stricter, more protective standards will be required of each source emitting the criteria pollutant depending on whether the facility is located in either a NAAQS NA region or in an attainment area.

III.   NATIONAL AMBIENT AIR QUALITY STANDARDS (NAAQS)

A.   INTRODUCTION

The 1970 CAA contained provisions for EPA to set national ambient air quality standards, known as NAAQS.[52] These standards limit the maximum concentration levels of pollutants in the ambient (outdoor) air necessary to protect the public health and welfare.[53] Consequently, NAAQS are not concerned with air quality within buildings.

NAAQS are measured in parts of pollutant per million (micrograms per cubic meter) of ambient air. Thus, a NAAQS is measured by the level of concentration of pollutants detected in an outdoor air region (known as an air quality control region (AQCR)) not to exceed a specified amount in a specified time period. For example, for carbon monoxide, the NAAQS goal is that there shall be no more than 9 parts per million of carbon monoxide in the air of an AQCR during an eight hour period.[54] Generally, if monitoring devices detect air more polluted than the allowable amounts, the AQCR violates the NAAQS.

The NAAQS must be attained in each AQCR throughout the country. They are designed as an air quality standard and not a performance standard directly applicable to individual pollution sources. For example, the goals of the CAA are met when the air quality of both Houston, Texas and Newport, Rhode Island meet the NAAQS. This is because the NAAQS give states a target

---

[52]   40 C.F.R. § 51.166(m)(ii).

[53]   40 C.F.R. § 51.166(k)(3)(vi)(c); *see*, David M. Driesen, Should Congress Direct the EPA to Allow Serious Harms to Public Health to Continue?: Cost Benefit Tests and NAAQS under the Clean Air Act, 11 Tul.Envtl. L.J. 217 (1998).

[54]   40 C.F.R. § 50.8(a)(1).

pollution limit. The goal of the NAAQS for each state, through their own state implementation plans, is to monitor and regulate each AQCR and each individual pollution source located within its boundaries. Individual source regulation is accomplished by the state's imposition of specific performance standards upon individual pollution sources from a source's CAA permit.

Finally, the CAA mandates that the NAAQS be met by specific statutorily-defined target dates. The dates were initially set to convert the NAAQS from a goal into a reality. However, these target dates have been revised and postponed because Congress highly underestimated the complexity and difficulty involved in attainment of the NAAQS.

B.   STATUTORY SCHEME

The CAA directs EPA to establish air quality standards through the administrative rulemaking process.[55] The NAAQS establish ceilings for industry pollutant concentrations that should not be exceeded anywhere in the United States. The pollution level within an area determines the degree of control that will be imposed on new and existing pollution sources in that area. If air quality is better than the NAAQS in a particular area, then the PSD program applies. If it is worse, then the NA program applies. Despite their critical importance to the CAA, NAAQS are not directly enforceable. They are the controlling force behind the development and implementation of industry-wide regulations promulgated by EPA. These provisions are known as standards of performance, emission limitations, and work practice standards. They are imposed upon the regulated community as conditions to operating permits. Thus, it is the emissions limitations and standards of performance written into a specific permit that are actually enforced against polluters rather than the NAAQS themselves.

1.   Relevant Statutory Sections

Sections 107 through 110 are the general NAAQS sections of the CAA.[56] Section 107 describes how air quality control regions (AQCRs) are to be established. Section 108 gives EPA authority to create a list of air pollutants to

---

[55]   CAA § 109(a); 42 U.S.C.A. § 7409(a).

[56]   CAA §§ 107-110; 42 U.S.C.A §§ 7407-7410; *see*, William F. Penderson, Science and Public Policy: New Ambient Air Quality Standards under the Clean Air Act, 16 Pace Envtl. L. Rev. 15 (1998).

be regulated under this program. Section 109 requires that EPA establish both primary and secondary national ambient air quality standards called NAAQS. Finally, section 110 mandates state implementation plans (SIPs) and specifies SIP requirements.

2.   The Federal Role

Congress envisioned that each program under the CAA be jointly created and implemented by EPA and the states. In each program, the CAA establishes specific federal and state roles for implementation and enforcement of the program's goals. The federal role includes creating an air pollutants list, establishing air quality criteria, issuing air pollution control techniques, setting primary and secondary NAAQS, and reviewing and approving state implementation plans.

a.   Air Pollutants List

EPA's first step toward establishing NAAQS for a pollutant is to add it to the air pollutants list. This list is compiled by EPA and consists of air pollutants "which may reasonably be anticipated to endanger public health or welfare[.]"[57] No later than 12 months after listing an air pollutant under Section 108(a), EPA must issue "air quality criteria" for the pollutant.[58]

b.   Air Quality Criteria

Air quality criteria refers to a document prepared by EPA that provides a scientific basis for promulgation of air quality standards for an air pollutant. Air quality criteria for an air pollutant "shall accurately reflect the latest scientific knowledge useful in indicating the kind and extent of all identifiable

---

[57]   CAA § 108(a)(1); 42 U.S.C.A. § 7408(a)(1) ("for the purpose of establishing national primary and secondary ambient air quality standards, the administrator shall within 30 days after Dec. 31, 1970, publish, and shall from time to time thereafter revise, a list that includes each air pollutant- (A) which in his judgment has an adverse effect on public health or welfare; (B) the presence of which in the ambient air results from numerous or diverse mobile or stationary sources; and (C) for which air quality criteria had not been issued before Dec. 31, 1970, but for which he plans to issue air quality criteria under this section.").

[58]   CAA § 108(a)(2); 42 U.S.C.A. § 7408(a)(2).

effects on public health or welfare that may be expected from the presence of such pollutant in the ambient air in varying quantities."[59]

"Public health in this context means the health of any group of the population, including sensitive or vulnerable groups."[60] Public welfare "includes, but is not limited to, effects on soils, water, crops, vegetation, manmade materials, animals, wildlife, weather visibility, and climate, damage to and deterioration of property, and hazards to transportation, as well as effects on economic values and on personal comfort and well-being."[61] In other words, the air quality criteria documents include all relevant data demonstrating the levels of pollution and lengths of exposure that affect the public health or welfare.

c. Air Pollution Control Techniques

Simultaneously with the issuance of air quality criteria, EPA shall issue to the states and appropriate air pollution control agencies information on air pollution control techniques. This information is valuable because it allows the regulatory agencies to comply with the CAA by requiring pollution sources to achieve the "highest emission control level that is technologically and economically feasible."[62] The control techniques include data relating to the cost of installation and operation, energy requirements, emission reduction benefits, and environmental impact of emission control technology, as well as data on alternative fuels, production processes and operating methods that will eliminate or significantly reduce emissions.

The issuance of air quality criteria and information on air pollution control techniques must be published in the Federal Register and copies made available to the general public.[63] At the same time, EPA issues air quality criteria and control techniques for pollutants, it must also publish proposed

---

[59] CAA § 108(a)(2); 42 U.S.C.A. § 7408(a)(2).

[60] S.Rep. No. 6196, 91st Cong., 2d Sess. 9-10 (1970), in 1 Legis.Hist. at 409-10.

[61] CAA § 302(h); 42 U.S.C.A. § 7602(h).

[62] *See*, Bunker Hill Company v. United States EPA, 572 F.2d 1286 (9th Cir.1977).

[63] CAA § 108(d); 42 U.S.C.A. § 740.

national primary and secondary ambient air quality standards (NAAQS) for the same pollutants.[64]

d. Setting the Standards

NAAQS are standards "the attainment and maintenance of which in the judgment of the Administrator, based on such criteria and allowing an adequate margin of safety, are requisite to protect the public health."[65] EPA must establish "primary ambient air quality standards" to protect public health and "secondary ambient air quality standards" to protect public welfare.[66]

EPA must submit the proposed primary and secondary ambient air quality standards for public comment in a rulemaking proceeding,[67] and must respond to public comments.[68] Within six months of publication of the proposed primary and secondary standards, the administrator must promulgate final primary and secondary ambient air quality standards for the pollutant.[69] Once EPA has promulgated final national ambient air quality standards, responsibility under the CAA shifts from the federal government to the states.

i. Primary Standards

Primary standards must be set at levels to protect health with an adequate margin of safety.[70] Primary standards define the air quality required to prevent

---

[64] CAA § 109(a)(2); 42 U.S.C.A. § 7409(a)(2).

[65] CAA § 109(b)(1); 42 U.S.C.A § 7409(b)(1).

[66] CAA § 109(b); 42 U.S.C.A. § 7409(b).

[67] CAA § 307(d); 42 U.S.C.A. § 7607(d).

[68] APA § 553(c); 5 U.S.C.A. § 553(c).

[69] CAA § 307(d)(10); 42 U.S.C.A. § 7607(d)(10).

[70] CAA § 109(b)(1); 42 U.S.C.A. § 7409(b)(1).

any detrimental impact on human health. The primary standards must be met in all parts of the country whether inhabited or uninhabited.[71]

ii.   Secondary Standards

Secondary standards must be set at levels necessary to protect the public welfare from any known or anticipated adverse effects associated with the presence of air pollutants in the ambient air.[72] Secondary standards protect against any adverse effects on soil, water, crops, vegetation, animals, property, visibility, or on personal comfort and well-being.[73]

e.   Approval of State Implementation Plans (SIPs)

Within three years of promulgation of the final standards, each state must prepare and submit to EPA for approval, a state implementation plan (SIP).[74] After reviewing the submission, EPA proposes either to approve, disapprove, or conditionally approve the SIP.[75]

In a 1973 case, the Seventh Circuit stated that SIP approval is dependent on EPA's determination that the plan conforms with the requirements of Section 110.[76] Such requirements include:

1)   certain schedules and timetables for compliance;

---

[71]   Lead Industries v. United States EPA, 647 F.2d 1130, 1180 (D.C. Cir.1980), *cert. denied*, 449 U.S. 1042; 101 S.Ct. 621; 66 L.Ed.2d 503 (1980).

[72]   CAA § 109(b)(2); 42 U.S.C.A. § 7409(b)(2).

[73]   52 Fed. Reg. 24670.

[74]   CAA § 110(a)(1); 42 U.S.C.A. § 7410(a)(1).

[75]   CAA § 110; 42 U.S.C.A. § 7410; *see also*, Union Electric v. United States EPA, 427 U.S. 246; 96 S.Ct. 2518; 49 L.Ed.2d 474 (1976) (court upholds EPA's approval of the Missouri SIP in spite of arguments that the SIP included restrictions that were economically and technologically infeasible).

[76]   *See*, Indiana & Michigan Electric v. United States EPA, 509 F.2d 839, 840 (7th Cir.1973).

2)   provisions for the establishment and operation of appropriate devices and procedures for monitoring and analyzing ambient air quality data;

3.   procedures for reviewing the location of new sources to which the standards apply;

4)   adequate provisions for intergovernmental cooperation;

5)   assurances that the state will have adequate personnel, funding, and authority to monitor and enforce compliance; and

6)   provisions for modification of the plan to account for revisions in the NAAQS or the availability of improved and more expeditious methods for achieving compliance.[77]

If EPA approves the SIP, the elements of the submission become the applicable law for purposes of the CAA. If it disapproves the SIP, the state must submit a revised SIP. EPA has several sanctions available if a state does not submit an adequate SIP.[78]

If EPA approves the SIP, it formally promulgates the elements of the SIP. This gives the SIP the status of federal law, and is enforceable as federal law as well. Also, if a state changes an element of its SIP, the changes must be approved by EPA. These SIPs must contain emission limitations and all other measures necessary to attain the primary standards "as expeditiously as practicable," but no later than three years after EPA has approved implementation of the plan. The secondary standards must merely be met within a reasonable period.[79]

---

[77]   *Id.*

[78]   *See*, City of Highland Park v. Train, 519 F.2d 681 (7th Cir.1975).

[79]   CAA § 110(a)(2)(A) & (B); 42 U.S.C.A. § 7410(a)(2)(A) & (B).

3. The State's Role

The state's role within the NAAQS program includes drafting a detailed SIP, which helps establish air quality control regions and meets specific federal requirements. The state must submit the SIP to EPA for approval.[80]

A SIP is the primary mechanism for achieving CAA goals. Section 110(a) requires that every state prepare a SIP that provides for the "implementation, maintenance, and enforcement" of each NAAQS.[81] Within their plans, states must determine whether each air quality control region (AQCR) in their state has attained the NAAQS for each of the criteria pollutants.[82]

a. Air Quality Control Regions (AQCRs)

Though the ultimate responsibility for development and implementation of SIPs lies with the states, the CAA requires designation of AQCRs. These regions are interstate or intrastate areas which, because of common meteorological, industrial, and socioeconomic factors, should be treated as a single unit for air pollution control purposes.[83]

Thus, air quality is not measured on a state-by-state basis. Two different states may be held accountable for an AQCR and its attainment of the NAAQS within their respective states if the communities share a common air pollution problem. The act envisions that much of the attainment, assessment, and planning be regional rather than based on state boundaries.

---

[80]   CAA § 110; 42 U.S.C.A. § 7410; *see*, People of the State of California v. Department of the Navy, 431 F.Supp. 1271 (N.D.Cal.1977); *see also*, Ridge, John Hiski, Deconstructing the Clean Air Act: Examining the Controversy Surrounding Massachusetts's Adoption of the California Low Emission Vehicle Program, 22 B.C.Envtl.Aff.L.Rev. 163 (1994).

[81]   CAA § 110(a); 42 U.S.C.A. § 7410(a).

[82]   CAA § 110; 42 U.S.C.A. §7410.

[83]   CAA § 107; 42 U.S.C.A. § 7407.

AQCRs are designated by EPA or the governor of a state with EPA approval. Once a state determines whether an AQCR is in attainment of the NAAQS, it must develop an inventory of existing sources of air pollution in each AQCR. For areas that exceed the NAAQS, states must determine what emission limits must be imposed upon each individual source so that the NAAQS can be attained within the CAA's specified time lines.

b.   Contents of a SIP

Section 110(a)(2) of the CAA provides that each SIP shall:

1)   include enforceable emission limitations and other control measures as may be necessary to meet the applicable CAA requirements;

2)   provide for the appropriate devices, methods, systems and procedures to monitor, compile and analyze data on ambient air and to make such data available to EPA;

3)   include a description of the state's enforcement program designed to assure that NAAQS are achieved;

4)   contain adequate provisions demonstrating that the State will not allow activities within its boundaries that will contribute to air pollution or interfere with the SIP;

5)   assure EPA that the State will have adequate personnel, funding and legal authority to carry out the CAA requirements;

6)   require sources to install and maintain adequate equipment, and submit and make publicly available periodic emissions reports;

7)   provide for emergency and contingency plans to protect the public health and welfare from imminent and substantial endangerment;

8)   provide for SIP revisions as may be necessary;

9)   assure EPA that NA requirements are met;

10)   assure EPA that consultation, public notification and PSD requirements are met; and

11)   provide for air quality modeling.[84]

c.   Submission of SIPs to EPA

The state shall adopt and submit its SIP to EPA within three years after EPA promulgates a NAAQS. The SIP should provide for the implementation, maintenance and enforcement of the NAAQS in each of the state's AQCRs.[85]

C.   CURRENT NAAQS POLLUTANTS

Presently, six criteria pollutants are listed for which NAAQS have been set. These pollutants are found all over the United States and can injure health, harm the environment and cause property damage. The standards for these pollutants are designed to protect especially sensitive persons.[86] These six pollutants are: carbon monoxide (CO), lead (Pb), nitrogen dioxide (NO_2), ozone (O_3), particulate matter (PM_{10}) and sulfur dioxide (SO_2).

1.   CO: Carbon Monoxide

CO is a colorless, odorless and very toxic gas primarily emitted from the exhaust of gasoline powered vehicles. Inhalation of high concentrations of this gas will cause serious injury or death. Specifically, carbon monoxide affects the ability of the blood to carry oxygen, which in turn affects the cardiovascular, nervous and pulmonary systems of the human body.

2.   Pb: Lead

Lead is a heavy metal that is hazardous to health if breathed or swallowed. Its use in gasoline, paints and plumbing compounds has been sharply

---

[84]   CAA § 110(a)(2); 42 U.S.C.A. § 7410(a)(2).

[85]   CAA § 110(a)(1); 42 U.S.C.A. § 7410(a)(1); *see*, United States v. Ford Motor Company, 814 F.2d 1099, 1102 (6th Cir.1987), *cert. denied*, 484 U.S. 822 (1987).

[86]   CAA § 108(a)(1)(A)-(C); 42 U.S.C.A. § 7408(a)(1)(A)-(C).

restricted or eliminated by federal laws and regulations. Lead is known to cause retardation and brain damage, especially in children.

3. Nox/NO₂: Nitrogen Oxides

Nitrogen Oxides are the product of combustion from mobile transportation and stationary sources that burn fossil fuels. These pollutants react photochemically in the atmosphere with volatile organic compounds (VOCs) to form ozone. Nox contributes to the environmental problems posed by acid rain and particulate matter. In humans, these pollutants cause respiratory illnesses and lung damage.[87]

4. O₃: Ozone

O₃ is a pungent, colorless and toxic gas commonly referred to as smog. It is found in two layers of the atmosphere, the stratosphere and the troposphere. In the stratosphere (the atmospheric layer beginning seven to 10 miles above the earth's surface), ozone naturally shields the earth from ultraviolet radiation's harmful effects on humans and the environment. In the troposphere (the layer extending up to seven to 10 miles from the earth's surface), ozone is a chemical oxidant and major component of photochemical smog.

Ozone in the troposphere can seriously affect the human respiratory system and is one of the most prevalent and widespread of all the criteria pollutants regulated under the CAA.[88] Specifically, ozone causes breathing difficulty and reduces lung function. Asthma, eye irritation, nasal congestion, reduced resistance to infection, and possibly premature aging of lung tissue are aggravated by ozone in the air.

5. PM₁₀: Particulate Matter

Particulate matter (PM₁₀) includes fine particles (10 microns or less in diameter) for which a health-based NAAQS has been established under Section 109, and total suspended particulates (TSPs) for which NAAQS have been set to protect the environment. TSPs are any material, except water in uncombined

---

[87]   *See, State of New York v. U.S. EPA*, 133 F.3d 987 (7th Cir. 1998).

[88]   *See,* American Petroleum Institute v. Costle, 665 F.2d 1176 (D.C. Cir.1981) (details the process to set ozone levels under the NAAQS).

form, that is or has been airborne and exists as a liquid or a solid under normal conditions. Fine particulates pose a great health hazard because they can pass through the body's natural defenses and penetrate deep into the lungs. Specifically, particulates cause eye and throat irritation, impaired visibility, bronchitis and lung damage.

6.   SO₂: Sulfur Dioxide

SO_2 is a heavy, pungent and colorless gas emitted by sources using sulfur-bearing fossil fuels such as natural gas, coal and oil. These emissions also cause "acid rain" and are the principal target of the acid rain control program. They are considered very dangerous to plants, animals and humans. In humans, this pollutant causes respiratory tract problems and permanent harm to lung tissue.[89]

Although the concept of fixing NAAQS is awkward and complicated, the alternative of the states establishing and enforcing their own ambient air quality standards would be even more confusing.[90] Though Congress calls for EPA to set the NAAQS, the 1990 CAA did not ignore the importance of state participation in implementation of a clean air program.

The CAA grants states an important role in implementation and enforcement of its air programs. Once primary and secondary standards are set by EPA, the states step in to designate areas within their boundaries as being in nonattainment or in attainment of each NAAQS. Thereafter, the state must comply with the CAA in establishing the corresponding nonattainment program (NA) and the prevention of significant deterioration program (PSD).

---

[89]   *See*, American Lung Association v. United States EPA, 134 F.3d 388 (D.C.Cir. 1998).

[90]   *See*, American Trucking Associations, Inc. v. United States EPA, 175 F.3d 1027 (D.C.Cir. 1999). In this case, the NAAQS revisions for ozone and particulate matter were disputed. *See also*, Clean Air Implementation Project v. United States EPA, 150 F.3d 1200 (D.C.Cir. 1998).

IV.   NONATTAINMENT AREAS (NA) PROGRAM

A.   INTRODUCTION

A nonattainment area (NA) is an area that fails to meet the limitations set by the NAAQS. This is commonly referred to as "exceeding" the NAAQS."[91] The policy of the NA program is to implement strict regulatory requirements upon sources located in nonattainment areas to allow the region to attain and maintain the NAAQS.

The CAA was initially adopted with the goal of nationwide attainment of NAAQS by 1975. Meeting the standards is an enormous technical and economic challenge. Under the original program, an estimated 200,000 stationary sources, plus the automobile industry, were given three years to comply with costly and sometimes technically difficult requirements. The result was extensive noncompliance throughout the country.

Congress recognized the extent of noncompliance and responded when it overhauled the CAA in 1977. "Nonattainment areas" were officially recognized in this statute. The 1977 amendments extended the compliance date for nonattainment areas to December 31, 1982, and authorized further extensions for the pollutants proving most difficult to control (ozone and carbon monoxide) up to December 31, 1987. The 1977 amendments also authorized the "offset program." The offset program allows new and modified facilities to be constructed only if reductions of the criteria air pollutants proposed for emission are acquired at a greater than one to one ratio. Thus, it must be shown that if allowed to construct, the total amount of pollutants in the area will be sufficiently less than before the source's construction and operation.

In 1990, Congress amended the CAA because some parts of the nation were still exceeding the NAAQS for compliance with ozone and carbon monoxide. The 1990 amendments imposed additional responsibilities on NA regions depending on the severity of the problem. Below, we discuss the NA program as applied after the 1990 amendments.

---

[91]   CAA § 171(2); 42 U.S.C.A. § 7501(2); *see,* Thomas O. McGarity, Missing Milestone: A Critical Look at the Clean Air Act's VOC Emissions Reduction Program in Non-Attainment Areas, 18 V.A. Envtl. L.J. 41 (1999).

B.   STATUTORY SCHEME

1.   Relevant Statutory Sections

Sections 171 through 179 are the general NA sections of the CAA.[92] These sections apply to major existing, new, and modified sources of NAAQS pollutants. "Major" sources under this program are defined as those that directly emit or have the potential to emit, 100 tons per year or more of any NAAQS pollutant.[93] "Existing" sources are those facilities in existence at the time of passage of the regulations under this section. "New" sources are facilities to be constructed after the passage of regulations under this section. "Modifications" regulated by this program are physical changes in, or changes in the method of operation of, a stationary source that increases the amount of any air pollutant emitted or which results in the emission of any air pollutant not previously emitted.[94]

2.   The Federal Role

a.   Standards of Performance

The role of EPA under the NA program is to set reasonably available control technology (RACT) standards for implementation by existing sources and lowest achievable emissions rate (LAER) standards for implementation by new sources and for modifications of existing sources. LAER is the strictest standard of performance set by the CAA.[95]

b.   EPA Designates and Classifies Areas

EPA designates areas as nonattainment areas, after it reviews a state's list of regions a state deems not in attainment of the NAAQS. Once an area has been designated as NA, EPA classifies it according to the severity of nonattainment

---

[92]   CAA §§ 171-179; 42 U.S.C.A. §§ 7501-7509.

[93]   CAA § 302(j); 42 U.S.C.A. § 7602(j).

[94]   CAA §§ 171(4), 111(4); 42 U.S.C.A. §§ 7501(4), 7411(4).

[95]   CAA §§ 172(c)(1), 173(a)(2); 42 U.S.C.A. §§ 7502(c)(1), 7503(a)(2).

as either a marginal, moderate, serious, severe or extreme area.[96] Marginal areas are the least polluted; extreme areas are the most polluted. EPA will likewise designate attainment areas and areas that are not classifiable due to lack of information or data.[97]

The most polluted NA regions must comply with additional regulatory requirements, and use more advanced control technology than less polluted areas. Also, an area's classification determines the amount of offset emissions reductions required before a new source permit can be approved. For example, the offset ratio for a moderate area may be 1.15 to 1 and for an extreme area it might be 2 to 1. Similarly, a marginal area must meet the NAAQS requirements within three years where an extreme area must meet them in 20 years. The differences represent Congress' acceptance that more polluted areas will take longer to attain the NAAQS even after imposing more stringent requirements on its pollution sources.

c.   Review and Approve State Permit Programs

EPA must review and approve a state's NA permit program. If a state fails to submit an approved program, EPA may adopt and administer the permit program for that state. Once permit program approval has been received, the state has primary permit writing responsibilities for facilities within its boundaries. The state must then submit all permit applications and proposals to EPA for review. EPA may object and request permit revisions. If revisions are not met, EPA may administer the permit instead of the state.

3.   The State Role

a.   SIP Submission to EPA

The state's primary role is to demonstrate to EPA, through its SIP and permit program, how it will comply with the NAAQS. The state must submit its SIP and identify whether an area is in attainment or nonattainment of each NAAQS. In addition to including all the information required under the SIPs

---

[96]   CAA § 172; 42 U.S.C.A. § 7502.

[97]   CAA § 107(d); 42 U.S.C.A. § 7407(d).

(discussed above), the state must include the information requested under Section 172(c) for NA areas.[98]

b.   Section 172(c) Requirements

i.   RACM/RACT

Section 172(c) requires a plan to include implementation of all reasonably available control measures (RACM) and all reasonably available control technology (RACT) standards of performance from existing sources in the area (including emissions reductions) to ensure attainment of the NAAQS.[99] On the other hand, new sources must comply with a much stricter standard of LAER.[100]

ii.   Reasonable Further Progress

The plan shall require reasonable further progress. "Reasonable further progress" means such annual reductions in pollution emissions to ensure timely attainment of the NAAQS.

iii.   Inventory

The plan shall also include a comprehensive inventory of actual emissions from all pollutant sources.

iv.   Identification and Quantification

The plan must identify and calculate the total amount of emissions allowed for all permits for the construction and operation of major new or modified sources in each area. The plan shall demonstrate that the total emissions allowed will be consistent with the achievement of reasonable further progress and will not interfere with timely attainment of the NAAQS.

---

[98]   CAA § 172(c); 42 U.S.C.A. § 7502(c).

[99]   CAA § 172(c); 42 U.S.C.A. § 7502(c).

[100]   *See*, State of Michigan v. Thomas, 805 F.2d 176 (6th Cir.1986); *see also*, Lewis, William H., Jr. & Prillaman, Hunter L., Reasonably Available Control Technology under the Clean Air Act: Is EPA Following its Statutory Mandate?, 16 Harv. Envtl. L. Rev. 343 (1992).

v.   Permits

The plan shall require permits for the construction and operation of new or modified major sources in nonattainment areas.

vi.   Other Measures

The plan shall also include enforceable emission limitations, and such other control measures necessary to provide for timely attainment of the NAAQS.

vii.   Compliance

The plan shall meet the applicable provisions of Section 110 of the CAA discussed above.

c.   Section 173 Permit Requirements

The CAA requires either the state or EPA to implement a permit program for all new sources and for modifications of existing sources.[101] To obtain a permit, the source must demonstrate compliance with offsets, LAER, and statewide compliance with all CAA requirements.[102]

i.   Offsets

An offset is the reduction of a criteria pollutant by an amount greater than the planned increase that would occur if a new company were to construct or if an existing company were to expand or modify a production process or increase its output of a criteria air pollutant.

A unique permit requirement is that a new or modified source must obtain sufficient offsetting emissions reductions for its NAAQS pollutants. In short, the source must demonstrate that after it receives its permit the total amount of air pollutants in the area will be sufficiently less than before the source's new or modified construction and operation. The offsets may be obtained from the same source being modified or from other pollution sources

---

[101]   CAA § 173; 42 U.S.C.A. § 7503.

[102]   *Id.*

in the same NA region. In addition, the offset must be for the same NAAQS pollutant the permittee plans to emit.[103] For example, if Company A plans to modify its facility and the modification would increase SO_2 emissions by 100 tons per year, it must convince Company B to reduce its SO_2 emissions by an amount significantly greater than 100 tons per year. Thus, slowly but surely, the NA region keeps moving toward attainment; thus, demonstrating reasonable further progress.[104]

The state may allow a source to obtain emission reductions in a completely different NA regions if (a) the other area has an equal or higher NA classification than the area in which the new source is located, and (b) emissions from such other area contribute to a violation of the NAAQS in the NA region in which the new source is located.[105]

ii.   Offsetting Exemption

A source may be exempt from obtaining offsetting emissions reductions if the source will be located in a zone within the NA region that has been identified as an "economic development zone."[106] EPA and the Secretary of Housing and Urban Development jointly designate economic development zones for purposes of this CAA requirement.

iii.   Lowest Achievable Emission Rate

Another permit requirement is that the proposed new source must comply with the lowest achievable emission rate ("LAER").[107] LAER is the strictest standard of performance required under the new CAA.

---

[103]   *See*, Mostaghel, Deborah M., State Reactions to the Trading of Emissions Allowances under Title IV of the Clean Air Act Amendments of 1990, 22 B.C. Envtl. Aff. L. Rev. 201 (1995) (for a discussion of some of the problems arising from emissions trading).

[104]   CAA §§ 172(c)(2), 182(b)(1); 42 U.S.C.A. §§ 7502(c)(2), 7511a(b)(1).

[105]   CAA § 173; 42 U.S.C.A. § 7503(c)(1).

[106]   40 C.F.R. § 52.

[107]   CAA § 173(a)(2); 42 U.S.C.A. § 7503(a)(2).

iv.   Statewide Compliance

Another permit requirement is that the owner or operator of the proposed new or modified source must demonstrate that all of its major stationary sources in the state are in compliance with all applicable CAA emission limitations and standards.   In addition, upon analysis of alternative sites, sizes, production processes, and environmental control techniques for the proposed source EPA must determine that the SIP is being adequately implemented by the state and that the benefits outweigh the environmental and social costs imposed by its location, construction, or modification.

C.   JUDICIAL INTERPRETATIONS

Key decisions involving the NA program are discussed below.

1.   Partial SIP Approval Allowed

In *City of Seabrook v. United States EPA*, the Appeals Court upheld EPA's proposed "partial" and "conditional" approvals of nonattainment area SIPs (under the 1977 CAA) and the imposition of a ban on construction of new sources in areas without such approvals.[108]

2.   SIP Provisions Disallowed

In *Abromowitz v. United States EPA*, the Appeals Court found that EPA exceeded its authority under the 1977 CAA by approving the South Coast Basin in southern California for carbon monoxide and ozone control measures without requiring attainment of the NAAQS before December 31, 1987 as required by the 1977 CAA. As a result, the Appeals Court ordered EPA to disapprove the relevant SIP provisions.[109]

3.   Bubble Policy Allowed

In *Chevron, U.S.A., Inc. V. Natural Resources Defense Council, Inc.*, the Supreme Court upheld EPA's decision to allow states to treat all of the pollution-emitting devices within the same industrial grouping as though they

---

[108]   City of Seabrook v. United States EPA, 659 F.2d 1349 (5th Cir.1981).

[109]   Abromowitz v. United States EPA, 832 F.2d 1071 (9th Cir.1987).

were encased within a single "bubble" as a reasonable interpretation of the term "stationary source" under Section 172(b)(6).[110]

4. Denial of County Redesignation Upheld

In *State of Ohio v. Ruckelshaus*, the Appeals Court upheld EPA's decision to refuse a state's request to redesignate a single county from "nonattainment" to "attainment" even though the data from the county showed that the county's ambient air met the required ambient standard. EPA argued that although the one county was in attainment, pollution sources originating in that county added significantly to the ozone levels in the surrounding counties, all of which constituted one air quality control region.[111]

The NA program is an innovative program. It tailors preventative measures by the severity of the pollution in an area and sets strict (hopefully realistic) deadlines for reaching clean air goals. It is a comprehensive approach to reducing the six criteria air pollutants found nationwide. Another CAA program protects our nation's "clean air" areas, and is known as the PSD program.

V. PREVENTION OF SIGNIFICANT DETERIORATION PROGRAM (PSD)

A. INTRODUCTION

The PSD program mandates that the government control and regulate, to whatever extent necessary, areas that meet or exceed the NAAQS. These "clean air" areas are known as PSD areas.[112] The PSD program is a complex counterpart to the NA program. EPA is required to design and implement a program that prevents unlimited industrial growth from degrading air quality

---

[110] Chevron, U.S.A. Inc. v. Natural Resources Defense Council, Inc., 467 U.S. 837, 104 S.Ct. 2778, 81 L.Ed. 2d 694 (1984), *rehearing denied* 468 U.S. 1227, 105 S.Ct. 29, 82 L.Ed. 2d 921 (1984).

[111] State of Ohio v. Ruckelshaus, 776 F.2d 1333 (6th Cir.1985).

[112] *See, e.g.*, Hsiao, Peter, New Developments and Trends in Clean Air Act Litigation and Enforcement, C127 ALI-ABA 299 (1995).

where the NAAQS are being met so as to ensure the preservation of clean air.[113] The PSD program sustains attainment areas by incorporating:

1) strict performance standards requiring any new major facility to incorporate the best available control technology (BACT);

2) an increment limitations system that allows only a limited and planned amount of pollution in these areas to prevent any single project from having undue effects on air quality; and

3) a scheme of procedural and technical permit requirements imposed upon area sources to ensure compliance with performance standards and the increment limitations system.

B.   STATUTORY SCHEME

1.   Relevant Statutory Sections

Sections 160-169B are the PSD sections of the CAA.[114] These sections apply to major new and modified sources of any air pollutants. "Major" sources are defined as those that directly emit or have the potential to emit, 100 tons per year or more of any air pollutant from 28 listed types of stationary sources or any other source with the potential to emit 250 tons per year or more of any air pollutant.[115]

"New" sources are defined as stationary sources constructed or modified after section 111 regulations are published by EPA.[116]

---

[113]   CAA § 161; 42 U.S.C.A. § 7471.

[114]   CAA §§ 160-169B; 42 U.S.C.A. §§ 7470-7479; *see*, Frank B. Friedman, The State Implementation Plan Process, Non-Attainment, PSD, and other Clean Air Act Issues, C473 ALI-ABA 213, 243 (1990).

[115]   CAA § 169(1); 42 U.S.C.A. § 7479(1); *see also*, Alabama Power Co. v. Costle, 636 F.2d 323, 352-355 (D.C. Cir.1979).

[116]   CAA § 111(a); 42 U.S.C.A. § 7411(a).

"Modifications" are those in which any physical change in, or change in the operation of, a stationary source that increases (by more than a "de minimis" amount) the amount of any air pollutant emitted or which results in the emission (by more than a "de minimis" amount) of any air pollutant not previously emitted.[117] De minimis amounts are defined by EPA regulations. The de minimis thresholds range from 0.0004 to 100 tons for each pollutant regulated under the CAA.[118] Increases above these de minimis levels are considered "significant" and thus require a permit. As with the NA program, the PSD program also incorporates both federal and state implementation.

2.   The Federal Role in Subclassifying Geographic Areas

EPA's role in the PSD program primarily consists of classifying areas to establish the amount of protection needed to prevent future air pollution. EPA subclassifies all PSD areas into three categories: Class I, II, or III depending on the amount of protection needed to prevent future air pollution.

a.   Class I Areas

Class I areas are the most protected and include all international parks, national wilderness areas larger than 5,000 acres, national memorial parks larger than 5,000 acres, and national parks larger than 6,000 acres.[119] These areas are to be kept in strictly pristine conditions and cannot deviate from the absolute mandates of the PSD program. In other words, the policy is one of "no tolerance" where air quality degradation of a PSD area is concerned.

Redesignation of Class I areas into Class II or III areas is strictly limited because the redesignation would allow air quality degradation. However, Class II areas may be redesignated as Class I, or in limited circumstances, into Class III areas.[120] For example, in *Nance v. United States EPA*, the Ninth Circuit held that the Northern Cheyenne Reservation could reclassify its area from Class II

---

[117]   CAA § 111(a)(4); 42 U.S.C.A. § 7411.

[118]   40 C.F.R. §§ 51.166(b)(23)(i), 51.21(b)(23)(i).

[119]   CAA § 162(a); 42 U.S.C.A. § 7472.

[120]   CAA § 164(a)(2)(A), (B), (C).

to Class I in order to strictly protect the area's air from degradation.[121] Very little to no development is allowed in a Class I area in order to prevent further deterioration of the air quality.

b. Class II Areas

Class II areas are all other areas (not in the Class I category) designated as being in attainment of the NAAQS or unclassifiable due to lack of information or data.[122] Some economic growth is allowed in Class II areas, but only in very limited amounts that do not significantly deteriorate air quality. These additional amounts of pollutants are called "allowable increments" and are part of the increments limitations system mentioned earlier in this chapter. The increments allowed in Class II areas are closely monitored to ensure the air quality does not fall below the NAAQS.

c. Class III Areas

Class III areas allow more economic growth than Class II areas. Thus, the allowable increments are greater. No Class III areas have been specifically designated by the CAA. However, Congress declared that Class III areas be jointly designated by EPA with a state governor's approval.[123] As with Class II areas, the increments allowed in Class III areas must be closely monitored to ensure the air quality does not fall below the NAAQS.

3. The State Role

The state's role in the PSD program consists of listing air quality control regions that have attained the NAAQS, working with EPA to redesignate area classifications, incorporating a PSD plan in its SIP, and implementing and enforcing a PSD permit system for new or modified facilities in PSD areas.

---

[121] Nance v. United States EPA, 645 F.2d 701, 704 (9th Cir.1981) cert. denied 454 U.S. 1081, 102 S.Ct. 635, 70 L.Ed.2d 615 (1981); *see also*, Administrator, State of Arizona v. United States EPA, 151 F.3d 1205 (9th Cir. 1998).

[122] CAA § 162(b); 42 U.S.C.A. § 7472.

[123] CAA § 164; 42 U.S.C.A. § 7474.

a. Listing

The governor of each state shall submit to EPA a list of all AQCRs within their respective states that meet the national primary or secondary NAAQS.[124]

b. Area Class Redesignation

If a state is not satisfied with EPA's Class designation then it may redesignate an area to either offer more protection or to allow for more development. To protect certain "environmentally sensitive areas," the CAA states that areas that exceed 10,000 acres in size, and are national monuments, national primitive areas, national preserves, national recreation areas, national wild and scenic rivers, national wildlife refuges, national lakeshores, and seashores and national parks or wilderness areas established after Aug. 7, 1977, may only be redesignated as Class I or II.[125]

To allow for more development, a state may redesignate some Class II areas as Class III. Any area not deemed "environmentally sensitive" may be redesignated as Class III if specifically approved by EPA and the state governor. In addition, redesignation must not cause or contribute to concentrations of any air pollutant that exceeds any maximum allowable increments permitted under the classifications of any other areas. EPA must also notify the federal land manager and provide public hearings. Under no circumstances is the quality of the air in these areas to deteriorate below NAAQS levels.

i. Impact Analysis

Prior to redesignation, an in-depth analysis of the health, environmental, economic, social and energy effects of the proposed redesignation shall be prepared and made available for public inspection and comment. The impact analysis is to be considered by the redesignating authorities.

---

[124] CAA § 107(d)(1)(A)(ii); 42 U.S.C.A. § 7407(d)(1)(A)(ii).

[125] CAA §§ 164(a)(1), (2); 42 U.S.C.A. §§ 7474(a)(1), (2).

ii.   Public Notice

Prior to redesignation, public notice shall be given and public hearings conducted in areas to be redesignated and in areas that may be affected by the proposed redesignation.[126] The notice and hearings allow all interested persons to participate and comment on the proposed redesignation.

c.   PSD and the State Implementation Plan

The state must also include a PSD implementation plan in its SIP. The plan shall contain facility-specific emission limitations and such other measures necessary to prevent significant deterioration of air quality in PSD areas.[127] The SIP must also demonstrate how the state intends to implement Section 165 permit requirements.

d.   Section 165 Permit Requirements

Section 165 requires preconstruction review and issuance of a permit prior to the construction or modification of any major facility in a PSD area.[128] As part of the review process, the owner or operator of the facility must demonstrate that emissions will not further contribute to air pollution in excess of the NAAQS, will not cause any applicable emission standard or standard of performance to be altered, and will not cause or contribute to air pollution in excess of any maximum allowable air quality increment.[129]

---

[126]   CAA § 164(b); 42 U.S.C.A. § 7476.

[127]   CAA § 161; 42 U.S.C.A. § 7471.

[128]   CAA § 165; 42 U.S.C.A. § 7475; *see*, Montana Power Company v. United States EPA, 608 F.2d. 334 (9th Cir.1979) (*see* discussion on whether facilities may be grandfathered under the PSD program and not be subject to PSD review).

[129]   CAA § 165(a)(3); 42 U.S.C.A. § 7475(a)(3). In Detroit Edison Co. v. Michigan Dept. of Environmental Quality, 39 F.Supp.2d 875 (E.D. Mich.1999), the court held that the electric utility company could not restart and operate the power plant after a decade of non-use without first obtaining a PSD and New Source Review permit.

i.   Air Quality Increments

The PSD program requires major new and modified sources to demonstrate that their emissions will not cause air quality to deteriorate beyond specified numerical increments. The increments are designated by Congress (as expressly stated in the CAA for sulfur dioxide and total suspended particulates) or by EPA regulations.[130]

The increment size is determined by whether the area is designated Class I, II or III. Class I has the most restrictive increments and Class III the least restrictive. The increments for each class were chosen as a rough measure of whether an area should be kept at its present air quality, or whether moderate or greater growth is appropriate. It is expected that once new sources use up the allowable increments, no new industrial growth is to be allowed in the PSD area.

ii.   BACT

The standard of performance for new and modified facilities under this program is the best available control technology (BACT). BACT "imposes a responsibility on the permit applicant to identify the particular available technology that will produce the maximum degree of reduction of each regulated pollutant to be emitted from the proposed facility."[131]

iii.   Permitting Process

The state shall give EPA a copy of each permit application received and shall provide notice to EPA of each state action related to the facility's permit approval. Thereafter, EPA shall provide notice of the permit application to the federal land manager and the federal official managing any lands within a Class I area that may be affected by emissions from the proposed facility.[132]

---

[130]   CAA §§ 163, 166; 42 U.S.C.A. §§ 7473, 7476.

[131]   Citizens for Clean Air v. United States EPA, 959 F.2d 839, 845 (9th Cir.1992).

[132]   CAA § 164(b)(1)(B); 42 U.S.C.A. § 7474(b)(1)(B).

iv.   Impact Analysis and Air Quality Monitoring

A preconstruction impact analysis and continuous air quality monitoring at the proposed site, and in areas that may be affected by emissions from a facility must be conducted by the facility owner or operator for each regulated pollutant emitted from the facility. A permit shall not be issued unless the owner or operator demonstrates that emissions of particulate matter and sulfur dioxide (causing smog and haze) will not cause or contribute to concentrations that exceed the maximum allowable increases for a Class I area. Compliance may be demonstrated with air quality monitoring and modeling.[133]

v.   Exemptions

Exemptions to permit requirements, also known as variances, may be granted where the owner or operator demonstrates to the state governor that the facility cannot be constructed without such a variance and the state is convinced that the benefits of the facility outweigh the environmental and economic costs. The federal land manager and the President shall participate in the decision on whether a variance shall be issued. If such a variance is granted, a permit may be issued for such source.[134]

C.   JUDICIAL INTERPRETATIONS

Key decisions involving the PSD program are discussed below.

1.   Air Deterioration Prohibited

In *Sierra Club v. Ruckelshaus* the District Court prohibited EPA from approving SIPs that allowed air quality to deteriorate to the level of the NAAQS. The court failed to provide details about how this goal was to be accomplished. In response to opinions like this one Congress eventually amended the CAA to establish the PSD program.[135]

---

[133]   CAA § 165(d), (e); 42 U.S.C.A. § 7475(d), (e).

[134]   CAA § 165(d)(2)(D); 42 U.S.C.A. § 7475(d)(2)(D).

[135]   Sierra Club v. Ruckelshaus, 344 F.Supp. 253 (D.D.C.1972).

2. Judicial Review of PSD Regulations

In *Alabama Power Co. v. Costle*, the Appellate Court's opinion reviews EPA's initial PSD regulations upholding the validity of some and requiring comprehensive and highly detailed revision of others. For example, one of the holdings was that the CAA obligated EPA to take emissions controls into account in determining a facilities "potential to emit" beyond the 100/250 ton threshold.[136]

3. New Refinery Allowed in a PSD Area

In *Citizens Against the Refinery's Effects v. United States EPA* the Appellate Court upheld EPA's decision to issue a PSD permit to build the first refinery in more than 20 years on the east coast in Portsmouth, Virginia, a Class II area for SO_2.[137]

4. Redesignation to Class I Area Allowed

In *Nance v. United States EPA*, the Appellate Court did a cost/benefit analysis to balance benefits to a tribe in the Northern Cheyenne Reservation against disadvantages to others in deciding to uphold EPA's decision allowing the reservation to be redesignated from a Class II area to a Class I area.[138]

5. Nonattainment Area Redesignated as a PSD Area

In *Southwestern Pennsylvania Growth Alliance v. Browner*, the Appellate Court upheld EPA's decision to redesignate an Ohio air quality control region from a moderate ozone nonattainment area to an attainment area.[139]

---

[136] Alabama Power Co. v. Costle, 636 F.2d 323 (D.C. Cir.1979).

[137] Citizens Against the Refinery's Effects v. United States EPA, 643 F.2d 178 (4th Cir.1981).

[138] Nance v. United States EPA, 645 F.2d 701 (9th Cir.1981), *cert. denied* 454 U.S. 1081, 102 S.Ct. 635, 70 L.Ed.2d 615 (1981).

[139] *See*, Southwestern Pennsylvania Growth Alliance v. Browner, 144 F.3d 984 (6th Cir. 1998).

The PSD program has assumed considerable importance in the effort to protect our national parks from encroachment by development in nearby areas. But in its attempt to discourage new growth in remote, unpopulated, clean air areas, it encourages polluting facilities to locate in urban, highly populated dirty areas. Also, it is hard to imagine that PSD areas will ban all new growth completely once the allowable growth increments are used up. Yet, without a protective scheme, these clean air areas would be quickly developed and as polluted as their NA counterparts. The most beneficial effect of the PSD program is that it forces industry to invent new, clean technology that allows for both economic growth and protection of our ambient air.

VI.   NATIONAL EMISSION STANDARDS FOR HAZARDOUS AIR POLLUTANTS (NESHAPs)

A.   INTRODUCTION

The National Emission Standards for Hazardous Air Pollutants (NESHAPs) Program mandates that government control and regulate hazardous pollutants to protect health, without regard to costs or technological feasibility. Hazardous air pollutants include substances known to cause cancer, leukemia, birth defects, reproductive problems, lung diseases, nervous system disorders and other major health problems.[140] These sources must meet new technology-based emission standards for all stationary sources, whether the source is new, existing, or modified. The emission standard for major new, existing, or modified sources that emit hazardous pollutants is the maximum achievable control technology (MACT).[141]

For hazardous air pollutants (HAPs), "major" is defined as any source "that emits or has the potential to emit . . . 10 tons per year or more of any hazardous air pollutant or 25 tons per year or more of any combination of hazardous air pollutants."[142] A modification under this program means "any

---

[140]   CAA § 112(b)(1); 42 U.S.C.A. § 7412(b)(1); *see*, Eric M. Johnson, National Emission Standards for Hazardous Air Pollutants for Source Categories, 6 S.C. Envtl. L.J. 121 (1997).

[141]   CAA § 112(d)(2), (3); 42 U.S.C.A. § 7412(d)(2), (3).

[142]   CAA § 112(a)(1); 42 U.S.C.A. § 7412(a)(1); *see*, National Mining Association v. United States EPA, 59 F.3d 1351 (D.C. Cir.1995).

physical change in, or change in the method of operation of, a major source which increases the actual emission of any hazardous air pollutant emitted by the source by more than a de minimis (minimal) amount or which results in the emission of any hazardous air pollutant not previously emitted by more than a de minimis amount."[143] Pollutant-specific de minimis amounts are set by EPA regulation.[144]

Sources of HAPs that are not "major" because they do not meet the 10/25 tons per year threshold are called "area sources." The standard of performance for area sources is the generally available control technology (GACT) or management practices available.[145]

B.   STATUTORY SCHEME

1.   Relevant Statutory Section

Section 112 of the CAA authorizes EPA to set health-based standards for the emissions of hazardous pollutants known as the National Emission Standards for Hazardous Air Pollutants (NESHAPs).[146] Under the NESHAPs program, EPA must list as a hazardous air pollutant any substance known to cause, or that may reasonably be anticipated to cause adverse effects to human health or adverse environmental effects.[147] Congress wants EPA to regulate, at a minimum, the 189 listed air pollutants known to cause cancer, leukemia, birth defects, reproductive problems, lung diseases, and other major health problems.[148]

---

[143]   CAA § 112(a)(5); 42 U.S.C.A. § 7412(a)(5).

[144]   CAA § 112(a)(5); 42 U.S.C.A. § 7412(a)(5).

[145]   CAA § 112(a); 42 U.S.C.A. § 7412(a).

[146]   CAA § 112; 42 U.S.C.A. § 7412.

[147]   CAA § 112(b)(2); 42 U.S.C.A. § 7412(b)(2).

[148]   CAA § 112(b)(1); 42 U.S.C.A. § 7412(b)(1).

2.   The Federal Role

a.   Hazardous Air Pollutants List

Congress specifically lists 189 pollutants to be regulated as HAPs.[149] In addition, Congress authorizes EPA to modify the list by adding or deleting pollutants as necessary.[150] The administrator is to base such decisions upon whether the "substance may reasonably be anticipated to cause any adverse effects to the human health or adverse environmental effects."[151]

b.   Categories and Subcategories List

EPA must also publish a list of all categories and subcategories of major and area sources of the listed HAPs. The categories and subcategories shall be consistent with the source categories established pursuant to Section 111 for NSPS.[152]

c.   Emission Standards for Major Sources

EPA must promulgate regulations establishing emission standards for each category or subcategory of major and area sources of HAPs, applying the appropriate standard of performance as either MACT or GACT.[153] The 1990 CAA amendments revised this program to include a provision that would grant sources a six-year extension of compliance with the MACT standards if they voluntarily reduced emissions by 90 percent or more before the MACT standards were proposed.[154] Once a source satisfies EPA (or in some instances, the state)

---

[149]   *Id.*

[150]   CAA § 112(b)(2); 42 U.S.C.A. § 7412(b)(2).

[151]   CAA § 112(b)(2)(C); 42 U.S.C.A. § 7412(b)(2)(C).

[152]   CAA § 112(c)(1); 42 U.S.C.A. § 7412(c)(1).

[153]   CAA § 112(d); 42 U.S.C.A. § 7412(d).

[154]   CAA § 112(i)(5); 42 U.S.C.A. § 7412(i)(5).

that a reduction will be achieved, the actual reductions become an "alternative emission limitation" that is fully enforceable as a primary emissions limitation.[155]

d.   Emissions from Area Sources to be Studied

EPA must also study the health and environmental effects of pollutants emitted from area sources, specifically those affecting urban areas. The study must include ambient air monitoring, analysis of health risks and consideration of atmospheric transformation and other factors that can elevate public health risks. Upon completion of the study, EPA must give to Congress a comprehensive strategy to control emissions of HAPs from area sources.[156]

3.   The State Role

a.   State HAPs Program

Each state may develop, and submit to EPA for approval, a program for the implementation and enforcement of emission standards and permit requirements for HAPs. State standards must be at least as stringent as federal standards.[157] EPA may withdraw approval of a state program if it finds that the state is not administering and enforcing their program adequately.[158]

b.   Permit Requirements

Major sources of HAPs must receive a permit for the discharge of these pollutants. This permit must include facility-specific emissions limits for HAPs to be emitted.[159]

---

[155]   CAA § 112(i)(5)(B); 42 U.S.C.A. § 7412(i)(5)(B).

[156]   CAA § 112(k); 42 U.S.C.A. § 7412(k).

[157]   CAA § 112(l)(1); 42 U.S.C.A. § 7412(l)(1).

[158]   CAA § 112(l)(6); 42 U.S.C.A. § 7412(l)(6).

[159]   CAA § 505(d); 42 U.S.C.A. § 7661(d).

C.   JUDICIAL INTERPRETATIONS

Various interpretations and implementation of Section 112 has been the source of controversy and litigation. Below are two examples of cases that directly impacted the interpretation of issues regarding Section 112.

1.   Emission Standards Required for Listed HAPs

In *Sierra Club v. Gorsuch* the District Court ordered EPA to issue proposed regulations establishing emission standards for radionuclides[160] after EPA listed radionuclides as a HAP but failed to propose regulations establishing emission standards within 180 days as required by the CAA.[161]

2.   EPA Interpretations Upheld

In *Natural Resources Defense Council (NRDC) v. United States EPA*, the NRDC sued EPA, arguing that Section 112 did not allow BAT regulations specifically, and the consideration of costs and feasibility generally, to be considered in the formulation of emission standards. The final decision affirmed EPA's interpretation of the CAA, that:

1)   vinyl chloride emissions caused adverse health effects;

2)   EPA must make an initial determination of a "safe" level of emissions;

3)   "safe" did not mean completely risk-free; and

4)   that EPA had discretion to define an emissions level that constituted an "acceptable" health risk.

---

[160]   *See*, Eblen, *supra* note 12 at 590 (Exposure to radionuclides from radiation emissions can cause such health problems as fatigue, nausea, vomiting, loss of teeth and hair, and damage to blood cells, possibly causing death).

[161]   Sierra Club v. Gorsuch, 551 F.Supp. 785 (N.D.Cal.1982); *see also*, Sierra Club v. Ruckelshaus, 602 F.Supp. 892 (N.D.Cal.1984).

Furthermore, the court ruled EPA had acted reasonably in considering economic and technological feasibility after defining a "safe" level to further tighten the standard.[162]

The NESHAPs program protects human health and the environment from the debilitating and deadly effects of hazardous air pollutants. These pollutants cause cancer, leukemia, birth defects, reproductive problems, lung diseases, nervous system disorders and other major health problems. Hazardous air pollutants are released from motor vehicles, small stationary sources, such as dry cleaners and auto paint shops, and large stationary sources, such as chemical factories and incinerators.

This program mandates EPA to regulate and control 189 named hazardous air pollutants and encourages industry to voluntarily reduce emissions by 90 percent. The permit requirements together with the strict technology-forcing MACT standards will eventually improve the quality of life for many Americans by lowering exposure to these pollutants and lessening the number of deaths resulting from exposure to these contaminants.

VII.   ENFORCEMENT PROVISIONS

A.   INTRODUCTION

The CAA includes specific enforcement powers to ensure compliance with all of its programs and regulations. The goal is to provide tough, effective means of deterring potential polluters and of punishing violators. Upon application for approval of state CAA programs, states must demonstrate to EPA that their state laws have enforcement provisions at least as stringent as the federal CAA.

On the administrative side, the CAA requires facilities to obtain a permit prior to construction and operation. The permit requires the facility owner and operator to keep records, monitor activities and periodically report information to either a state or federal regulatory agency, depending upon which program is

---

[162]   Natural Resource Defense Counsel (NRDC) v. United States EPA, 824 F.2d 1146 (D.C. Cir.1987) (en banc), *rev'd.* 804 F.2d 710 (D.C. Cir.1986).

being administered.[163] The permit also authorizes the regulatory agency to enter a facility at reasonable times and obtain copies of records, inspect monitoring equipment and sample air emissions.[164]

Like many other environmental statutes, the CAA authorizes EPA to impose administrative, civil and criminal enforcement actions.[165] If violations are found or suspected, the agency may initiate administrative actions, including notice of deficiencies, notice of violations, permit suspensions or modifications, and administrative fines. The CAA authorizes EPA to impose administrative penalties of up to $200,000.[166] Larger penalties are also allowed if the Administrator and the Attorney General jointly determine that a larger penalty is appropriate.[167] These remedies are implemented and agreed to by both parties in a consent agreement, or issued by an administrative law judge through an administrative order.[168]

If violations are so serious that the enforcing agency determines that penalties stricter than administrative penalties are necessary, then the agency may pursue civil remedies. Civil remedies impose higher fines and offer permit revocations and injunctions calling for corrective action. In determining the amount of any civil penalty, the Administrator takes into account:

1)   the gravity of the violation;

2)   the economic benefit or savings resulting from the violation;

3)   the size of the violator's business;

---

[163]   CAA § 114(a)(1); 42 U.S.C.A. § 7414(a)(1); see, Peter Hsiao, Clean Air Act Litigation and Enforcement, SE98 ALI-ABA 1007 (2000).

[164]   CAA § 114(a)(2)(A); 42 U.S.C.A. § 7414(a)(2)(A).

[165]   CAA § 113(a)(3); 42 U.S.C.A. § 7413(a)(3).

[166]   CAA § 205(c)(1); 42 U.S.C.A. § 7524(c)(1).

[167]   Id.; see, Olin Corporation v. Yeargin Incorporated, 146 F.3d 398 (6th Cir.1998) (where defendants settled CAA claim for $1,000,000).

[168]   CAA § 205(b); 42 U.S.C.A. § 7524(b).

4)   the violator's historical record of compliance;

5)   any actions taken to remedy the violation;

6)   the effect of the penalty on the violator's business; and

7)   other appropriate matters.[169]

These remedies are implemented after a hearing and are issued and signed by both parties and a civil court judge in a consent decree. If the parties cannot come to an agreement, then the judge issues a civil enforcement order.

Because traditional administrative and civil remedies may not always deter misconduct, the CAA also authorizes criminal enforcement actions. Willful acts, conducted with intent or knowledge, that pose an imminent danger to human health, welfare or the environment are punishable by criminal sanctions.

Criminal felony sanctions for knowing violations, with fines of up to $25,000 per day, plus imprisonment of up to thirty years are authorized under this act.[170] Fines against organizations for up to $2,000,000 per violation for "knowingly endangering" human health or the environment are also allowed.[171] These enforcement provisions make the 1990 CAA one of the most "penalty driven" environmental statutes to date.

The CAA does not centralize its enforcement provisions into one particular part of the statute. For example, government enforcement authority for stationary source compliance with SIPs and national emission limitations is found in Section 113.[172] Similar enforcement provisions with respect to mobile sources are found in Sections 203-205.[173] Additionally, citizen's enforcement

---

[169]   CAA § 205(c)(2); 42 U.S.C.A. § 7425(c)(2).

[170]   CAA § 113(c); 42 U.S.C.A. § 7413(c).

[171]   CAA § 113(c)(5)(A); 42 U.S.C.A. § 7413(c)(5)(A).

[172]   CAA § 113; 42 U.S.C.A. § 7413.

[173]   CAA §§ 203-205; 42 U.S.C.A. §§ 7522-7524.

provisions are found in Section 304.[174] Below we more fully discuss some of the enforcement sections of the CAA.[175]

B.   GENERAL PERMIT REQUIREMENTS

1.   Introduction

The 1990 amendments included the CAA's first national permit system for all major sources of air pollution.[176] While these requirements complicate the SIP process, they also add much greater specificity for permittees, regulators, and concerned citizens.[177]

Permits are the driving force for implementing all the provisions and regulations of the CAA programs. A permit, usually several hundred pages in length, resembles a license. Most major sources of air pollution, such as power plants, chemical factories, and in some cases, smaller polluters are required to obtain a permit prior to construction and operation of a facility. A permit includes a comprehensive list of all the regulated pollutants of a source. It also includes information about which pollutants are being released, how much the source is allowed to release, and the program that will be used to meet pollutant release requirements.

EPA has broad authority to expand categories of industries subject to permit requirements. States will administer permits unless EPA has disapproved part or all of a state permit program, then EPA will issue the permits in that state. To receive EPA approval to administer permits, a state must meet

---

[174]   CAA § 304; 42 U.S.C.A. § 7604.

[175]   *See*, Miskiewicz, James & Rudd, John S., Civil and Criminal Enforcement of the Clean Air Act after the 1990 Amendments, 9 Pace Envtl. L. Rev. 281 (1992) (for an excellent explanation of the civil and criminal enforcement provisions of the CAA).

[176]   For additional reading on the permit program, *see*, Williamson, Timothy L., Fitting Title V into the Clean Air Act: Implementing the New Operating Permit Program, 21 Envt. L. 2085 (1991); *see*, David P. Novello, The New Clean Air Act Operating Permit Program: EPA's Final Rules, 23 ELR 10080 (1993).

[177]   Percival, Robert V., Environmental Regulation: Law, Science, and Policy, at 791 (1992).

minimum requirements for staffing, collection of fees and administrative procedures.[178]

2. Relevant Statutory Sections

Sections 501 through 507 set out the general requirements and procedures for permits to be issued under the NSPS, NESHAPS, PSD, and NA programs.[179]

a. Definitions

Section 501 sets definitions for terms used in this Subchapter of the CAA.[180]

b. Permit Contents

Section 502 authorizes EPA to promulgate regulations that establish minimum measures (e.g., applications, monitoring and reporting requirements and fee systems) for a permit program to be administered by an air pollution control agency. For example, a permittee must pay fees based on the size of emission which provides an economic incentive for reductions. The fees offset administrative costs incurred by states in implementing a permit program. The fee program generally must collect in the aggregate at least $25 per ton of regulated pollutant. All fees must be used solely to support the program.[181] Section 502 also allows facilities with multiple sources, which qualify to be regulated by multiple CAA programs, to be issued a single permit that covers all the necessary provisions of each of the applicable programs under the CAA.[182]

---

[178] *Id.* at 792.

[179] CAA §§ 501-507; 42 U.S.C.A. §§ 7661-7661f.

[180] CAA § 501; 42 U.S.C.A. § 7661.

[181] CAA § 502(b); 42 U.S.C.A. § 7661(b).

[182] CAA § 502(c); 42 U.S.C.A. § 7661(c).

c.   Time lines for Permit Applications

Section 503 sets out time lines for completion of permit applications, and requires submission of a compliance plan describing how the source will comply with all requirements.[183]

d.   Permit Conditions

Section 504 sets permit conditions such as enforceable emission standards, monitoring, inspections, entry and reporting requirements. This section also provides that a permit may be used as a "shield" preventing government imposition of new non-permit requirements upon a permitted facility.[184] This exempts application of new regulations upon existing permitted facilities until the expiration and revision or reissuance of a new permit.

e.   Notifications

Section 505 requires states to notify EPA of each air permit request. States must also notify contiguous states of permit requests by facilities whose air emissions may affect the neighboring state's air.[185]

f.   Self Regulation by States

Section 506 allows a state or interstate permitting authority to establish additional permitting requirements.[186]

g.   Compliance Assistance for Small Businesses

Section 507 allows a state to adopt as part of the SIP, a small business stationary source technical and environmental compliance assistance program.[187]

---

[183]   CAA § 503; 42 U.S.C.A. § 7661b.

[184]   CAA § 504; 42 U.S.C.A. § 7661.

[185]   CAA § 505; 42 U.S.C.A. § 7661d.

[186]   CAA § 506; 42 U.S.C.A. § 7661e.

[187]   CAA § 507; 42 U.S.C.A. § 7661f.

The permit system is the driving force for implementing and enforcing the CAA programs and their regulations. A facility owner should pay special attention to meeting all of the application requirements and should expect to work closely with the issuing agency and its permit writers. Once issued, the permit is the law with which a facility must comply.

Although the permit process is lengthy and expensive, it is an essential tool that incorporates science, technology, economics, health concerns and environmental protection in such a way that a tailored balance of needs is achieved. Voluntary compliance with an issued permit is the key to protecting human health, welfare and the environment.

C.   GOVERNMENT ACTIONS

Section 113 authorizes various federal enforcement actions and grants specific authority for EPA to initiate administrative, civil and criminal proceedings against violators.[188] The following is a list and description of the relevant statutory sections authorizing government enforcement actions.

1.   Administrative Remedies

Section 113(a) authorizes administrative remedies against a state when the state:

1)   fails to comply with its SIP;

2)   fails to enforce its SIP or permit program; or

3)   fails to comply with new source requirements.

EPA may issue an administrative order, assess an administrative penalty, or bring a civil action against a state. Similar actions are allowed if EPA finds that a person or entity is violating any SIP requirement, permit requirement, or otherwise not complying with new source requirements.[189]

---

[188]   CAA § 113; 42 U.S.C.A. § 7413.

[189]   CAA § 113(b); 42 U.S.C.A. § 7413(b); *see*, United States v. Pan American Grain Manufacturing Co., Inc., 29 F.Supp.2d 53 (D.Puerto Rico 1998).

Section 120 provides the administrator with authority to issue regulations requiring EPA (or a state) to assess and collect a noncompliance penalty against stationary sources not in compliance with any emission limitation, standard, schedule of compliance, or other CAA requirement.[190]

Section 167 allows EPA (or a state) to enforce PSD requirements, including the issuance of an order, or injunctive relief to prevent the construction or modification of major emitting facilities failing to comply with PSD requirements.[191]

Section 179 allows EPA to sanction states that do not comply with their own state SIPs. For example, EPA may deny awarding federal highway dollars to a state and may apply stricter offset requirements under the NA program of at least 2 to 1. Also, a state may be required to revise their SIP to include "such additional measures that can be feasibly implemented in the area in light of technological achievability, costs, and any non-air quality and other air quality-related health and environmental impacts."[192]

Section 185 requires that major stationary sources in "severe and extreme ozone nonattainment areas" pay a fee of up to $5,000 per ton[193] of VOC emitted by the source during the calendar year in excess of 80 percent of the baseline amount if the area failed to meet the primary NAAQS for ozone.[194]

Sections 203-205 list a number of prohibited acts regarding mobile sources (motor vehicles) and allow for administrative and civil enforcement actions in amounts of up to $25,000 per day per violation.[195]

---

[190] CAA § 120; 42 U.S.C.A. § 7420.

[191] CAA § 167; 42 U.S.C.A. § 7477.

[192] CAA § 179(d)(2); 42 U.S.C.A. § 7509(d)(2).

[193] This amount is adjusted according to inflation. *See*, CAA § 185(b)(1), (3); 42 U.S.C.A. § 7511d(b)(1), (3).

[194] CAA § 185; 42 U.S.C.A. § 7511d.

[195] CAA §§ 203-205; 42 U.S.C.A. §§ 7522-7524.

In case of an emergency, Section 303 allows EPA to take whatever action is necessary to stop any polluting activity that presents an imminent and substantial endangerment to public health, welfare, or the environment.[196]

2. Civil Remedies

Section 113(b) authorizes civil remedies, including injunctions and civil penalties of not more than $25,000 per day for each violation for any person who has violated:

1)   a SIP or permit;[197]

2)   any rule, order, waiver, or fee issued under the CAA; or

3)   any new source requirements for attempting to construct or modify a major stationary source.[198]

3. Criminal Remedies

Section 113(c) authorizes criminal remedies to include fines of up to $2,000,000 for each violation and confinement for up to 30 years. Section 113 addresses five types of criminal violations.[199] Four are for "knowing" violations and one is for a "negligence" violation:

1)   Any person who "knowingly" violates any requirement or prohibition of a SIP shall be punished by a fine or by imprisonment not to exceed 5 years, or both. If a conviction of any person under this paragraph is for a violation committed after a previous "first" conviction, the maximum punishment

---

[196]   CAA § 303; 42 U.S.C.A. § 7603.

[197]   *See*, L.E.A.D. v. Exide Corporation, 1999 W.L. 124473, *15 (E.D. Pa. 1999).

[198]   CAA § 113(b); 42 U.S.C.A. § 7413(b); *see*, Lisa M. Schenck, Lets Clear the Air: Enforcing Civil Penalties Against Federal Violators, 6 Envtl. Law 839 (2000); *see*, Miskiewizz, *supra* note 175 at 281.

[199]   CAA § 113(c); 42 U.S.C.A. § 7413(c).

shall be doubled with respect to both the fine and imprisonment.[200]

2)   (A) Any person who "knowingly" makes any false material statement, representation, or certification in, or omits material information from, or "knowingly" alters, conceals, or fails to file or maintain any notice, application, record, report, plan, or other document required under the CAA;[201]

(B) Any person who "knowingly" fails to notify or report as required under the CAA;[202]

(C) Any person who "knowingly" falsifies, tampers with, renders inaccurate, or fails to install any monitoring device or method required to be maintained or followed under the CAA.[203]

The punishment for these violations shall be a fine or imprisonment for not more than 2 years, or both. The punishment may be doubled for repeat offenders with respect to both the fine and imprisonment.

3)   Any person who "knowingly" fails to pay any fee owed the United States under the CAA shall, upon conviction, be punished by a fine or by imprisonment for not more than 1 year, or both. For repeat offenders the maximum punishment shall be doubled with respect to both the fine and imprisonment.[204]

---

[200]   CAA § 113(c)(1); 42 U.S.C.A. § 7413(c)(1); *see*, United States v. Banks, 1999 W.L. 257647 (E.D. Pa. 1999).

[201]   CAA § 113(c)(2)(A); 42 U.S.C.A. § 7413(c)(2)(A); *see*, United States v. Fern, 155 F.3d 1318 (11th Cir. 1998).

[202]   CAA § 113(c)(2)(B); 42 U.S.C.A. § 7413(c)(2)(B).

[203]   CAA § 113(c)(2)(C); 42 U.S.C.A. § 7413(c)(2)(C).

[204]   CAA § 113(c)(3); 42 U.S.C.A. § 7413(c)(3).

4)   Any person who "negligently" releases into the ambient air any hazardous air pollutant listed pursuant to Section 7412 of this title or any extremely hazardous substance listed pursuant to Section 11002(a)(2) of this title that is not listed in Section 7412 of this title, and who at the time negligently places another person in imminent danger of death or serious bodily injury shall, upon conviction, be punished by a fine, or by imprisonment for not more than 1 year, or both. For repeat offenders the maximum punishment shall be doubled with respect to both the fine and imprisonment.[205]

5)   Any person who knowingly releases into the ambient air any hazardous air pollutant listed pursuant to Section 7412 or any extremely hazardous substance listed pursuant to Section 11002(a)(2) that is not listed in Section 7412, and who knows at the time that he places another person in imminent danger of death or serious bodily injury shall, upon conviction, be punished by a fine or imprisonment of not more than 15 years, or both. Organizations convicted of this violation shall be subject to a fine of not more than $1,000,000 for each violation. For repeat offenders, the maximum punishment shall be doubled with respect to both the fine and imprisonment.[206]

D.   CITIZEN ACTIONS

In addition to government actions, the CAA allows for and encourages citizens to enforce its provisions with the use of citizen suits.[207] Under Section 304, citizens may sue to enforce CAA provisions against polluters or government agencies.[208]

---

[205]   CAA § 113(c)(4); 42 U.S.C.A. § 7413(c)(4).

[206]   CAA § 113(c)(5); 42 U.S.C.A. § 7413(c)(5).

[207]   Belden, Roy S., Preparing for the Onslought of Clean Air Act Citizen Suits: A Review of Strategies and Defenses, 1 Envtl.Law. 377 (1995).

[208]   CAA § 304; 42 U.S.C.A. § 7604.

Specifically, Section 304 allows citizens to sue on their own behalf against:

1)   any person, including the United States, and any other government agency to the extent permitted by the 11th Amendment of the Constitution, who is alleged to be in violation of either an emission standard or limitation, or an order issued by EPA or a State with respect to such a standard or limitation;[209]

2)   EPA where there is an allegation that EPA has failed to perform an act or duty that is non-discretionary;[210] or

3)   any person who proposes to construct or constructs any new or modified, major emitting facility without a required permit.[211]

These suits may be brought in any federal district court without regard to the amount in controversy or the citizenship of the parties. These suits are effectively used to enforce an emission standard or limitation, order EPA to perform a certain act or duty, and to apply appropriate civil penalties against polluters. Additionally, persons suing under section 304(a), may be awarded litigation costs, including reasonable attorney and expert witness fees as the court deems appropriate.[212]

Section 304(b) provides notice requirements for citizen suits.[213] A suit against any person who violates emissions standards or limitations must be

---

[209]   *See*, Committee for Environmentally Sound Development, Inc. v. The City of New York, 1998 W.L. 832606 (S.D.N.Y. 1998).

[210]   *See*, Environmental Defense Fund v. United States EPA, 167 F.3d 641 (D.C.Cir. 1999).

[211]   CAA § 304; 42 U.S.C.A. § 7604.

[212]   CAA §§ 113(b), 304(d), 307(f); 42 U.S.C.A. §§ 7413(b), 7604(d), 7607(f); *see also*, Ruckelshaus v. Sierra Club, 463 U.S. 680, 691; 103 S.Ct. 3274; 77 L.Ed.2d 938 (1983).

[213]   CAA § 304(b); 42 U.S.C.A. § 7604(b).

commenced no earlier than 60 days after the plaintiff has given notice of the violation to EPA, to the state in which the violation occurred, and to any alleged violator.[214] Note that where either EPA, or a State, has already sued the same entity to require compliance, no separate action may be commenced by any other person. However, an interested person may intervene in the existing suit as a matter of right.[215]

E. JUDICIAL INTERPRETATIONS

1. SIP Enforcement Allowed

In *General Motors Corp. v. United States*, the Supreme Court addressed whether EPA could enforce an existing SIP if it failed to complete a review of a SIP revision in a timely manner. A General Motors plant tried to extend a compliance deadline for installation of emission controls imposed by an existing SIP. Massachusetts authorities approved the extension and submitted it to EPA as a proposed SIP revision one day before the existing SIP compliance deadline. Twenty months later, while the proposed SIP revision was still pending, EPA filed an enforcement action alleging violations of the existing SIP deadline. The Supreme Court held that EPA could enforce the existing SIP even if it unreasonably delayed in acting on a proposed SIP revision.[216]

2. Aerial Photography Allowed Without a Warrant

In *DOW Chemical Co. v. United States*, the Supreme Court held that the government's use of aerial photography to perform a site inspection was not a "search" requiring a warrant and was upheld as a legal enforcement tool for government agencies.[217]

---

[214] CAA § 304(b)(1); 42 U.S.C.A. § 7604(b)(1); *see*, Anderson v. Farmland Industries, Inc., 45 F.Supp.2d 863 (D.Kan.1999).

[215] CAA § 304(b)(1)(B); 42 U.S.C.A. § 7604(b)(1)(B); *see also*, Ruckelshaus v. Sierra Club, 463 U.S. at 691 (1983).

[216] General Motors Corp. v. United States, 496 U.S. 530; 110 S.Ct. 2528; 110 L.Ed.2d 480 (1990).

[217] DOW Chemical Co. v. United States, 476 U.S. 227; 106 S.Ct. 1819; 90 L.Ed.2d 226 (1986).

3.   EPA Must Issue Final Standards

In *Sierra Club v. Ruckelshaus*, citizens effectively sued under CAA Section 304 to force EPA to meet its nondiscretionary duty to issue final standards for radionuclides emissions.[218]

VIII.   CONCLUSION

The CAA, one of the most far-reaching regulatory programs ever to be enacted, is an attempt to close the gap between the goal and the reality of clean air in the United States. The 1990 amendments to the CAA has created laws that attempt to control acid rain, urban smog, hazardous air pollutants, ozone protection, and allows for marketing pollution rights through its offsetting program. The CAA attempts to balance economic needs with environmental protection by using the availability of technological solutions.

The programs established under the CAA are comprehensive and complex and will take many years to fully implement. If federal, state, and local governments, as well as consumers and industry, cooperatively fund and implement these programs, the goals of the CAA will be met and our air will become much cleaner.

---

[218]   Sierra Club v. Ruckelshaus, 602 F.Supp. 892 (N.D.Cal.1984).

CHAPTER 6

THE CLEAN WATER ACT
(CWA)

*"[N]obody can be in good health if he does not
have all the time, fresh air, sunshine, and good
water."*

- Flying Hawk, Oglala Sioux Chief

CHAPTER 6: THE CLEAN WATER ACT

I.   INTRODUCTION

Clean water is essential to human health, productive economies, and
robust ecosystems. Without water, life on Earth as we know it could not exist.
Water is used for many purposes in today's world and is considered necessary
to most human endeavors. However, many human activities contaminate our
waters.   Water pollution has increased substantially since the Industrial
Revolution. This increase is due to such factors as increasing human population,
greater per capita use of water for hygienic, manufacturing, and luxury purposes,
and the use of natural waters for disposal of an increasing array of waste
products.[1] After recognizing the need for action to help clean and maintain our
nation's navigable waters, Congress enacted the Federal Water Pollution Control
Act (FWPCA)[2] in 1972 which was substantially supplemented by the Clean

---

[1]   THE ENCYCLOPEDIA OF THE ENVIRONMENT, pg. 557 (Ruth A. Eblen & William
R. Eblen, eds. 1994).

[2]   33 U.S.C.A. §§ 1251-1376; Pub.L. No. 92-500; 86 Stat. 816.

Water Act of 1977.[3] Both acts and their subsequent amendments[4] in 1981, 1987, and 1993), are commonly referred to as the "Clean Water Act." The Clean Water Act (CWA) is a comprehensive and technically rigorous piece of legislation that seeks to protect the nation's navigable waters from pollution. To do this, the CWA specifically regulates pollutant discharges into the "navigable waters" of the United States[5] by implementing two concepts: setting water quality standards for surface water and limiting effluent discharges into such waters.

The policy objectives of the CWA are to restore and maintain the "chemical, physical and biological integrity of the nation's waters."[6] To achieve these objectives, the CWA[7] and its judicial interpretations[8] originally set the following national goals:

    1)   that pollutant discharges into the navigable waters be eliminated by 1985;

---

[3]   33 U.S.C.A. §§ 1251-1387; Pub.L. No. 95-217; HR 3199 - Dec. 27, 1977 (Codified in various sections of 33 U.S.C.A.).

[4]   *See* Amendments in 1981, 1987, 1993; Pub.L. No. 103-431 (1994) "Ocean Pollution Reduction Act" which amended § 1311; Pub.L. No. 101-596 (1990) "Great Lakes Critical Program Act" which amended §§ 1268, 1334 and enacted § 1270, and the "Long Island Sound Imp. Act" which amended § 1324(d)(2) and enacted § 1269, and the "Lake Champlan Special Designation Act" which amended § 1324(d) and enacted § 1270.

[5]   CWA § 101; 33 U.S.C.A. § 1251.

[6]   CWA § 101(a); 33 U.S.C.A. § 1251(a).

[7]   CWA § 101(a)(1)-(7); 33 U.S.C.A. § 1251(a)(1)-(7).

[8]   *See*, Train v. City of New York, 420 U.S. 35; 95 S.Ct. 839; 43 L.Ed.2d 1 (1975) (CWA is a comprehensive program for controlling and abating water pollution); United States v. Borowski, 977 F.2d 27 (1st. Cir.1992) (CWA is not designed to protect individual workers because its objective is to restore and maintain the chemical, physical, and biological integrity of the nation's waters); Quivira Mining Co. v. United States EPA, 765 F.2d 126 (10th. Cir.1985) (intent of CWA is to cover, as much as possible, all United States waters); United States v. Earth Sciences, Inc., 599 F.2d 368 (10th Cir.1979) (CWA was designed to regulate, to the fullest extent possible, sources that emit pollution into rivers, streams and lakes).

2)   that wherever attainable, an interim goal of water quality that provides for the protection and propagation of fish, shellfish, and wildlife and also provides for recreation in and on the water be achieved by July 1, 1983;

3)   that the discharge of toxic pollutants in toxic amounts be prohibited;

4)   that federal financial assistance be provided to construct Publicly Owned Treatment Works;

5)   that local and regional waste treatment management planning processes be developed and implemented to assure adequate control of pollutant sources in each State;

6)   that a major research and demonstration effort be made to develop technology necessary to end the discharge of pollutants into the navigable waters, waters of the contiguous zone, and the oceans; and

7)   that programs for the control of nonpoint sources of pollution be developed and implemented in an expeditious manner to enable CWA goals to be met through the control of both point and nonpoint sources of water pollution.

A.   SOURCES OF POLLUTION

The CWA divides pollution into two fundamental categories: pollution from point sources and pollution from nonpoint sources.

1.   Point Sources

A point source is "any discernible, confined and discrete conveyance, including but not limited to any pipe, ditch, channel, tunnel conduit, well, discrete fissure, container, rolling stock, concentrated animal feeding operation, or vessel or other 'floating craft'[9] from which pollutants are or may be

---

[9]   United States v. West Indies Transport, 127 F.3d 299 (3d Cir. 1997) (floating craft), *cert. denied* 118 S.Ct. 700.

discharged."[10] Thus, most point sources are commercial or industrial facilities or Publicly Owned Treatments Works (POTWs). POTWs are waste treatment facilities designed to treat domestic waste waters and are usually owned by a state, local municipality, or Indian tribe. Additional examples of point sources may include:

1)   mining spoil piles;[11]

2)   bulldozers, backhoes,[12] and dump trucks;[13]

3)   redeposit material from land clearing operations;[14]

4)   culverts running under a railway at the boundary of a landfill connecting two portions of a marsh;[15]

5)   concentrated animal feeding operations (CAFOs);[16]

6)   deep injection wells;[17]

---

[10]   CWA § 502(14); 33 U.S.C.A. § 1362(14); *but see*, Hersperger, Stephanie L., A Point Source of Pollution under the Clean Water Act: A Human Being Should be Included, 5 Dick. J. Envtl. L. & Pol'y 97 (1996).

[11]   Sierra Club v. Abston Construction Co., Inc., 620 F.2d 41 (5th Cir.1980).

[12]   Avoylelles Sportsmen's League, Inc. v. Marsh, 715 F.2d 897 (5th Cir.1983); *see also*, United States v. Holland, 373 F.Supp. 665, 668 (M.D.Fla.1974).

[13]   United States v. Weisman, 489 F.Supp. 1331 (M.D.Fla.1980).

[14]   Avoyelles Sportsmen's League, Inc. v. Marsh, 715 F.2d 897 (5th Cir.1983).

[15]   Dague v. City of Burlington, 935 F.2d 1343 (2d Cir.1991).

[16]   Carr v. Alta Verde Industries, Inc., 931 F.2d 1055 (5th Cir.1991); *but see* Oregon Natural Desert Association v. Domdeck, 172 F.3d 1092, 1095 (9th Cir. 1998) (cattle grazing is not a point source).

[17]   Inland Steel Co. v. United States EPA, 901 F.2d 1419 (7th Cir.1990).

7) pipes and spillways;[18]

8) leachate from reserve sumps;[19]

9) raw sewage discharge from privately owned septic systems;[20]

10) culverts through which water flowed from a city landfill into adjacent wetlands;[21]

11) hazardous waste lagoon overflows;[22] and

12) target launchers and shooting platforms at a skeet shooting range.[23]

In the 1987 CWA amendments, Congress classified storm water runoff as a point source.[24] "Storm water runoff" is defined as wastewater generated by rainfall that flows over terrain into navigable waters that picks up pollutants along the way.[25] The CWA requires that storm water runoff from industrial activities and municipal storm sewer systems be regulated under the National Pollution Discharge Elimination System (NPDES) permit program. Thus, industrial activities that add pollutants to storm water runoff, such as that resulting from food and tobacco processing facilities, sawmills, paper, and pulp mills, chemical plants, oil producing plants, and waste treatment, storage, and

---

[18] National Wildlife Federation v. Gorsuch, 693 F.2d 156, (D.C. Cir.1982).

[19] United States v. Earth Sciences, Inc., 599 F.2d 368 (10th Cir.1979).

[20] Friends of Sakonnet v. Dutra, 738 F.Supp. 623 (D.R.I.1990).

[21] Dague v. City of Burlington, 732 F.Supp. 458 (D.Vt.1989).

[22] Fishel v. Westinghouse Elec. Corp., 640 F.Supp. 442 (M.D.Pa.1986).

[23] Long Island Soundkeeper v. New York Athletic Club, WL 131863 (S.D.N.Y. 1996).

[24] CWA § 402(p); 33 U.S.C.A. § 1342(p).

[25] Natural Resources Defense Council v. Costle, 568 F.2d 1369, 1377 (D.C. Cir.1977).

disposal facilities must include storm water conditions in their NPDES permits. Note that municipalities with populations greater than 100,000 have had to apply with similar permit requirements by 1991, for a permit that would be issued by 1993, and with the permit providing for expeditious compliance, but not later than three years after issuance.[26]

There exist certain exemptions from the NPDES program. For example, agricultural storm water runoff or return flows from irrigated farmland are generally exempt from the storm water runoff permit requirements.[27] Also, this exemption includes not just random run-off of rain but almost all agricultural discharges. Much litigation has centered around this exception and courts have held that the exemption does not apply to:

1)   deliberate emptying of a wastewater holding pond servicing a concentrated animal feeding station after the pond had been filled with heavy rain;[28] nor to

2)   the disposal of 80 gallons of agricultural chemicals down a storm sewer.[29]

Although point source pollution, including storm water discharges from industrial activities and municipalities, accounts for a significant amount of water pollution, some water pollution originates from what are called "nonpoint sources."

2.   Nonpoint Sources

A "nonpoint source" is a source of water pollution without a single point of origin or, in other words, pollution that is not introduced into a receiving

---

[26]   CWA § 402(p)(4)(B); 33 U.S.C.A. § 1342(p)(4)(B).

[27]   CWA § 502(14); 33 U.S.C.A. § 1362(14); *see also*, United States v. Samuel Gratz, 1993 WL 19733 (E.D.Penn.1993).

[28]   Carr v. Alta Verde Industries, Inc., 931 F.2d 1055 (5th Cir.1991).

[29]   United States v. Samuel Gratz, 1993 WL 19733 *7 (E.D. Penn.1993).

body of water from a specific outlet.[30] Some examples of nonpoint sources may include agriculture,[31] forestry, urban development, mining, construction, dams, channels, land disposal, saltwater intrusion, and city streets.

State plans to identify and control nonpoint sources are under way throughout the United States. Control involves a process that:

1)   identifies and locates pollution problem areas;

2)   designates critical watershed zones vulnerable to pollution and ideal for pollution control efforts;

3)   selects appropriate Best Management Practices (BMPs) that may mitigate pollution;

4)   conducts a public education campaign;

5)   selects and implements the appropriate BMPs; and

6)   evaluates and re-evaluates performance, as necessary.[32]

B.   TYPES OF POLLUTANTS

The primary pollutants in our nation's waters fall into one of three categories: conventional, toxic, and nonconventional pollutants.

1.   Conventional Pollutants

Conventional pollutants are those commonly expected to pollute navigable waters. They include but are not limited to, biological oxygen demand

---

[30]   *See e.g.*, Donahue, Debra L., The Untapped Power of Clean Water Act Section 401, 23 Ecology L. Q. 201 (1996).

[31]   Zanng, David, Agriculture, Nonpoint Source Pollution, and Regulatory Control: The Clean Water Act's Bleak Present and Future, 20 Harv. Envtl. L. Rev. 515 (1996).

[32]   *See* Eblen, *supra* note 12 at 560.

(BOD), suspended solids, fecal coliform, and pH.[33]   Commonly known substances such as organic waste, sediment, acid, bacteria, viruses, nutrients, salts, oil and grease, and heat are also considered conventional pollutants.

2.   Toxic Pollutants

"Toxic pollutants" are identified as those substances that can cause death, disease, behavioral abnormalities, cancer, genetic mutations, physical malformations/deformations or birth defects in organisms and their offspring[34] and include: heavy metals (cadmium, silver, lead, copper, mercury, zinc, chromium, and nickel), hazardous wastes, and pesticides.[35]   Under Section 307(a)(1), EPA must publish a list of toxic pollutants taking into account toxicity, persistence, degradability, and the nature and extent of effects on organisms in any waters.[36]

3.   Nonconventional Pollutants

"Nonconventional pollutants" are identified as substances that do not fit the definition of either a conventional or toxic pollutant.[37]   These include ammonia, chlorine, color, iron, and total phenols and any other pollutant EPA lists as a nonconventional pollutant.[38]

---

[33]   CWA § 304(a)(4); 33 U.S.C.A. § 1314(a)(4).

[34]   CWA § 502(13); 33 U.S.C.A. § 1362(13).

[35]   *Id.*

[36]   CWA § 307(a)(1); 33 U.S.C.A. § 1317(a)(1).

[37]   CWA § 301(b)(1)(F); 33 U.S.C.A. § 1311(b)(1)(F).

[38]   CWA § 301(g)(1), (4); 33 U.S.C.A. § 1311(g)(1), (4).

C. STATUTORY SCHEME

As part of its overall structure, the CWA prohibits any "person"[39] from "discharging"[40] "pollutants,"[41] including dredged or fill materials, into "navigable waters"[42] of the United States without a permit. These terms, as defined by the CWA, regulations, and judicial opinions, are explained below.

1. Person

Under the CWA, a "person" is "an individual, corporation, partnership, association, State, municipality, commission, or political subdivision of a State, or any interstate body."[43] The CWA includes government entities (such as states[44]) as persons in order to hold them directly accountable for environmental harm they cause. Inclusion of the United States as a "person" occurs only in clauses subjecting the United States to suit.[45]

"Persons" also include federal employees who violate the CWA. For example, in *United States v. Curtis*, the director of the Adak Naval Air Station in Alaska was criminally indicted on five counts of dumping jet fuel into an abandoned discharge line that opened into the Bering Sea.[46]

---

[39]   CWA § 502(5); 33 U.S.C.A. § 1362(5).

[40]   CWA § 502(12); 33 U.S.C.A. § 1362(12).

[41]   CWA §§ 502 (12), (19); 33 U.S.C.A. §§ 1362 (12), (19).

[42]   CWA § 101(a)(1); 33 U.S.C.A. § 1251(a)(1).

[43]   CWA § 502(5); 33 U.S.C.A. § 1362(5).

[44]   CWA § 505(a)(1); 33 U.S.C.A. § 1365(a)(1); *see also*, City of Milwaukee, et al. v. States of Illinois and Michigan, 451 U.S. 304; 101 S.Ct.1784; 68 L.Ed.2d 114 (1981).

[45]   United States Dept. of Energy v. Ohio, 503 U.S. 607, 617-618; 112 S.Ct. 1627, 1634-1645; 118 L.Ed.2d 255, 267-268 (1992) (the United States must specifically waive its sovereign immunity in order to be sued).

[46]   United States v. Curtis, 988 F.2d 946 (9th Cir.1993).

2. Discharge

A "discharge" of a pollutant is "any addition of any pollutant to navigable waters from any point source, [and] any addition of any pollutant to the waters of the contiguous zone or the ocean from any point source other than a vessel or other floating craft."[47] EPA has successfully argued that to "discharge" a pollutant, a facility must "add" pollutants to navigable waters from the "outside world."[48] This does not include natural organic material already present in the water.[49] Some examples of activities that constitute a "discharge" include:[50]

1) landowners' wetlands filling activities;[51]

2) landowners' removal of vegetation from wetlands and redeposit of the vegetation back into the wetlands;[52]

3) pouring wet cement on top of a fill that was previously placed in a wetlands area, to create a patio for a house trailer;[53]

---

[47] CWA § 502(12); 33 U.S.C.A. § 1362(12); *see* United States v. West Indies Transport, 127 F.3d 299 (3d Cir. 1997), *cert. denied* 118 S.Ct. 700 (1998) (a barge is a point source).

[48] National Wildlife Federation v. Gorsuch, 693 F.2d 156, 174-175 (D.C. Cir.1982).

[49] *Id.*

[50] *See*, State of Missouri ex rel. Ashcroft v. U.S. Army Corps of Engineers, 526 F.Supp. 660 (W.D.Mo.1980), aff'd 672 F.2d 1297 (8th Cir.1982) (discusses what is not a discharge).

[51] *See*, United States v. Pozsgai, 999 F.2d 719 (3d Cir.1993); Fox Bay Partners v. U.S. Army Corps of Engineers, 831 F.Supp. 605 (N.D.Ill.1983); United States v. Lambert, 589 F.Supp. 366 (M.D.Fla.1984).

[52] Avoyelles Sportsmen's League, Inc. v. Marsh, 715 F.2d 897 (5th Cir.1983).

[53] United States v. Robinson, 570 F.Supp. 1157 (M.D.Fla.1983).

4)   indirect, accidental, or unintentional releases;[54] and

5)   placing clean fill dirt on dry land.[55]

3.   Pollutants

"Pollutants" are "any dredged spoil, solid waste, incinerator residue, sewage, garbage, sewage sludge, munitions, chemical wastes, biological materials, radioactive materials, heat, wrecked or discarded equipment, rock, sand, cellar dirt and industrial, municipal, and agricultural waste discharged into water."[56] Note that there exists debate over whether certain substances should be considered a pollutant under the CWA.[57]

Although oil is not specifically included as a pollutant under the CWA, it is not expressly excluded either.[58] For example, in *United States v. Hamel*, the Court of Appeals adopted a broad definition of "pollutant" and held that

---

[54]   *See*, e.g., SED, Inc. v. City of Dayton, 519 F.Supp. 979, 989 (S.D.Ohio 1981); United States v. Earth Sciences, Inc., 599 F.2d at 374.

[55]   United States v. Mills, 817 F.Supp. 1546, 1548 (N.D. Fla.1993), aff'd 36 F.3d 1052 (11th Cir.1994).

[56]   CWA § 502(6); 33 U.S.C.A. § 1362(6).

[57]   *See* National Crushed Stone Association v. United States EPA, 601 F.2d 111 (4th Cir.1979), *rev'd on other grounds at* 449 U.S. 64, 101 S.Ct. 295, 66 L.Ed.2d 268 (crushed stone from mining is a are pollutant); Avoyelles Sportsmen's League, Inc. v. Marsh, 715 F.2d 897 (5th Cir.1983) (dredged material is a pollutant even where it comes from same water it is being discharged to); United States v. Pozsgai, 999 F.2d 719 (3d Cir.1993) (pollutants include dredged soil, rock, sand, concrete rubble and cinder blocks); United States v. Schallom, 998 F.2d 196 (4th Cir.1993) (pollutants also include "shotcrete," a combination of sand and cement); United States v. Weisman, 489 F.Supp. 1331 (M.D.Fla.1980) (fill material dumped and spread on defendant's property for construction of a road constituted a "pollutant"); United States v. Bradshaw, 541 F.Supp. 880, 884 (D.Md.1981) (demolition debris and sand used by property owner to fill wetlands were considered "pollutants" under the CWA).

[58]   CWA § 502(6); 33 U.S.C.A. § 1362(6).

petroleum products are pollutants under the CWA.[59]   The Appeals Court reasoned that although the definition could have been more clearly written to include petroleum products, it did not exclude petroleum products. The Appeals Court further reasoned that petroleum products are included in the definition of "pollutant" as a "man-made or man-induced alteration of the chemical, physical, biological, and radiological integrity of the water."[60]

4.   Navigable Waters of the United States

"Navigable waters" are defined as "waters of the United States, including the territorial seas."[61]   EPA regulations more specifically define "navigable waters" to also include any water from intrastate waters to prairie potholes;[62] wetlands;[63] intermittently flowing tributaries;[64] the territorial seas;"[65] and bodies of water wholly within a state whose use or misuse could affect interstate commerce.[66]

---

[59]   United States v. Hamel, 551 F.2d 107, 110 (6th Cir.1977).

[60]   *Id.*; *but see* Waste Action Project v. Dawn Mining Corp., 137 F.3d 1426 (9th Cir. 1998) (uranium mine tailings are not pollutants under the CWA).

[61]   CWA § 502(7); 33 U.S.C.A. § 1362(7).

[62]   40 C.F.R. §§ 110.1, 117.1(i).

[63]   33 C.F.R. § 323.3(a)(3).

[64]   United States v. Texas Pipeline Co., 611 F.2d 345 (10th Cir.1979); *see also,* United States v. Pozsgai, 999 F.2d 719 (3d Cir.1993) (landowners' wetland filling activities constituted a discharge of pollutants into water within meaning of the CWA).

[65]   CWA § 502(7) & (8); 33 U.S.C.A. § 1362(7) & (8); *see also,* Remy, Carol Elizabeth, United States Territorial Sea Extension: Jurisdiction And International Environmental Protection, 16 Fordham Int'l L.J. 1208, 1222-1223 (1993) (territorial seas extend seaward a distance of between 3 and 12 miles from the shore line).

[66]   Hoffman Homes, Inc. v. United States EPA, 999 F.2d 256, 260 (7th Cir.1993).

In addition to the traditional definitions of "navigable waters,"[67] federal courts have defined "waters of the United States" to also include intermittent waste streams,[68] tidal creeks,[69] dry arroyos,[70] canals,[71] rivers and streams,[72] and the contiguous zone. However, "navigable waters" do not include groundwater.[73] For example, a citizens' suit could not be maintained against the federal government for the Coast Guard's release of contaminants into ground water even though contaminants eventually migrated into a nearby bay.[74]

To regulate the discharge of pollutants into navigable waters, the CWA is based on two concepts to implement its major programs: 1) state water quality

---

[67]   United States v. Oxford Royal Mushroom Products, Inc., 487 F.Supp. 852 (E.D.Pa.1980) (navigable waters of the United States do not require navigability in fact).

[68]   Municipal Power Agency v. United States EPA, 836 F.2d 1482 (5th Cir.1988).

[69]   United States v. Weisman, 489 F.Supp. 1331 (M.D.Fla.1980).

[70]   United States v. Phelps Dodge Corp., 391 F.Supp. 1181 (D.C.Ariz.1975).

[71]   United States v. Holland, 373 F.Supp. 665 (M.D.Fla.1974) (waters of nonnavigable, man-made mosquito canals, which emptied into a bayou arm of Tampa Bay, were "waters of the United States" within the CWA).

[72]   United States v. Texas Pipe Line Co., 611 F.2d 345 (10th Cir.1979) (waters of unnamed tributary, which flowed, at least during times of significant rainfall, into a major river, were "navigable waters" within meaning of this chapter even if the stream was not discharging water continuously into a river navigable in the traditional sense); United States v. Earth Sciences, Inc., 599 F.2d 368 (10th Cir.1979) (stream that supported trout and beaver and was used for irrigation was a navigable water despite the fact that it was not used to transport goods or materials); United States v. Zanger, 767 F.Supp. 1030 (N.D.Cal.1991) (intermittent stream was one of the "waters of the United States" within scope of the CWA where it either was or could be used for recreational purposes, had been used for commercial fishing and was a tributary of other water of the United States).

[73]   Kelley for and on Behalf of the People of the State of Michigan v. United States, 618 F.Supp. 1103 (W.D.Mich.1985); see also, United States v. GAF Corp., 389 F.Supp. 1379 (S.D.Tex.1975) (disposal of chemical wastes into underground waters that do not flow into or affect surface water does not constitute "discharge of a pollutant").

[74]   Kelley for and on Behalf of the People of the State of Michigan v. United States, 618 F.Supp. 1103 (W.D. Mich.1985).

standards; and 2) federal effluent limitations. State water quality standards are controls which the states enforce under Section 303 of the CWA, and which focus on "the capacity of the receiving water to absorb or dilute a given pollutant."[75] These water quality standards, also called ambient water standards, are "legal expressions of permissible amounts of pollutants allowed in a defined water segment."[76] In contrast, effluent limitations are technology-based controls that focus on the treatment of pollutants prior to their discharge into navigable waters. The NPDES program[77] implements and regulates these effluent limitations.

II.   STATE WATER QUALITY STANDARDS

Water quality standards are controls that focus on the capacity of navigable waters to absorb or dilute a given pollutant. State water quality standards function in two ways. First, as a measure of performance, the standards establish the maximum level of pollution allowable in interstate waters. Second, the standards provide for a legal cause of action against polluters. If the wastes discharged by polluters reduce water quality below established standards, polluters may be subject to enforcement actions.

A.   DESIGNATING USES

Under CWA Section 303, States are designated that authority to set water quality standards[78] in conformance with the CWA's antidegradation policy that is strictly enforced by EPA.

1.   Antidegradation Policy

The CWA authorizes EPA to establish and enforce an antidegradation policy.[79]

---

[75]   *Id.*

[76]   Bogardus, Lisa M., State Certification of Hydroelectric Facilities under Section 401 of the Clean Water Act, 12 Va. Envtl. L.J. 43 (1992).

[77]   CWA § 402; 33 U.S.C.A. § 1342.

[78]   CWA § 303; 33 U.S.C.A. § 1313.

[79]   CWA § 303(d)(4)(B); 33 U.S.C.A. § 1313(d)(4)(B).

The policy which prohibits deterioration of water bodies when their quality equals or exceeds levels necessary to attain applicable water quality standards. In other words, the goal is to keep clean waters clean. The designated use for these pristine bodies of water should be at least fishable or swimmable. The policy allows limited lowering of high water quality standards, only when "it is necessary to accommodate important economic or social development in the area in which the waters are located,"[80] even though such exceptions are sparingly granted.[81]

2.   Five Designated Uses

The CWA authorizes states to establish water quality standards designating one of five possible water uses for each water body or segments of water bodies. These five uses include: public water supplies, propagation of fish and wildlife, recreation, agriculture, and industry.[82] Under the CWA, the goal for all navigable waters should be at least "fishable and swimmable."[83] These use designations must be reviewed every three years.[84]

States must also determine the criteria that establishes the maximum amount of pollutants to be discharged into a specific segment of water so that the designated use is attained. These can either be numerical or narrative and can be rejected by EPA.[85] For example, a state might set the water quality standard for a certain creek by designating it as a "fishing area" (the use) and requiring the chloride concentration be no greater than 250 milligrams per liter of water (the criteria).

---

[80]   40 C.F.R. § 131.12(a)(2).

[81]   CWA §§ 101(a)(2) & 303(c)(3); 33 U.S.C.A. §§ 1251(a)(2) & 1313(c)(3); 40 C.F.R. § 131.10(g)(6), (j).

[82]   CWA § 303(c)(2)(A); 33 U.S.C.A. § 1313(c)(2)(A).

[83]   CWA § 101(a)(2); 33 U.S.C.A. § 1251(a)(2).

[84]   CWA § 303(c)(1); 33 U.S.C.A. § 1313(c)(1). Note that new TMDL regulations were proposed in 1999.

[85]   40 C.F.R. § 131.11.

Once a use is designated, the water quality must be tested to see if it is above or below standards that would allow for the designated use. To create a consistent and uniform testing method, EPA has developed a "mixing zone" concept. If testing results show the water quality to be above the designated use, then the water is cleaner than the designated use and the "antidegradation policy" takes effect. In contrast, if testing results show the water quality to be below the designated use, then the water is dirtier then the designated use and violates the CWA. If a state finds it impossible to attain a designated use, then "downgrading" may be allowed.

B.   TESTING WATER QUALITY AND MIXING ZONES

Once a use is designated for a water body, the water must be periodically tested to see if its quality is in compliance with its designated use. Since concentrations of pollutants within the immediate proximity of any discharge are so high as to exceed (violate) water quality standards, and because industry and technology are not yet available to guarantee "no pollutant discharges," it is necessary to establish a boundary allowing pollution dispersement. EPA created the concept of a mixing zone to allow a discharge to disseminate and become diluted prior to water quality testing.[86] A mixing zone is the distance extending 100 meters in all directions from the effluent discharge point.[87]

Water quality testing should be conducted on the outer edges of the mixing zone.[88] The results of testing should demonstrate compliance with the designated water quality standard. If not, the polluter is held accountable.

C.   DOWNGRADING DESIGNATED USES

In situations where the water body is extremely polluted and will only support limited aquatic species, the designated use (and national goal) of fishable/swimmable may be very difficult to attain. For this reason, EPA regulations allow for a "downgrading" of the designated use from the higher level of fishable and swimmable to a lower level such as industrial use. For EPA to approve downgrading the state must conduct a "use attainability analysis"

---

[86]   Puerto Rico Sun Oil Company v. United States EPA, 8 F.3d 73 (1st Cir.1993).

[87]   40 C.F.R. § 125.121(c).

[88]   Marathon Oil Co. v. United States EPA, 830 F.2d 1346, 1349 (5th Cir.1987).

designed to demonstrate that attainment of the initial designated use is not feasible.[89] EPA allows for downgrading by states if the designated use is not feasible when:

1)   naturally occurring pollutant concentrations prevent the attainment of the use;

2)   natural low flow conditions or low water levels prevent attainment of the use;

3)   human-caused conditions or pollution sources prevent the attainment of the use and cannot be remedied or would cause more environmental damage to correct them;

4)   dams, diversions or other types of hydrologic modifications preclude attainment;

5)   physical conditions related to natural features of the water body, cover, flow, depth, pools, riffles and the like, unrelated to water quality, preclude attainment of aquatic life protection uses; or

6)   controls more stringent than those required by Section 301(b) and Section 306 of the CWA would result in widespread and substantial economic hardships.[90]

Downgrading is not allowed if the water is an outstanding natural resource such as waters of national and state parks and wildlife refuges, and waters of exceptional recreational or ecological significance.[91]

---

[89]   CWA § 303(c)(2)(A); 33 U.S.C.A. § 1313(c)(2)(A) and 40 C.F.R. § 131.10 (1998).

[90]   40 C.F.R. § 131.10(g).

[91]   40 C.F.R. § 131.12(a)(3).

III.   FEDERAL EFFLUENT LIMITATIONS

A.   FEDERAL ROLE

Effluent limitations restrict the quantities, types, and concentrations of specified substances discharged from point sources.[92] Effluent limitations can vary. For example, in *Natural Resources Defense Council, Inc. v. Texaco Refining & Marketing, Inc.*, EPA issued two types of effluent limitations.[93] The first limitation was based on maximum daily limits of a particular pollutant that could be discharged from an outfall.[94] The second effluent limitation was based on daily average limits calculated as the maximum average amount that could be safely discharged over the course a calendar month.[95]

The CWA authorizes EPA to set effluent limitations for point sources (except POTWs) in order to regulate discharges into our nation's waters. The purpose of effluent limitations is to assure that water quality standards will be met.[96] The effluent limitations are set by federal regulation and will be specifically incorporated into a facility's permit as a prerequisite for approval to operate the facility.

B.   STATE ROLE

The CWA allows states to impose effluent limits more stringent than the federal limits whenever a source interferes with water quality.[97] EPA has no authority to set aside nor modify these limitations and must include in the permit

---

[92]   CWA §§ 301, 304; 33 U.S.C.A. §§ 1311, 1314.

[93]   Natural Resources Defense Council, Inc. v. Texaco Refining & Marketing, Inc., 2 F.3d. 493, 496 (3rd Cir.1993).

[94]   *Id.*

[95]   *Id.*

[96]   CWA § 301; 33 U.S.C.A. § 1311.

[97]   CWA § 510; 33 U.S.C.A. § 1370; *see, e.g.*, Mississippi Commission on Natural Resources v. Costle, 625 F.2d 1269 (5th Cir.1980).

any such modifications.[98] EPA's only authority regarding water quality standards is to determine whether the standards meet the applicable CWA requirements.[99] If they do not, then EPA can set the water quality standards.[100]

The CWA provides that a state must certify that effluent limits comply with water quality standards.[101] States must establish a "Total Maximum Daily Load" (TMDL) for waters where effluent limits are not stringent enough to achieve water quality standards.[102] These TMDLs apply to all navigable waters that fail water quality standards, even after the application of technology based limits.[103]

The CWA establishes several major programs that rely on the water quality standards and effluent limitations. These programs include: 1) NPDES Permit Program; 2) Wetlands Protection and Dredge and Fill Program; 3) Oil Spill Program; and 4) Nonpoint Source Pollution Program.

IV.   THE NATIONAL POLLUTION DISCHARGE ELIMINATION SYSTEM (NPDES) PERMIT PROGRAM

The National Pollution Discharge Elimination System (NPDES) permit program requires a permit for almost all point source discharges, except for oil and gas operations, prior to construction and/or for operations.[104] The NPDES permit gives the permittee the right to discharge specific pollutants from certain

---

[98]   United States Steel Corp. v. Train, 556 F.2d 822 (7th Cir.1977).

[99]   CWA § 303; 33 U.S.C.A. § 1313.

[100]   CWA § 302(a); 33 U.S.C.A. § 1312(a).

[101]   CWA § 401; 33 U.S.C.A. § 1341.

[102]   CWA § 303(d)(1)(C); 33 U.S.C.A. § 1313(d)(1)(C).

[103]   *Id.* TMDLs are to be set with a factor of safety for seasonal variations in flow and unknown conditions.

[104]   CWA § 402; 33 U.S.C.A. § 1342. Additional pollutants exempted from the NPDES program include sewage from vessels, discharges from some agricultural and silvicultural activities, discharges into POTWs, and discharges in compliance with instructions from an On-Scene Coordinator responding to a spill. 40 C.F.R. § 122.3.

point sources, and lasts approximately 5 years. In some instances, permits for internal waste streams above the final discharge point are also required.[105] The internal monitoring and treatment requirement is referred to as the "internal waste stream rule"[106] which provides the EPA with an enhanced ability to regulate and monitor the discharge of pollutants, to ensure the effectiveness of treatment processes, and to prevent the use of dilution as a treatment method."[107]

All NPDES permits contain effluent limitations (including technological requirements) necessary to achieve compliance with water quality standards. Additionally, NPDES permits require that the permit holder constantly monitor its discharges as well as the quality of the receiving waters.[108] The permit holder must also maintain records and periodically report discharge information to EPA (or a delegated State).[109]

A.   STATE DELEGATION

Under Section 306(c) of the CWA, states are delegated the authority to administer the NPDES program.[110] Under the CWA, permit program delegation has succeeded to the extent that more than fifty-seven states and territories currently administer the NPDES program under delegated authority. While EPA issues permits in the remaining states and territories, in a number of instances

---

[105]   Public Service Company of Colorado, Fort St. Train Station v. United States EPA, 949 F.2d 1063 (10th Cir.1991); *see also*, Texas Municipal Power Agency v. United States EPA, 836 F.2d 1482, 1486-1487 (5th Cir.1988).

[106]   40 C.F.R. § 122.45(h); *see also*, Texas Municipal Power Agency v. United States EPA, 836 F.2d 1482 (5th Cir.1988) (outlines internal waste stream rule).

[107]   Morris, James C. III & Deatherage, Scott D., Fifth Circuit Survey June 1987-May 1988 Environmental Law, 20 Tex. Tech L. Rev. 407 (1989).

[108]   40 C.F.R. § 122.48 (1998); *see also*, Chemical Manufacturers Ass'n. v. United States EPA, 870 F.2d 177 (5th Cir.1989).

[109]   CWA § 308 (a)(4)(A); 33 U.S.C.A. § 1318(a)(4)(A); *see also*, 40 C.F.R. § 122.6.

[110]   CWA § 306(c); 33 U.S.C.A. § 1316(c). State-issued permits under the NPDES program are often referred to as State Pollution Discharge Elimination System ("SPDES") permits. *See*, e.g. 40 C.F.R. Part 123.

non-delegated states administer their own permit programs under state law.[111] States that have the authority to administer their own NPDES programs must ensure that their programs are at least as stringent as the federal program. However, states may implement requirements that are more stringent than the federal program.[112]

B.   PERMIT CONDITIONS

1.   Broad Discretion

EPA is given broad discretion to carry out permit functions and to prescribe necessary regulations.[113] These expansive grants of power are given great deference by the courts.[114]

2.   Application

A NPDES permit application[115] must be submitted to EPA (or the delegated state) by anyone wishing to discharge pollutants into navigable waters from a point source. The application must be filed at least 180 days prior to the date of the proposed discharge or at least 180 days prior to the date an existing

---

[111] Copeland, Claudia, Comprehensive Clean Air and Clean Water Permits: Is the Glass Still Just Half Full? 21 Envtl. L. 2135, 2154-2156 (1991) (Principal reason some states do not seek delegation is lack of resources to administer the federal program. For others, the issue is how to effectively coordinate multiple agencies with jurisdiction over some portion of a state's water quality programs. Failure to seek delegation carries no explicit CWA penalty, but delegation presumably is one factor that EPA considers when awarding cooperative financial assistance agreements under Section 106).

[112] 40 C.F.R. 123.1(i).

[113] CWA § 501(a); 33 U.S.C.A. § 1361(a).

[114] *See*, American Meat Institute v. United States EPA, 526 F.2d 442 (7th Cir.1975).

[115] EPA applications include: Form 1 (general information), Form 2C (more detailed information for existing sources), Form 2D (detailed information for new sources and new discharges), Form 2E (for facilities that discharge only non-process wastewater), and Form 2F (for storm water discharges). *See* 40 C.F.R. § 122.21 for a complete discussion of the information required in NPDES permit forms.

permit is to expire,[116] and must include such general information as the location of the point source, amounts of the pollutant/effluent flow, effluent characteristics, and the average flow rate.[117]

If the permit is for a new discharge, sufficient information must be included for EPA to determine whether the discharge is a "new source,"[118] which may mean compliance with more detailed environmental review requirements under NEPA.[119] Also, states must certify that the discharge will comply with its own water quality standards.[120]

3.   Permit Issuance Process

If a state has been delegated authority to implement the NPDES permit program, then the state drafts the NPDES permit and submits it to EPA for review.[121] EPA then has 90 days to object to the proposed permit. EPA may object if it finds that waters in another state could be affected by emissions from the same permitted point source or that the proposed permit is "outside the guidelines and requirements" of the CWA.[122] If EPA objects, there must be a period for public comment and, if requested by the state or an interested party, the request must be made within 90 days of receipt of objections, and there must be a public hearing.[123] EPA must then modify, withdraw, or reaffirm its objections.[124]

---

[116]   40 C.F.R. § 121.21(c) and (d).

[117]   40 C.F.R. § 121.21(a)(1).

[118]   CWA § 306(a)(2); 33 U.S.C.A. § 1316(a)(2).

[119]   CWA § 511(c); 33 U.S.C.A. § 1371(c).

[120]   CWA § 402(b)(1)(A); 33 U.S.C.A. § 1342(b)(1)(A).

[121]   CWA § 402(d); 33 U.S.C.A. § 1342(d).

[122]   CWA § 402(d)(2); 33 U.S.C.A. § 1342(d)(2).

[123]   40 C.F.R. § 123.44 (e).

[124]   40 C.F.R. § 123.44(g).

If EPA reaffirms its objections, the state and EPA may proceed in one of two ways. The state may modify the terms of the proposed permit within 30 days of EPA's decision to stand by its objections. If the state modifies its permit in accordance with EPA, it must allow another comment period and public hearing before issuance. If the state refuses to modify the proposed permit, EPA has exclusive authority to issue the final permit.[125] However, before EPA can issue its own final permit, is should solicit public comments and conduct a public hearing.[126] Before issuing a final permit, either the state or EPA (depending on which entity has the authority) must present the proposed permit for public comment and public hearing.[127] A public notice of the hearing must be published and include:

1) mailing of notice to permit applicants and appropriate federal and state authorities; and

2) the mailing of a notice to any person or group who has requested placement on the NPDES permit mailing list for actions affecting the geographical area.[128]

After public comments are received and a hearing is held, EPA (or the delegated State) must respond to comments and issue a final permit that will become effective 30 days after issuance.[129]

---

[125] CWA §§ 402(d)(1), (4); 33 U.S.C.A. §§ 1342 (d)(1), (4).

[126] 40 C.F.R. §§ 124.6, 124.10, 124.12.

[127] Costle v. Pacific Legal Foundation, 445 U.S. 198; 100 S.Ct. 1095; 63 L.Ed.2d 329 (1980) (EPA extended to Los Angeles a temporary permit for a waste water treatment plant without a hearing. The United States Supreme Court held that it is reasonable to extend permits without a hearing when the public has exhibited no degree of interest in the permit); Natural Resources Defense Council (NRDC) v. United States EPA, 859 F.2d 156 (D.C. Cir.1988) (CWA promotes public participation in permit process through notice and opportunity for hearing); Trustees for Alaska v. United States EPA, 749 F.2d 549 (9th Cir.1984) (EPA was required to conduct a public hearing to allow parties challenging pollutant discharge permits issued to Alaska gold miners to present evidence on effluent limitations for arsenic and mercury, as well as monitoring requirements).

[128] 40 C.F.R. § 124.10(c).

[129] 40 C.F.R. § 124.12 (public hearings); 124.15(b) (1998) (30 days).

4.   Term

Generally, a NPDES permit is effective for a term of five years.[130] Note that upon expiration, the NPDES permit continues in effect so long as a renewal application is timely filed. A limited permit term ensures that at intervals not greater than five years, the terms and conditions of the permit be re-evaluated by EPA and the public.[131]

5.   Anti-Backsliding Policy

Backsliding means a regression or a decline in the amount or level of protection. The anti-backsliding policy limits the extent to which point sources can increase discharges above permitted levels. In most instances, an NPDES permit may not be modified to become more lenient (e.g. allow for backsliding).[132] The CWA requires that "a permit may not be renewed, reissued, or modified . . . to contain effluent limitations that are less stringent than the comparable effluent limitations in the previous permit except in compliance with [Section 303(d)(4), the TMDL section.]"[133]

However, there are limited circumstances where the CWA allows technology-based limits to be modified to contain a less strict standard in future permits.[134] For example, backsliding may be allowed if:

---

[130]   CWA § 402(b)(1)(B); 33 U.S.C.A. § 1342(b)(1)(B).

[131]   *See*, Pacific Legal Foundation v. Watt, 539 F.Supp. 841 (C.D.Cal.1982) (NPDES permits issued for less than the maximum five-year period may be extended up to but not beyond the five-year maximum); Natural Resources Defense Council (NRDC) v. United States EPA, 915 F.2d 1314, 1319 (9th Cir.1990) (Although NPDES permits are issued for no more than five years, administrative delays can extend their duration).

[132]   CWA § 402(o)(1); 33 U.S.C.A. § 1342(o)(1).

[133]   *Id.*

[134]   CWA § 402(o)(2); 33 U.S.C.A. § 1342(o)(2).

1)   material and substantial alterations or additions to the permitted facility occur after permit issuance which justify less stringent limitations;[135]

2)   where the permittee is unable to meet its present limitation despite installation, operation, and maintenance of necessary equipment;[136] or

3)   where new information was not available at the time the permit was issued.[137]

In other rare circumstances, backsliding may be allowed if courts view EPA's action to be arbitrary and capricious. For example, in *Puerto Rico Sun Oil Co. v. United States EPA*, the Court of Appeals held that if EPA had "mouse trapped" the discharger into standards that could not be relaxed later because of anti-backsliding provisions then such action was arbitrary and capricious.[138]

Although it is important to understand the general NPDES permit conditions, the most important part of a NPDES permit is the portion setting the standards of performance or effluent limitations applicable to a facility.

C.   STANDARDS OF PERFORMANCE

The CWA authorizes EPA to set effluent limitations for all point source discharges except for those from POTWs.[139] POTWs are not regulated by effluent limitations standards. However, they must meet secondary treatment requirements. Effluent limitations are determined by type and quantity of

---

[135]   CWA § 402(o)(2)(A); 33 U.S.C.A. § 1342(o)(2)(A); *see* e.g., Natural Resources Defense Council (NRDC) v. United States EPA, 859 F.2d 156 (D.C. Cir.1988).

[136]   CWA § 402(o)(2)(E); 33 U.S.C.A. § 1342(o)(2)(E).

[137]   CWA § 402(o)(2)(B)(i); 33 U.S.C.A. § 1342(o)(2)(B)(i); *see*, In the Matter of City of Tulsa, Oklahoma, NPDES Appeal No. 88-10, NPDES Permit No. OK0026221, 1991 NPDES LEXIS 14,15, 3 E.A.D. 505, 513, (January 31, 1991).

[138]   Puerto Rico Sun Oil Co. v. United States EPA, 8 F.3d 73 (1st Cir.1993).

[139]   CWA § 304(b)(4)(B); 33 U.S.C.A. § 1314(b)(4)(B).

pollutants.   The C.F.R. lists regulated industry by category and sets the appropriate effluent limitation standards for each pollutant commonly discharged by that industry.[140]   An effluent limitation standard is the "standard of performance" required for the covered industrial source.

The CWA requires different levels or types of standards of performance depending on whether a source is new or existing, whether its discharges will be of "conventional"[141] pollutants (biochemical oxygen demand, suspended solids, fecal coliform, pH, and oil and grease), "toxic"[142] pollutants (126 hazardous "priority pollutants" listed in the CWA) or "nonconventional pollutants" (pollutants that are neither "conventional" nor "toxic," as so defined), and whether the source releases pollutants directly into receiving waters (direct dischargers) or through a publicly owned treatment works (POTW) (indirect dischargers).[143]

The five standards of performance that apply to today's direct dischargers are BCT, BAT, BDT, secondary treatment, and ICS. BCT, BAT, and BDT standards control the degree of allowable pollution according to the level of technological achievement within the industry.   Secondary treatment applies specifically to POTWs and ICS applies to facilities discharging "toxic" pollutants into very polluted waters.

1.   Best Conventional Pollutant Control Technology (BCT)

BCT is a technology-based effluent limitation whose level of control is no less stringent than is generally described as the "average of the best" technology in use to control conventional pollutants.

---

[140]   CWA § 304(b)(1)(A), (B); 33 U.S.C.A. § 1314(b)(1)(A), (B).

[141]   40 C.F.R. § 401.16.

[142]   40 C.F.R. § 401.15; *see also*, Wiygul, Robert B., The Structure of Environmental Regulation on the Outer Continental Shelf: Sources, Problems, and the Opportunity for Change, 12 J. Energy Nat. Resources & Envtl. L. 75, 180 (1992).

[143]   Bobertz, Bradley C., The Tools of Prevention: Opportunities for Promoting Pollution Prevention under Federal Environmental Legislation, 12 Va. Envtl. L.J. 1, 15 (1992).

a.   BCT Applied

Existing facilities discharging conventional pollutants had to achieve BCT by March 31, 1989.[144] Section 304(a)(4) authorized EPA to publish information identifying conventional pollutants. They include "pollutants classified as biological oxygen demanding, suspended solids, fecal coliform, pH levels, grease and oil."[145]

b.   Factors Considered

Factors considered in assessing the BCT (including measures and practices) consists of balancing effluent reduction costs with the resulting benefits. EPA takes into account the age of equipment and facilities involved, the process employed, the engineering aspects of various control techniques, process changes, and non-water quality environmental impacts (including energy requirements).[146]

EPA also compares the cost for an industrial source to remove an additional pound of pollutant with the cost for a POTW to remove an additional pound of pollutant above the same level. If the cost to the industry is less than the cost to the POTW, the additional level of control for the industrial source will be considered reasonable and will be incorporated into the BCT standards, and similarly incorporated into a source's permit as a condition for operation. If the costs is more, then EPA will probably not incorporate the standard into a source's permit.

2.   Best Available Technology Economically Achievable (BAT)

BAT considers the "best existing" technology available in the industry instead of just the "average of the best" used for BCT.[147] Specifically, BAT

---

[144]   CWA § 301(b)(2)(E); 33 U.S.C.A. § 1311(b)(2)(E).

[145]   40 C.F.R. § 401.16.

[146]   CWA § 304(b)(1)(B); 33 U.S.C.A. § 1314(b)(1)(B).

[147]   Rodgers, William H., Jr., 2 Environmental Law Air and Water, §§ 4.1 - 4.43, § 4.29, at 427 (1986) [citing, 118 Cong. Rec. 33696 (1972), in 1 Legis. Hist. at 170

effluent limitations are developed from data that comes from the average performance measures of the best performing plant in an industrial field, category or class.[148] Therefore, BAT is more stringent than BCT.[149]

a.   BAT Applied

BAT applies to existing facilities discharging toxic pollutants[150] and nonconventional pollutants.[151] Facilities discharging these pollutants had to achieve BAT by March 31, 1989. Under the C.F.R., BAT standards have been set for the following toxic pollutants:

1)   Aldrin/Dieldrin;

2)   DDT--"DDT" means the compounds DDT, DDD, and DDE;

3)   Endrin;

4)   Toxaphene;

5)   Benzedrine;

6)   Polychlorinated Biphenyls (PCBs).[152]

(statement of Sen. Muskie)].

[148]   *Id.*

[149]   Deck, Carol, Teter, Katharine J., & Widner, Robert C., Long Arm of Uncle Sam: Federal Environmental Issues in Siting Decisions, 7-WTR Nat. Resources & Env't 9, 46 (1993).

[150]   CWA § 301(b)(2)(C), (D); 33 U.S.C.A. § 1311(b)(2)(C), (D); *see also*, 40 C.F.R. § 129.4 (42 Fed.Reg. 2613, Jan. 12, 1977, as amended at 42 Fed.Reg. 2620, Jan. 12, 1977; 42 Fed.Reg. 6555, Feb. 2, 1977).

[151]   CWA § 301(b)(2)(F); 33 U.S.C.A. § 1311(b)(2)(F).

[152]   40 C.F.R. § 129.4.

b. Factors Considered

The factors considered for BAT standards include the process employed, the engineering aspects of various control techniques, the cost of achieving effluent reduction, and environmental impacts upon water quality.[153] Cost can be taken into account, but there is no balancing those costs against benefits reaped as is done with BCT. BAT includes standards that must be both capable of economical implementation and technologically available."[154]

Under BAT, EPA may push for technology which is readily available, but not in routine use and often not in use at all. EPA may look beyond the best performer in the industry and apply technologies that have not been applied as long as there is a reasonable basis to believe that the technology will be available soon and that it will result in greater protection of the quality of our waters.[155]

3. Best Demonstrated Control Technology (BDT)

A third and distinct effluent standard for industrial sources of water pollution is the Best Demonstrated Control Technology (BDT) which is found in the new source performance standards (NSPS) of Section 306. The NSPS are based upon the BDT and are technology-based standards that apply to new sources. A new source is "any source, the construction of which is commenced after the publication of proposed regulations prescribing a standard of performance."[156] Construction is "any placement, assembly, or installation of facilities or equipment, including contractual obligations to purchase such

---

[153] CWA § 304(b)(2)(B); 33 U.S.C.A. § 1314(b)(2)(B); *see also*, Funk, William, The Exception that Proves the Rule: FDF Variances under the Clean Water Act, 13 B.C. Envtl. Aff.L.Rev. 1, 4-5 (1985).

[154] Bremberg, Blair P., Pre-Rulemaking Regulatory Development Activities and Sources as Variables in the Rulemaking Fairness Calculus: Taking a Soft Look at the Ex-APA Side of Environmental Policy Rulemakings, 6 J. Min. L. & Pol'y 1, 48, fn.83 (1990).

[155] Rodgers, *supra* note 147 at 427.

[156] CWA § 306(a)(2); 33 U.S.C.A. § 1316(a)(2).

facilities or equipment, at the premises where such equipment will be used, including preparation work at such premises."[157]

States are required to establish NSPS program plans and submit them to EPA for approval. EPA must approve the state plans if they are at least as stringent as the federal regulations. However, states are not allowed to impose more stringent provisions than those set forth by federal regulations on a new source until 10 years after construction.[158]

a.   BDT Applied

BDT is the performance standard for all new facilities. It is a technology-based effluent limitation and is the most stringent standard established under the CWA. The BDT standards must reflect "the greatest degree of effluent reduction . . . achievable through application of the best available demonstrated control technology [BDT], processes, operating methods, or other alternatives, including, where practicable, standards permitting no discharge of pollutants."[159]

Congress decided to establish such stringent requirements for new sources to assure that the design and operation of new stationary sources of pollution minimized the discharge of pollutants to the maximum extent possible. BDT requires the maximum use of available means to prevent new pollution problems and to attain a goal of "no discharge." Congress realized that it is much more effective and feasible to implement the strictest control technology prior to facility construction than after construction has already begun.[160] Thus, new sources are expected to implement more costly technology than existing sources in order to achieve long-term pollution prevention goals.

---

[157]   CWA § 306 (a)(5); 33 U.S.C.A. § 1316(a)(5).

[158]   CWA § 306(d); 33 U.S.C.A. § 1316(d).

[159]   CWA § 306(a)(1); 33 U.S.C.A. § 1316(a)(1).

[160]   Maloney, Kathleen, Assessing NEPA's Effect on NPDES New Source Permit Issuance: Do the New NPDES Regulations Strike the Proper Balance?, 38 Sw.L.J. 1231, 1235 (1985).

b.　　Factors Considered

The factors considered for BDT standards include the cost of achieving effluent reduction, and any non-water quality, environmental impact and energy requirements.[161] EPA is allowed to distinguish among classes, types, and sizes within categories of new sources and should also consider the type of process employed including whether it is a batch or continuous process.[162]

Under BDT, Congress expects new sources to outperform existing sources. The emphasis is on innovative technology that would allow the nation to someday comply with the "no discharge policy."[163] Thus, BDT is technology-forcing. A technology may be "demonstrated" if it is based upon a reasonable extension of prior developments.[164] Although costs are considered they are not a determinative factor.[165]

c.　　NEPA Applies

Under Section 511(c)(1), an EPA permit for a new source is subject to EIS analysis under NEPA.[166] The legislative history of the CWA indicates that Congress believed that new source owners or operators have a degree of adaptability in planning, design, construction, and location not available to existing sources. Congress concluded that persons proposing to build new sources would benefit if, prior to construction, they are forced to implement the NEPA process requiring the review and consideration of environmental impacts of the proposed project and of alternative actions and options.[167]

---

[161]　CWA § 306(b)(1)(B); 33 U.S.C.A. § 1316(b)(1)(B).

[162]　CWA § 306(b)(2); 33 U.S.C.A. § 1316(b)(2).

[163]　Rodgers, *supra* note 147 at 430-31.

[164]　Rodgers, *supra* note 147 at 430.

[165]　Rodgers, *supra* note 147 at 433-34.

[166]　CWA § 511(c); 33 U.S.C.A. § 1371(c) (action of the administrator was deemed major federal action covered by NEPA).

[167]　Maloney, *supra* note 160; *see* e.g., Municipality of Anchorage v. United States, 980 F.2d 1320 (9th Cir.1992).

4.   Treatment Levels

Generally, wastewater treatment can be controlled to attain various levels of waste removal. These levels are known as primary, secondary, and tertiary treatment levels.

a.   Primary Treatment Levels

Specifically, primary treatment removes almost all floating or settleable solids by using flotation screens, filters and sedimentation processes. For example, primary treatment removes about 30 percent of the carbonaceous biochemical oxygen demand from domestic sewage.

b.   Secondary Treatment Levels

Secondary treatment is the level most POTWs implement and is the minimum level required by the CWA.[168] This treatment level combines waste, bacteria and oxygen in trickling filters or in an activated sludge process and removes about 90 percent of the oxygen-demanding substances and suspended solids. Disinfection is the final stage.

EPA numerically quantified secondary treatment for three conventional water quality parameters: biochemical oxygen demand (BOD), suspended solids, and acidity (pH).[169] Federal regulations have also made special provisions for upward revisions of secondary treatment effluent limits when necessary to take into account:[170]

1)   storm water infiltration into combined sewers during wet weather periods; and

2)   effluent limitations from major industrial dischargers into treatment works that exceed effluent design criteria by 10

---

[168]   CWA § 301(b)(1)(B); 33 U.S.C.A. § 1311(b)(1)(B); *see also*, Honig, Ron I., Sludge Compensation: Remedying a Clean Water Act Remedial Order: The Boston Harbor Cleanup Example, 73 B.U.L.Rev. 215, 235, n.25 (1993).

[169]   40 C.F.R. § 133.102.

[170]   40 C.F.R. § 133.103.

percent. Here, the POTW could exceed its secondary treatment criteria but discharges could be no greater than the industrial waste received from other treatment facilities.

In the 1981 amendments to the CWA, Congress revised the definition of secondary treatment to allow less expensive biological treatment methods such as oxidation ponds, lagoons, ditches, and trickling filters.[171]

c. Tertiary Treatment Levels

Tertiary treatment is the most advanced treatment level. This stage goes beyond the secondary or biological stage. It removes numerous nutrients such as phosphorus and nitrogen and most suspended solids.

5. Individual Control Strategies (ICS)

"[I]t is the national policy that the discharge of toxic pollutants be prohibited."[172] The CWA empowers EPA to impose effluent standards that prohibit the discharge of toxic pollutants based on health and environmental factors such as toxicity, degradability and persistence.[173] If a body of water has been identified by the state as being "toxic" or a "hot spot" then the state is authorized to impose Individual Control Strategies (ICSs) for facilities that discharge into that body of water. This allows the state to impose even stricter standards upon these facilities than the general BAT or BDT to attain compliance with water quality standards.[174]

The various standards of performance (BCT, BAT, BDT, secondary treatment, and ICS) described above are the standards for direct dischargers. Indirect dischargers are regulated under the CWA though they are not required to apply for and receive a NPDES permit. The CWA requires indirect dischargers to implement pretreatment standards prior to sending their wastes to a POTW.

---

[171] CWA § 304(d)(4); 33 U.S.C.A. § 1314(d)(4).

[172] CWA § 101(a)(3); 33 U.S.C.A. §1251(a)(3).

[173] CWA § 307(a)(2); 33 U.S.C.A. § 1317 (a)(2).

[174] CWA § 304(l); 33 U.S.C.A. § 1314(l).

D.   PRETREATMENT STANDARDS

Many industrial facilities discharge into POTWs instead of directly into navigable waters to avoid the strict and expensive requirements of the NPDES permit program. These facilities are known as "indirect dischargers." Congress recognized that pollutants from indirect dischargers could interfere with the POTWs or at least pass through treatment systems without adequate treatment. Therefore, the CWA requires indirect dischargers to pretreat their wastewater to achieve, together with the POTW, a final discharge into navigable waters meeting BAT (the standard required of a direct discharger).

1.   Implementation

The CWA requires EPA to promulgate pretreatment standards for introduction of waste streams into POTWs by indirect dischargers.[175] The pretreatment standards are incorporated into an indirect discharger's service agreement with a POTW. A POTW must monitor and enforce the service agreements with customers to ensure compliance with the pretreatment standards.

2.   Three Types of Standards

Pretreatment standards consist of "general" prohibitions, "specific" prohibitions, and "categorical" pretreatment standards.

a.   General Prohibitions

"General" prohibitions focus on certain types of discharges from all industrial users of a POTW. They forbid discharges that "pass through" a POTW or "interfere" with its operation.[176] A "pass through" is a discharge sent to a POTW for treatment whose contents nonetheless exit the POTW into navigable waters of the United States in quantities or concentrations that, alone or in conjunction with other discharges, cause a POTW to violate its NPDES permit.[177] An "interference" is a discharge which, alone or in conjunction with discharges from other sources, disrupts a POTW process - and the disruption in

---

[175]   CWA § 307(b); 33 U.S.C.A. § 1317(b).

[176]   40 C.F.R. § 403.5(a).

[177]   40 C.F.R. § 403.3(n).

turn causes the POTW to violate its NPDES permit or prevents the POTW from employing its chosen sludge use or practice.[178]

b. "Specific Prohibitions"

"Specific" prohibitions forbid the discharge of specific materials that can harm POTW collection and treatment systems. Specific prohibitions may include heat (inhibits biological activity) and certain pollutants whose characteristics are likely to cause a fire or explosive hazard, cause corrosive damage, obstruct the flow within a POTW, or are discharged in concentrations or flow rates that interfere with a POTW.[179]

c. Categorical Pretreatment Standards

"Categorical Pretreatment Standards" apply to enumerated categories of industrial sources and are technology-based numerical discharge limitations. If a POTW is capable of super-treating the discharges it receives from indirect dischargers, then the CWA allows the POTW to issue the indirect discharger "removal credits" which relax the indirect discharger pretreatment requirements.

3. Removal Credits Program

Removal credits reflect pollutant removal by POTWs above and beyond the secondary treatment level. This includes the ability to remove pollutants expected to be initially removed by the indirect discharger through pretreatment standards. Thus, removal credits are granted to avoid redundant treatment by industry and POTWs.[180] A POTW is required to have an EPA approved pretreatment program before it may grant removal credits to indirect dischargers.[181]

---

[178] 40 C.F.R. § 403.3(i).

[179] 40 C.F.R. § 403.5(b).

[180] Garrett, Theodore L., The Clean Water Act Amendments of 1987, C266 ALI-ABA 323, 335, (1988).

[181] National Ass'n of Metal Finishers v. United States EPA, 719 F.2d 624 (3d Cir.1983), rev'd on other grounds by Chemical Manufacturing Association v. Natural Resource Defense Counsel, Inc., 470 U.S. 116; 105 S.Ct. 1102; 84 L.Ed.2d 90 (1985).

"Removal credits are intended to be the mechanism for relieving indirect dischargers from pretreatment standards when the POTW and other users are capable of meeting the standards . . . [R]emoval credits simply reallocate between the POTW and the indirect dischargers the responsibility for removing the total amount of pollutants necessary to achieve the applicable limit."[182] However, removal credits are subject to two limitations:

1)   the resulting POTW discharge must conform to effluent limitations that would apply to a specific toxic pollutant from the discharger if it were directly discharged into the water by the indirect discharger; and

2)   the indirect discharger's release of toxics into a POTW must not stop sludge use or disposal by the POTW in accordance with the sludge disposal guidelines of Section 405 of the CWA.[183]

The standards of performance for direct and indirect dischargers have the force and effect of the law for facilities to follow and are strictly enforced by state and federal agencies. To pacify indirect dischargers' concerns, Congress expressly assures them that EPA will not impose additional requirements when a POTW "is not meeting the requirements of a permit . . . as a result of inadequate design or operation of such treatment works."[184] Yet, in reality there are situations in which it is not possible for a discharger to comply with its strict standard. The CWA acknowledges these situations by allowing a permitting agency to issue a "variance" or exemption from the required standard of performance.

E.   VARIANCES

A variance is an exemption from certain specific regulations and permit provisions. If a variance is granted, the permit holder is allowed to implement a more relaxed or less stringent standard of performance. A variance is granted

---

[182]   *Id.*; *see also*, Chemical Manufacturers' Ass'n v. United States EPA, 885 F.2d 253, 260 (5th Cir.1989).

[183]   *See*, Chicago Association of Commerce v. United States EPA, 873 F.2d 1025 (7th Cir.1989).

[184]   CWA § 402(m); 33 U.S.C.A. §1342(m).

to a permit holder only under special circumstances.[185] The CWA allows several types of variances for: nonconventional pollutants, processes using fundamentally different factors,[186] thermal discharges, pretreatment standards, and deepwater discharges.

1.   Nonconventional Pollutants Variances

Section 301(c) provides a variance for direct dischargers of nonconventional pollutants if the owner or operator shows that the modified requirements will represent the maximum use of technology within the economic capability of the owner or operator and will result in reasonable further progress toward the elimination of the discharge of pollutants.[187]

In addition, Section 301(g) allows a variance for "certain nonconventional pollutants" such as: ammonia, chlorine, color, iron, and total phenols.[188] This variance can be obtained under three conditions:

1)   a showing that the modified requirements will comply with the appropriate standard of performance, either BCT or BAT;

2)   that the modified requirements will not result in additional requirements on any other point or nonpoint source; and

3)   that the modification will not interfere with the attainment or maintenance of water quality standards (so as to protect public

---

[185]   Chemical Manufacturers Ass'n v. United States EPA, 870 F.2d 177, 236, (5th Cir.1989), cert. denied (In promulgating nationwide pollutant effluent limitations, EPA need not consider hardships faced by a particular plant. Congress intended "fundamentally different" characteristics of particular plants to be considered by EPA in a Section 301(n) variance proceeding).

[186]   These are factors other than those used by EPA to establish a standard of performance or effluent limitation.

[187]   CWA § 301(c); 33 U.S.C.A. § 1311(c); *see also*, Kopper Company, Inc. v. United States EPA, 767 F.2d 57 (3rd Cir.1985).

[188]   CWA §301(g); 33 U.S.C.A. § 1311(g).

water supplies and not pose an unacceptable risk to human health or the environment).[189]

2.   Fundamentally Different Factors (FDF) Variance

In issuing national performance standards, EPA tests specific categories of sources and looks at certain factors such as processes employed, control techniques, costs, and water quality impacts. It is not uncommon for EPA to transfer data for tested categories of sources to other "untested" sources in setting effluent standards. To insure that untested categories of sources are not unfairly burdened, the CWA provides variances for "fundamentally different factors" (FDF). To receive this variance, the permit holder must show that effluent limitations to his facility should be less stringent because his facility operates in a "fundamentally different" fashion than the "tested" industry or industry as a whole.[190] In issuing an FDF variance, EPA considers: the age and size of the facility, land availability, age and size of equipment, processes employed at the plant, non-water quality impacts, and engineering aspects of the control technology. Factors not considered include the cost of installing technology within the time frame that the act allows and the impact of the discharge in question on the quality of the receiving water. A proposed alternative has to be no less stringent than that justified by the fundamental difference of the facility, and it must not result in environmental impacts that are worse than if the required technology was used.[191]

3.   Thermal Discharge Variance

Thermal discharge is heated water from industrial processes. This type of discharge is considered a pollutant because it can kill or injure aquatic organisms. Generally, thermal discharge is regulated by permit conditions setting the allowable temperatures and volumes of such discharges to protect aquatic life and wildlife. The CWA provides variances for thermal discharges.[192]

---

[189]   CWA § 301(g)(2); 33 U.S.C.A. § 1311(g)(2).

[190]   CWA § 301(n); 33 U.S.C.A. § 1311(n).

[191]   40 C.F.R. §§ 125.31, 124.62(e)(1); 40 C.F.R. § 63 (provides procedures for variance when EPA is the permitting authority).

[192]   CWA § 316; 33 U.S.C.A. § 1326.

The permit holder requesting the variance must assure the issuing agency that the modified requirement will nonetheless protect aquatic life and the wildlife dependent on that body of water.[193]

4. Pretreatment Standard Variance

A Pretreatment Standard Variance is available under Section 307(e)[194] and allows indirect dischargers to implement "innovative control systems" if the system has the potential for industry-wide application in the future and if it will not cause the receiving POTW to be in violation of its NPDES permit.[195]

5. Deepwater Discharge Variance

Section 301(h) provides POTWs with a waiver from secondary treatment standards if the POTW discharges into certain marine waters.[196] Section 403 allows a similar marine water discharge waiver from BAT or BDT standards for direct industrial dischargers.[197] These sections allow discharges into deep waters of the territorial sea or the waters of the contiguous zone, or into saline estuarine waters where there is a strong tidal movement and other related hydrological and geological characteristics.[198] The CWA requires EPA to issue guidelines regarding the degradation of marine waters to protect human health or welfare and marine life.[199]

Some deepwater discharge controls that EPA has imposed include monitoring requirements based on samples of aquatic biota and water quality

---

[193]   *Id.*

[194]   CWA § 307(e); 33 U.S.C.A. § 1317(e); CWA § 402(m); 33 U.S.C.A. § 1342(m).

[195]   CWA § 402(m); 33 U.S.C.A. § 1342(m).

[196]   CWA § 301(h); 33 U.S.C.A. § 1311(h); *see also,* Hanmer, Rebecca W., The Clean Water Act: As Amended by the Water Quality Act of 1987, 144 PLI/Lit 7 (1987).

[197]   CWA § 403; 33 U.S.C.A. §1343.

[198]   CWA §§ 301(h), 403; 33 U.S.C.A. §§ 1311(h), 1343.

[199]   CWA § 403(c); 33 U.S.C.A. § 1343(c).

standards.   However, whether adequate monitoring can be realistically established for a deepwater offshore discharge is debatable.   In *Kilroy v. Ruckelshaus*, the Court of Appeals looked to the Congressional Record and held that Congress has expressly prohibited the discharge of sewage sludge into marine waters.[200]

Regardless of whether a variance is granted, once a permit is final it becomes "the law" for a specific source.   If any permit condition is violated the facility owner and operator may be held liable and are thus subject to fines and penalties.   These fines and penalties may be avoided if the defendant raises and proves a legitimate defense.   In the CWA, Congress expressly provides two defenses applicable in emergency situations.

F.   DEFENSES

EPA recognizes that bypasses and upsets of effluent discharges will inevitably occur and may be unavoidable in emergency situations.   Therefore, the CWA and EPA regulations allow affirmative defenses to the charges of violations for certain bypasses and upsets that occur at a treatment facility.   A bypass is an intentional diversion of wastewater from any portion of a treatment facility.[201] An upset is defined as an exceptional incident in which there is unintentional and temporary noncompliance because of factors beyond reasonable control.   By definition, both bypasses and upsets will likely result in a violation of a facility's permit and other CWA regulations.   Generally, unless the bypass or upset occurs under an extreme emergency situation, the permittee will face both civil and criminal penalties.   The burden of proof is on the permittee to establish a valid bypass or upset.

---

[200]   Kilroy v. Ruckelshaus, 738 F.2d. 1448, 1453-54 (9th Cir.1984) (Los Angeles entered into a consent decree to terminate all ocean sludge disposal); 127 Cong. Rec. HB 9515 (1981) (congressional record of the 1981 Municipal Waste Water Construction Grant Amendments).

[201]   40 C.F.R. § 122.41(m)(1)(i).

1. Bypass

Generally, bypasses that do not exceed effluent limits are allowed in order to perform essential maintenance to ensure efficient operations.[202] The regulations also permit bypasses that cause effluent limits to be greater than allowed under the permit if such bypasses are unavoidable to prevent loss of life, personal injury, severe property damage, or if the permittee can show that there was no feasible alternative to the bypass.[203] A facility owner or operator must notify EPA 24 hours in advance of conducting a bypass. In the event of an unanticipated bypass, EPA must be notified within 24 hours after the bypass occurs.

In most bypass (and upset) situations, it is unlikely a court will allow the use of the defense to avoid liability. Courts are more likely to give great weight to expert testimony stating that the facility had other viable, less environmentally damaging options available at the time of the bypass or upset. For example, in *United States v. Weitzenhoff*, the court held that Weitzenhoff did not have a valid reason to dump 436,000 pounds of pollutant solids (sewer sludge) into the ocean. Here, the Appellate Court stated that the sludge could have been trucked off the site, and a bypass would only be allowed to prevent loss of life, personal injury, or severe property damage.[204]

In another case, *United States v. Boldt*, a discharger was prosecuted for knowingly bypassing industrial wastewater containing high concentrates of toxic metals into a municipal sewer line.[205]

2. Upset

An "upset" is an exceptional incident in which there is unintentional and temporary non-compliance with technology based effluent limitations because of

---

[202] 40 C.F.R. § 122.41(m)(2).

[203] 40 C.F.R. § 122.41(m)(4); *see also*, Natural Resources Defense Council (NRDC) v. United States EPA, 822 F.2d 104 (D.C. Cir.1986).

[204] United States v. Weitzenhoff, 1 F.3d 1523 (9th Cir.1993) modified at 35 F.3d 1275 (9th Cir.1993).

[205] United States v. Boldt, 929 F.2d 35 (1st Cir.1991).

factors beyond the reasonable control of the permittee.[206] An upset constitutes an affirmative defense to an action brought for noncompliance with such technology based effluent limitations. Generally permit violations due to operational errors, improperly managed facilities, inadequate facilities, lack of preventative maintenance, or careless or improper operations are not considered to be allowable defenses. To successfully claim an upset defense, the permittee must identify specific causes for the upset, show that the facility was working properly at the time of the upset, provide notice to EPA of the upset and show compliance with any applicable remedial measures.[207] Notice to EPA must be provided within 24 hours after the event.[208]

For example, in *United States v. City of Sarasota*, the District Court allowed the City of Sarasota to discharge municipal waste into a local bayou under an upset defense where:

1)   overloading was due to excessive rainfall; or

2)   any other event, including local, federal, or state regulations, would preclude the use of the system and would be beyond the control of, and without fault of the city.[209]

The NPDES Permit Program and each of its elements is an integral part of the CWA, but it only addresses direct dischargers. Other human activities also degrade and pollute our nation's waters. Thus, the CWA established various other programs to address those activities. One of those programs is the Wetlands Protection and Dredge and Fill Permit Program.

V.   WETLANDS PROTECTION AND THE DREDGE AND FILL PERMIT PROGRAM

Wetlands are transitional lands between terrestrial and aquatic systems, where the water table is usually at or near the surface or the land is covered by

---

[206]   40 C.F.R. § 122.41(n)(1).

[207]   40 C.F.R. § 122.41(n)(2) and (3).

[208]   40 C.F.R. § 122.41(n)(2)(iii).

[209]   United States v. City of Sarasota, No. 87210CWT15B (M.D.Fla.1988).

shallow water. Wetlands include, among numerous other areas, marshes, swamps, bogs, wet meadows, prairie potholes, sloughs, and river over-flow lands, as well as shallow lakes and ponds.[210] Wetlands serve important ecological and economic functions. Inland wetlands control floods and their potential for related damage. In coastal areas, wetlands are excellent storm buffers and are necessary to help prevent shoreline erosion. Also, wetlands help maintain and improve the water quality of rivers, lakes, and other bodies of water by removing and retaining nutrients, processing chemical and organic wastes, and reducing sediment to receiving waters.[211] Wetlands serve as critical habitats for a wide variety of plants and animals; even wetlands smaller than one acre support an abundance of life forms. Ducks, geese, and swans are some of the larger wildlife species to make use of wetlands. A large number of threatened and endangered species rely on wetlands. About 5,000 species of plants, 190 species of amphibians, and 270 species of birds rely on or exist in America's wetlands. Many of these species are designated as threatened or endangered and depend directly or indirectly on wetlands.[212]

Economically, wetlands serve as the cradle of the world's seafood industry. It has been estimated that the annual economic value of wetlands habitat to the United States economy is about $14 billion. Thus, for both ecological and economic reasons, it is very important that our wetlands be protected from many dredge and fill activities.[213] To control the loss of wetlands, Congress created the Wetlands Protection and Dredge and Fill Permit Program under CWA Section 404.

A.   DREDGE AND FILL PERMIT

Section 404 prohibits a person from discharging or placing "dredged or fill materials" into navigable waters, including wetlands[214] without a permit.

---

[210]   33 C.F.R. § 328.3; 42 Fed. Reg. 37128.

[211]   Eblen, *supra* note 12 at 814-816.

[212]   *Id.*

[213]   *Id.*

[214]   33 C.F.R. § 328.3(a); 40 C.F.R. § 230.3(s) (broad definition of navigable waters includes wetlands).

"Dredged material" is material that is excavated or dredged from the waters of the United States.[215] "Fill material" is any material used for the primary purpose of replacing an aquatic area with dry land or of elevating the bottom of a body of water.[216] Dredged or fill materials are "pollutants" under the CWA.[217] Thus, their discharge into navigable waters of the United States is prohibited.[218] Under certain circumstances, the CWA allows for "dredged or fill material" at certain specified wetlands sites, but only by persons receiving a Section 404 permit.

The Section 404 permit program (otherwise known as the Dredge and Fill Permit Program) is administered by the United States Secretary of the Army Corps. of Engineers (USACOE).[219] Under federal regulations, the discharge of fill material includes such activities as site development fills, causeways, dams and dikes, artificial islands, riprap, and groins.[220] None of these activities may be initiated without first obtaining a Section 404 permit.

Litigation over whether specific activities require a Section 404 permit are common. For example the courts have required a Section 404 permit for activities such as:

    1)   a home development project on the shores of a lake;[221]

---

[215]   33 C.F.R. § 323.2(c).

[216]   40 C.F.R. § 323.2(e).

[217]   CWA § 502(6); 33 U.S.C.A. § 1362(6).

[218]   CWA § 101(a); 33 U.S.C.A. § 1251(a).

[219]   CWA § 404; 33 U.S.C.A. § 1344; *see also*, United States v. Riverside Bayview Homes, Inc., 474 U.S. 121; 106 S.Ct. 455; 88 L.Ed.2d 419 (1985); *but see* United States v. Wilson, 133 F.3d 251 (4th Cir. 1997) (Corps' definition of "waters of the United States" exceeded Congressional authority); United States v. Hallmark Construction, 14 F.Supp. 1065 (N.D.Ill. 1998) (wetland's use by migratory birds does not exceed Congress' Commerce Clause powers); *see* excellent discussion on wetlands, Chertok, Mark A., Federal Regulation of Wetlands, SE98 ALI-ABA 715 (2000).

[220]   33 C.F.R. § 323.2(f).

[221]   United States v. Riverside Bayview Homes, Inc., 474 U.S. 121; 106 S.Ct. 455; 88 L.Ed.2d 419 (1985) (this home development project on the shores of Lake St. Clair,

2)   land clearing operations on 20,000 acres of wetlands;[222] and

3)   excavations of ditches or barriers, and any disturbing activity on natural river berms, or beach dunes.[223]

As with other portions of the CWA, Congress recognized the economic importance of certain human activities and has allowed limited exemptions to the Section 404 permit requirement. Thus, discharge of dredged and fill material from exempt activities is allowed without obtaining a permit.

B.   EXEMPTIONS

The following activities may be exempt from the Section 404 permit program:

1)   farming activities;[224]

2)   maintenance or reconstruction of dams, breakwaters, and other similar structures;

3)   farm ponds or irrigation and drainage ditches;

4)   temporary sediment basins;

5)   construction of farm roads, forest roads or roads for mining; and

---

Michigan required a Section 404 permit).

[222]   Avoyelles Sportsmen's League, Inc. v. Marsh, 715 F.2d 897 (5th Cir.1983) (80 % of the lands in question had been appraised as "wetlands" by EPA).

[223]   United States v. Lee Wood Contracting, Inc., 529 F.Supp. 119, 120 (E.D.Mich.1981) (truckload was "filling" with 500 cubic yards of bricks); *see also* 33 C.F.R. § 323.3 (wetlands may be separated from other waters by dykes, barriers, berms and dunes).

[224]   *But see*, Gunn v. United States Department of Agriculture, 118 F.3d 1233 (8th Cir. 1998), *cert denied* 118 S.Ct. 1042 (1998) (under U.S. Department of Agriculture's swampbuster program, farmers could lose certain federal farm aid benefits for farming certain wetlands).

6)   activities under a state approved nonpoint source management program.[225]

Exemptions for farmlands are regularly litigated and the courts are placed in the position of interpreting the act and deciding who must obtain a Section 404 permit and who is exempt.[226]   For example, in *Avoyelles Sportsmen's League, Inc. v. Marsh*, the Court of Appeals found that large scale deforestation close to wetlands is not normal farming activity, and therefore, not entitled to an exemption under Section 404(f).[227]

The Wetlands Protection and Dredge and Fill Permit Program establishes a high priority on control and regulation of activities that are potentially damaging to our nation's wetlands. Similarly, the Oil Spill Program under the CWA, places a high value on protecting our nation's waters from the environmental harm caused by oil spills.

VI.   OIL SPILL PROGRAM

An oil spill occurs when crude or refined oil is discharged or leaked onto land, inland water, or the open seas. Most of the world's oil resources are found in distant locations. This makes transportation of huge quantities of crude oil a necessity and greatly increases the chances for accidents involving spills. The largest and most publicized spills, however, are caused by tanker accidents during maritime transport. Not all spills are accidental, some of the oil found in waterways is from open sea bilge pumping and the rinsing of tanks by maritime transporters to take on new cargo.[228]

Spilled oil presents a great hazard to wildlife and local economies dependent on fishing or tourism. Animals that rely on insulating fur or feathers to survive, such as sea otters and waterfowl, become coated with oil and are no longer able to keep warm. They eventually die of hypothermia or intestinal

---

[225]   CWA § 404(f)(1); 33 U.S.C.A. § 1344(f)(1).

[226]   United States v. Larkins, 852 F.2d 189 (6th Cir.1988).

[227]   Avoyelles Sportsmen's League, Inc. v. Marsh, 715 F.2d 897 (5th Cir.1983) (where defendant acted to drain, reshape and level wetlands).

[228]   Eblen, *supra* note 12 at 499-500.

problems due to ingestion of oil. In addition, entire regions suffer as fishing industries struggle to survive, tourism declines because of polluted seashores, and property values can decline.[229] The CWA addresses oil spill problems under Section 311.

A. NO DISCHARGE POLICY

Section 311 declares that "it is the policy of the United States that there should be no discharges of oil or hazardous substances into or upon the navigable waters of the United States."[230] This section authorizes EPA to conduct any necessary studies and issue any appropriate regulations to meet the "no discharge" policy.

B. REGULATIONS

The regulations prohibit discharges of oil and other hazardous wastes in quantities that violate water quality standards or that cause a film, sheen, or discoloration of the water's surface or adjoining shorelines, or cause sludge or emulsion to be deposited beneath the surface of the water or upon the adjoining shorelines.[231] Note that the appearance of a sheen of oil on the water's surface presumes harm on the environment.[232]

The sheen test prohibits any discharge that the President deems is harmful to the environment, and there is no limitation to time, location, circumstances, or conditions.[233] A visual sheen test to determine if Section 311 has been violated due to oil based drilling mud and cuttings is valid.[234]

---

[229]   *Id.*

[230]   CWA § 311(b)(1); 33 U.S.C.A. § 1321(b)(1).

[231]   40 C.F.R. § 110.3(b).

[232]   Chevron U.S.A. Inc. v. Yost, 919 F.2d 27, 30 (5th Cir. 1990).

[233]   CWA § 311(b)(3), (4); 33 U.S.C.A. § 1321(b)(3), (4).

[234]   American Petroleum Institute v. United States EPA, 787 F.2d 965, 983 (5th Cir. 1986) (court allowed a new test to be used in Alaska where long hours of darkness and frozen sea conditions made the visual sheen test impossible. This new test is called the "static sheen test" and involves testing a discharge before going into the waters. The

Discharges from a properly functioning vessel are excluded from the "sheen test."[235]

C.   ENFORCEMENT

Facility owners are liable without a showing of fault for costs of cleaning up hazardous waste and oil spills. This standard has been described as strict liability with limitations. In addition, the Oil Pollution Act (OPA)[236] is now the primary source of liability for oil spills, and compliments Section 311 by offering financial penalties.   Thus, facility owners may be ultimately liable for administrative, civil, and criminal penalties.

So far, this chapter has addressed three of the four major programs established by the CWA: the NPDES Program, the Wetlands Protection and Dredge and Fill Program, and the Oil Spill Program. A fourth major program under the CWA is the Nonpoint Source Pollution Program.

VII.   NONPOINT SOURCE POLLUTION PROGRAM

Nonpoint sources of pollution are land uses that cause pollution. Nonpoint source pollution includes sediments, minerals, nutrients, pesticides, organic wastes, livestock wastes, crop debris, wastes oils, and thermal pollution.[237]   While the main focus of the CWA has been on point source pollution, nonpoint source pollution is estimated to have caused 65% of our stream pollution, 76% of our lake pollution, and 45% of our estuary's pollution.[238]

---

material is placed in a container of sea water and stirred for a period of time. Next, the surface of the water is examined for oil slicks).

[235]   United States v. Chevron Oil Company, 583 F.2d 1357, 1358 (5th Cir.1978); upheld in Chevron U.S.A. Inc. v. Yost, 919 F.2d 27 (5th Cir.1990).

[236]   Oil Pollution Act (OPA) of 1990, OPA §§ 1001-7001; 33 U.S.C.A. §§ 2701-2761.

[237]   Rodgers, *supra* note 147 at 124-125.

[238]   Malone, Linda A. & Tabb, William M., Environmental Law: Cases and Materials, 542-594 (1992).

The 1987 amendments to the CWA placed a high priority on nonpoint source pollution by stating that "it is the national policy that programs for control of nonpoint sources of pollution be developed and implemented in an expeditious manner so as to enable the goals of this act to be met through both point and nonpoint sources of pollution."[239] Control of nonpoint sources are left primarily to the states under sections 319 and 208 of the CWA.[240]

A.   NONPOINT SOURCE MANAGEMENT PROGRAMS

Section 319 requires the Governor of each State to submit to EPA a state assessment report and a state management program plan that identify and address control strategies for navigable waters adversely affected by nonpoint source pollution. The state assessment report must:

1)   identify waters that without additional control on nonpoint source pollution cannot be expected to attain or maintain the goals and requirements of the CWA;

2)   identify categories as well as individual sources that cause waters to fail water quality standards;

3)   describe processes to control nonpoint sources; and

4)   identify state and local programs for controlling pollution.[241]

The management program addresses and delineates best management practices, and measures to be undertaken to reduce pollutants from nonpoint sources.[242] EPA must approve or disapprove the report and program within 180 days after a state's submission.

---

[239]   CWA § 101(a)(7); 33 U.S.C.A. § 1251(a)(7).

[240]   CWA §§ 319, 208; 33 U.S.C.A. §§ 1329, 1288.

[241]   CWA § 319(a)(1); 33 U.S.C.A. § 1329(a)(1).

[242]   CWA § 319(b); 33 U.S.C.A. § 1329(b).

B.   AREA WIDE WASTE TREATMENT PROGRAMS

Section 208 authorizes EPA to issue guidelines for the identification of areas with substantial water quality control problems resulting from urban-industrial concentrations of pollutants. Once identified as an "urban-industrial problem area" by the Governor of each State, the State should designate local government agencies and local elected officials to develop effective area wide waste treatment management plans.

These plans address (1) the industrial waste treatment needs of an area over a 20-year period, (2) the construction, and financing of such treatment works, (3) the regulatory programs for these facilities, (4) the identification of mine-related, construction, and other nonpoint source related pollution, and (5) the measures to control this nonpoint source related pollution. The local program must be approved by the lead state agency and EPA prior to implementation.[243]

To encourage state implementation of nonpoint source pollution programs, some federal funds and grants are made available.[244] No grant may be made to a State that failed in the preceding year to make satisfactory progress toward implementation of the plan.[245] For example in *Natural Resources Defense Council v. Costle*, the District Court authorized EPA to withhold federal funds from states who failed to achieve Section 208 planning requirements.[246]

C.   TRANSBOUNDARY POLLUTION

If one State's pollution significantly affects another State's waters (transboundary pollution) and keeps the receiving state from meeting its own water quality standards or the CWA's requirements, the adversely affected state may petition EPA for a conference with the polluting State in hopes of reaching a transboundary pollution prevention agreement. EPA will notify the polluting State and convene a conference within 180 days after receiving notice of alleged

---

[243]   CWA § 208; 33 U.S.C.A. § 1288.

[244]   CWA § 319(h)(3); 33 U.S.C.A. § 1329(h)(3).

[245]   CWA § 319(h)(8); 33 U.S.C.A. § 1329(h)(8).

[246]   Natural Resources Defense Council v. Costle, 564 F.2d 573 (D.C. Cir.1977).

violations.[247] EPA has no final action authority and can only mediate and encourage an agreement. However, EPA can deny federal environmental protection funds to a noncooperative state.

Another option available to the receiving state, is that of filing a common law nuisance suit against the polluting state. For example, in *Illinois v. City of Milwaukee*, Illinois sued four Wisconsin cities for polluting Lake Michigan. Ultimately, the United States Supreme Court said that a state with a high water quality standard can bring an action to require that its strict standards be honored, and that the receiving state need not be compelled to lower its standards to that of neighboring states.[248]

VIII. ENFORCEMENT PROVISIONS

A. INTRODUCTION

The CWA, like the other major federal environmental statutes, authorizes the government to take enforcement action in several of the available forums: administrative, civil, or criminal. On the administrative side, the CWA requires facilities to obtain an NPDES permit prior to a discharge into navigable waters. The NPDES permit program is discussed above in Part IV. of this chapter. The CWA also requires a permit prior to "dredging and filling" of any navigable waters and wetland areas. This permit program is discussed above in Part V. of this chapter. Other administrative enforcement provisions, such as record keeping, inspections, and compliance orders are discussed below. Discussion of government civil and criminal enforcement actions will follow. Lastly, citizen enforcement actions will be addressed.

---

[247]   CWA § 319(g)(1); 33 U.S.C.A. § 1329(g)(1).

[248]   Illinois v. City of Milwaukee, 406 U.S. 91; 92 S.Ct. 1385; 31 L.Ed.2d 712 (1972).

B.   GOVERNMENT ACTIONS

1.   Administrative Remedies

a.   Records, Reports and Inspections

EPA has broad authority under Section 308 to require the owner or operator of any point source to maintain records, make reports, install, use, and maintain monitoring equipment, sample effluents and allow for facility and record inspections by EPA and their authorized representatives.[249]

b.   Compliance Orders

The CWA allows EPA to issue administrative compliance orders if it determines that a violation is occurring.[250] Such orders must state a time for compliance not to exceed thirty days for violations of interim compliance schedules or operation and maintenance requirements. For violations of final deadlines, EPA may allow a reasonable time for compliance, taking into account the seriousness of the violation and any good faith effort to comply with the applicable requirements.

c.   Administrative Penalties

EPA may assess administrative penalties for violation of compliance orders and for violation of enumerated statutory sections of the CWA.[251] These penalties are broken down into two classes: Class I and Class II penalties.[252] In

---

[249]   CWA § 308; 33 U.S.C.A. § 1318.

[250]   CWA § 309(a)(3); 33 U.S.C.A. § 1319(a)(3) (these orders are also referred to as "administrative orders").

[251]   CWA § 301; 33 U.S.C.A. § 1311 (basic prohibition of discharges without a permit), CWA § 302; 33 U.S.C.A. § 1312 (water quality-related effluent limitations), CWA § 306; 33 U.S.C.A. § 1316 (national performance standards for new sources), CWA § 307; 33 U.S.C.A. § 1317 (toxic and pretreatment effluent standards), CWA § 308; 33 U.S.C.A. § 1318 (records, reporting and inspections), CWA § 318; 33 U.S.C.A. § 1328 (aquaculture provisions), or CWA § 405; 33 U.S.C.A. § 1345 (disposal or use of sewage sludge).

[252]   CWA § 309(g); 33 U.S.C.A. § 1319(g).

determining the class and amount of such penalties, EPA, or the U. S. Army Corps of Engineers, considers the nature, circumstances, extent and gravity of the violation, the violator's ability to pay, prior history of violations, culpability, economic benefit or savings resulting from the violation and other matters as justice may require.[253]

i.   Class I Penalties

A Class I penalty may not exceed $10,000 per violation, and the total penalty may not exceed $25,000.[254]

ii.   Class II Penalties

A Class II penalty may not exceed $10,000 per day for each day of violation, and the total penalty may not exceed $125,000.[255]

d.   Public Notice and Hearing Required

EPA is required to give public notice of a proposed order assessing an administrative penalty. It must also allow the public an opportunity to comment on a proposed order and to participate in any hearing.[256] If the person being assessed a penalty does not request a hearing, any commentor may petition for a hearing and one shall be granted if the supporting evidence is material and not previously considered.[257] Whenever EPA denies such a petition, notice of the denial and the reasons for it shall be given to the petitioner and published in the Federal Register.[258] Defendants of Class I and II penalties are entitled to request a hearing within thirty days of issuance of an order. For Class I orders the hearing is informal and is to provide "...a reasonable opportunity to be heard and

---

[253]   CWA § 309(g)(3); 33 U.S.C.A. § 1319(g)(3).

[254]   CWA § 309(d); 33 U.S.C.A. § 1319(g)(2)(A) (Class I Penalty).

[255]   CWA § 309(g)(2)(B); 33 U.S.C.A. § 1319(g)(2)(B) (Class II Penalty).

[256]   CWA § 309(g)(4); 33 U.S.C.A. § 1319(g)(4).

[257]   *Id.*

[258]   *Id.*

to present evidence."[259] Defendants of Class II penalties are entitled to request a formal "on the record" hearing pursuant to APA Section 554.[260]

2. Civil Remedies

Sections 309(b) and (d) set out the authority for civil enforcement of certain CWA violations.[261] The Administrator may "commence a civil action for appropriate relief, including a permanent or temporary injunction, for any violation for which he is authorized to issue an administrative compliance order."[262] Appropriate relief may include civil penalties for violations,[263] injunctions,[264] government recovery for cleanup costs,[265] contempt penalties,[266]

---

[259] CWA § 309(g)(2)(A); 33 U.S.C.A. § 1319(g)(2)(A).

[260] APA § 554; 5 U.S.C.A. § 554.

[261] CWA §§ 309(d); 33 U.S.C.A. §§ 1319(d) ("Any person who violates section 301, 302, 306, 308, 318 or 405 of this Act, or any permit condition or limitation implementing any of such sections in an permit issued under section 402 of this Act by the Administrator, or by a state, or in a permit issued under section 404 of this Act by a state, and any person who violates any order issued by the Administrator under subsection (a) of this section shall be subject to a civil penalty not to exceed $25,000 per day of such violation").

[262] CWA § 309(b); 33 U.S.C.A. § 1319(b).

[263] CWA § 309(d); 33 U.S.C.A. § 1319(d); *see* United States v. Buntin, Civ. No. 76-64 (M.D.Tenn.1976) (civil fine of $4,904.20 was imposed on a private homeowner for a leaking oil tank that discharged effluent into a nearby creek).

[264] *See*, Weinberger v. Romero-Barcelo, 456 U.S. 305; 102 S.Ct. 1798; 72 L.Ed.2d 91 (1982) (it is difficult to obtain injunctions, but they are an available remedy).

[265] Frederick E. Bouchard, Inc. v. United States, 583 F.Supp. 477 (D.C. Mass. 1984).

[266] United States v. City of Providence, 492 F.Supp. 602 (D.R.I.1980).

and a court appointed receivership.[267] In addition, the government may seek a civil compliance order.[268]

Parties who violate certain provisions of the CWA, for example, discharging without a permit or discharging in violation of an existing permit, are subject to civil penalties of up to $25,000 per day for each violation.[269] Additionally, the CWA allows the court to award attorney's fees to "prevailing or substantially prevailing parties."[270]

3.   Criminal Remedies

Section 309(c) authorizes criminal remedies including fines of up to $1,000,000 and confinement of up to 30 years. Section 309 provides for six criminal actions. Two for "negligence" and four for "knowing" violations as follows:

    1)   Any person who "negligently" violates specified sections of the CWA or any permit issued under the CWA may be subject to a fine of no less than $2,500 nor more than $25,000 per day of violation, and up to one year in prison, or both.[271] Repeat

---

[267]   United States v. City of Detroit, 476 F.Supp. 512 (E.D.Mich.1979) (mayor of Detroit was appointed the receiver of city's wastewater treatment system).

[268]   CWA § 309(a)(1); 33 U.S.C.A. § 1319(a)(1) ("Whenever, on the basis of any information available to him, the Administrator finds that any person is in violation of any condition or limitation which implements sections 1311, 1312, 1316, 1317, 1318, 1328, or 1345 of this title in a permit issued by a state under an approved permit program under section 1342 or 1344 of this title he shall proceed under his authority in paragraph (3) of this subsection or he shall notify the person in alleged violation and such state of such finding. If beyond the thirtieth day after the Administrator's notification the state has not commenced appropriate enforcement action, the Administrator shall issue an order requiring such person to comply with such condition or limitation or shall bring a civil action in accordance with subsection (b) of this section").

[269]   CWA §§ 309(d); 33 U.S.C.A. §§ 1319(d).

[270]   CWA § 505(d) ; 33 U.S.C.A. § 1365(d).

[271]   CWA § 309(c)(1); 33 U.S.C.A. § 1319(c)(1).

offenders may be subject to a fine of not more than $50,000 per day of violation, imprisonment of up to 2 years, or both.[272]

2)   Any person who "negligently" introduces into a sewer system or into a POTW any pollutant or hazardous substance which such person knew or reasonably should have known could cause personal injury or property damage or causes such treatment works to violate any effluent limitation or permit condition shall be punished by a fine of not less than $2,500 nor more than $25,000 per day of violation, or by imprisonment for not more than 1 year, or both. Repeat offenders may be subject to a fine of not more than $50,000 per day of violation, or by imprisonment of not more than 2 years, or both.[273]

3)   Any person who "knowingly" violates specified sections of the CWA or any permit condition or limitation or any requirement imposed in a pretreatment program shall be punished by a fine of not less than $5,000 nor more than $50,000 per day of violation, or by imprisonment for not more than 3 years, or both. Repeat offenders may be subject to a fine of not more than $100,000 per day of violation, or by imprisonment of not more than 6 years, or both.[274]

4)   Any person who "knowingly" introduces into a sewer system or into a POTW any pollutant or hazardous substance which such person knew or reasonably should have known could cause personal injury or property damage or which causes such treatment works to violate any effluent limitation or condition in its permit, shall be punished by a fine of not less than $5,000 nor more than $50,000 per day of violation, or by imprisonment for not more than 3 years, or both. Repeat offenders may be

---

[272]   CWA § 309(c)(1)(A); 33 U.S.C.A. § 1319(c)(1)(A).

[273]   CWA § 309(c)(1); 33 U.S.C.A. § 1319(c)(1).

[274]   CWA § 309(c)(2)(A); 33 U.S.C.A. § 1319(c)(2)(A).

subject to a fine of not more than $100,000 per day of violation, or by imprisonment of not more than 6 years, or both.[275]

5)   Any person who "knowingly" violates specified sections of the CWA or any permit condition or limitation in a permit and who "knows" at that time that he thereby places another person in "imminent danger of death or serious bodily injury," shall, upon conviction be subject to a fine of up to $250,000, and imprisonment for up to 15 years, or both.[276] An organization can be fined up to $1,000,000 for each violation. For repeat offenders, the fine and imprisonment may be doubled.[277]

6)   Any person who "knowingly" makes any false statements or who knowingly tampers with records or monitoring devices shall be subject to a fine of up to $10,000, imprisonment for up to 2 years, or both.[278] A repeat offender may be subject to a fine of up to $20,000 per day of violation, imprisonment of up to 4 years, or both.[279]

C.   CITIZEN ACTIONS

In addition to government actions, the CWA allows for and encourages citizens to enforce its provisions with the use of citizen suits.[280] Under Section 505 a citizen may sue the government for its failure to enforce provisions of the

---

[275]   CWA § 309(c)(2)(B); 33 U.S.C.A. § 1319(c)(2)(B).

[276]   CWA § 309(c)(3); 33 U.S.C.A. § 1319(c)(3).

[277]   *Id.*

[278]   CWA § 309(c)(4); 33 U.S.C.A. § 1319(c)(4).

[279]   *Id.*

[280]   *See* 77 Wash.U.L.Q. 533 (1999) (discussing "standing" for citizens' suits).

CWA.[281] In addition, citizens may sue other citizens for violations such as discharging without a permit or discharging in violation of an existing permit.[282]

Citizens suits are limited to violations of either effluent standards or administrative orders and such violations must be continuing or threaten to recur.[283] The United States Supreme Court has ruled that under the CWA, a citizens group cannot maintain an action for purely past violations.[284] However, a violation may not be considered "wholly past" if there is a series or pattern of past violations that indicate the likelihood that violations will occur in the future.[285] In *Gwaltney of Smithfield, Ltd. v. Chesapeake Bay Foundation, Inc.*, the United States Supreme Court permitted an action to proceed so long as the plaintiff advanced a "good-faith allegation of continuous or intermittent violations."[286]

No action may be commenced under a citizen's suit without a sixty day notice to the Administrator, state or violator (depending on which entity is being sued).[287] Note however, that where the government has already "commenced and is diligently prosecuting" a criminal action against a violator, a citizen suit may

---

[281]   CWA § 505(a); 33 U.S.C.A. § 1365(a) (specific waiver of federal sovereign immunity).

[282]   *Id.*

[283]   CWA § 505(a)(1); 33 U.S.C.A. § 1365(a)(1).

[284]   Gwaltney of Smithfield, Ltd, v. Chesapeake Bay Foundation, 484 U.S. 49; 107 S.Ct.872; 93 L.Ed.2d 827 (1987) (though efforts may be underway to allow citizens to sue water polluters for "wholly past violations"); *see*, Leonard, Arne R., When Should an Administrative Enforcement Action Preclude a Citizen Suit under the Clean Water Act?, 35 Nat.Resources J. 555, 556 (1995).

[285]   Gwaltney of Smithfield, Ltd, v. Chesapeake Bay Foundation, 484 U.S. 49; 107 S.Ct. 872; 93 L.Ed.2d 827 (1987).

[286]   *Id.*

[287]   CWA § 505(b)(1)(A); 33 U.S.C.A. § 1365(b)(1)(A); *see also*, Proffitt v. Commissioners, 754 F.2d 504 (3d Cir.1985); Walls v. Waste Resource Corp., 761 F.2d 311 (6th Cir.1985); Garcia v. Cecos Int'l Inc., 761 F.2d 76, 82 (1st Cir.1985); Hallistrom v. Tillamook County, 844 F.2d 598, 601 (9th Cir.1988).

not be brought.[288] These provisions typically allow for litigation costs, including reasonable expert witness and attorneys fees to be awarded to the prevailing party.[289] Penalties assessed in citizen suits are to be paid to the federal government.[290] It is important to note that civil enforcement under the CWA does not provide citizens an opportunity to recover damages for injury to persons or to property.[291] These damages are more properly recovered in tort actions.

IX. CONCLUSION

Clean water is essential to the survival of the Earth's ecological systems. For humans, it must be suitable for drinking and for many other activities (such as for the production of electricity, crops, and of many goods and materials). However, many human activities contaminate our waters and thus deplete our sources of clean water.

The CWA seeks to protect and manage the nation's water resources. It addresses point source and nonpoint sources of pollution and regulates conventional, toxic, and nonconventional pollutants. The CWA establishes a bifurcated system where both state and local governments must work closely with the federal government to attain clean water. Potential polluters are not to discharge into the navigable waters without first receiving a permit. Compliance with the CWA and its regulations allows our waters to be used and enjoyed in ways that benefit the human environment without unduly endangering our ecological resources.

---

[288] CWA § 505(b)(1)(B); 33 U.S.C.A. § 1365(b)(1)(B).

[289] CWA § 505(d); 33 U.S.C.A. § 1365(d).

[290] Austin, Jeannette L., The Rise of Citizen-Suit Enforcement in Environmental Law: Reconciling Private and Public Attorney's General, 81 NW.U.L.Rev. 220, 239-240 (1987).

[291] Scott, Shay S., Combining Environmental Citizen Suits & Other Private Theories of Recovery, 8 J.Envtl.L. & Litig. 369, 378 (1994).

TABLE OF CASES

A.

Abbott Laboratories v. Gardner, 38, 40, 41
Abromowitz v. United States EPA, 266
Administrator, State of Arizona v. United States EPA, 270
Alabama Power Co. v. Costle, 268, 275
Alpine Lakes Protection Society v. Schlapfer, 84
American Automobile Mfr's Assn. v. Massachusetts Dept. of Environmental Protection, 43
American Lung Association v. United States EPA, 259
American Meat Institute v. United States EPA, 315
American Mining Congress v. United States EPA, 95, 99, 100, 101
American Petroleum Institute v. Costle, 258
American Petroleum Institute v. United States EPA, 341
American Petroleum Institute v. United States EPA, 127
American Trucking Associations, Inc. v. United States EPA, 259
Amland Properties Corp. v. Aluminum Co. of America, 203
Amoco Oil Co. v. Borden, Inc., 194
Animal Defense Fund v. Hodel, 34, 92
Apache Powder Co. v. United States, 142, 143
Appalachian Mountain Club v. Brinegar, 84
Appalachian Power Company v. United States EPA, 239
Arlington Coalition on Transportation v. Volpe, 65
Artesian Water Co. v. New Castle County, 203
Asarco, Inc. v. United States EPA, 247
Asiana Airlines v. Federal Aviation Admin., 9
Association of Data ProcessingService Organizations, Inc. v. Camp, 39
Atlanta Coalition on Transportation Crisis, Inc. v. Atlanta Regional Commission, 65
Avoylelles Sportsmen's League, Inc. v. Marsh, 298, 304, 305, 339, 340

B.

Barlow v. Collins, 39
Bessemer Mountain, Rissler & McMurry Co. v. Council on Environmental Quality, 8
Block v. Community Nutrition Institute, 36
Blue Circle Cement, Inc. v. Board of Commissioner's of Rogers County, 96
Blue Legs v. United States Bureau of Indian Affairs, 150
Blue Legs v. United States EPA, 148
Blue Ocean Preservation Society v. Watkins, 80
Boles v. Onton Dock, Inc., 77
Bonner v. City of Prichard, 77
Boundary Waters Wilderness v. Dombeck, 57
Brewer v. Raven, 202

Bunker Hill Company v. United States EPA, 251

C.

C & A Carbone, Inc. v. Town of Clarkstown, 147
Calvert Cliffs' Coordinating Committee, Inc. v. United States Atomic Energy Commission, 56
Carr v. Alta Verde Industries, Inc., 298, 300
Catellus Development Corp. v. United States, 99
Central Vermont Quality Services, Inc. v. City of Rutland, Vt., 147
Central Wayne Energy Recovery, L.P. v. United States EPA , 244
Chemical Manufacturers' Ass'n v. United States EPA, 128
Chemical Manufacturers' Ass'n. v. United States EPA, 314, 331
Chemical Manufacturers' Ass'n v. United States EPA, 330
Chemical Manufacturing Association v. Natural Resource Defense Counsel, Inc., 329
Chemical Waste Management, Inc. v. United States EPA, 144, 145
Chevron, U.S.A. Inc. v. Natural Resources Defense Council, Inc., 267
Chevron U.S.A. Inc. v. Yost, 341, 342
Chicago Association of Commerce v. United States EPA, 330
Citizens Against the Refinery's Effects v. United States EPA, 275
Citizens for a Better Henderson v. Hodel, 79, 86
Citizens for Clean Air v. United States EPA, 273
Citizens to Preserve Overton Park, Inc. v. Volpe, 34, 47
City of Boston v. Volpe, 59
City of Carmel by the Sea v. United States Department of Transportation, 57
City of Chicago v. Environmental Defense Fund, 109, 112, 114, 147
City of Chicago v. Environmental Defense Fund, 109
City of Davis v. Coleman, 72
City of Gallatin v. Cherokee County, 148
City of Highland Park v. Train, 254
City of Milwaukee, et al. v. States of Illinois and Michigan, 303
City of New York v. Exxon Corp., 192
City of Rochester v. United States Postal Service, 84, 85
City of Seabrook v. United States EPA, 266
Clean Air Implementation Project v. United States EPA, 259
Coburn v. Sund Chemical Corp., 202
Columbia River Service Corp. v. Gilman, 207
Conductron Corp. v. Gladys P. Williams, 207
Connecticut Coastal Fisherman's Assn v. Remington Arms, Co., Inc., 98, 99
Conner v. Burford, 80

Conservation Council of North Carolina v. Froehlke, 57
Cook v. Rockwell Intern, 202
Costle v. Pacific Legal Foundation, 317
County of Suffolk v. Secretary of Interior, 57
CP Holdings, Inc. v. Goldberg-Zoino & Associates, Inc., 174
Crockett v. Uniroyal, Inc., 114, 125

D.

D'Agnillo v. United States Department of Housing and Urban Development, 85
DOW Chemical Co. v. United States, 293
Dague v. City of Burlington, 298, 299
Davis Enterprises v. United States EPA, 35
Dedham Water Co. v. Cumberland Farms Dairy, Inc., 158, 172, 193
Dickerson v. United States EPA, 231, 232
Dopico v. Goldschmidt, 32, 33, 34

E.

Eagle-Picher Industries, Inc. v. United States EPA, 167, 232, 233
Edison Electric Institute v. United States EPA, 127
Ellison v. Connor, 45
Ely v. Velde, 66
Environmental Defense Fund v. Andrus, Inc., 80
Environmental Defense Fund, Inc. v. Corps of Engineers of U.S. Army, 62
Environmental Defense Fund, Inc. v. Wheelabrator Technologies, Inc., 112, 117, 121, 144
Environmental Defense Fund v. United States EPA, 292

F.

FMC Corp. v. Northern Pump Co., 128
FMC Corp. v. United States Department Of Commerce, 173
Far East Conf. v. United States, 43
Fishel v. Westinghouse Elec. Corp., 299
Foundation for North American Wild Sheep v. United States Dept. of Agriculture, 77
Fox Bay Partners v. U.S. Army Corps of Engineers, 304
Frederick E. Bouchard, Inc. v. United States, 348
Friends of Ompompanoosuc v. Federal Energy Regulatory Commission, 74
Friends of Sakonnet v. Dutra, 299
Friends of the Payette v. Horseshoe Bend Hydroelectric Co., 90
Fritiofson v. Alexander, 88
Furrer v. Brown, 154, 155

G.

Gade v. National Solid Wastes Management Ass'n, 136
Garcia v. Cecos Int'l Inc., 352
Gee v. Boyd, 76
General Electric Co. v. Litton Industrial Automation Systems, Inc., 195

General Motors Corp. v. United States, 293
George E. Warren Corp. v. United States EPA, 40
Goldberg v. Kelly, 32
Goose Hollow Foothills League v. Romney, 66
Goss v. Lopez, 13
Grazing Fields Farm v. Goldschmidt, 76
Great N. Railway v. Merchants Elevator Co., 44
Greene County Planning Board v. Federal Power Commission, 62
Grolier Inc. v. Federal Trade Commission, 15
Gunn v. United States Department of Agriculture, 339
Gwaltney of Smithfield, Ltd, v. Chesapeake Bay Foundation, 352

H.

Hallistrom v. Tillamook County, 352
Hallstrom v. Tillamook County, 155
Hanly v. Mitchell (Hanly I), 68
Hanly v. Kleindiest (Hanly II), 65, 71, 76
Harman Mining Company v. Layne, 32
Hazardous Waste Treatment Council v. United States EPA, 106, 119, 122
Hindes v. Federal Deposit Insurance Corp., 38, 39
Hoffman Homes, Inc. v. United States EPA, 306
Horsehead Resource Development Co., Inc., v. Browner, 112

I.

ICC v. Brotherhood of Locomotive Engineers, 35
Idaho Conservation League v. Mumma, 86, 87
Illinois v. City of Milwaukee, 345
Illinois v. Panhandle E., 44
In re T.P. Long Chemical, Inc., 175
Indiana & Michigan Electric v. United States EPA, 253
Indianapolis Power & Light Company v. United States EPA, 238
Inland Steel Co. v. United States EPA, 298
IT&T Corp. v. International Brotherhood of Electrical Workers, 6
Izaak Walton League v. Schlesinger, 66

J.

J.V. Peters & Co., Inc. v. Ruckelshaus, 230
Jicarilla Apache Tribe v. Federal Energy Regulatory Comm., 47
Jones v. Gorgon, 73
Julis v. City of Cedar Rapids, Iowa, 65

K.

Kaiser Aluminum and Chemical Corp. v. Catellus Development Corp., 181
Kelley v. Thomas Solvent Company, 206
Kilroy v. Ruckelshaus, 334
Kleppe v. Sierra Club, 72, 85, 89
Kopper Company, Inc. v. United States EPA, 331
Lead Industries v. United States EPA, 253
Levin Metals v. Parr-Richmond Terminal Company, 207

355

Long Beach Unified School District v. Dorothy B. Godwin California Living Trust, 181
Lumbermens Mutual Casualty Co. v. Belleville Industries Inc., 215

M.

Marathon Oil Co. v. United States EPA, 310
Mardan Corp v. C.G.C. Music, Ltd., 129
Marmon Group, Inc. v. Rexnord, Inc., 191
Marsh v. Oregon Natural Resources Council, 78
Maryland Conservation Council, Inc. v. Gilchrist, 64
Mathews v. Eldridge, 14
Matter of Penn Central Transportation Co., 185
Matter of Romero & Busot, Inc., 20
McDowell v. Schlesinger, 88
McKart v. United States, 41
Metropolitan Edison Co. v. People Against Nuclear Energy, 67, 68
Middlesex County Bd. of Chosen Freeholders v. N.J. Dept. of Environmental Protection, 148
Milburn Colliery Company v. Hicks, 16
Mississippi Commission on Natural Resources v. Costle, 312
Mobil Oil Corp. v. United States EPA, 109
Mobil Oil Corp. v. United States EPA, 146
Montana Power Company v. United States EPA, 272
Morehead Marine Services, Inc. v. Washnock, 16
Motor Vehicle Manufacturers Ass'n v. State Farm Mutual Auto Insurance Co., 48
Mountain States Corp. v. Petroleum Corp., 44
Mraz v. Canadian Universal Insurance Co., Ltd., 129, 193
Municipal Power Agency v. United States EPA, 307, 314
Municipality of Anchorage v. United States, 325

N.

NL Industries, Inc. v. Kaplan, 165, 203
Nance v. United States EPA, 269, 270, 275
National Ass'n of Metal Finishers v. United States EPA, 329
National Crushed Stone Ass'n v. United States EPA, 305
National Mining Association v. United States EPA, 276
National Railroad Passenger Corp. v. New York City Housing Authority, 174
National Solid Wastes Management Ass'n v. Alabama Dept. of Environmental Management, 144
National Wildlife Federation v. Gorsuch, 299, 304
Natural Resource Defense Counsel (NRDC) v. United States EPA, 281
Natural Resources Defense Council, Inc. v. Morton, 57, 87
Natural Resources Defense Council, Inc. v. Texaco Refining & Marketing, Inc., 312
Natural Resources Defense Council (NRDC) v. United States EPA, 317, 318, 319, 335
Natural Resources Defense Council v. Costle, 299, 344
Natural Resources Defense Council v. United States Nuclear Regulatory Commission, 42

New York Natural Resources Defense Council, Inc. v. Kleppe, 56, 79
New York v. United States, 191
Nucleus of Chicago Homeowners Assn. v. Lynn, 76

O.

O'Connor v. Heckler, 8
O'Neil v. Picillo, 214
Old Bridge Chemicals, Inc. v. New Jersey Dept. of Environmental Protection, 120, 121, 125
Olin Corporation v. Yeargin Inc., 149, 175, 176, 177, 187, 282
Olmstead Citizens For A Better Community v. United States, 67
Oregon Natural Desert Ass'n v. Domdeck, 298
Owen Electric Steel Co. of South Carolina, Inc. v. Browner, 101

P.

Pacific Legal Foundation v. Watt, 318
Panhandle Producers & Royalty Owners Association v. Economic Regulatory Administration, 68
Pease & Curren Refining, Inc. v. Spectrolab, Inc., 195
Pennsylvania v. Union Gas Co., 176, 182
Pennzoil Co. v. Federal Energy Regulatory Commission, 41
Penobscot Air Services, Ltd. v. Federal Aviation Administration, 15, 46
People of the State of California v. Department of the Navy, 255
People of the State of Michigan v. United States, 307
Philadelphia v. Stepan Chemical Co., 203
Primeco Personal Communications L.P. v. Village of Fox Lake, 199
Prisco v. A&D Carting Corp., 168 F.3d 593 (2d Cir.1999), 199
Proffitt v. Commissioners, 352
Public Citizen v. Carlin, 10
Public Service Company of Colorado, Fort St. Train Station v. United States EPA, 314
Puerto Rico Sun Oil Company v. United States EPA, 310, 319

Q.

Quivira Mining Co. v. United States EPA, 296

R.

Redwing Carriers, Inc. v. Saraland Apartments, 199
Reid State Park in Maine, Citizens for Reid State Park v. Laird, 58
Robbins v. Cyprus Cumberland Coal Company, 15
Robertson v. Methow Valley Citizens Council, 57, 87, 90
Ruckelshaus v. Sierra Club, 292, 293

S.

SED, Inc. v. City of Dayton, 305

Sabine River Authority v. United States Department of Interior, 76, 78
San Juan New Materials High Tech, Inc. v. International Trade Commission, 18
Sand Springs Home v. Interplastic Corp., 211, 214
Save Our Ten Acres v. Kreger, 77
Save Our Wetlands v. Sands, 60
Secretary of the Interior v. California, 88
Shell Oil Co. v. United States EPA, 102, 105, 106, 108, 110
Sierra Club v. Abston Construction Co., Inc., 298
Sierra Club v. Costle, 245, 247
Sierra Club v. Gorsuch, 280
Sierra Club v. Marsh, 71, 72, 87, 88, 89
Sierra Club v. Morton, 37, 39, 40, 79
Sierra Club v. Peterson, 38, 77, 78
Sierra Club v. Ruckelshaus, 274, 280, 294
Silva v. Romney, 58
Solite Corp. v. United States EPA, 112, 134
Southland Corp. v. Ashland Oil, Inc., 199
Southern Pacific Transportation Co. v. California, 191
Southwestern Pennsylvania Growth Alliance v. Browner, 275
State ex. rel. Brown v. Georgeoff, 188
State of Colorado v. Idarado Mineral Co., 175, 215
State of Idaho v. Bunker Hill Co., 180, 181
State of Michigan v. Thomas, 263
State of Mississippi v. Marsh, 88
State of Missouri ex rel. Ashcroft v. U.S. Army Corps of Engineers, 304
State of Missouri v. Independent Petrochemical Corp., 187, 188
State of New York v. Shore Realty Corp., 178, 184, 193, 206, 210
State of New York v. United States EPA, 258
State of Ohio v. Ruckelshaus, 267
State of Wyoming v. Hathoway, 59
Steel Manufacturers Ass'n v. United States EPA, 99, 145
Stockman v. Federal Election Commission, 37

T.

Texas & Pacific Railway v. Abilene Cotton Oil Co., 43
Texas v. United States of America, 41
The Movement Against Destruction v. Trainor, 238
Thomas v. Peterson, 83, 84
Township of Lower Alloways Creek v. Public Service Electric & Gas Co., 76
Township of Ridley v. Blanchette, 65
Train v. City of New York, 296
Trinity Episcopal School Corp. v. Romney, 71
Trout Unlimited v. Morton, 79
Trustees for Alaska v. United States EPA, 317

U.

Union Electric v. United States EPA, 253
United States Dept. of Energy v. Ohio, 303
United States EPA v. Environmental Waste Control, Inc., 130, 131, 138, 139, 140
United States Steel Corp. v. Train, 313

United States v. A & F Materials Co., 212
United States v. A & N Cleaners and Launderers, Inc., 180
United States v. Alcan Aluminum Corp., 172, 192, 213
United States v. Atlantic Richfield Co., 245
United States v. Bliss, 175
United States v. Boldt, 335
United States v. Borowski, 296
United States v. Bradshaw, 305
United States v. Buckley, 210
United States v. Buntin, 348
United States v. Carolina Transformer Co., Inc., 208
United States v. Carr, 165, 174
United States v. Chem-Dyne Corp., 214
United States v. Chevron Oil Company, 342
United States v. Chrysler Corporation, 9
United States v. City of Detroit, 349
United States v. City of Providence, 348
United States v. City of Sarasota, 336
United States v. Conservation Chemical Co., 187, 188, 189, 210, 230
United States v. Curtis, 303
United States v. Dickerson, 231
United States v. EKCO Housewares, Inc., 139, 140
United States v. Earth Sciences, Inc., 296, 299, 305, 307
United States v. Fern, 290
United States v. Fleet Factors Corp., 183, 185, 220, 221
United States v. Ford Motor Company, 257
United States v. GAF Corp., 307
United States v. Hallmark Construction, 338
United States v. Hamel, 305, 306
United States v. Hardage, 184
United States v. Haves Int'l Corp., 154
United States v. Holland, 298, 307
United States v. Hooker Chemicals and Plastic Corp., 159, 209
United States v. ILCO, Inc., 103
United States v. Indiana Woodtreating Corp., 134, 135, 136, 137, 139, 140
United States v. International Minerals & Chem. Corp., 153
United States v. Iron Mountain Mines, Inc., 111
United States v. Lambert, 304
United States v. Larkins, 340
United States v. Laughlin, 153, 165
United States v. Lee Wood Contracting, Inc., 339
United States v. Maryland Bank & Trust Co., 218
United States v. McDonald & Watson Waste Oil Co., 109, 128
United States v. Metate Asbestos Corp., 175
United States v. Mexico Feed and Seed Co., 207
United States v. Mills, 305
United States v. Monsanto Co., 210
United States v. Mottolo, 181
United States v. New Castle County, 179
United States v. Nicolet, Inc., 185
United States v. NEPCCO, 188, 199, 210, 230
United States v. Ottati & Goss, Inc., 185, 186, 210
United States v. Oxford Royal Mushroom Products, Inc., 307
United States v. Peterson Sand and Gravel, Inc., 181

United States v. Phelps Dodge Corp., 307
United States v. Plaza Health Laboratories, Inc., 25
United States v. Pozsgai, 26, 304, 305, 306
United States v. R.W. Meyer, Inc., 210
United States v. Recticel Foam Corp., 104
United States v. Riverside Bayview Homes, Inc., 338
United States v. Robinson, 304
United States v. Rohm & Hass Co., 195
United States v. Schallom, 305
United States v. Seymour Recycling Corp., 230
United States v. Shell Oil Co., 210, 216, 218, 219
United States v. South Carolina Recycling and
Disposal, Inc., 185, 186
United States v. Stringfellow, 187, 215
United States v. T & S Brass and Bronze
Works, Inc., 115, 156
United States v. Texas Pipeline Co., 306, 307
United States v. Villages, 25
United States v. Wagner, 154
United States v. Ward, 175, 187, 210
United States v. Weisman, 298, 305, 307
United States v. Weitzenhoff, 335
United States v. West Indies Transport, 297, 304
United States v. Western Pacific Railroad Co., 43
United States v. Western Processing Co., 192
United States v. Wilson, 338
United States v. Zanger, 307
United Technologies Corp. v. United States EPA, 99
Universal Camera Corp. v. National Labor
Relations Board, 49

V.

Vermont Yankee Nuclear Power Corp. v. Natural
Resources Defense Council, Inc., 33
Violet v. Picillo, 172, 218
Voluntary Purchasing Groups, Inc. v. Reilly, 193

W.

Walls v. Waste Resource Corp., 352
Warm Springs Dam Task Force v. Gribble, 89
Waste Action Project v. Dawn Mining Corp., 306
Webster v. U.S. Department of Energy, 45
Weinberger v. Romero-Barcelo, 348
Winnebago Tribe of Nebraska v. Ray, 77
Wisconsin Electric Power v. Reilly, 244
Wyoming Outdoor Coordinating Council v. Butz, 77

358

ACRONYMS

A

AAQS: Ambient Air Quality Standards

ALJ: Administrative Law Judge

APA: Administrative Procedure Act

AQC: Air Quality Criteria

AQCR: Air Quality Control Region

ARAR: Applicable or Relevant and Appropriate Standards, Limitations, Criteria and Requirements

ATSDR: Agency for Toxic Substances and Disease Registry

B

BACM: Best Available Control Measures

BACT: Best Available Control Technology

BAT: Best Available Technology Economically Achievable

BADT: Best Available Demonstrated Control Technology

BCT: Best Conventional Pollutant Control Technology

BDAT: Best Demonstrated Available Technology

BDT: Best Demonstrated Control Technology

BMP: Best Management Practice(s)

BOD: Biochemical Oxygen Demand; Biological Oxygen Demand

BPCT: Best Practicable Control Technology

BPJ: Best Professional Judgment

BPT: Best Practicable Control Technology; Best Practicable Treatment

C

CAA: Clean Air Act

CATX: Categorical Exclusion

CBEC: Concentration-Based Exemption Criteria

CE: Conditionally Exempt Generators

CEQ: Council on Environmental Quality

CERCLA: Comprehensive Environmental Response, Compensation, and Liability Act

CERCLIS: Comprehensive Environmental Response, Compensation, and Liability Information System

CFC: Chlorofluorocarbons

C.F.R.: Code of Federal Regulations

CMI: Corrective Measures Implementation

CMS: Corrective Measures Study

CO: Carbon Monoxide

CTG: Control Technique Guidelines

CWA: Clean Water Act (aka FWPCA)

CZMA: Coastal Zone Management Act

D

DDD: Dichloro-diphenyl-dichloro-ethane

DDE: Dichloro-diphenyl-ethane

DDT: Dichloro-diphenyl-trichloro-ethane

DHHS: Department of Health and Humans Services

DO: Dissolved Oxygen

DOJ: U.S. Department of Justice

DOT: U.S. Department of Transportation

E

EA: Environmental Assessment

EIS: Environmental Impact Statement

EPA: U.S. Environmental Protection Agency

EPCRA: Emergency Planning and Community Right to Know Act (part of the Superfund Amendments and Reauthorization Act, Title III)

ESA: Endangered Species Act

F

FDF: Fundamentally Different Factors

FIFRA: Federal Insecticide, Fungicide, and Rodenticide Act

FFCA: Federal Facility Compliance Act

FONSI: Finding Of No Significant Impact

FR: Federal Register; Final Rulemaking

FS: Feasibility Study

FWPCA: Federal Water Pollution Control Act

G

GACT: Generally Available Control Technology

GSA: General Services Administration

H

HAP: Hazardous Air Pollutant

HEW: U.S. Dept. of Health, Education and Welfare

HRS: Hazardous Ranking System

HW: Hazardous Waste

HWI: Hazardous Waste Index

HWM: Hazardous Waste Management

HSWA: Hazardous and Solid Waste Amendments

HUD: U.S. Dept. of Housing and Urban Development

HWIR: Hazardous Waste Identification Rule

I

IDLH: Immediately Dangerous to Life and Health

I/M: Inspection and Maintenance

IRAA: Indoor Radar Abatement Act

L

LAER: Lowest Achievable Emission Rate

LIA: Lead Industries Association

LQG: Large Quantity Generator

M

MACT: Maximum Achievable Control Technology

MPRSA: Marine Protection, Research & Sanctuaries Act; *also known as the Ocean Dumping Ban Act (ODBA)*

MSDS: Material Safety Data Sheet

MSWLF: Municipal Solid Waste Landfill

N

NA: Nonattainment Area

NAAQS: National Ambient Air Quality Standards

NBAR: Non-Binding Preliminary Allocation of Responsibility

NCP: National Contingency Plan

NEPA: National Environmental Policy Act

NESHAPs: National Emission Standards for Hazardous Air Pollutants

NIPDWSs: National Interim Primary Drinking Water Standards

NO$_2$: Nitrogen Dioxide

NOHSCP: National Oil and Hazardous Substances Contingency Plan

NOD: Notice of Deficiencies

NOI: Notice of Intent

NOV: Notice of Violations

NPL: National Priorities List

NPDES: National Pollution Discharge Elimination System

NSPS: New Source Performance Standards

NSR: New Source Review

O

O$_3$: Ozone

ODBA: Ocean Dumping Ban Act; *also known as the Marine Protection, Research and Sanctuaries Act (MPRSA)*

O/M: Operation and Maintenance

OPA: Oil Pollution Act

OSHA: Occupational Safety and Health Act

P

PA: Preliminary Assessment

Pb: Lead

PCB: Poly-Chlorinated Biphenyls

PJD: Primary Jurisdiction Doctrine

PM: Particulate Matter

POTW: Publicly Owned Treatment Works

POWTW: Publicly Owned Waste Treatment Works

PPA: Pollution Prevention Act

PPB: Parts Per Billion

PPM: Parts Per Million

PRP: Potentially Responsible Party

PSD: Prevention of Significant Deterioration

R

RA: Remedial Action

RACM: Reasonably Available Control Measures

RACT: Reasonably Available Control Technology

RCRA: Resource Conservation and Recovery Act

RFA: RCRA Facility Assessment

RFI: RCRA Facility Investigation

RFP: Reasonable Further Progress

RI: Remedial Investigation

RI/FS: Remedial Investigation/Feasibility Study

ROD: Record of Decision

RQ: Reportable Quantity

S

SARA: Superfund Amendments and Reauthorization Act of 1986

SDWA: Safe Drinking Water Act

SEPA: State Environmental Protection Act

SIP: State Implementation Plan

SO2: Sulfur Dioxide

SQG: Small Quantity Generator

SRAP: Superfund Remedial Accomplishment Plan

SWDA: Solid Waste Disposal Act

SWMU: Solid Waste Management Unit

T

TCLP: Total Concentrate Leachate Procedure; Toxicity Characteristic Leaching Procedure

TMDL: Total Maximum Daily Load

TRS: Total Reduced Sulfur

TSCA: Toxic Substances Control Act

TSD: Treatment, Storage and Disposal

TSDF: Treatment, Storage and Disposal Facility

TSM: Transportation System Management

TSS: Total Suspended Solids

U

UMTRCA: Uranium Mill Tailings
Radiation Control Act

UIC: Underground Injection Control

USACOE: U.S. Army Corps of
Engineers

UST: Underground Storage Tank

V

VOC: Volatile Organic Compounds

GLOSSARY

A

Abatement: Reducing the degree or intensity of, or eliminating, pollution.

Absorption: The uptake of water or dissolved chemicals by a cell or an organism (as tree roots absorb dissolved nutrients in soil).

Acid Deposition/Acid Rain: A complex chemical and atmospheric phenomenon that occurs when emissions of sulfur and nitrogen compounds and other substances are transformed by chemical processes in the atmosphere, often far from the original sources, and then deposited on earth in either wet or dry form. The wet forms, popularly called "acid rain," can fall as rain, snow, or fog. The dry forms are acidic gases or particulates.

Action Levels: In the Superfund program, the existence of a contaminant concentration in the environment high enough to warrant action or trigger a response under SARA and the National Oil and Hazardous Substances Contingency Plan. The term is also used in other regulatory programs.

Activated Sludge: Product that results when primary effluent is mixed with bacteria-laden sludge and then agitated and aerated to promote biological treatment, speeding the breakdown of organic matter in raw sewage undergoing secondary waste treatment.

Acute Exposure: A single exposure to a toxic substance which results in severe biological harm or death. Acute exposures are usually characterized as lasting no longer than a day, as compared to longer, continuing exposure over a period of time.

Acid Rain: *See Acid Deposition.*

Acid Rain Precursors: Sulfur and nitrogen compounds and other substances which cause acid rain. *See also, Acid Deposition.*

Acute Toxicity: The ability of a substance to cause poisonous effects resulting in severe biological harm or death soon after a single exposure or dose. Also, any severe poisonous effect resulting from a single short-term exposure to a toxic substance. *See Chronic Toxicity, Toxicity.*

Administrative Law Judge (ALJ): One who presides at an administrative hearing with power to administer oaths, take testimony, rule on questions of evidence, and make determinations of fact. Also known as a "hearing officer" or "hearing examiner."

Administrative Order on Consent: A legal agreement signed by EPA and an individual, business, or other entity through which the violator agrees to pay for correction of violations, take the required corrective or cleanup actions, or refrain from an activity. It describes the actions to be taken, may be subject to a comment period, applies to civil actions, and can be enforced in court.

Administrative Order: A legal document signed by EPA directing an individual, business, or other entity to take corrective action or refrain from an activity. It describes the violations and actions to be taken, and can be enforced in court. Such orders may be issued, for example, as a result of an administrative complaint whereby the respondent is ordered to pay a penalty for violations of a statute.

Administrative Procedure Act (APA): A law that sets forth procedures and requirements related to the promulgation of regulations.

Administrative Record: All documents which EPA considered or relied on in selecting the response action at a Superfund site, culminating in the Record of Decision for remedial action.

Agricultural Pollution: Farming wastes, including runoff and leaching of pesticides and fertilizers, erosion and dust from plowing, improper disposal of animal manure and carcasses, crop residues, and debris.

Airborne Particulates: Total suspended particulate matter found in the atmosphere as solid particles or liquid droplets. Chemical composition of particulates varies widely depending on location and time of year. Airborne particulates include: windblown dust, emissions from industrial processes, smoke from the burning of wood and coal, and motor vehicle or non-road engine exhausts.

Air Pollutant: Any substance in the ambient air that could, in high enough concentrations, harm people, other animals, vegetation, or material. Pollutants may include almost any natural or artificial composition of matter capable of being airborne. They may be in the form of solid particles, liquid droplets, gases, or a combination thereof. Generally, they fall into two main groups; (1) those emitted directly from identifiable sources, and (2) those produced in the air by interaction between two or more primary pollutants,

or by reaction with normal atmospheric constituents with or without photoactivation.

Air Pollution Control Device: Mechanisms or equipment that cleans emissions generated by, (for example, an incinerator) removing pollutants that would otherwise be released to the atmosphere.

Air Pollution: The presence of contaminant or pollutant substances in the ambient air that do not disperse properly and that interfere with human health or welfare, or produce other harmful environmental effects.

Air Quality Control Region (AQCR): Federally designated area that is required to meet and maintain federal ambient air quality standards. May include nearby locations in the same state or nearby states that share common air pollution problems.

Air Quality Criteria (AQC): The levels of pollution and lengths of exposure above which adverse health and welfare effects may occur.

Air Quality Standards: The level of pollutants prescribed by regulations that may not be exceeded during a given time in a defined area.

Air Toxics: Also known as hazardous air pollutants or HAPs, they are any air pollutant for which a national ambient air quality standard (NAAQS) does not exist (i.e., these do not include ozone, carbon monoxide, PM-10, sulfur dioxide, nitrogen oxide) that may reasonably be anticipated to cause cancer, developmental effects, reproductive dysfunctions, neurological disorders, heritable gene mutations, or other serious or irreversible chronic or acute health effects in humans.

Alkaline: The condition of water or soil which contains a sufficient amount of alkali to raise the pH above 7.0.

Alternate Method: Any method of sampling and analyzing for an air pollutant that is not a reference or equivalent method but that has been demonstrated in specific cases -- to EPA's satisfaction -- to produce results adequate for compliance monitoring.

Ambient Air: Any unconfined portion of the atmosphere: open air, surrounding air.

Ambient Air Quality Standards: *See Criteria Pollutants, National Ambient Air Quality Standards, Primary Standard, and Secondary Standard.*

Antidegradation Policy: Part of federal air quality and water quality requirements prohibiting deterioration where pollution levels are above the legal limit. *See Nondegradation Policy.*

Applicable or Appropriate Requirements (ARARs): Any state or federal statute that pertains to the protection of human life and the environment in addressing specific conditions or use of a particular cleanup technology at a Superfund site.

Aquatic: Growing or living in or around water.

Arbitrary and Capricious: In administrative law, the standard of review used by the court to determine whether an agency action or decision is unreasonable or intolerable. Under this standard the court is very tolerant of agency decisions and gives great deference to agency discretion and interpretations.

Area Source: Any small source of non-natural air pollution that is released over a relatively small area but which cannot be classified as a point source. Such sources may include vehicles and other small engines, small businesses, and household activities.

Arsenic: *See Heavy Metals.*

Attainment Area: An area considered to have air quality as good as or better than the national ambient air quality standards as defined in the Clean Air Act. An area may be an attainment area for one pollutant and a nonattainment area for others.

B

Background Level: In air pollution control, the concentration of air pollutants in a definite area during a fixed period of time prior to the starting up or on the stoppage of a source of emission under control. In toxic or hazardous substances it represents the average and normal presence of such substances in the environment.

Beneficiation: The dressing or processing of ores for the purpose of (1) regulating the size of, or recovering, the ore or product, (2) removing unwanted constituents from the ore, and (3) improving the quality, purity, or assay grade of a desired product.

Berm: A narrow shelf, path, or lodge typically at the top or bottom of a slope.

Best Available Control Measures (BACM): Under the Clean Air Act, a term used to refer to the most effective measures (according to EPA guidance) for controlling small or dispersed particulates from sources such as roadway dust, soot and ash from wood stoves and open burning of brush, timber, grasslands, or trash.

Best Available Control Technology (BACT): Under the Clean Air Act, an emission limitation based on the maximum degree of emission reduction (considering energy, environmental, and economic impacts) achievable through application of production processes and available methods, systems, and techniques. BACT is the standard of performance required for new and modified facilities under the PSD program of the Clean Air Act. BACT does not permit emissions in excess of those allowed under any other applicable Clean Air Act provision. Use of the BACT concept is allowable on a case-by-case basis for major new or modified emissions sources in attainment areas and applies to each regulated pollutant.

Best Available Demonstrated Technology (BADT): Under the Clean Water Act, the most effective commercially available means of controlling pollutant discharges from all new sources.

Best Available Technology Economically Achievable (BAT): Under the Clean Water Act, this level of control is generally described as the best technology currently in use and includes controls on toxic pollutants.

Best Conventional Pollutant Control Technology (BCT): Under the Clean Water Act, this level of control is generally described as the best technology available that controls "conventional" pollutants.

Best Demonstrated Available Technology (BDAT): Under the Resource Conservation and Recovery Act, the most effective commercially available means of treating specific types of hazardous waste as identified by the EPA. The BDATs may change with advances in treatment technologies.

Best Management Practice (BMP): Under the Clean Air Act, methods that have been determined to be the most effective, practical means of preventing or reducing pollution from non-point sources.

Best Practicable Control Technology; Best Practicable Treatment (BPT): Under the Clean Water Act, this level of control technology is described as the "average of the best" technology currently in use to control wastes from a specific industry.

Bilge: The part of the underwater body of a ship between the flat of the bottom and the vertical topsides.

Bioaccumulants: Substances that increase in concentration in living organisms as they take in contaminated air, water, or food because the substances are very slowly metabolized or excreted.

Biochemical Oxygen Demand (BOD): A measure of the amount of oxygen consumed in the biological processes that break down organic matter in water. The greater the BOD, the greater the degree of pollution.

Biological Oxygen Demand (BOD): An indirect measure of the concentration of biologically degradable material present in organic wastes. It usually reflects the amount of oxygen consumed in five days by biological processes breaking down organic waste.

Biota: The animal and plant life of a given region.

Bottom Ash: The non-airborne combustion residue from burning pulverized coal in a boiler; the material which falls to the bottom of the boiler and is removed mechanically; a concentration of the non-combustible materials which may include toxics.

Breakwater: An offshore structure (e.g. a wall) used to protect a harbor or beach from the force of the waves.

Bubble: Under the CAA, a system where existing emissions sources can propose alternate means to comply with a set of emissions limitations; under the bubble concept, sources are controlled more than required at one emission point where control costs are relatively low in return for a comparable relaxation of controls at a second emission point where costs are much higher. *See Emissions Trading, Netting, Offsets.*

Bubble Policy: *See Bubble, Emissions Trading, Netting, Offsets.*

By-product: Material, other than the principal product, produced as a consequence of an industrial process.

C

Cadmium: *See Heavy Metals.*

Cap: A layer of clay, or other impermeable material installed over the top of a closed landfill or other site where wastes have been remediated to prevent entry of rainwater and minimize leachate or migration of any remaining contaminants.

Carbon Monoxide (CO): A colorless, odorless, poisonous gas produced by incomplete fossil fuel combustion, such as the burning of carbon-based fuels, including gasoline, oil and wood. When carbon monoxide gets into the body, it combines with chemicals in the blood and prevents the blood from bringing oxygen to cells, tissues, and organs. High level exposures to carbon monoxide can cause serious health effects including death from sustained exposures. Symptoms of exposure to carbon monoxide can include vision problems, reduced alertness, and general reduction in mental and physical functions.

Carbon Tetrachloride: A colorless nonflammable toxic liquid that has an odor resembling that of chloroform and is used as a solvent and a refrigerant.

Carcinogen: Any substance that can cause or aggravate cancer.

Categorical Exclusion: A class of actions which either individually or cumulatively would not have a significant effect on the human environment, and therefore, would not require preparation of an environmental assessment or environmental impact statement under the National Environmental Policy Act (NEPA).

Characteristic: Any one of the four categories used in defining hazardous waste: ignitability, corrosivity, reactivity, and toxicity.

Chlorofluorocarbons (CFCs): A family of inert, nontoxic, and easily liquefied chemicals used in refrigeration, air conditioning, packaging, insulation, or as solvents and aerosol propellants. Because CFCs are not destroyed in the lower atmosphere, they drift into the upper atmosphere where their chlorine components destroy the stratospheric ozone layer which protects the Earth's surface from harmful effects of radiation from the sun.

Chromium: *See Heavy Metals.*

Chronic Effect: An adverse effect on a human or animal in which symptoms recur frequently or develop slowly over a long period of time.

Chronic Toxicity: The capacity of a substance to cause long-term poisonous human health effects. *Also see, Acute Toxicity.*

Class I Area: Under the Clean Air Act, a Class I area is one in which visibility is protected more stringently than under the national ambient air quality standards; includes national parks, wilderness areas, monuments, and other areas of special national and cultural significance. Little or no economic growth is allowed in this area.

Class II Area: Under the Clean Air Act, a Class II area is an area in attainment of the NAAQS that has not been designated as a Class I area. Some limited economic growth is allowed in this area, but it must not significantly deteriorate the quality of the air.

Class III Area: Under the Clean Air Act, a Class III area is one in attainment of the NAAQS which is jointly designated as a Class III by the EPA and a state's governor. Class III areas allow more economic growth than Class II areas.

Cleanup: Actions taken to deal with a release or threat of release of a hazardous substance that could affect humans and/or the environment. The term "cleanup" is sometimes used interchangeably with the terms remedial action, removal action, response action, or corrective action.

Closed-Loop Recycling: Reclaiming or reusing wastewater for non-potable purposes in an enclosed process.

Closure: The procedure a landfill operator must follow when a landfill reaches its legal capacity for solid waste: ceasing acceptance of solid waste and placing a cap on the landfill site.

Coastal Zone Management Act (CZMA): The act which protects lands and waters adjacent to the coast that exert an influence on the uses of the sea and its ecology, or inversely, whose uses and ecology are affected by the sea.

Coke: Bituminous coal from which the volatile components have been driven off by heat, leaving fixed carbon and ash fused together.

Coking Process: An industrial process which converts coal into coke; it is one of the basic materials used in blast furnaces for the conversion of iron ore into iron.

Combustion: (1) Burning, or rapid oxidation, accompanied by release of energy in the form of heat and light. A basic cause of air pollution. (2) Refers to controlled burning of waste in which heat chemically alters organic compounds converting them into stable inorganics such as carbon dioxide and water.

Comment Period: Time provided for the public to review and comment on a proposed EPA action or rulemaking after publication in the Federal Register.

Commercial Waste: All solid waste emanating from business establishments such as: stores, markets, office buildings, restaurants, shopping centers, and theaters.

Compliance Monitoring: Collection and evaluation of data, including self-monitoring reports, and verification to show whether pollutant concentrations and loads contained in permitted discharges are in compliance with the limits and conditions specified in the permit.

Compliance Schedule: A negotiated agreement between a pollution source and a government agency that specifies dates and procedures by which a source will reduce emissions and, thereby, comply with a regulation.

Concentration-Based Exemption Criteria (CBEC): An alternative approach to hazardous waste identification. Each hazardous constituent is assigned a numerical exemption criterion based on risk treatment technology. If all hazardous constituents in a waste, waste mixture or waste derivative fall below the exemption criteria, the waste is not subject to the Hazardous Waste Management regulations of Subtitle C of RCRA (the land disposal restrictions). The mixture and derived from rules would still determine whether a waste would enter the RCRA regulatory system, but the CBEC approach would define whether and when the waste could exit the system. *See Derived from Rule, Mixture Rule.*

Conditionally Exempt Generators (CE): Persons or enterprises which produce less than 220 pounds of hazardous waste per month. Exempt from most regulation, they are required merely to determine whether their waste is hazardous, notify appropriate state or local agencies, and ship it by permitted transporter for proper disposal. *See Small Quantity Generator.*

Consent Decree: A legal document, approved by a judge, that formalizes an agreement reached between EPA and potentially responsible parties (PRPs) through which PRPs will conduct all or part of a cleanup action at a Superfund site; cease or correct actions or processes that are polluting the environment; or otherwise comply with EPA initiated regulatory enforcement actions to resolve the contamination at the Superfund site involved. The consent decree describes the actions PRPs will take and may be subject to a public comment period.

Conservation: Preserving and renewing, when possible, human and natural resources. The use, protection, and improvement of natural resources according to principles that will assure their highest economic or social benefits.

Construction Ban: If, under the Clean Air Act, EPA disapproves an area's planning requirements for correcting nonattainment, EPA can ban the construction or modification of any major stationary source of the pollutant for which the area is in nonattainment.

Contamination: Any physical, chemical, biological, or radiological substance or matter that has an adverse affect on air, water, or soil.

Contiguous: Touching along a boundary or at a point; adjacent.

Contiguous Zone: The zone of the high seas, established by the United States under Article 24 of the Convention on the Territorial Sea and Contiguous Zone, which is contiguous to the territorial sea and which extends nine miles seaward from the outer limit of territorial sea.

Contingency Plan: A document setting out an organized, planned, and coordinated course of action to be followed in case of a fire, explosion, or other accident that releases toxic chemicals, hazardous waste, or radioactive materials that threaten human health or the environment. *Also see, National Oil and Hazardous Substances Contingency Plan.*

Continuous Discharge: A routine release into the environment that occurs without interruption, except for infrequent shutdowns for maintenance, process changes, etc.

Control Technique Guidelines (CTG): A series of EPA documents designed to assist states in defining reasonable available control technology (RACT) for major sources of volatile organic compounds (VOC).

Conventional Pollutants: Statutorily listed pollutants understood well by scientists. These may be in the form of organic waste, sediment, acid, bacteria, viruses, nutrients, oil and grease, or heat.

Corrosion: The dissolution and wearing away of metal caused by a chemical reaction such as between water and pipes, chemicals touching a metal surface, or contact between two metals.

Corrosive: A chemical agent that reacts with the surface of a material causing it to deteriorate or wear away.

Cost/Benefit Analysis: A quantitative evaluation of the costs which would be incurred by implementing an environmental regulation versus the overall benefits to society of the proposed action.

Cost-Effective Alternative: An alternative corrective method identified as being the best available in terms of reliability, performance, and cost. Although costs are one important consideration, regulatory and compliance analysis does not require EPA to choose the least expensive alternative. For example, when selecting or approving a method for cleaning up a Superfund site the agency balances costs with the long-term effectiveness of the methods proposed and the potential danger posed by the site.

Cost Recovery: A legal process by which potentially responsible parties who contributed to contamination at a Superfund site can be required to reimburse the Trust Fund for money spent during any cleanup actions by the federal government.

Cradle-to-Grave or Manifest System: A procedure in which hazardous materials are identified and followed as they are produced, treated, transported, and disposed of by a series of permanent, linkable, descriptive documents (e.g., manifests). Commonly referred to as the cradle-to-grave system under the Resource, Conservation and Recovery Act.

Criteria Pollutants: The 1970 amendments to the Clean Air Act required EPA to set National Ambient

371

Air Quality Standards for certain pollutants known to be hazardous to human health. EPA has identified and set standards to protect human health and welfare for six pollutants: ozone, carbon monoxide, total suspended particulates, sulfur dioxide, lead, and nitrogen oxide. The term, "criteria pollutants" derives from the requirement that EPA must describe the characteristics and potential health and welfare effects of these pollutants. It is on the basis of these criteria that standards are set or revised.

Criteria: Descriptive factors taken into account by EPA in setting standards for various pollutants. These factors are used to determine limits on allowable concentration levels, and to limit the number of violations per year. When issued by EPA, the criteria provide guidance to the states on how to establish their standards.

Culvert: (1) A transverse drain. (2) A conduit for a culvert. (3) A bridge over a culvert.

D

DDT: Dichloro-diphenyl-trichloro-ethane. The first chlorinated hydrocarbon insecticide. it has a half-life of 15 years and can collect in fatty tissues of certain animals. It is a toxic substance. EPA banned registration and interstate sales of DDT for virtually all but emergency uses in the United States in 1972 because of its persistence in the environment and accumulation in the food chain.

Decontamination: Removal of harmful substances such as noxious chemicals, harmful bacteria or other organisms, or radioactive material from exposed individuals, rooms and furnishings in buildings, or the exterior environment.

Degradability: The ability of a chemical substance to become reduced in complexity.

Deep-Well Injection: Deposition of raw or treated, filtered hazardous waste by pumping it into deep wells, where it is contained in the pores of permeable subsurface rock.

Degradability: The ability of a chemical substance to become reduced in complexity.

Delegated State: A state (or other governmental entity such as a tribal government) that has received authority to administer an environmental regulatory program in lieu of a federal counterpart. As used in connection with the NPDES programs, the term does not connote any transfer of federal authority to a state.

Delist: Use of the petition process to have a facility's toxic designation rescinded.

De Minimis: Minimal; in small amounts.

Derived from Rule: Under this Resource Conservation and Recovery act regulation, Any substance "derived from" a listed hazardous waste is treated as a "hazardous waste," and any substance "derived from" a characteristic hazardous waste" only if it continues to exhibit a hazardous characteristic, such as ignitability, corrosivity, toxicity, and reactivity.

Designated Pollutant: An air pollutant which is neither a criteria nor hazardous pollutant, as described in the Clean Air

Act, but for which new source performance standards exist. The Clean Air Act does require states to control these pollutants which include: acid mist, total reduced sulfur (TRS), and fluorides.

Designated Uses: Those water uses identified in state water quality standards that must be achieved and maintained as required under the Clean Water Act. Uses can include cold water fisheries, public water supply, irrigation, etc.

Detection Criterion: A predetermined rule to ascertain whether a tank is leaking or not. Most volumetric tests use a threshold value as the detection criterion. *See Volumetric Tank Tests.*

Dike: A low wall that can act as a barrier to prevent a spill from spreading.

Diluent: Any liquid or solid material used to dilute or carry an active ingredient.

Dilution Ratio: The relationship between the volume of water in a stream and the volume of incoming water. It affects the ability of the stream to assimilate waste.

Dioxin: Any of a family of compounds known chemically as dibenzo-p-dioxins. Concern about them arises from their potential toxicity and contaminants in commercial products. Tests on laboratory animals indicate that they are some of the more toxic artificial compounds.

Direct Discharger: A municipal, commercial, or industrial facility which introduces pollution through a defined conveyance or system such as outlet pipes; a point source.

Direct Runoff: Water that flows over the ground surface or through the ground directly into streams, rivers and lakes.

Discharge: Flow of surface water in a stream or canal or the outflow of groundwater from a flowing artesian well, ditch, or spring. Can also apply to discharge of liquid effluent from a facility or to chemical emissions into the air through designated venting mechanisms.

Discrete Fissure: A distinct, clearly identifiable, narrow opening or crack of considerable length and depth, usually occurring from some breaking or parting.

Disinfection: The chemical or physical process that kills pathogenic organisms in water. Chlorine is often used to disinfect sewage treatment effluent water supplies, wells, and swimming pools.

Disposal: Final placement or destruction of toxic, radioactive, or other wastes; surplus or banned pesticides or other chemicals; polluted soils; and drums containing hazardous materials from removal actions or accidental releases. Disposal may be accomplished through use of approved secure landfills, surface impoundments, land farming, deep-well injection, ocean dumping, or incineration.

Dissolved Oxygen (DO): The oxygen freely available in water, vital to fish and other aquatic life and for the prevention of odors. DO levels are considered a most important indicator of a water body's ability to support desirable aquatic life. Secondary and advanced waste treatment are generally designed to ensure adequate DO in waste-receiving waters.

373

Distillation: The act of purifying liquids through boiling, so that the steam condenses to a pure liquid and the pollutants remain in a concentrated residue.

Diversion: (1) Use of part of a stream flow as water supply. (2) A channel with a supporting ridge on the lower side constructed across a slope to divert wastes at a non-erosive velocity to sites where they can be used and disposed of.

Domestic Waste: *See Household Waste.*

DOT Reportable Quantity: The quantity of a substance specified in U.S. Department of Transportation regulation that triggers labeling, packaging and other requirements related to shipping such substances.

Double Lining: Placing two relatively impermeable barriers/liners designed to keep leachate inside a landfill. For example, placing landfill materials over layers of dense clay and plastic.

Draft Permit: A preliminary permit drafted and published by EPA; subject to public review and comment before final action on the application.

Dredged Material: Any material excavated or dredged from the navigable waters of the United States. Dredged material often contains high levels of toxic and other pollutants that have precipitated into bottom sediments. Disposal in navigable waters requires a CWA Section 404 permit.

Dredging: Removal of mud from the bottom of water bodies. This can disturb the ecosystem and cause silting that kills aquatic life. Dredging of contaminated muds can expose biota to heavy metals

and other toxics. Dredging activities may be subject to regulation under Section 404 of the Clean Water Act.

Dump: (1) A site used to dispose of solid waste without environmental controls. (2) A solid waste disposal site having no environmental restrictions. *Also, see Open Dump.*

E

Ecological Impact: The effect that an artificial or natural activity has on living organisms (biotic) and their non-living (abiotic) environment.

Effluent: Wastewater, treated or untreated that flows out of a treatment plant, sewer, or industrial outfall.

Effluent Guidelines: Technical EPA documents which set effluent limits for industries and pollutants.

Effluent Limitation: Restrictions established by a state or EPA on quantities, rates, and concentrations in wastewater discharges.

Effluent Standard: *See Effluent Limitation.*

Emergency (Chemical): A situation created by an accidental release or spill of hazardous chemicals that poses a threat to the safety of workers, residents, the environment, or property.

Emission: Pollution discharged into the atmosphere from smokestacks, other vents, and surface areas of commercial or industrial facilities; from residential chimneys; and from motor vehicle, locomotive, or aircraft exhausts.

Emission Standard: The maximum amount of air polluting discharge legally allowed from a single source, mobile, or stationary.

Emissions Trading: The creation of surplus emission reductions at certain stacks, vents or similar emissions sources and the use of this surplus to meet or redefine pollution requirements applicable to other emissions sources. This allows one source to increase emissions when another source reduces them, maintaining an overall constant emission level. Facilities that reduce emissions substantially may "bank" their "credits" or sell them to other facilities or industries.

Endangered Species: Animals, birds, fish, plants, or other living organisms threatened with extinction by manmade or natural changes in their environment. Requirements for declaring a species endangered are contained in the Endangered Species Act.

Endangerment Assessment: A study to determine the nature and extent of contamination at a site on the National Priorities List and the risks posed to public health or the environment. EPA or the state conducts the study when a legal action is to be taken to direct potentially responsible parties to clean up a site or pay for it. An endangerment assessment supplements a remedial investigation.

Enforcement: EPA, state, or local legal actions to obtain compliance with environmental laws, rules, regulations, or agreements and/or obtain penalties or criminal sanctions for violations. Enforcement procedures may vary depending on the requirements of different environmental laws and related implementing regulations. Under

CERCLA, for example, EPA will seek to require potentially responsible parties to clean up a Superfund site, or pay for the cleanup; whereas, under the Clean Air Act, the agency may invoke sanctions against cities failing to meet ambient air quality standards, possibly preventing certain types of construction or federal funding. In other situations, if investigations by EPA and state agencies uncover willful violations, criminal trials and penalties are sought.

Environment: The sum of all external conditions affecting the life, development, and survival of an organism.

Environmental Assessment(EA): An environmental analysis prepared pursuant to the National Environmental Policy Act to determine whether a federal action would significantly affect the environment, and thus, require a more detailed environmental impact statement.

Environmental Audit: An independent assessment of the current status of a party's compliance with applicable environmental requirements, or of a party's environmental compliance policies, practices, and controls.

Environmental Impact Statement (EIS): A document required of federal agencies by the National Environmental Policy Act for major projects or legislative proposals significantly affecting the environment. A tool for decision making, it describes the positive and negative effects of the undertaking and cites alternative actions.

Exposure: The amount of radiation or pollutant present in a given environment that represents a potential health threat to living organisms.

Extraction Procedure (EP Toxic): Determining toxicity by a procedure which simulates leaching; if a certain concentration of a toxic substance can be leached from a waste, that waste is considered hazardous, i.e., "EP Toxic."

Extremely Hazardous Substances: Any of 406 chemicals identified by EPA as toxic, and listed under SARA Title III. The list is subject to periodic revision.

F

Feasibility Study: (1) Analysis of the practicability of a proposal; e.g., a description and analysis of potential cleanup alternatives for a site such as one on the National Priorities List. The feasibility study usually recommends selection of a cost-effective alternative. It usually starts as soon as the remedial investigation is underway; together, they are commonly referred to as the "RI/FS". (2) A small-scale investigation of a problem to ascertain whether a proposed research approach is likely to provide useful data.

Federal Implementation Plan: Under current law, a federally implemented plan to achieve attainment of air quality standards, used when a state is unable to develop an adequate plan.

Feedstock: (1) The raw materials supplied to manufacturing or processing plants for use in the production of goods or for treatment, respectively. Waste from one industry may be the feedstock for another industry. (2) The crude oil

and natural gas liquids fed to the topping units.

Fill Material: Dirt, mud, and other materials deposited into aquatic areas to create more dry land, usually for agricultural or commercial development purposes. Such activities often damage the ecology of the area.

Financial Assurance for Closure: Documentation or proof that an owner or operator of a facility such as a landfill or other waste repository is capable of paying the projected costs of closing the facility and monitoring it afterwards as provided in RCRA regulations.

Finding Of No Significant Impact (FONSI): A document prepared by federal agency showing why a proposed action would not have a significant impact on the environment and would not require preparation of an Environmental Impact Statement. A FONSI is based on the results of an environmental assessment.

Fissure: A narrow opening or crack.

Flashpoint: The lowest temperature at which evaporation of a substance produces enough vapor to form an ignitable mixture with air.

Fleet: A group (of buses, cars, trucks, ships, or planes) operated under unified control.

Floodplain: The flat or nearly flat land along a river or stream or in a tidal area that is covered by water during a flood.

Flue Gas: The air coming out of a chimney after combustion in the burner. It can include nitrogen oxides, carbon oxides, water vapor, sulfur oxides, particles, and many chemical pollutants.

Fly Ash: Non-combustible residual particles expelled by flue gas.

Fossil Fuel: Fuel derived from ancient organic remains, e.g., peat, coal, crude oil, and natural gas.

Fugitive Emissions: Emissions not caught by a capture system.

Fundamentally Different Factors (FDF): A type of permit variance allowing a permit holder to implement a different or less stringent effluent or emission limitation because the affected facility operates in a "fundamentally different" fashion than industry as a whole.

Future Liability: Refers to potentially responsible parties' obligations to pay for additional response activities beyond those specified in the Record of Decision or Consent Decree.

G

Garbage: Animal and vegetable waste resulting from the handling, storage, sale, preparation, cooking, and serving of foods.

Generally Available Control Technology (GACT): Under the Clean Air Act, NESHAPS program standard of performance for area sources. GACT means the use of that technology that is already generally available and currently used by most members of industry.

Generator: (1) A facility or mobile source that emits pollutants into the air or produces regulated wastes. (2) Any person, by site, whose act or process produces regulated medical waste or whose act first causes such waste to become subject to regulation. In a case where more than one person (e.g.,

doctors with separate medical practices) is located in the same building, each business entity is a separate generator.

Greenhouse Effect: The warming of the Earth's atmosphere attributed to a build-up of carbon dioxide or other gases; some scientists think that this build-up allows the sun's rays to heat the Earth, while infra-red radiation makes the atmosphere opaque to a counterbalancing loss of heat.

Groin: A rigid structure (such as a concrete wall) built out from a shore to protect the shore from erosion, to trap sand, or to direct a current for scouring a channel.

Groundwater: The supply of fresh water found beneath the Earth's surface, usually in aquifers, which feeds wells and springs. Because groundwater is a major source of drinking water, there is growing concern over contamination from leaching agricultural or industrial pollutants or leaking underground storage tanks.

H

Habitat: The place where a population (e.g., human, animal, plant, microorganism) lives and its surroundings, both living and non-living.

Halons: Bromine-containing compounds with long atmospheric lifetimes whose breakdown in the stratosphere can cause a depletion of the atmospheric ozone. Halons are often used in fire-fighting.

Hazardous Air Pollutants (HAPs): Air pollutants which are not covered by ambient air quality standards but which, as defined in the Clean Air Act, may reasonably be expected to cause or contribute to irreversible illness or death. Such pollutants include asbestos, beryllium, mercury benzene, coke oven emissions, radionuclides, and vinyl chloride, which are released by sources such as chemical plants, dry cleaners, printing plants, and motor vehicles (cars, trucks, buses, etc.) Health effects include cancer, birth defects, nervous system problems, and death due to massive accidental releases.

Hazardous Chemical: An EPA designation for any hazardous material requiring a Material Safety Data Sheet (MSDS) under OSHA's Hazard Communication Standard. Such substances are capable of producing fires and explosions or adverse health effects like cancer and dermatitis. Hazardous chemicals are distinct from hazardous waste. *See Hazardous Waste.*

Hazardous Ranking System (HRS): The principle screening tool used by EPA to evaluate risks to public health and the environment associated with abandoned or uncontrolled hazardous waste sites. The HRS calculates a score based on the potential of hazardous substances spreading from the site through the air, surface water, or ground water, and on other factors such as density and proximity of human population. This score is the primary factor in deciding if the site should be on the National Priorities List and, if so, what ranking it should have compared to other sites on the list.

Hazardous Substance: (1) Any material that poses a threat to human health and/or the environment. Typical hazardous substances are toxic, corrosive, ignitable, explosive, or chemically reactive. (2) Any substance designated by EPA to be reported if a designated quantity of the substance is spilled in the waters of the United States or if otherwise released into the environment.

Hazardous Waste (HW): By-products of society that can pose a substantial or potential hazard to human health or the environment when improperly managed; wastes that possess at least one of four characteristics (ignitability, corrosivity, reactivity, or toxicity), or appears on special EPA lists.

Hazardous Waste Landfill: An excavated or engineered site where hazardous waste is deposited and covered.

Health Assessment: An evaluation of available data on existing or potential risks to human health posed by a Superfund site. The Agency for Toxic Substances and Disease Registry (ATSDR) of the Department of Health and Human Services (DHHS) is required to perform such an assessment at every site on the National Priorities List.

Heavy Metals: Metallic elements with high atomic weights, e.g., mercury, chromium, cadmium, arsenic, and lead; can damage living things at low concentrations and tend to accumulate in the food chain.

Hexavalent State: An element having 6 as the whole number that represents or denotes the combining power of one element with another. It is determined by the valence electrons. Valence electrons, in the outermost shell of an atom, determine chemical properties.

Holding Pond: A pond or reservoir, usually made of earth, built to store polluted runoff.

Household Waste (Domestic Waste): Solid waste, composed of garbage and rubbish which normally originated in a private home or apartment house. Domestic waste may contain a significant amount of toxic or hazardous waste.

Human Health Risk: The likelihood that a given exposure or series of exposures may or will damage the health of individuals.

Hydrochlorofluorocarbons: An aqueous solution of chlorofluorocarbons.

I

Identification Code or EPA I.D. Number: The unique code assigned to each generator, transporter, and treatment, storage, or disposal facility by regulating agencies to facilitate identification and tracking of chemicals or hazardous waste.

Ignitable: Capable of burning or causing a fire.

Immediately Dangerous to Life and Health (IDLH): The maximum level to which a healthy individual can be exposed to a chemical for 30 minutes and escape without suffering irreversible health effects or impairing symptoms. Used as a "level of concern."

Impoundment: A body of water or sludge confined by a dam, dike, floodgate, or other barrier.

Incineration: A treatment technology involving destruction of waste by controlled burning at high temperatures, e.g., burning sludge to remove the water and reduce the remaining residues to a safe, non-burnable ash that can be disposed of safely on land, in some waters, or in underground locations.

Incinerator: A furnace for burning waste under controlled conditions.

Indirect Discharge: Introduction of pollutants from a non-domestic source into a publicly owned waste-treatment system. Indirect dischargers can be commercial or industrial facilities whose wastes enter local sewers.

Indoor Air: The breathing air inside a habitable structure or conveyance.

Industrial Waste: Unwanted materials from an industrial operation; may be liquid, sludge, solid, or hazardous waste.

Injection Well: A well into which fluids are injected for purposes such as waste disposal, improving the recovery of crude oil, or solution mining.

Injection Zone: A geological formation receiving fluids through a well.

Innovative Technologies: New or inventive methods to treat effectively hazardous waste and reduce risks to human health and the environment.

Inorganic Chemicals: Chemical substances of mineral origin, not of basically carbon structure.

In-Situ Stripping: Treatment system that removes or "strips" volatile organic compounds from contaminated ground or surface water by forcing an airstream through the water and causing the compounds to evaporate.

Inspection and Maintenance (I/M): (1) Activities to assure that vehicles' emissions-controls work properly. (2) Also applies to wastewater treatment

379

plants and other anti-pollution facilities and processes.

Interim (Permit) Status: Period during which treatment, storage, and disposal facilities are temporarily permitted to operate while awaiting a permanent permit.

Inventory: Inventory of chemicals produced pursuant to Section 8(b) of the Toxic Substances Control Act.

Irreversible Effect: Effect characterized by the inability of the body to partially or fully repair injury caused by a toxic agent.

Irrigation: Applying water or waste water to land areas to supply the water and nutrient needs of plants.

Irrigation Return Flow: Surface and subsurface water which leaves the field following application of irrigation water.

L

Land Ban: Phasing out of land disposal of most untreated hazardous wastes as mandated by the 1984 HSWA amendments to RCRA.

Landfill: A method for final disposal of solid waste on land. The refuse is spread and compacted and a cover of soil applied so that effects on the environment (including public health and safety) are minimized. Under current regulations, landfills are required to have liners and leachate treatment systems to prevent contamination of groundwater and surface waters. An industrial landfill disposes of non-hazardous industrial wastes. A municipal landfill disposes of domestic waste including garbage, paper, etc.

Leachate: Water that collects contaminants as it trickles through wastes, pesticides or fertilizers. Leaching may occur in farming areas, feedlots, and landfills, and may result in hazardous substances entering surface water, groundwater, or soil.

Lead (Pb): A heavy metal that is hazardous to health if breathed or swallowed. Its use in gasoline, paints, and plumbing compounds has been sharply restricted or eliminated by federal laws and regulations. *See Heavy Metals.*

Liner: (1) A relatively impermeable barrier designed to keep leachate inside a landfill. Liner materials include plastic and dense clay. (2) An insert or sleeve for sewer pipes to prevent leakage or infiltration.

List: Shorthand term for EPA list of violating facilities or firms barred from obtaining government contracts because they violated certain sections of the Clean Air or Clean Water Acts. The list is maintained by The Office of Enforcement and Compliance Monitoring.

Listed Waste: Wastes listed as hazardous under RCRA but which have not been subjected to the Toxic Characteristics Listing Process because the dangers they present are considered self-evident.

Lowest Achievable Emission Rate (LAER): Under the Clean Air Act, the rate of emissions that reflects (1) the most stringent emission limitation in the implementation plan of any state for such source unless the owner or operator demonstrates such limitations are not achievable; or (2) the most stringent emissions limitation achieved in practice, whichever is more stringent. A proposed new or modified source may not emit pollutants in excess of existing new source standards.

M

Major Modification: This term is used to define modifications of major stationary sources of emissions with respect to Prevention of Significant Deterioration and New Source Review under the Clean Air Act.

Major Stationary Sources: Term used to determine the applicability of Prevention of Significant Deterioration and New Source Regulations. In a nonattainment area, any stationary pollutant source with potential to emit more than 100 tons per year is considered a major stationary source. In PSD areas, the cut off level may be either 100 or 250 tons per year depending upon the source. Under the NESHAPS, program the threshold level is 25 tons per year of any hazardous air pollutant.

Manifest System: Tracking of hazardous waste from "cradle to grave" (generation through disposal) with accompanying documents known as manifests. *See also Cradle-to-Grave.*

Margin of Safety: Maximum amount of exposure producing no measurable effect in animals (or studied humans) divided by the actual amount of human exposure in a population.

Maritime: Of or relating to navigation or commerce on the sea.

Maximum Achievable Control Technology (MACT): Under Clean Air Act, NESHAPs program, generally, the best available control technology, taking into account cost and technical feasibility. It is the required standard of performance for "major" new existing or modified sources emitting hazardous air pollutants. "Major" for this program is defined as any source that emits or has the potential to emit 10 tons per year or more of any hazardous air pollutant or 25 tons per year or more of any combination of hazardous air pollutants.

Medical Waste: Any solid waste generated in the diagnosis, treatment, or immunization of human beings or animals, in research pertaining thereto, or in the production or testing of biologicals excluding hazardous waste identified or listed under 40 C.F.R. Part 261 or any household waste as defined in 40 C.F.R. Sub-section 261.4(b)(1).

Mercury: *See Heavy Metals.*

Meteorological: Dealing with the atmospheric phenomena and weather of a region.

Mining Overburden: Any material overlying an economic mineral deposit which is removed to gain access to that deposit.

Mitigation: Measures taken to reduce adverse impacts on the environment.

Mixed Funding: Settlements in which potentially responsible parties and EPA share the cost of a response action.

Mixture Rule: This Resource Conservation and Recovery Act rule states that any solid non-hazardous waste mixed with a listed hazardous waste is treated as a "hazardous waste." And that any solid non-hazardous waste mixed with a characteristic hazardous waste is treated as a "hazardous waste only if it exhibits hazardous waste characteristics.

Mobile Source: Any non-stationary source of air pollution such as cars, trucks, motorcycles, buses, airplanes and locomotives.

Modeling: An investigative technique using a mathematical or physical representation of a system or theory that accounts for all or some of its known properties. Models are often used to test the effect of changes of system components on the overall performance of the system.

Modified Source: The enlargement of a major stationary pollutant source is referred to as a "modified " source. Modification of a source implies that the source will be emitting more emissions than before the modification.

Monitoring: Periodic or continuous surveillance or testing to determine the level of compliance with statutory requirements and/or pollutant levels in various media or in humans, plants, and animals. Enhanced monitoring programs may include keeping records on materials used by the source, periodic inspections, and installation of continuous emission monitoring systems.

Monitoring Well: (1) A well used to obtain water quality samples or measure groundwater levels. (2) Well drilled at a hazardous waste management facility or Superfund site to collect groundwater samples for the purpose of physical, chemical, or biological analysis to determine the amounts, types, and distribution of contaminants in the groundwater beneath the site.

Moratorium: During the negotiation process, a period of 60 to 90 days during which EPA and potentially responsible parties may reach settlement but no site response activities can be conducted.

Municipal Discharge: Discharge of effluent from waste water treatment plants which receive waste water from households, commercial establishments, and industries. Combined sewer/separate storm overflows are included in this category.

Municipal Sewage: Wastes (mostly liquid) originating from a community; may be composed of domestic waste waters and/or industrial discharges.

Municipal Solid Waste Landfill (MSWL): The disposal site for residential and commercial solid waste generated, collected, and processed within a community.

Munitions: Armament, ammunition.

N

National Ambient Air Quality Standards (NAAQS): Standards established by EPA that apply to outside air throughout the country. *See Criteria Pollutants, State Implementation Plans, Emissions Trading, Primary Standards, and Secondary Standards.*

National Contingency Plan (NCP): *See National Oil and Hazardous Substances Contingency Plan.*

National Emissions Standards For Hazardous Air Pollutants (NESHAPs): Emissions standards set by EPA for an air pollutant not covered by NAAQS that may cause an increase in fatalities or in serious, irreversible, or incapacitating illness. Primary standards are designed to protect human health, secondary standards to protect public welfare (e.g., building facades, visibility, crops and domestic animals).

National Interim Primary Drinking Water Regulations: Commonly referred to as NIPDWRs.

National Oil and Hazardous Substances Contingency Plan (NOHSCP): The federal regulation that guides determination of the sites to be corrected under both the Superfund program and the program to prevent or control spills into surface waters or elsewhere.

National Pollutant Discharge Elimination System (NPDES): A provision of the Clean Water Act which prohibits discharge of pollutants into waters of the United States unless a special permit is issued by EPA, a state, or, where delegated, a Native American tribal government.

National Priorities List (NPL): EPA's list of the most serious uncontrolled or abandoned hazardous waste sites identified for possible long-term remedial action under Superfund. The list is based primarily on the score a site receives from the Hazard Ranking System. EPA is required to update the NPL at least once a year. A site must be on the NPL to receive money from the Trust Fund for remedial action.

National Response Center: The federal operations center that receives notifications of all releases of oil and hazardous substances into the environment; open 24 hours a day, is operated by the U.S. Coast Guard, which evaluates all reports and notifies the appropriate agency.

Navigable Waters: Traditionally, surface waters sufficiently deep and wide for navigation, but now including waters adjacent to or connected to waters navigable in fact.

Netting: A concept in which all emission sources in the same area that are owned or controlled by a single company are treated as one large source, thereby allowing flexibility in controlling individual sources in order to meet a single emissions standard. *See Bubble, Bubble Policy, Emissions Trading.*

Neutralization: Decreasing the acidity or alkalinity of a substance by adding alkaline or acidic materials, respectively.

New Source: Any stationary source built or modified after publication of final or proposed regulations that prescribe a given standard of performance.

New Source Performance Standards (NSPS): Uniform national EPA air emission and water effluent standards which limit the amount of pollution allowed from new sources or from modified existing sources.

New Source Review (NSR): Clean Air Act requirement that State Implementation Plans must include a permit review that applies to the construction and operation of new and modified stationary sources in nonattainment areas to assure attainment of national ambient air quality standards.

Nitrogen Dioxide (NO$_2$): The result of nitric oxide combining with oxygen in the atmosphere; major component of photochemical smog.

Nitrogen Oxides (NOx): A criteria air pollutant. Nitrogen oxides are produced from burning fuels including gasoline and coal. They are a major component of photochemical smog and of acid rain.

Nonattainment Area (NA): An area that does not meet one or more of the National Ambient Air Quality Standards for the criteria pollutants designated in the Clean Air Act.

Non-Binding Preliminary Allocation of Responsibility (NBAR): Process for EPA to propose a way for potentially responsible parties to allocate costs among themselves.

Nonconventional Pollutant: Any pollutant not statutorily listed or which is poorly understood by the scientific community.

Nondegradation Policy: An environmental policy which disallows any lowering of naturally occurring quality regardless of preestablished health standards.

Nonpoint Source: Diffuse pollution sources (i.e., without a single point of origin or not introduced into a receiving stream from a specific outlet). The pollutants are generally carried off the land by stormwater. Common non-point sources are agriculture, forestry, mining, construction, dams, channels, land disposal, saltwater intrusion, and city streets.

Notice of Deficiency (NOD): An EPA written notice to a facility owner or operator identifying areas in a permit application which do not meet the agency requirements. This notice typically requests additional information from the facility.

Notice of Intent (NOI): A written announcement to Federal, State and local agencies, and to interested persons that a draft environmental impact statement will be prepared. The notice shall briefly describe the EPA action, its location, and the issues involved. Its purpose is to involve other government agencies and interested persons as early as possible in the planning and evaluation of actions which may have significant environmental impacts.

Notice of Violation (NOV): An EPA written notice to the facility owner or operator identifying specific facility or permit violations. This notice typically requests the facility owner or operator to contact the agency within a certain time frame, and it may additionally set administrative fines and notify recipient of her rights to request an agency conference or hearing.

O

Offsets: A method used in the 1990 Clean Air Act to give companies which own or operate large (major) sources in nonattainment areas flexibility in meeting overall population reduction requirements when changing production processes. If the owner or operator of the source wishes to increase release of a criteria air pollutant, an offset (reduction of a somewhat greater amount of the same pollutant) must be obtained either at the same plant or by purchasing offsets from another company. *See also Bubble, Emissions Trading, Netting.*

Offsite Facility: A hazardous waste treatment, storage, or disposal area that is located away from the generating site.

Onsite Facility: A hazardous waste treatment, storage, or disposal area that is located on the generating site.

Onboard Controls: Devices placed on vehicles to capture gasoline vapor during refueling; they route it to the engine or engines when the vehicle is starting so that it can be efficiently burned.

Open Burning: Uncontrolled fires in an open dump.

Open Dump: An uncovered site used for disposal of waste without environmental controls. *See Dump.*

Operable Unit: Term for each of a number of separate activities undertaken as part of a Superfund site cleanup. A typical operable unit would be removal of drums and tanks from the surface of a site.

Operating Conditions: Conditions specified in a RCRA permit that dictate how an incinerator must operate as it burns different waste types. A trial burn is used to identify operating conditions needed to meet specified performance standards.

Operation and Maintenance (O/M): (1) Activities conducted after a Superfund site action is completed to ensure that the action is effective. (2) Actions taken after construction to assure that facilities constructed to treat waste water will be properly operated and maintained to achieve normative efficiency levels and prescribed effluent limitations in an optimum manner.

Operator: The person responsible for the overall operation of a facility.

Organic Chemicals/Compounds: Animal or plant-produced substances containing mainly carbon, hydrogen, nitrogen, and oxygen.

Outfall: The place where effluent is discharged into receiving waters.

Oxidant: A substance containing oxygen that reacts chemically in air to produce a new substance; the primary ingredient of photochemical smog.

Oxidation: The addition of oxygen that breaks down organic waste or chemicals such as cyanides, phenols, and organic sulfur compounds in sewage by bacterial and chemical means.

Ozone (O_3): Found in two layers of the atmosphere, the stratosphere and the troposphere. In the *stratosphere* (the atmospheric layer 7 to 10 miles or more above the earth's surface) ozone is a natural form of oxygen that provides a protective layer shielding the earth from ultraviolet radiation. In the *troposphere* (the layer extending up 7 to 10 miles from the earth's surface), ozone is a chemical oxidant and major component of photochemical smog. It can seriously impair the respiratory system and is one of the most widespread of all the criteria pollutants for which the Clean Air Act required EPA to set standards. Ozone in the troposphere is produced through complex chemical reactions of nitrogen oxides which are among the primary pollutants emitted by combustion sources; hydrocarbons, released into the atmosphere through the combustion, handling and processing of petroleum products, and sunlight.

Ozone Layer: The protective layer in the atmosphere, about 15 miles above the ground, that absorbs some of the sun's ultraviolet rays, thereby reducing the amount of potentially harmful radiation that reaches the earth's surface.

P

Packaging: The assembly of one or more containers and any other components necessary to assure minimum compliance with a program's storage and shipment packaging requirements.

Parameter: A variable, measurable property whose value is a determinant of the characteristics of a system; e.g., temperature, pressure, and density are parameters of the atmosphere.

Particulates: A criteria air pollutant. Particulate matter is fine liquid or solid particles such as dust, smoke, mist, fumes, or smog found in air or emissions that are released into and move around in the air. Particulates are produced by many sources including burning of diesel fuels by trucks and buses, incineration of garbage, mixing and application of fertilizers and pesticides, road construction, industrial processes such as steel making, mining operations, agricultural burning, and operation of fireplaces and wood stoves. Particulates can cause eye, nose, and throat irritation and other health problems.

Particulate Matter (PM$_{10}$): A standard for measuring the amount of solid or liquid matter suspended in the atmosphere, i.e. the amount of particulate matter over 10 micrometers in diameter; smaller PM-10 particles penetrate to the deeper portions of the lung, affecting sensitive population groups such as children and individuals with respiratory ailments.

Parts Per Billion (ppb)/Parts Per Million (ppm): Units commonly used to express contamination ratios as in establishing the maximum permissible amount of a contaminant in water, land, or air.

Performance Standards: (1) Regulatory requirements limiting the concentrations of designated organic compounds, particulate matter, and hydrogen chloride in emissions from incinerators.
(2) Operating standards established by EPA for various permitted pollution control systems, asbestos inspections, and various program operations and maintenance requirements.

Permit: An authorization, license, or equivalent control document issued by EPA or an approved state agency to implement the requirements of an environmental regulation; e.g., a permit to operate a waste water treatment plant or to operate a facility that may generate harmful emissions.

Persistence: Refers to the length of time a compound stays in the environment once introduced. A compound may persist for less than a second or indefinitely.

Pesticide: Substances or mixture thereof intended for preventing, destroying, repelling, or mitigating any pest. Also, any substance or mixture intended for use as a plant regulator, defoliant, or desiccant.

Photochemical Oxidants: Air pollutants formed by the action of sunlight on oxides of nitrogen and hydrocarbons.

Photochemical Smog: Air pollution caused by chemical reactions of various pollutants emitted from different sources.

Point Source: A stationary location or fixed facility from which pollutants are discharged; any single identifiable source of pollution, e.g., a pipe, ditch, ship, ore pit or factory smokestack.

Pollutant: Generally, any substance introduced into the environment that adversely affects the usefulness of a resource.

Pollution: Generally, the presence of matter or energy whose nature, location, or quantity produces undesired environmental effects. Under the Clean Water Act, for example, the term is defined as the manmade or man-induced alteration of the physical, biological, chemical, and radiological integrity of water.

Polychlorinated Biphenyls (PCBs): A mixture of compounds composed of the biphenyl molecule which has been chlorinated to varying degrees.

Post-Closure: Time period following the shutdown of a waste management or manufacturing facility; for monitoring purposes, often considered to be 30 years.

Potentially Responsible Party (PRP): Any individual or company -- including owners, operators, transporters or generators -- potentially responsible for, or contributing to a spill or other contamination at a Superfund site. Whenever possible, through administrative and legal actions, EPA requires PRPs to clean up hazardous sites they have contaminated.

Precursor: In photochemistry, a compound antecedent to a volatile organic compound (VOC). Precursors react in sunlight to form ozone or other photochemical oxidants.

Preliminary Assessment (PA): The process of collecting and reviewing available information about a known or suspected waste site or release.

Pretreatment: Processes used to reduce, eliminate, or alter the nature of waste water pollutants from non-domestic sources before they are discharged into publicly owned treatment works (POTWs).

Prevention of Significant Deterioration (PSD): EPA program in which state and/or federal permits are required in order to restrict emissions from new or modified sources in places where air quality already meets or exceeds primary and secondary ambient air quality standards.

Primary Standards: Primary standards are set for criteria air pollutants. They are a pollution limit based on health effects which are designed to protect human health with an adequate margin of safety. *See National Ambient Air Quality Standards, Secondary Standards.*

Primary Waste Treatment: First step in wastewater treatment; screens and sedimentation tanks are used to remove most materials that float or will settle. Primary treatment removes about 30 percent of carbonaceous biochemical oxygen demand from domestic sewage.

Public Comment Period: The time allowed for the public to express its views and concerns regarding an action by EPA (e.g., a *Federal Register* notice of proposed rulemaking, a public notice of a draft permit, or a Notice of Intent to Deny).

387

Public Hearing: A formal meeting at which EPA officials hear the public's views and concerns about an EPA action or proposal. EPA is required to consider such comments when evaluating its actions. Public hearings must be held upon request during the public comment period.

Public Notice: (1) Notification by EPA informing the public of agency actions such as the issuance of a draft permit or scheduling of a hearing. EPA is required to ensure proper public notice including publication in newspapers and broadcast media. (2) In the safe drinking water program, water suppliers are required to publish and broadcast notices when pollution problems are discovered.

Publicly Owned Treatment Works (POTW): A waste treatment works owned by a state, unit of local government, or Indian tribe, usually designed to treat domestic wastewaters.

R

Radiation: Transmission of energy through space of any medium. Also known as radiant energy.

Radioactive Substances: Substances that emit ionizing radiation. Human exposure to radiation can cause radiation sickness which is commonly marked by fatigue, nausea, vomiting, loss of teeth and hair, and in more severe cases by damage to blood-forming tissue with a decrease in red and white blood cells and with bleeding.

Reactive or Reactive Waste: A substance which can easily undergo a chemical transformation.

Reasonable Further Progress (RFP): Annual incremental reductions in air pollutant emissions as reflected in a State Implementation Plan that EPA deems sufficient to provide for the attainment of the applicable national ambient air quality standards by the statutory deadline.

Reasonably Available Control Measures (RACM): A broadly defined term referring to technological and other measures for pollution control.

Reasonably Available Control Technology (RACT): Control technology that is reasonably available and both technologically and economically feasible. Usually applied to existing sources in nonattainment areas; in most cases, it is less stringent than new source performance standards.

Receiving Waters: A river, lake, ocean, stream, or other watercourse into which waste water or treated effluent is discharged.

Reclamation: (In recycling) Restoration of materials found in the waste stream to a beneficial use which may be for purposes other than the original use.

Record of Decision (ROD): A public document that explains which cleanup alternative(s) will be used at National Priorities List sites where, under CERCLA, Trust Funds pay for the cleanup.

Recycle/Reuse: Minimizing waste generation by recovering and reprocessing usable products that might otherwise become waste (i.e. recycling of aluminum cans, paper and bottles, etc.).

Reduction: The addition of hydrogen, removal of oxygen, or addition of electrons to an element or compound.

Refuse: *See Solid Waste.*

Regulated Medical Waste: Under the Medical Waste Tracking Act of 1988, any solid waste generated in the diagnosis, treatment, or immunization of human beings or animals, in research pertaining thereto, or in the production or testing of biologicals. Included are cultures and stocks of infectious agents, human blood and blood products, human pathological body wastes from surgery and autopsy, contaminated animal carcasses from medical research, waste from patients with communicable diseases, and all used sharp implements, such as needles and scalpels, etc., and certain unused sharps.

Release: Any spilling, leaking, pumping, pouring, emitting, emptying, discharging, injecting, escaping, leaching, dumping, or disposing into the environment of a hazardous or toxic chemical or extremely hazardous substance.

Remedial Action (RA): The actual construction or implementation phase of a Superfund site cleanup that follows remedial design.

Remedial Investigation (RI): An in-depth study designed to gather data needed to determine the nature and extent of contamination at a Superfund site, establish site cleanup criteria, identify preliminary alternatives for remedial action, and support technical and cost analyses of alternatives. The remedial investigation is usually done with the feasibility study. Together they are usually referred to as the "RI/FS."

Remedial Response: Long-term action that stops or substantially reduces a release or threat of a release of hazardous substances that is serious but not an immediate threat to public health.

Remediation: (1) Cleanup or other methods used to remove or contain a toxic spill or hazardous materials from a Superfund site. (2) For the Asbestos Hazard Emergency Response program, abatement methods include: evaluation, repair, enclosure, encapsulation, or removal of greater than 3 linear feet or square feet of asbestos-containing materials from a building.

Removal Action: Short-term immediate actions taken to address releases of hazardous substances that require expedited response. *See Cleanup.*

Reportable Quantity (RQ): Quantity of a hazardous substance that triggers reports under CERCLA. If a substance exceeds its RQ the release must be reported to the National Response Center, the State Emergency Response Center, and community emergency coordinators for areas likely to be affected.

Residual: Amount of a pollutant remaining in the environment after a natural or technological process has taken place, e.g., the sludge remaining after initial wastewater treatment, or particulates remaining in air after it passes through a scrubbing or other process.

Residue: The solids remaining after the evaporation of a sample of water or sludge.

Resource Recovery: The process of obtaining matter or energy from materials formerly discarded.

Response Action: (1) Generic term for actions taken in response to actual or potential health-threatening environmental events such as spills, sudden releases, and asbestos abatement/management problems. (2) A CERCLA-authorized action involving either a short-term removal action or a long-term removal response. This may include but is not limited to: removing hazardous materials from a site to an EPA-approved hazardous waste facility for treatment, containment or treating the waste on-site, identifying and removing the sources of groundwater contamination and halting further migration of contaminants. *See Cleanup.*

Responsible Party: The person or entity likely to be called on to answer or to account as a liable cause of an occurrence.

Restoration: Measures taken to return a site to pre-violation conditions.

Reuse: Using a product or component of municipal solid waste in its original form more than once, e.g., refilling a glass bottle that has been returned or using a coffee can to hold nuts and bolts.

Riprap: (1) A foundation or sustaining wall of stones or chunks of concrete thrown together without order (as in deep water). (2) A layer of this or similar material on an embankment slope to prevent erosion.

Risk: A measure of the probability that damage to life, health, property, and/or the environment will occur as a result of a given hazard.

Risk Assessment: Qualitative and quantitative evaluation of the risk posed to human health and/or the environment

by the actual or potential presence and/or use of specific pollutants.

Rolling Stock: The wheeled vehicles owned and used by a railroad or motor carrier.

Runoff: That part of precipitation, snow melt, or irrigation water that runs off the land into streams or other surface water. It can carry pollutants from the air and land into receiving waters.

S

Safe: Condition of exposure under which there is a practical certainty that no harm will result to exposed individuals.

Sanctions: Actions taken by the federal government for failure to plan or implement a State Implementation Plan (SIP). Such action may include withholding of highway funds and a ban on construction of new sources of potential pollution.

Sanitary Landfill: *See Landfills.*

Scoping: A preliminary public discussion of the information to be developed, alternatives to be considered, and issues to be discussed in an EIS.

Scrap: Materials discarded from manufacturing operations that may be suitable for reprocessing.

Screening: Use of screens to remove coarse floating and suspended solids from sewage.

Secondary Standards: Secondary standards are set for criteria air pollutants. They are a pollution limit based on environmental effects which are designed to protect *welfare,* including effects on soils, water, crops, vegetation, manmade materials, animals, wildlife, weather, visibility, and climate; damage to property; transportation hazards; effects on economic values, and on personal comfort and well-being. *See also National Ambient Air Quality Standards, Primary Standards.*

Secondary Treatment: The second step in most publicly owned waste treatment systems in which bacteria consume the organic parts of the waste. It is accomplished by bringing together waste, bacteria, and oxygen in trickling filters or in the activated sludge process. This treatment removes floating and settleable solids and about 90 percent of the oxygen-demanding substances and suspended solids. Disinfection is the final stage of secondary treatment. *See Primary, Tertiary Treatment.*

Sediments: Soil, sand, and minerals washed from land into water, usually after rain. They pile up in basins, reservoirs, rivers, and harbors, destroying fish-nesting areas and holes of water animals, and clouding the water so that needed sunlight might not reach aquatic plants. Careless farming, mining, and building activities will expose sediment materials, contributing to their being washed off the land after rainfalls.

Segmenting: The breaking down of a NEPA action into small component parts in order to claim that the significance of any one part is not enough to trigger the EIS requirement. Segmenting is prohibited under CEQ regulation §1508.27(7).

Septic System: An onsite system designed to treat and dispose of domestic sewage. A typical septic system consists of a tank that receives waste from a residence or business and a system of tile lines or a pit for disposal of the liquid effluent (sludge) that remains after decomposition of the solids by bacteria in the tank; must be pumped out periodically.

Septic Tank: An underground storage tank for wastes from homes not connected to a sewer line. Waste goes directly from the home to the tank. *See Septic System.*

Sewage: The waste and wastewater produced by residential and commercial sources and discharged into sewers.

Sewage Sludge: Sludge produced at a publicly owned treatment works, the disposal of which is regulated under the Clean Water Act.

Sewer: A channel or conduit that carries wastewater and storm-water runoff from the source to a treatment plant or receiving stream. "Sanitary" sewers carry household, industrial, and commercial waste. "Storm" sewers carry runoff from rain or snow. "Combined" sewers handle both.

Significant Deterioration: Pollution resulting from a new source in previously "clean" areas. *See also Prevention of Significant Deterioration.*

Site: An area or place within the jurisdiction of the EPA and/or a state.

Site Assessment Program: A means of evaluating hazardous waste sites through preliminary assessments and site inspections to develop a Hazard Ranking System score.

Site Inspection: The collection of information from a Superfund site to determine the extent and severity of hazards posed by the site. It follows and is more extensive than a preliminary assessment. The purpose is to gather information necessary to score the site, using the Hazard Ranking System, and to determine if it presents an immediate threat requiring prompt removal.

Siting: The process of choosing a location for a facility.

Slough: A wet or marshy area.

Sludge: A semi-solid residue from any of a number of air or water treatment processes; can be a hazardous waste.

Slurry: A watery mixture of insoluble matter resulting from some pollution control techniques.

Small Quantity Generator (SQG): Persons or enterprises that produce 220-2200 pounds per month of hazardous waste; are required to keep more records than conditionally exempt generators. The largest category of hazardous waste generators, SQGs include automotive shops, dry cleaners, photographic developers, and a host of other small businesses.

Smog: Air pollution associated with oxidants. Smog can harm health, damage the environment and cause poor visibility. *See Photochemical Smog.*

Smoke: Particles suspended in air after incomplete combustion.

Socioeconomic: Involving a combination of social and economic factors.

Solder: Metallic compound used to seal joints between pipes. Until recently, most solder contained 50 percent lead. Use of lead solder containing more than 0.2 percent lead in pipes carrying drinking water is now prohibited.

Solid Waste: Generally, non-liquid, non-soluble materials ranging from municipal garbage to industrial wastes that contain complex and sometimes hazardous substances. However, as broadly defined under RCRA, solid wastes can also include sewage sludge, agricultural refuse, demolition wastes, and mining residues. Technically, under RCRA solid waste may also refer to liquids and gases in containers.

Solid Waste Disposal: The final placement of refuse that is not salvaged or recycled.

Solid Waste Management: Supervised handling of waste materials from their source through recovery processes to disposal.

Solid Waste Management Unit (SWMU): Any disposal or resource recovery system, program or facility used for the treatment of solid waste.

Source: Any place or object from which pollutants are released. A source can be a power plant, factory, dry cleaning business, gas station, farm land disposal site, manufacturing plant, pipes, valves, ditches, consumer products, and machines used in industry. Sources that stay in one place are referred to as stationary sources; sources that move around, such as cars or planes, are called mobile sources.

Source Reduction: Reducing the amount of materials entering the waste stream by redesigning products or patterns of production or consumption (e.g., using returnable beverage containers). Synonymous with waste reduction.

Source Separation: Segregating various wastes at the point of generation (e.g., separation of paper, metal and glass from other wastes to make recycling simpler and more efficient.)

Standards: Norms that impose limits on the amount of pollutants or emissions produced. EPA establishes minimum standards, but states are allowed to be stricter.

State Implementation Plans (SIP): EPA-approved state plans for the establishment, regulation, and enforcement of air pollution standards. A SIP is a detailed description of the programs a state will use to carry out its responsibilities under the Clean Air Act.

Stationary Source: A fixed-site producer of pollution, mainly power plants, gas stations, incinerators, and other facilities using industrial combustion processes.

Storage: Temporary holding of waste pending treatment or disposal; as in containers, tanks, waste piles, and surface impoundments.

Stratosphere: The layer of the atmosphere 7-10 or more miles above the earth's surface. Ozone in the stratosphere filters out harmful sun rays including a type of sunlight called ultraviolet B, which has been linked to health and environmental damage.

Sulfur Dioxide (SO₂): A pungent, colorless, gaseous pollutant formed primarily by the combustion of fossil fuels, most notably in power plants.

Some industrial processes, such as production of paper and smelting of metals, produce sulfur dioxide. Sulfur dioxide is a major component of the production of acid rain.

Sump: A pit or tank that catches liquid runoff for drainage or disposal.

Superfund: The program operated under the legislative authority of CERCLA and SARA that funds and carries out EPA hazardous substance emergency and long-term removal and remedial activities. These activities include establishing the National Priorities List, determining their priority, and conducting and/or supervising the cleanup and other remedial actions.

Surface Impoundment: Treatment, storage, or disposal of liquid hazardous wastes in ponds.

Surface Runoff: Precipitation, snow-melt, or irrigation water in excess of what can infiltrate the soil surface and be stored in small surface depressions; a major transporter of non-point source pollutants.

Surface Water: All water naturally open to the atmosphere (rivers, lakes, reservoirs, ponds, streams, impoundments, seas, estuaries, etc.) and all springs, wells, or other collectors directly influenced by surface water.

Suspended Solids: Small particles of solid pollutants that float on the surface of, or are suspended in, sewage or other liquids. They resist removal by conventional means.

T

Technology-Based Limitations: Industry-specific effluent limitations applied to a discharge when it will not cause a violation of water quality standards at low stream flows. Usually applied to discharges into large rivers.

Technology-Based Standards: Effluent limitations applicable to direct and indirect sources which are developed on a category-by-category basis using statutory factors, not including water-quality effects.

Terrestrial: Streams feeding larger streams or lakes.

Territorial Seas: The belt of the seas measured from the line of ordinary low water along that portion of the coast which is in direct contact with the open sea and the line marking the seaward limit of inland waters, and extending a distance of three miles.

Tertiary Treatment: Advanced cleaning of wastewater that goes beyond the secondary or biological stage, removing nutrients such as phosphorus, nitrogen, and most BOD and suspended solids.

Thermal Pollution: Discharge of heated water from industrial processes; can kill or injure aquatic organisms.

Total Concentrate Leaching Procedure: *See Toxicity Characteristic Leaching Procedure (TCLP).*

Total Suspended Particles: A method of monitoring particulate matter by total weight.

Total Suspended Solids (TSS): A measure of the suspended solids in wastewater, effluent, or water bodies, determined by tests for "total suspended non-filterable solids." *See also Suspended Solids.*

Toxic Pollutants: Materials that cause death, disease, or birth defects in organisms that ingest or absorb them. The quantities and exposures necessary to cause these effects can vary widely.

Toxic Substance: A chemical or mixture that may present an unreasonable risk of injury to health or the environment.

Toxic Waste: A waste that can produce injury if inhaled, swallowed, or absorbed through the skin.

Toxicity: The quality or degree of being poisonous or harmful to plant, animal or human life.

Toxicity Assessment: Characterization of the toxicological properties and effects of a chemical with special emphasis on establishment of dose-response characteristics.

Toxicity Characteristic Leaching Procedure (TCLP): A test designed to determine whether a waste is hazardous or requires treatment to become less hazardous; it also can be used to monitor treatment techniques for effectiveness.

Toxicity Characteristic Test: *See Toxicity Characteristic Leaching Procedure, Toxicity Testing.*

Toxicity Testing: Biological testing (usually with an invertebrate, fish, or small mammal) to determine the adverse effects of a compound or effluent.

Transporter: A person engaged in the off-site transportation of hazardous waste by air, rail, highway, or water.

Treatment: (1) Any method, technique, or process designed to remove solids and/or pollutants from solid waste, waste streams, effluents, and air emissions. (2) Methods used to change the biological character or composition of any regulated medical waste so as to substantially reduce or eliminate its potential for causing disease.

Treatment, Storage, and Disposal Facility (TSDF): Site where a hazardous substance is treated, stored, or disposed of. TSD facilities are regulated by EPA and states under RCRA.

Tributaries: Streams feeding larger streams or lakes.

Trickling Filter: A coarse treatment system in which wastewater is trickled over a bed of stones or other materials covered with bacteria that break down the organic waste and produce clean water.

Trivalent State: An element having 3 as the whole number that represents or denotes the combining power of one element with another. It is determined by the valence electrons. Valence electrons, in the outermost shell of an atom, determine chemical properties.

Troposphere: The atmospheric layer extending up 7 to 10 miles from the earth's surface.

Trust Fund: A fund set up under the Comprehensive Environmental Response, Compensation and Liability Act (CERCLA) to help pay for cleanup of hazardous waste sites and for legal action to force those responsible to clean the sites.

U

Underground Storage Tank (UST): A tank located at least partially underground and designed to hold gasoline or other petroleum products or chemicals.

V

Variance: Government permission for a delay or exception in the application of a given law, ordinance, or regulation.

Volatile Organic Compound (VOC): Any organic compound that participates in atmospheric photochemical reactions causing smog. Volatile organic chemicals include gasoline, industrial chemicals such as benzene, solvents such as toluene and xylene, and tetrachloroethylene (a principal dry cleaning solvent). Many VOCs are also hazardous air pollutants; for example benzene causes cancer.

Volumetric Tank Tests: One of several tests to determine the physical integrity of a storage tank; the volume of fluid in the tank is measured directly or calculated from product-level changes. A marked drop in volume indicates a leak.

W

Waiver: *See Variance.*

Waste: (1) Unwanted materials left over from a manufacturing process. (2) Refuse from places of human or animal habitation.

Waste Load Allocation: (1) The maximum load of pollutants each discharger of waste is allowed to release into a particular waterway. Discharge limits are usually required for each specific water quality criterion being, or expected to be, violated. (2) The portion of a stream's total assimilative capacity assigned to an individual discharge.

Waste Minimization: Measures or techniques that reduce the amount of wastes generated during industrial production processes; term is also applied to recycling and other efforts to reduce the amount of waste going into the waste stream.

Waste Treatment Lagoon: Impoundment made by excavation or earth fill for biological treatment of wastewater.

Waste Treatment Plant: A facility containing a series of tanks, screens, filters, and other processes by which pollutants are removed from water.

Waste Treatment Stream: The continuous movement of waste from generator to treater and disposer.

Wastewater: The spent or used water from a home, community, farm, or industry that contains dissolved or suspended matter.

Water Pollution: The presence in water of enough harmful or objectionable material to damage the water's quality.

Water Quality Criteria: Levels of water quality expected to render a body of water suitable for its designated use. Criteria are based on specific levels of pollutants that would make the water harmful if used for drinking, swimming, farming, fish production, or industrial processes.

Water Quality Standards: State-adopted and EPA-approved ambient standards for water bodies. The standards prescribe the use of the water body and establish the water quality criteria that must be met to protect designated uses. For example, in a stream which is used for trout habitat and propagation, the concentration of iron should not exceed 1 mg/l.

Water Quality-Based Limitations: Effluent limitations applied to dischargers when mere technology-based limitations would cause violations of water quality standards. Usually applied to discharges into small streams.

Watershed: The land area that drains into a stream.

Water Supply System: The collection, treatment, storage, and distribution of potable water from source to consumer.

Water Table: The level of groundwater.

Wetlands: An area that is saturated by surface or groundwater with vegetation adapted for life under those soil conditions, as in swamps, bogs, fens, marshes and estuaries.

Wildlife Refuge: An area designated for the protection of wild animals within which hunting and fishing are either prohibited or strictly controlled.

INDEX

References are to page numbers.

Acid Rain Regulations 238
Act of God 214, 215, 217
Act of War 214-217
Adjudication 6, 13-15, 18, 35, 45, 51
Administrative Fines 17-19, 282, 381
Administrative Hearings 6, 15
Administrative Law Judge 282, 356, 361
Administrative Orders . . . .
18, 20, 21, 36, 151, 161, 230, 233, 346, 352
Administrative Procedures Act 8
Agricultural Waste 305
Air Pollutants List 250, 278
Air Pollution Control Act 236
Air Pollution Control Techniques 250, 251
Air Quality Control Regions . . 249, 255, 270
Air Quality Criteria 250, 251, 356, 362
Air Quality Increments 273
Antidegradation Policy 308, 310, 362
Anti-backsliding 318, 319
Applicable or Relevant and Appropriate
   Requirements 198, 204
ARARS 198, 204, 362
Arbitrary and Capricious Standard . . 47, 48, 76
Area Class Redesignation 271
Area Wide Waste Treatment 344
Attorney's Fees 194, 349
Best Available Technology Economically
   Achievable 321, 356, 363
Best Conventional Pollutant Control
   Technology 320, 356, 363
Best Demonstrated Available
   Technology 145, 356, 363
Best Demonstrated Control
   Technology 323, 356
Best Management Practices 301, 343
Biochemical Oxygen
   Demand 320, 326, 356, 364, 384
Bubble Policy 247, 266, 364, 379
Burden of Proof 26, 203, 218, 334
Bureau of Land Management 1
Bureau of Solid Waste Management 4
Bypass 90, 334, 335
Cash-out 223, 225, 228, 229
Categorical . . . 60, 72, 245, 328, 329, 356, 365
Categorical Exclusion 356, 365
Categorical Exclusions 60, 72
Causation 171-173, 186, 201, 210, 218
CERCLA 6-38,
51, 93, 124, 140, 142, 152, 155, 158-161,
163-166, 168-179, 182-235, 356, 371, 385,
386, 389, 391
CERCLA Requirements 197
Citizen Actions 291, 351

Civil Remedies   23, 24, 152, 282, 283, 289, 348
Class I Areas 269
Class II Areas 269-271, 365
Class III Areas 269, 270, 365
Classifications 270, 271
Clean Air Act 164, 190, 236, 238, 243, 248,
249, 255, 263, 265, 267, 268, 282, 284, 291,
356, 362, 363, 365, 367-369, 371, 373, 374,
377, 380-382, 389
Clean Water Act 3, 4, 129, 160, 189, 295, 296,
298, 301, 308, 323, 326, 329,333, 352, 357,
363, 369, 370, 379, 383, 388
Closed Clean 139
Co: Carbon Monoxide 257, 356
Coastal Zone Management Act . . . 5, 357, 365
Code of Federal Regulations 6, 356
Compliance Orders 150, 345, 346
Concentration-based Exemption Criteria 356, 366
Consent Agreements and Consent Decrees . . 18
Contiguous Zone 297, 304, 307, 333, 367
Contract Carriers 182, 183
Contribution 161, 171, 212-214, 228
Conventional Pollutants   301, 302, 320, 321, 367
Corporations 17, 24, 53, 181, 208
Corrective Measures Implementation . 142, 356
Corrective Measures Study 142, 356
Corrosivity 106, 107, 111, 157, 189, 365
Cost Recovery Action 171, 173, 229, 233
Cost Recovery Actions 155, 171
Council on Environmental Quality 1, 8, 53, 54,
66, 356
Covenants Not to Sue 223, 229
Covered Persons 176, 205, 208
Criminal 6, 16, 17, 20, 23-27, 44, 51, 97, 150,
152, 153, 157, 282-284, 287, 289, 334, 342,
345, 349, 352, 371
Criminal Remedies 23, 26, 289, 349
Current Owners and Operators 177, 205
Damages for Loss of Natural Resources . . 200
De Minimis . 187, 223, 225-229, 269, 277, 369
De Novo Review 34, 45, 47
Deepwater Discharge 333
Deepwater Discharge Variance 333
Defenses 214, 259, 291, 334, 336
Derived from Rule 109, 110, 366, 369
Designating Uses 308
Direct Discharger 328, 369
Disaster Relief and Emergency Assistance Act196
Discarded Material 98, 100
Divisibility 211, 214, 226
Downgrading Designated Uses 310
Dredge and Fill Permit 336-338, 340
Dredge and Fill Program 313, 342

Due Process 13, 14, 209
Effluent Limitations 308, 312-314, 317-319, 322, 326, 330-332, 335, 336, 346, 381, 390, 392
Effluent Limits 312, 313, 326, 335, 371
EIS 22, 56-66, 68, 69, 71-76, 78-90, 200, 325, 357, 372, 387
Emergency Planning and Community Right to Know Act 357
Emissions from Area Sources 279
Endangered Species 22, 70, 149, 337, 357, 371
Endangered Species Act 70, 357, 371
Environmental Assessment 58, 60, 73, 357, 365, 372, 373
Environmental Impact Statement 22, 56, 58, 62, 200, 357, 365, 372, 373, 380
Environmental Policy 2, 3, 52-55, 60, 61, 92, 323, 358, 365, 372, 380
Environmental Protection Agency 1, 3, 17, 35, 163, 239, 357
EPA Identification Number 118, 119, 123-125, 133
Exclusion 190-192, 356, 365
Executive Branch 2
Exemptions 99, 109, 146, 182, 191, 274, 300, 339, 340
Existing Sources 240, 241, 243, 245, 256, 261, 263, 264, 315, 324, 325, 380, 385
F Wastes 104
Facility 6, 16, 18-20, 22, 84, 96, 98, 105, 118-122, 124-128, 130-132, 134-142, 144-146, 148, 150, 151, 153, 156, 163, 165, 172-174, 176-186, 201, 206, 214, 217-222, 224, 226, 227, 230, 233, 246-248, 265, 268, 272-274, 279, 281, 282, 284, 286, 287, 292, 304, 312, 319, 324, 332, 334-336, 342, 346, 357, 359, 369, 372, 373, 375, 378, 380, 381, 383, 386, 388, 389, 391, 392
Feasibility Study . 142, 169, 357, 359, 372, 385
Federal Effluent Limitations 308, 312
Federal Facility Compliance Act 96, 357
Federal Insecticide, Fungicide, and Rodenticide Act 5, 357
Federal Role in Subclassifying 269
Federal Water Pollution Control Act . . 295, 357
Federal Water Quality Administration 4
Final Agency Actions 155, 156
Final Order Rule 40, 41, 44
Financial Responsibility 131-133, 139
Finding of No Significant
Impact 61, 75, 77, 357, 372
Force Majeure 215
Formal Rulemaking 10-13, 16, 45, 48
Fundamentally Different
Factors 331, 332, 357, 373
General Permit Requirements 284
Generally Available Control
Technology 242, 277, 357, 373
Generator 108, 114-126, 134, 145, 146, 185-188, 209, 358, 359, 366, 373, 375, 388, 392
Geographic Areas 269
Government Actions 287, 291, 346, 351

Government Cleanup Options 229
Hard Look Doctrine 56
Hazard Ranking System 166, 379, 388
Hazardous Air Pollutants 240, 242, 276-278, 281, 294, 358, 362, 374, 377, 379, 392
Hazardous Air Pollutants List 278
Hazardous and Solid Waste
Amendments 96, 146, 357
Hazardous Ranking System 357, 374
Hazardous Substance . . . .
158, 163, 165, 172-174, 176, 177, 182, 184, 187-190, 194, 202, 207, 214-219, 221, 224, 227, 230-233, 291, 350, 365, 374, 385, 386, 389, 391
Hazardous Waste 22, 93-99, 101-111, 113-129, 131, 133-146, 150-153, 155-157, 159-164, 166-169, 178-183, 186, 189, 193, 198, 202, 207, 208, 211-213, 220-222, 229, 230, 234, 299, 342, 357, 363, 365-369, 374-379, 381, 386, 388, 391
Hazardous Waste Index 93, 167, 357
Hazardous Waste Response Fund 162
Health Assessment 194, 375
Hearing Record 12, 15, 16
History 4, 17, 23, 95, 191, 208, 325, 347
Hybrid 8, 10-13, 45
Hybrid Rulemaking 10-13, 45
Ignitability . 106, 111, 157, 189, 365, 369, 374
Imminent and Substantial Danger . 202, 230, 231
Imminent and Substantial
Endangerment 152, 230, 233, 256, 289
Imminently Hazardous 164, 165, 190
Incurrence of Response Costs 177, 186, 192, 193
Indirect Discharger 329, 330
Individual Control Strategies 327
Indoor Radon Abatement Act 5
Informal 8-14, 17, 18, 32, 45, 48, 347
Informal Rulemaking 8-12, 32, 45
Inheritance or Bequest 218, 222
Injunctions . . . 5, 18, 20-23, 29, 282, 289, 348
Innocent Landowner 214, 217-219, 222, 227, 228
Interim Status 118, 123, 128, 131, 132, 142, 151, 153
Joint and Several Liability 187, 211-214
Judicial Approach 86
Judicial Branch 2
Judicial Review . . . .
7, 11, 13, 30, 32, 35-43, 45, 51, 76, 90, 92, 97, 155, 156, 275
K Wastes 104
Land Ban 144, 146, 376
Lead Agency 60, 62, 63, 74, 75, 80-82, 86, 169, 170, 199
Legislative Branch 2
Legislative Function 7
Legislative Hearing 11
Lender 181, 183, 214, 220-222
Lessees 184
Listing . . 70, 102, 163, 244, 250, 270, 271, 377
Love Canal 159-161, 167

Lowest Achievable Emission
Rate 241, 265, 358, 377
Major Federal Actions 60, 63, 65, 72
Manifest 114, 115, 118, 120, 121, 124-126, 128, 133, 134, 136, 153, 157, 368, 377
Marine Waters 333, 334
Mining 32, 95, 99-101, 112, 215, 276, 296, 298, 301, 305, 306, 339, 376, 378, 380, 382, 387, 388
Mitigation 20, 57, 86, 89-91, 214, 378
Mixing Hazardous and Non-hazardous
Wastes 109
Mixing Zone 310
Mixture Rule 109, 110, 366, 378
Mobile Source Regulations 237, 238
Modifications or Revocations 18, 19
Mootness Doctrine 40, 42
National Air Pollution Control Administration 4
National Ambient Air Quality Standards 240, 248, 250, 252, 358, 362, 365, 368, 379, 380, 384, 387
National Contingency Plan 169, 173, 194, 197, 202, 203, 231, 232, 358, 379
National Emission Standards 240, 242, 276, 277, 358
National Emission Standards for Hazardous
Air Pollutants 240, 242, 276, 277, 358
National Environmental Policy
Act 3, 52, 60, 61, 92, 358, 365, 372
National Forest Service 1
National Pollution Discharge Elimination
System 99, 299, 313, 358
National Priorities List 93, 94, 163, 167, 168, 358, 371, 372, 374, 375, 379, 385, 389
National Response Center 165, 379, 386
Navigable Waters 160, 295-297, 299, 301, 303, 304, 306-309, 313, 315, 328, 337, 338, 341, 343, 345, 353, 370, 379
Necessary and Consistent .. 173, 199, 202, 203
Negotiated 10, 11, 366
Negotiated Rulemaking 10, 11
Nepa Applies 325
New and Modified Sources 240, 243-245, 248, 268, 273
New Source Performance Standards 240, 242, 243, 323, 358, 369, 380, 385
Nonattainment Areas 237, 241, 260, 261, 264, 288, 380, 381, 385
Nonconventional Pollutants 301, 302, 320, 322, 331, 353
Nonpoint Source 301, 313, 331, 340, 342-344, 380
Nonpoint Source Pollution Program .. 313, 342
Nonpoint Sources . 297, 300, 301, 342, 343, 353
Notice Letters 17, 18, 223
Notice of Intent 63, 80, 358, 380, 384
Nitrogen Oxides 258
O3: Ozone 258, 358
Ocean ... 5, 80, 304, 334, 335, 358, 370, 385
Ocean Dumping Ban Act 5, 358
Offsets 89, 264, 364, 381

Oil and Gas Exploration 56, 192
Oil Pollution Act 342, 358
Oil Spill Program 313, 340, 342
Onsite 118, 119, 122, 137, 149, 381, 387
Open Dump 150, 370, 381
Operator 115, 121, 122, 126, 128, 131-135, 137, 139, 146, 151, 176, 177, 179, 181, 183, 206, 207, 209, 213, 220-222, 266, 272, 274, 281, 331, 334, 335, 346, 365, 372, 377, 380, 381
Organizational 208
Organizational Liability 208
Owner 121, 126, 128, 131-135, 137, 139, 146, 151, 172, 176-178, 182-185, 207, 209, 211, 220-222, 233, 266, 272, 274, 281, 287, 305, 331, 334, 335, 346, 372, 377, 380, 381
Packaging and Labeling 121
Pb: Lead 257, 358
Penalty Policy 20, 21
Permit Conditions ... 130, 286, 315, 319, 332
Permit Decisions 155, 156
Permit Issuance Process 316
Permit Requirements 130, 154, 246, 264, 268, 272, 274, 279, 281, 284, 286, 300
Permits 5, 6, 15, 16, 18, 19, 21, 29, 39, 80, 99, 129, 130, 133, 141, 155-157, 249, 263, 264, 284, 285, 300, 314, 315, 317, 318, 383
Permitting 4, 128, 132, 273, 286, 324, 330, 332
Petroleum Exclusion 190-192
Point Source 297-300, 304, 313, 315, 316, 319, 342, 346, 353, 362, 369, 383, 390
Pollution Prevention Act 5, 359
Potentially Responsible Parties 160, 171, 176, 224, 234, 366, 368, 371, 378, 380
Preliminary Assessment 142, 166, 358, 383, 388
Pretreatment Standard Variance 333
Pretreatment Standards 327-331
Prevention of Significant Deterioration 240, 242, 259, 267, 359, 377, 383, 388
Primary Jurisdiction Doctrine 42, 359
Prior Owner 184
Program Delegation 245, 246, 314
Public Legislative Hearing 11
Public Policy 2, 184, 209, 234, 249
Publicly Owned Treatment Works 99, 129, 174, 297, 320, 359, 383, 384, 387
RCRA Facility Assessment 142, 359
Reactivity 106, 107, 111, 157, 189, 365, 369, 374
Reactivity. 157, 369
Reasonable Further Progress 263, 265, 331, 359, 384
Reasonableness Standard 48, 76
Reasonably Available Control
Measures 263, 359, 384
Reasonably Available Control
Technology 261, 263, 359, 384
Record of Decision 59, 91, 171, 198, 359, 361, 373, 385
Recordkeeping 124, 126, 131, 136, 153
Recycled Materials 100
Recycling 113, 185, 186, 230, 365, 385, 389,

392
Release or Threat of Release . 215-217, 227, 365
Relevant Statutory Sections 249, 261, 268, 285, 287
Remedial Actions 170, 193, 195, 196, 204, 205, 390
Remedial Investigation 142, 169, 359, 371, 372, 385
Remedial Investigation/feasibility Study 169, 359
Remedies 5, 17, 19-24, 26, 29, 41, 42, 44, 49, 141, 150, 152, 170, 199, 233, 282, 283, 287, 289, 346, 348, 349
Removal Actions 164, 195, 370
Removal Credits 329, 330
Removal Credits Program 329
Residue from Empty Containers 113
Resource Conservation and Recovery Act 3, 4, 93, 96, 160, 359, 363, 369
Response Costs 161, 162, 171-173, 177, 185-187, 189, 192-195, 199, 201-203, 208-214, 216, 218, 224-226
Responsibilities 97, 116, 118, 125, 133, 180, 203, 225, 237, 260, 262, 389
Responsibilities of 203
Retroactive 184, 188, 206, 208-210, 234
Ripeness Doctrine 40
Rule of Presumption of Judicial Review . . . 38
Rulemaking 1, 6-14, 16, 30-33, 45, 48, 50, 51, 91, 249, 252, 323, 357, 366, 384
Safe Drinking Water Act 4, 359
Sanitary Landfill 94, 148, 150, 387
SARA 5, 96, 161, 228, 234, 359, 360, 372, 389
Satellite Accumulation Rule 122, 123
Scope and Standard of Review 44-46
Scoping 63, 80-82, 169, 387
Section 104 . . . . 196, 229, 231, 233
Section 106 . . . . 229-231, 233, 234, 315
Section 107, 124, 171, 172, 178, 188, 189, 205, 207, 209, 214, 226, 230, 233. 249
Secured Creditors 185
Security Interest Owner 182, 183, 220
Security Interest Owners 183, 220
Settlements 222, 223, 225-229, 378
Sheen Test 341, 342
Significantly Affecting 60, 63, 372
So2: Sulfur Dioxide 259, 359
Solid Waste 93, 106, 111, 113, 127, 141, 142, 146-148, 150, 156, 157, 164, 189, 191, 213, 224, 305, 357-359, 365, 366, 370, 375-377, 379, 385, 386, 388, 389, 391
Solid Waste Disposal Act 55, 95, 147, 164, 189, 359
Sources of Pollution . . 297, 324, 342, 343, 353
Sovereign Immunity 37, 58, 96, 303, 351
Spill Response Requirements 126
Standards of Performance 244-246, 249, 261, 263, 319, 320, 327, 330
Standing 36, 37, 39, 44, 181
State and Local Government 182
State Authorization 115
State Delegation 314

State Environmental Protection Acts 53
State HAPS Program 279
State Implementation Plans 236, 249, 250, 253, 379, 380, 389
State Role 246, 262, 270, 279, 312
State Water Quality Standards 308, 369
Statutory Scheme . 243, 249, 261, 268, 277, 303
Stormwater 380
Strict Liability 21, 162, 172, 200, 210, 218, 342
Strict Scrutiny Standard 49
Substantial Evidence Standard 8, 48, 49
Subtitle C: Hazardous Waste 98
Subtitle D: Solid Waste 147
Superfund 96, 158-164, 166, 168, 169, 171, 194, 196, 200, 203, 211, 213, 223-226, 228, 229, 233, 234, 357, 359-362, 366-368, 371, 375, 378, 379, 381, 383, 385, 388, 389
Superfund Amendments and Reauthorization Act 96, 161, 203, 233, 357, 359
Territorial Seas 306, 390
Tertiary 326, 327, 387, 390
Testing Water Quality and Mixing 310
Thermal Discharge 332
Thermal Discharges 331, 332
Timing 36, 40, 79, 80, 82, 85
Total Maximum Daily Load 313, 359
Toxic Pollutant 164, 189, 302, 330
Toxic Pollutants . . 297, 302, 322, 327, 363, 390
Toxic Substances Control Act . 5, 190, 359, 376
Toxicity 102, 106, 108, 112, 113, 124, 146, 157, 170, 189, 212, 226, 302, 327, 359, 360, 365, 369, 372, 374, 390, 391
Transboundary Pollution 344
Transporter 114, 120, 121, 124-126, 176, 188, 189, 209, 366, 375, 390, 391
Treatment Levels 326, 327
Treatment Standards 111, 119, 145, 333
Treatment, Storage, and Disposal Facilities 98, 300, 376
TSDF 98, 114, 115, 121, 123, 124, 127-129, 132-141, 146, 151, 359, 391
Types of Pollutants 301
U & P Wastes 103, 105
Underground Injection Control Program . . 129
Underground Storage Tanks 93, 94, 96, 97, 374
Agency 3
Unreviewability 35, 36
Upset 334-336
Uranium Mill Tailings Radiation Control Act 5, 360
Use Attainability Analysis 310
Variance . . . 138, 274, 330-334, 373, 391, 392
Variances,138, 144, 146, 156, 274, 323, 330-332
Vessel, 165, 173, 176, 183, 184, 220, 297, 342
Waivers 96, 246
Watershed Zones 301
Wetlands 23, 25, 26, 60, 64, 70, 88, 90, 299, 304-306, 313, 336-340, 342, 393
Wetlands Protection and the Dredge and Fill Permit Program 336
Zones 265, 301, 310